To Ascend Into The Shining World Again

Rudolph Alexander, Jr., Ph.D.

Printed in the United States of America

ISBN: 0-9713672-0-5

Library of Congress Control Number: 2001118840

Chapter 1

My youngest sister, Cora Lee, screamed as I walked into the living room holding a bloody towel over my left eye. There seemed to be a mass of bodies in my living room. Besides my 15-year-old brother, Willie Lee, and my 10-year-old brother Sylvester, all my sisters were there—my oldest sister Mildred, who was 19, Betty, who was 13, and Cora Lee, who was 12. They, along with momma, were all in the living room watching television. I had not noticed that some of the guys that I worked with had followed me into the living room. Boot was behind me. Other co-workers came too.

"What happened to you?" my momma asked nervously.

"A guy at work cut me," I responded.

"Wake up Alexander," my momma said. This was the name she called my daddy. A few years ago, she told me that she didn't like the name Rudolph, suggesting that daddy had named me and decided when I was born that I would be Rudolph Alexander, Jr. From her, I developed a habit of calling some people by their last names rather than their first, like Bailey at work.

I walked into the bathroom, still holding the towel and wanting to see how much damage Lawrence had done to my eye. I could hear Boot trying to explain to momma what happened. My youngest sister angrily interrupted, "Who cut my brother?" "Who hurt my brother?" She was beginning to get a little hysterical. I could hear her going into my parents' room to hurry up Daddy, who was getting dressed. I was not sure what shift he was on. He worked a swing shift at Union Camp, and I believed that he was working the 11P.M. to 7A.M. shift or the 7A.M. to 3P.M. shift since he was in the bed. Daddy, with only his pants and shoes on, came out of his bedroom and asked where I was. Someone told him I was in the bathroom. Excitedly, Cora Lee was trying to tell him what happened.

My daddy appeared at the door of the bathroom and asked how bad was it. I turned to face him, taking the towel down from my face. I told him that I couldn't see. My daddy told my oldest sister Mildred to call the police, and she nervously asked for the telephone book.

1

"Come on," my daddy said, "I gonna take you to the emergency room. "Get my shirt," my daddy shouted to my brother Willie Lee. I began to follow him out of the living room, heading down the stairs of our house. We lived upstairs and my momma's cousin lived downstairs. As we were walking down the stairs, I could hear my sister telling the police dispatcher to send someone to 211 West 31st Street because someone had cut her brother, and he was hurt badly.

I got into the car, which was park directly in front of the house. My brother Willie Lee was coming, so I slid in the middle of the front seat, still holding the towel to my eye. I expected him to come because we seemed to have been a lot closer within the last year. As soon as daddy started the car, he hurriedly put it into drive and sped away. I could feel the rear tires spinning as he drove away.

Quickly, I began to realize that 1967 was not gonna be as good a year for me as I initially thought. The new year had just started, and I was very excited just a few weeks ago. I was more excited by this coming new year than any previous year.

I could even feel my excitement building in September when school started. I was 16 and a senior at Richard Arnold High School. My birthday was in November and I would turn 17. Also, in November, I met a new girl, Beulah Caldwell, and meeting her also gave me a positive feeling. She and her twin sister, Julia, would come into Foodtown Supermarket where I worked as a stockboy after school. Sometimes on Saturday, they would come into the store two or three times. At first, I thought that they were showing off because they were twins and wanted people looking at them. They also seemed to come down the aisle where I was putting can goods on the shelves. I began to talk to them. It seemed that one of them wanted me to talk to her more. So, I assumed that this one was looking to meet someone. She told me that her name was Beulah and gave me her telephone number. Most guys who worked at Foodtown collected a lot of girls' telephone numbers because girls were always coming into the store and flirting.

But more than anything else, I was looking forward to finishing high school and going into the Air Force as soon as I turned 18 in November of 1967. I had mentioned to momma earlier that I was planning to go into the Air Force and told her that I would need her or daddy's signature to enlist at 17. She didn't say anything, and her silence told me that she was not keen on me going into the service. I had thought that I might have to wait until I turned 18, and then I was gonna enlist without their signatures. My plan was to come home one day soon after my birthday and tell them both that I had enlisted.

Most of the boys in my neighborhood were talking about being drafted and going to Vietnam. I read in the newspaper that one of the boys that my oldest sister had gone to school with at Beach High had been killed in Vietnam. I was not thinking that much about dying, but I had thought about killing. I didn't wanna kill anyone. In fact, when I was 12, I told myself that I could never take someone's life because death is so permanent. I began to feel this way after accompanying a friend to a funeral home to see the body of a boy we both knew who had been killed after throwing some paint into a fireplace. Seeing him lying in the casket caused me to think seriously about death for the first time. Vietnam bothered me because I didn't wanna kill. I wanted to go into the Air Force because I wanted to be around airplanes.

One of the delights for me was staying up late for the conclusion of the television programming. Just before signing off at the end of the night, a segment would come on showing a jet high in the clouds with a poem being narrated about dancing on the clouds on silver wings. At one time, I thought about attending the Air Force Academy in Colorado, but I learned too late that I needed to have a 3.0 grade point average and had to be nominated by one of the two Georgia senators. I had not been serious about high school as a freshman and sophomore. I just did enough to pass, except for math. I liked math and put more effort into it. I knew, however, that I could still enlist in the Air Force and had planned to retire from the Air Force after 20 or 30 years. Now, my dreams and high hopes were all in jeopardy.

We arrived at Memorial Hospital on Waters Avenue, and my dad hurriedly took me in. We didn't have to wait, and I was immediately taken to a room where a nurse asked me to lie on the table.

The nurse asked my daddy what happened, and he told her that someone had cut me. She took the towel from my face and gently laid a white bandage over my left eye. A doctor came in the room, and my daddy left for a few minutes. I assumed he was going to be asked about his insurance. My daddy came back after a few minutes and told me that an eye specialist had been called and was on the way. Daddy stood beside me as I laid on the table. It was not very long before another doctor came in.

"What were you cut with?" the newly arrived doctor asked me as he began to examine my eye.

"A boxcutter, I believe. I never saw it, but they told me afterwards that it was a boxcutter."

The doctor looked a little puzzled.

"A boxcutter is something we used to open boxes. It has a razor blade in it."

"Well it hit your eye and I am gonna have to operate."

"When was the last time you ate?" the doctor asked.

"About 3 o'clock, I had a ham sandwich," wondering why he wanted to know when I last ate.

"Have you drank any alcohol?"

"No, Sir," I replied.

The doctor walked out of the room and told a nurse that I needed to be prepared for surgery.

The emotion in me began to swell although I was trying hard to contain it. But I couldn't. I began to cry and tears began to fall down the right side of my face. Daddy took out his handkerchief and wiped my face.

"Daddy, I scared," I sobbed. "Don't let them take out my eye."

"They're not gonna take out your eye," he assured me.

I believed him because he told me that in 1951, just after I had begun to walk, he refused to let some white doctors correct my legs, which were extremely bowed. They told him that I would be sent to a hospital in Atlanta, and my legs would be broken and then reset. Also, this service would be provided free and no charge to him. Unafraid of white folks and rejecting their free medical service, he told them that he wouldn't allow them to experiment on his boy's legs. He said that if my legs never straightened, it would be okay and he believed that they would straighten, as I grew older. My legs did straighten some, but they remained bowed, as I grew older. Whenever I was teased about my legs and how I ran, it didn't bother me. If my daddy had allowed those doctors to send me to Atlanta, they probably would have sawed my legs off to see if they could sew them back together. I am walking and that's okay.

A nurse began to take my shoes and socks off. Next, she unbuckled my pants and pulled them off. I kind of raised up a little and she took off my shirt and then gave me a strange-feeling gown to wear. I could feel her rubbing a wet cotton ball on my arm, and then I felt a needle slowing going in.

A police officer came into the room and began to talk to my dad. I heard him say that he went to the house and someone told him that I had been taken to the hospital. The police officer walked over to me on the table and asked who cut me. I told him the following:

A coworker named Lawrence got mad with me at work while we were mopping the store shortly after it had closed. Lawrence punched out before me and was waiting for me outside the store. When I walked out, he came up to me and hit me without warning. I hit him back and another coworker came between us and said we shouldn't fight. At this point, Lawrence took out his boxcutter, which I couldn't see because of the person between us. This person saw that Lawrence had a box cutter and stepped out of the way. As soon as he did, Lawrence swung at me and hit me in the left eye. I immediately knew something was wrong, and I put my hand to my eye. When I withdrew my hand, it was bloody. Someone, then, said, "Lawrence cut Rudolph."

The police officer asked, "What is Lawrence's last name?"

"Williams," I replied.

"Do you know where he stays?"

"No I don't. I never should have let him get that close to me," I said.

Someone came in and asked me to slide onto another table. I was then rolled out of the room. I was looking at the ceiling move, as I began to get sleepy. I knew the shot was taking effect and I began to lose consciousness.

When I awoke the next day, I was in a bed with the bars up on both sides. I looked around, conscious of a heavy bandage over my left eye. I was not in a room. I realized that I was at the end of a hall with a partition in front of my bed. I could hear footsteps in the hall, but they were not coming my way.

Later, I could hear someone walking down the hall and the sound of the steps began to get closer and closer. A lady in a white uniform came around the partition and said good morning. I said good morning to her. I had a difficult time trying to look at her because it was hard to open my right eye and there was a light just above my bed. But I could see that she was a Negro, around her late thirties.

"I need to give you a bath and change your sheets," she said. She applied a warm wash cloth to my face and began to gently wash my face. As she worked around the bandage on the left side of my face, she asked me what happened. I told her the same thing that I had told the police officer last night.

"How did you let this happened?"

"I couldn't help it, I didn't see a weapon, and it happened so fast that I couldn't block his hand or duck."

"Honey, you need to be careful. You only have one pair of eyes and when they are gone, you're blind."

She began washing my arms and hands. She was rubbing my hands hard because some blood had caked on my fingernails and between my fingers. Then, she told me to roll over on the left side of the bed, as she took the top sheet off me. I was on the edge with my back to her. I could feel her tugging at the right-side bottom sheet and pushing it to my back. She, then, put a clean sheet on the right half and it pulled it towards my back. Then, she instructed me to roll over on the right side of the bed. She stripped the bottom sheet off the left side and pulled the clean sheet over and tucked it in.

When she told me that she was gonna change the sheet, I thought that I would be getting up. I didn't know that someone could change sheets while a person was still in the bed. She told me that she would be back later and would feed me breakfast. Then she left.

A nurse came and gave me some pills to take. She told me that the hospital was full, and my doctor didn't want me moved. So, this was why I was in a hall and not in a room, I thought. I told her that I needed to urinate. She gave me a jug that looked like a pitcher, and I pulled it under the sheet. I rolled on my side and tried to take a piss. My bladder felt full, but nothing would come out. I waited patiently, but nothing.

The attendant came back, bringing a breakfast tray. She began to feed me, and I sipped on the milk she had brought me. I still had to take a piss, but I ate the breakfast and drank the milk. After she left, I tried to piss again in the jug. I was beginning to have a slight pain from needing to piss so bad, but still nothing would come out. Lying down and pissing was not something that I could easily do. I began to feel more miserable. I had to piss bad, and I was concerned about my eye. My bladder felt as if it was gonna burst.

My doctor came in and began to take the bandage off my eye. He told me that the surgery went well and that he had to put some stitches in the white part of my eye where the razor blade had hit. He also told me that I had several stitches in my eyelid and a cut on my lip. He gently pulled the bandage off and opened my eye gently with his fingers. He then put in some drops and some salve. He put on a fresh bandage and a sliver shield with holes in it over that. He told me that the hospital was full, and he didn't want me to be moved. He also told me that he didn't want me to get up and that I had to stay in bed for a while. Then he left.

I started to tell him that I couldn't piss, but didn't say anything. I didn't think anything was wrong, that it was from lying down. I turned on my side and tried again to piss in the jug. Nothing came out. I hated being in the hospital like this. Someone brought my lunch tray, but I didn't eat or drink anything. I had to piss since early this morning, and after lunch, I still was not able to do anything. I began to curse to myself. This was the most miserable time in my life. Finally, after about 7 hours of trying, I began to piss. It felt good to empty my bladder. When the nurse came to give me some pills, I gave her a full jug. Then, I dropped off to sleep. My daddy, momma, and brother Willie Lee woke me up.

"How come you didn't eat your food?" my daddy asked in a concerned tone.

"I didn't feel like eating," I said sleepily.

"When your operation was over, the nurse tried to wake you up, but she couldn't," my brother said.

"I remember drifting off to sleep as I was being rolled out of that room headed towards the operation room," I said. "I believe the nurse gave me a strong dose of whatever was in that needle. I don't like it here and wanna go home."

"Did the doctor say anything about when you'll be able to go home?" my daddy asked.

"No. He came this morning and changed my bandage and put some medicine in my eye," I said.

"I'm gonna talk to the doctor," he said. "I don't like you out in the hall like this."

They talked a little longer and then they left. I went back to sleep and woke up when I heard noise in the hall. It sounded as if someone was pushing a cart down the hall, and I guessed that it was the food trays. Someone bought me a tray and began to feed me. I couldn't keep my eye open because of the overhead light. After I finished eating, I went back to sleep. The nurse woke me up to give me some pills. She did it twice that night. I wondered why she didn't let me sleep and give me the medicine in the morning. It seemed as if she was always waking me to give me medicine.

Morning came. I was fed breakfast, and my sheets were changed again. The doctor came and changed my bandage and put some medicine in my eye. I went back to sleep.

I woke up and lay there with my eyes closed. I knew this was Wednesday. Boot came and brought my girlfriend Beulah with him. She grabbed my hand and was squeezing it tight. Her nails were digging into my hand. They asked how I was doing, and I told them okay. Boot was trying to cheer me up and said that everyone was concerned about me. They left after a while and said that they hoped that I get out of the hospital soon.

Later that afternoon, I heard someone coming down the hall. The steps were getting closer and I recognize Georgette Baker's voice. She told me that she had called my house and my momma told her what happened. She said my momma told her I was going home tomorrow and that they had just spoken with my doctor. It was good talking to her. She couldn't stay long because someone had given her a ride to the hospital, but I was glad she had come. I was also glad that I was getting out of the hospital the next day.

A sophomore, Georgette went to high school with me, and she has been after me since school started in the fall. It seemed that she was always searching for me in the school hall, and during lunchtime, she would come and sit with me. She was always grabbing me by the arm and reaching for my hand. Someone told me that she really liked me and talked about me often. She also began regularly to call me at home. She was rather cute and had a nice shape. I had a hard time choosing between her and Beulah. I met Georgette in October and Beulah in November of 1966. Also, I met two other girls at Richard Arnold. One was a freshman named Pam, who I took to the drive-in in October. When I went to pick up Pam, her mother wanted to see my driver license. Pam said that her mother said my voice was too heavy to be a teenager, and she was surprised that I was only 16 and a senior in high school. Pam was excited about going out, and I believe that this was the first time she had gone out with a guy in a car. In addition, I was talking to Bobbie. Her girlfriend told me that she was seriously thinking about quitting her boyfriend of several years for me and that she didn't know what to do. Thinking about Beulah, Georgetta, Pam, and Bobbie were the only pleasant thoughts that I had that cheered me up in this place. But thinking of them also made me worry. How would they react to me if I had to permanently wear a black patch over one eye like I had seen some people wear?

I was always a little shy with girls. I knew this would change as I got older, but girls didn't become real to me until I learned how to drive. I had learned how to drive a tractor when I spent summers on my aunt's' farm in Claxton, Georgia. I also moved daddy's car when he put it in the backyard for me to wash. When I turned 15, I got my learner's license. I became so good a driver that my daddy would take me with him whenever he took someone out of town, calling me his chauffeur. Momma didn't like me being around people drinking, but she was always relieved when I went with him to drive and bring daddy home when he had drank a lot. He was always doing favors for people without cars by taking them out of town, either the country in Georgia or South Carolina. Sometimes, they would pay him and sometimes he did it for nothing. He repeatedly told me that if I promised to do a favor for someone I should always do it. And if I promised to do a favor for someone and later saw that I couldn't do it, I ought to be a man and tell the person so the person could go somewhere else. My daddy told me that he didn't think much of people who, after promising to help him, didn't come through and didn't have the guts to tell him ahead of time. It was even worse when they avoided him afterwards. So, whenever he told people that he would take them out of town, he always showed up as promised. And the few occasions when he had to break his promise, he told them ahead of time so they could make other arrangements.

Once, we took some ladies to South Carolina to buy some roots to work spells off them. I did the driving to the root doctor's house, far back in the woods. His house was falling down, and I wondered why if he had so much power, he was living like this? I didn't believe in roots, but my momma and daddy did, like most uneducated people who had been raised in the country. On other occasions, my daddy would go somewhere in the country and get really drunk drinking moonshine. We would be somewhere far back in the woods, having turned numerous times on Georgia's dusty roads. I didn't know where I was but daddy always knew where he was. Leaving, he would drive back to the highway, and then tell me which way was back to Savannah. I was 15 then, and he was supposed to be awake to supervise my driving. I knew he and I both would get a ticket if we were stopped. Before getting in the backseat, he would tell me not to drive faster than 60. Then, he would get in the back seat and go to sleep. When I got to the house, I would wake him and tell him, Daddy, we're home.

The next day I was excited because I was going home. I had been in the hospital on my back since Monday and today was Thursday. I wanted to get up and move around a bit. I had learned to piss lying down, but I wasn't sure that I that I could have a bowel movement lying down. But I didn't have to worry about that yet. I wanted to go home. I was listening for my daddy's footsteps coming down the hall. The doctor came and confirmed that I was going home today. He told me that he wanted to see me in his office the next day.

By lunchtime, my daddy had not come, and I was beginning to get worried. I tried to think what shift he was working this week. At Union Camp, he worked three shifts, changing every week. I knew if he was on second or third shift, he would have been here by now. So, he must be working first shift and would be here when he got off work. I kept listening for his footsteps. Later in the afternoon, I heard faint footsteps that sounded like his. They became louder, and I knew the sound matched his pace when he walked fast. I was reminded of another day he walked fast.

On New Year's Eve, Beulah called me. She wanted me to come over to her house. I had known her for about a month then, and I had asked her for some pussy. She told me that she was not gonna do that. But I knew she was lying. Girls always try not to be too easy. She told me that there were seven girls in her school at Johnson High who were pregnant, and she didn't intend to have that to happen to her. I told her that I would wear a rubber, but she still said no. But on New Year's Eve, her tone was different. I told her that I didn't feel like going anywhere tonight and was planning on staying home. She told me that she had something for me, and I knew that this something was pussy.

My daddy was at Hog Shaw, a store on Anderson and Jefferson that sold beer and wine. My daddy likes to play checkers, and he went there to play in front of the store during the week. At times, he would drink beer there on the weekend, but he mostly drank gin, straight. He was playing checkers. I asked him if I could have the car. He always said yeah when I wanted to use the car to go out. He stopped the game and handed me the keys. He told me that he would walk home, which was only a block away.

I headed east on Anderson Street in the left lane. This street was east-bound only and the lights were synchronized. I thought that I could catch all the lights and be over at Beulah's house in no time. As I crossed Whitaker Street, a car suddenly pulled in front of me from the right lane without signaling. I blew my horn. I was in a hurry. As I was about to cross Bull Street, which divides the east side and west side, another car in the right lane that was only a few feet ahead of me turned left, trying to get on Bull street. I didn't have time to stop. I hit his left door. Daddy told me that if I hit another car I shouldn't move the car until the police came and saw the wreck. I got out of the car in the middle of Bull Street. The car I hit contained a white boy and a white girl. They were dressed up as if they were going to a formal dance. The white boy was angry. I told him that he should have been in the correct lane to turn left, and that the accident was his fault.

I called my daddy from a telephone booth nearby and told him that I had hit a car on Bull and Anderson. He told me that he would be there in a few minutes. He was three blocks away, and I saw him after a few minutes. He was walking faster than I had ever seen him walk. I told him what had happened. The police came and asked us to pull into Sears's parking lot. The car that I hit was following the car that initially pulled in front of me when I blew my horn. They were all trying to convince the police officer that I was at fault. I told the boy in the first car that I blew the horn at him for suddenly getting over, and I was not expecting another car to do the exact same thing. I said that you are not supposed to make a left turn from the right lane on a one-way street. The first white boy said that I was right, but the white boy whom I hit was still trying to make it my fault. The police officer told us both to be quiet. The white boy, however, continued to say that I hit him and therefore was the cause of the accident. I said back to him that he should have been in the correct lane. The police officer sternly said that he wanted both of us to stop talking. My daddy told me to stop, and I did. The officer handed me a report, which indicated that he was charging the white boy. I was not cited. My daddy and I got back in the car. He asked was I all right. I told him yeah that I was fine, and I still had somewhere to go. He asked for me to drop him back off at Hog Shaw. I did and headed east again. A little wreck was not gonna stop me from getting some pussy this New Year's Eve. I told Beulah what had happened on the way to her house, and I played it to my advantage. We left in the car. I wasn't disappointed. That night, there was no discussion about pregnant classmates, but she did ask me to wear a rubber.

I could hear my daddy walking fast down the hall. As he came around the partition with my clothes in his hand, I began to get up for the first time. I was almost about to cry. I told him that I thought he was not coming. He assured me that he would always come for me. He helped me to get dressed and told me to sit on the bed while he put my socks and shoes on. Then, he took me by the arm and began to lead me down the hall. He stopped at a desk, still holding me by the arm. The person behind the desk told him that his insurance had everything covered and that we could leave. As he led me outside, I had to close my right eye. The sun was too strong.

In the car, I began to have spasms in the neck and mouth, but I didn't know what it was.

"What wrong, Junior?" my daddy asked.

"I don't know, my head is turning," I said.

"We'll be home in a few minutes."

After getting home, I couldn't keep my head straight and my head would turn to the right. I was grinding my teeth also. After about 30 minutes, my daddy asked one of my sisters to get my coat. He took me to the emergency room of a hospital on Abercorn Street. My momma went too and we were in the back seat. I was strapped to a table and a doctor was trying to determine what was wrong. I explained to him that I couldn't keep my head from turning. It was beginning to hurt, and I was struggling against the straps. I twisted and turned so much that I was able to get from under the straps and sat up even with my parents trying to hold me down. After a few minutes, the doctor said he couldn't find anything wrong. They let me up, and then my parents took me to Dr. Friedman's office. When I was about 10, I went to him after my tonsils became swollen. That time he had given me a shot in the butt that hurt for 3 days.

This time, he was just looking down my throat. I was gagging as he attempted to force this flat stick in the back of my mouth. Exasperated, he said that he couldn't see anything because my tongue was in the way. My parents told me to sit still as best as I could. I did my best. He said that he couldn't see anything and wrote a prescription, nonetheless, for me.

When I returned home, I was exhausted. I went to my bed. My parents, brothers, and sisters were looking at me as I tried to go to sleep. The spasms had stopped. Neither the hospital nor Dr. Friedman said what was wrong and probably told my parents that it was in my head and related to me being hospitalized for the eye injury. I recalled, however, that all the time I was in the hospital, my head was turned to the right—away from the surgery on my left eye. I concluded that this was the problem and my neck muscles had gotten use to this position. Being hurt and hospitalized was hell, and I didn't wanna go through that again.

Chapter 2

The next day I went to see the doctor that had operated on my eye. His office was on Abercorn Street and his sign indicated that he was a specialist with several other specialists in his office. I learned that his name was Dr. Schultz. His waiting room was nice, and there was soft music playing. His waiting room was almost full and most people waiting had eye bandages on like me. Someone sitting next to my daddy asked him what had happened to me, and he explained what had happened. You should be relieved, said the person, because Dr. Schultz is the best eye doctor in Savannah.

A nurse came out and called my name. I went through the door with her. My daddy was holding my arm. I could only open my right eye briefly and kept it closed most of the time. I only had a brief look at the doctor on Monday night, but I studied him a little closer this morning, and he looked relatively young.

He took the bandage off and began to look at my eye, telling me to look down and to the right. I could see the light, but the doctor's face looked fuzzy. My vision was akin to looking through a heavy fog.

As he was examining my eye, he said, "I am gonna take your stitches out in a week or so."

"When can I go back to school?" I asked.

"Not for a few weeks. You won't be able to read with your right eye because it is weak."

"I'm supposed to graduate from high school in June, and I do not wanna repeat the twelfth grade."

"I understand that. You should be able to return next month. For now, I want you to continue taking these drops and putting in this salve at home."

Dr. Schultz asked my daddy to come over and showed him where the salve went.

"I want you to know now that you are gonna get a cataract on your eye as a result of the injury. I can't keep it from coming. It should be ready to come off in a few months, but I will postpone surgery until school is out so you won't miss more days than you absolutely have to." He bandaged my eye and we left.

"On Monday, we're going to the police station to swear out a warrant against the boy who did this to you," my daddy said.

When Monday arrived, we went to the police station. My daddy asked where did we need to go to swear out a warrant against someone. We were directed to a police officer behind a desk. I told him what happened the week before. I gave him Lawrence's name and told him who witnessed him cutting me. Then, I was told that I had to go to the judge and swear what I said happened. We were taken into a judge's office. Police court and the police department were in the same building. I remembered that I was supposed to have been in police court the week before to testify against this white boy whose car I hit. I thought I might be in trouble, but I remembered my daddy telling me that he went to court for me and explained that I had gotten hurt and was in the hospital.

The judge told me to raise my right hand and then he read the complaint. The judge wanted to know if I was swearing that this complaint was true, and I said yes. He told me that the arrest warrant would go out that day. Early the next morning, a subpoena came indicating that Lawrence had been arrested for assault and that he was going to police court that morning.

Shortly after we arrived, a lady came up to me and asked if I was Rudolph. I told her yes. She told me that she was Lawrence's mother and she didn't know anything had happened last week until she was told that Lawrence had been arrested. She told me that she was sorry and asked how my eye was. I told her. She began to talk to Daddy. I heard Daddy asked her why did her son have to cut me in the face.

As Daddy asked Lawrence's mother this question, I recalled hearing on the streets one day that a person who cuts someone around the neck or in the face intends to do serious or long-lasting harm to the person. I had heard that when some people threaten to cut someone's throat this generally meant that they were intending to cut the person's jugular vein, which generally caused death. I had also heard that someone who cuts someone in the face wants to disfigure the person so that the person would always be reminded whenever the person looked in the mirror or someone asked about the scar on the person's face.

Then I saw Lawrence sitting in the courtroom and wondered what his intentions were.

The first case called by the court bailiff was a guy who was caught with some moonshine in a wheelbarrow. He told the judge that he was helping a boy push the wheelbarrow and didn't know moonshine was in the wheelbarrow. The judge ignored his explanation and bound him over to state court, which tries misdemeanor cases.

Then, Lawrence was called, along with everyone connected with the case. I explained what happened, how we were mopping the store after it had closed. Lawrence started teasing me, and I teased him. I got the best of the teasing, and Lawrence got mad. He punched out before me and waited outside for me. After I punched out he came up to me and hit me in the face. I hit him back. Bailey came between us and said don't you fight. While Bailey was between us, Lawrence pulled out his boxcutter. As soon as Bailey stepped back, Lawrence swung and cut me. Bailey told about the same story, except he stated that he saw Lawrence take out the boxcutter, and this was why he moved out of the way.

Damn it, I thought. Why didn't someone tell me he was going for a weapon. I had heard that some guys do not let anyone come between them when there is an argument because they can't see what the other person is doing. Now I know why.

Lawrence testified and tried to blame me. He admitted that he started teasing me first. But his justification for cutting me was that I continued after he had stopped.

I started to get angry hearing this. I didn't say what the teasing was about, but he said something about my momma. I asked him to hand me a mop and he stated that I should tell my ma to get it. Everyone laughed, but I was not mad about what he said. I wasn't gonna say anything about his parents, but I was gonna say something about those funny clothes he wore to work. I guess the truth hurts. Many guys would have fought him for saying something just about their mommas. I didn't and instead talked about his clothes and then he got mad. If he had not say anything to me that night, I wouldn't have said anything to him. I know some people who can't take teasing, but generally these people do not tease others. Lawrence starts it and then gets mad when he doesn't get the best of it.

The judge told him that was not an excuse for hurting me like he did, and he was gonna bind this case to state court. Lawrence's head dropped. We all left police court.

On the day the doctor was taking the stitches out of my eye, my daddy refused to go. He said he didn't wanna be there then. I understood. So, my momma took me. The chair was tilted back and a nurse was brought in to assist. The doctor kept telling me to look down and to the right while this nurse was holding my eye lids open. It felt like she was gonna rip my eyelids. When I returned home, I told daddy that it hurt. He told me that he knew it would and wouldn't be able to watch it.

Henry Beasley, my best friend, came by after school and asked how I was doing. He told me that a lot of classmates were asking about me. He had two senior pictures of me that were taken in the fall along with the entire senior class. He asked which one did I want to go into the yearbook. In one of the pictures, I was smiling. I chose the picture in which I wasn't smiling. Beasley asked was I sure and stated that the other picture looked better to him. I told him that I was sure. I was not in a smiling mood.

I finally went back to school. I spoke to all my teachers, and they all indicated that I was not in jeopardy of failing any of my classes. I was relieved. A few of my teachers asked what happened. A few girls came over to me and put their arms around me and told me how sorry they were that I had gotten hurt. I appreciated their concern, but I didn't feel comfortable wearing a bandage over my eye.

Beulah came to see me at home one Saturday and had walked over to my house. My daddy told me that I could drive her home. This was the first time that I had driven since my injury, and I was leery of my side vision. But I was able to drive her home. Before going into her house, I decided to get a coke from the store on the corner. Beulah stayed about three houses from the corner.

Since I had been coming to see Beulah, this was the first time that I had gone into that store. Most of the time, there were a group of guys standing on the corner in front of the store. Swinton, who I subsequently introduced to Beulah's twin sister Julia, knew some of them, and he would go talk to them. Swinton, whom some people called Blue, had lived on Grapevine Avenue with us years ago. After moving from Grapevine, his family moved on the east side briefly before moving back west. So, he knew some of the guys who hung out in front of this store. When we would go over to Beulah and Julia's house, he would sometimes go up on the corner, but I didn't. They were not the type of guys that I associated with. As I walked passed them, someone asked what happened to me. I told them briefly and they wanted to know if my eye was taken out. I said no, but that I was having a hard time seeing. I went on into the store and bought a coke. I decided to take it with me and gave the clerk a deposit on the bottle. I crossed East Broad and went into Beulah's house. Her sisters and mother expressed concern for me. I spoke with them for a while and then I carefully drove back home.

My daddy and I had to go to court three times before Lawrence was eventually tried. Defendants in state court sit in a chair facing the judge, while the witnesses stand near the defendant. The first time the judge asked if Lawrence wanted a lawyer, and he and his mother indicated that they would like to have a lawyer. So, the case was put off. It was also put off again for another reason. By the third time, I didn't have to tell the prosecutor anything before court started because he remembered the case.

Lawrence came up to me in the hall and spoke, "I am sorry that I hurt you and apologize for what I did." He offered his hand to me and he seemed sincere.

"I accept your apology," as I shook his hand. "But I do not ever want you to say anything to me. If we later see each other on the street, don't say anything to me and I won't say anything to you."

Lawrence's lawyer came up to me and asked me if there would be any problems between Lawrence and me when this case was over. I told him that Lawrence apologized, and I accepted his apology and shook his hand. But we were never gonna be friends.

When the case was tried, the judge asked me about my vision. I told him that I couldn't see well out of left eye and that I was legally blind in it. I told him that I had to have surgery soon for a cataract that had come because of the injury. The judge seemed very concerned and found Lawrence guilty and gave him a fine of 500 dollars or 6 months. He also gave him 4 months and no fine. He subsequently served 2 months and paid the fine.

I knew that I would see Lawrence again, given that Savannah was not a large city, and it was made even smaller by the limited places Negroes went. One night I was in a cafe on Barnard Street, just around the corner from my house that was about two blocks away. It was about 11 o'clock. I had ordered a sandwich and fries to go, and while I was sitting at the counter, Lawrence walked in. Our eyes met, but he didn't say anything and I didn't say anything. He didn't even nod his head in recognition. He walked passed me. I got my order and left. On another occasion, I saw him, but he didn't see me.

Later, someone asked me if I was satisfied with the outcome of the case. My feeling was that no amount of time given to Lawrence would make me feel good. I wanted the vision that I had at the beginning of the year. I wanted to go back and prevent something like that from ever happening in the first place.

As graduation neared, I was beginning to feel better. The bandage was off my eye, but I had to start wearing sunglasses because my eyes had become sensitive to light. When our prom was nearing, Georgette asked me to take her. For some reason, it was decided that only Richard Arnold students could attend the prom. So, I couldn't take Beulah to Richard Arnold's prom. I did agree, however, to take her to Johnson High School's prom. I told her that I was taking Georgette to the prom and why. Beulah seemed a little jealous, but understood. Some of her sisters were trying to make more of my taking Georgette. Besides Beulah's twin sister, Julia, there were Alma and Liz who were younger. Brenda was the youngest, and she was about 9 or 10. After Beulah's prom, she and I decided to stop seeing each other. But it was mostly me who wanted to see other girls.

Near graduation, several students at Richard Arnold organized a bus trip to Brunswick for the day. None of the white students went, however. Most social events at school were segregated, and white students kept to themselves.

There were lots more Negroes at school that year. The year before, the first year Richard Arnold was integrated, there were few of us. I recall the white principal and counselor coming to Beach High early in 1965 to explain a new high school that was being created from a junior high school. The thing that attracted me was not the opportunity to go to school with whites, but to go to a school that prepared students for vocational training. The principal said that the school would offer welding, brick masonry, sheet metal work, barbering, food service, and others. Students would take a half day of vocational training and a half day of regular classes. Beasley and I were told that if we wanted to go to college we still could go with a diploma from Richard Arnold. At that time, I was in the tenth grade and planning to go into the Air Force, but I thought that I could learn a trade and still go into the Air Force. So, I asked my daddy could I transfer to Richard Arnold, which was located on Bull Street, and he said yes.

The first year was a little difficult. Many of the white students had a major problem with us being there. On the first day, when Beasley and I walked into our homeroom, one of the white girls said in a low voice—"Oh shucks, we got two of them." One Negro student in another class was called a black monkey and he complained to the teacher. One white boy I was watching pulled a knife out and pretended like he was shaving. I ignored him. I knew that some white boys had beaten up one of my neighbors, and they were certainly capable of attacking people, but most of them, I learned, tried to intimidate. As I walked alone into the bathroom one day, a group of white boys were in there talking. One of them was saying that he didn't like any niggers, black or white. When they saw me, they became quiet. I pissed in the urinal with my back turned to them, and when I finished, I walked out. I didn't have any major problems that year.

The next year, my senior year, there were a lot more Negroes and the white students were a lot milder. Those who couldn't stand us transferred. Some of the newer Negro students were more willing to fight. On the first day, William Ruff had a pistol in his back pocket. I knew him from around Ogeechee Road.

Ruff, Donald Williams, who used to live across the street from me, and another guy were playing half-rubber before school started one morning. Ruff was batting with a broomstick. He swung but missed the rubber ball and it sailed away as Donald missed catching it. The ball hit a car, containing a white boy who was talking to a girl that was standing beside the car. The white boy, who was not a student at the school, jumped out of the car and said something to Ruff and Donald. He was huge and looked to be about 6'6", 250 pounds. He approached them as if he was gonna fight them. Ruff, with the stick in his hand, approached him cursing. Donald, in a menacing stance, was on one side of the white guy and the other guy was on the other side in a like manner. Although they had the white guy outnumbered, I wasn't sure that they could beat him. He looked tough. Ruff quickly swung the stick and hit the white boy in the head, breaking the stick in two pieces. The white guy rubbed his head and backed off. The stick upside his head took the fight out of him. I heard later that Ruff knocked out another white boy for cursing his girlfriend. It seemed that a lot of white students were backing off.

On the day of the trip to Brunswick, Georgia I was looking for a girl to talk to. I saw one girl who appeared to be alone and started talking to her. I had seen her around school, but had not said much to her. She was a freshman or sophomore, but she appeared to be mature. She told me that her name was Sylvia. By the time, we got to the beach, we were holding hands as if we had been gone together for months. She told me she was glad that I was talking to her and that she had been watching me for a long time. We kissed and held hands all over the beach. We continued on the bus backed to Savannah. She asked me to come to her house that night. I had learned always to go to a girl's house when she has extended an invitation. Many times they are home alone.

When I arrived at her house, she told me that I had to put my shirttail in because her aunt was home and her aunt was strict. I did, and she took me into the living room. She sat on one end of the couch and I sat on the other. I knew that there would be no kissing and holding hands, or anything else, here. After talking for about 45 minutes, the cuckoo in the clock came out. Sylvia jumped up as if she had been touched with a cattle prod.

"It is 9 o'clock, you have to go home," Sylvia said.

"What?"

"I can't have company after 9 o'clock. Leave."

I got up and left. I decided that I was not coming back. Maybe in a few years she would have more freedom. Perhaps we could get together then. My mind went to Beulah.

I knew Beulah was seeing Ronald. Ronald lived a block from me on 31st Street between Barnard and Whitaker Street. I told him that I didn't have a problem with him seeing her because I was seeing someone else. He told me that he thought that Beulah still liked me and wanted to get back together. In a few weeks, I decided to call her and we talked for a while. Finally, we both admitted that we had broken up hastily. We agreed to start seeing each other again. Ronald was out of the picture.

My eye operation to remove the cataract was scheduled for July. My daddy checked me into the hospital the day before the surgery. This time I was at the hospital on Bull Street near Washington Avenue. I was sharing a large room with about four or five beds in it. Beside me was an elderly man, who was also there for cataract surgery. We both had the same doctor. Across the room were several beds with curtains around them. Several doctors were behind one curtain working on a man who was bleeding profusely from the nose. He was cursing the doctors and his wife. The doctors were telling him to be nice to his wife and they were doing everything to stop the bleeding. It gave me an eerie feeling. An attendant came and clipped my eyelashes. A doctor came and checked to see if everything was ready for tomorrow morning.

That night the elderly man got out of bed and got down on his knees to pray. He asked God to guide the doctor's hand tomorrow morning so that both of us would have a successful operation. I watched him as he prayed. I never thought about praying. I shouldn't be here. This man's cataract came about naturally as he looked to be over 60 years old. I was 17 and in the hospital for cataract surgery. This isn't right, I felt. I shouldn't be here.

The next day, I was given a shot and later put on a table to be rolled into the operating room. I was wide awake as I was moved into the operating room. After I was put on the table, the doctor asked if I was ready to go to sleep. Before I could answer, he had put something in my face and I immediately lost consciousness. When I woke up, I was back in the room, and my daddy and Beulah were there. The next day I left with another bandage over my eye.

Chapter 3

All year long, I had felt that my life had been derailed. Earlier in the year, I had emergency surgery to save the vision in my left eye. I missed a lot of school in January and February, and I was afraid that I wouldn't graduate in June. Then, I had surgery again for a cataract that had come on my eye as a result of the injury. My vision was not good, and I felt that my dream of going in the Air Force was over. Things couldn't get worse, I thought. But little did I know that things in the last half of 1967 were gonna get worse than they were in the first half of 1967.

"Rudolph, my club is giving a party to raise money, and I would like for you to come," said Beulah.

"Okay, I'll come. When is it?" I asked.

"Next Friday night."

When Friday came, Swinton and I went together. Julia, whom Swinton was seeing, had invited him. I couldn't drive this night because there was something wrong with my daddy's car. So, we had to walk. The party was at one of Beulah friends' homes. It was across the railroad tracks, further east from East Broad Street.

Beulah told me that she was gonna arrive early to help set up. When Swinton and I arrived, the party was going on in the backyard. As we went through the iron fence, I could see that someone had strung lights across the backyard and there was a record player playing. The Supreme's song, "Reflection," was playing. I said hello to Beulah, and she introduced me to some of her girlfriends. I went over and sat in a chair. I really didn't wanna be there, and I only came because Beulah asked. I thought that I would stay awhile and then leave. I had to be at work early in the morning.

I began to look around to see who was there. Swinton drifted to the other side of the yard and was talking to some guys. I didn't know the guys Swinton was talking to but I knew they lived on the east side and I had seen them standing in front of the store on the corner of East Broad and Duffy. I never approached them to talk with them on that corner, but Swinton frequently did.

I did recognize some faces and knew them a little because they would sometimes be on Beulah's porch whenever I went to see Beulah. One of Beulah's friends was named Sarah. Sarah's brother Willie was there and his cousin, Thomas. Sarah was always at Beulah's house and I thought at one time that Sarah was another one of Beulah's sisters. Beulah told me that Sarah was a good friend. One day, a guy was on Beulah's porch and Beulah introduced him as Sarah's brother, Willie. I told him that I had a brother named Willie Lee. Another time, Willie was there, but another guy was with him. I was told that he was Willie's cousin and he was introduced to me as Thomas Williams.

I only recognized Willie and Thomas at the party. There were others, but I didn't know them. I sat alone for most of the evening and I was looking for an excuse to leave. I bought a hot dog and some punch, but they were not that good. The music was good and I was enjoying that. They were playing some of the Temptations, but they kept playing the Supreme's "Reflection" and that tune began to resonate in my head. Swinton seemed to be spending most of his time on the other side of the yard, talking with the guys. But I didn't think this was odd.

"Beulah, I have to get up early tomorrow and go to work, so I need to leave," I said. I wondered if she expected me to walk her home.

"I'm sorry that I didn't spend much time with you, but I had promised to help out."

"That's okay."

"I need to stay and help clean up later."

"Swinton, I really need to leave," glancing over to him.

Swinton got up, and all the other guys got up to leave too. I figured that they were gonna walk and talk with Swinton until we got to East Broad Street and then they would go to their hangout in front of the store on Duffy and East Broad. As we crossed East Broad Street, I noticed that the guys were still with us, but still I was not alarmed. But then an odd thing happened.

"Is your name Rudolph?" asked Thomas.

I thought why is he asking me that when he knows my name perfectly well. He and Willie used to be on Beulah's front porch a lot and I met him on the porch one day.

"Yeah, my name is Rudolph," I said as I turned to face him.

Thomas stared at me for about 10 or 15 seconds, not saying a word. Then, he turned and walked away, with all the other guys following him. I thought that this was odd, but I really didn't sense that I was in danger. I had never had any words with those guys on the east side and I was not expecting any trouble. I thought that he was just trying to be funny although he was not smiling or laughing. I dismissed it, and wondered instead if Beulah and I were on good terms. I wondered if I did something tonight to make her mad with me. We didn't have a lot to say and I had not been too sociable. I thought that I should return to the party and see if everything was all right between the two of us.

"I need to talk with Beulah, I'm going back." I said.

"You can go. I am going home," Swinton responded.

I start walking back to the house, which was only four or five blocks away. I didn't think anything was amiss until after someone behind me shouted angrily, "Hey, you."

From the tone of the guy's voice, I knew then that there was a problem. As I turned, there were three guys facing me, one had a gun out on me. I could also see that there were four or five other guys hanging back as if there was gonna be some trouble and they didn't wanna be too close.

"I heard you were messin with one of our boys," the guy with the gun said. I felt the blood draining from my head, and this gave me a very sinking feeling. This was the first time that anyone had ever drawn a gun on me. I was watching the guy with the gun, but I moved my eyes a little to see the other two. One was Thomas, who had just asked my name. He had something in his hand. The other guy whom I didn't know was standing by Thomas. He too looked as if he had a weapon in his hand, but I couldn't see clearly.

"If you move, I'll blow your chest out," the guy with the gun said menacingly. "Are you gonna apologize to my man?" nodding over at Thomas. Thomas reached over and pulled my watch from my wrist. I didn't resist.

"I don't know what you talking about, I haven't done anything to you gu . . ." I was not able to get the last word out when, one of the guys hit me in the eye. I saw the hand coming at me out of the corner of my eye, but I was too scared to move and it was happening very fast. Then, Thomas hit me with something near my face. Something was wrong as I couldn't see anything with my right eye. I couldn't see, and I immediately thought about what happened to me in January. I panicked. I moved backward from the attack and was trying to get away. I knew I was bleeding and I couldn't see well. I stumbled backward, but Thomas kept coming forward and hitting me with something. I thought he was stabbing me because I felt a sharp pain. I heard someone say, "Fuck him up, fuck him up bad." I really panicked then and start running. Thomas was behind me, continuing to hit me in the back. I could hear the guy shout to Thomas to come back because they got me. Thomas stopped and apparently was going back. Then, I heard a gun shot. I began to feel my back. I knew I was bleeding from the face, but I was not sure about whether I had been stabbed or shot in the back. I frantically searched my back with my hands for blood. I wiped my eye and I could see better, but I felt a burning sensation as some sweat got into the wound I knew I had just above my right eye. Since I was retreating east, I had to circle around to get back west.

I had a mixture of emotions—anger and fear. The bleeding had stopped, but my clothes were torn. I was afraid to go home. I decided to go first to Swinton's house.

"Swinton, those sons-of-bitches jumped me, " I said after I arrived at Swinton's house. I generally did not cuss, but the emotions in me couldn't be restrained. "I need to see a mirror," I said, as I walked into his house, which was two blocks from my house.

"They were talking about jumping you at that party. I wanted to tell you, but I didn't get a chance. That's why I didn't go back with you."

I got a mirror and looked at my eye. There was a deep gash in my right eyebrows. I knew that this was a knife wound and would need stitches. This meant I had to tell my daddy. "Damn," I said. Also, my clothes were torn, and as soon as I walked into my living room, they all were gonna know that I had been in some type of fight.

I walked the two blocks home dejectedly. When I got there, immediately my momma asked what happened. I told her that some guys ganged me on the east side. My daddy was coming out of the bedroom. "Come here boy," my daddy commanded. I walked up to him. "This shit is gonna stop. Call the police," he said. I got the telephone book and called the police. I told what happened and told the dispatcher I knew one of the boys. She asked for my address and stated that she would send a patrol car to my house. However, I really didn't expect a patrol car to come, for the police, after talking with me briefly in the emergency room last January, never came back to the hospital or to my house afterwards. This was not important enough for them, I thought.

Solemnly, my daddy, my brother Willie Lee, and I got into the car to ride to the emergency room at Memorial Hospital. My daddy was not in a hurry this time like he was in January. I felt as if I had a ton on my head because I was looking down at the floor of the car. I thought to myself as we headed towards the emergency room that this was my third trip to the hospital in 1967. I went in January, July, and now was on the way for a third trip in August. I didn't like hospitals and seeing blood, especially my own. I hated hospitals. As we neared the sign that said Memorial Hospital, I swore to myself that this would be the last time I would go to the hospital. The next time, the other person is going to the hospital, not me.

Chapter 4

The next day, I didn't go to work. I called in and told Douglas, the manager of Foodtown, that I wouldn't be in. I didn't go into a lot of details but told him I had a problem. He wasn't too pleased because Saturday is a busy day for grocery shopping. I could have worked though. My right eye was a little swollen, and I had taken several stitches in my eyebrows. I was most unhappy about the doctor cutting some of my eyebrows so he could sew up my cut. Girls and women had always told me how cute my eyes were, that my eyebrows were bushy and sexy. I felt that my life was continuing to come apart—piece-by-piece.

Then, the situation began to get worse. My daddy had gone over to the store near Beulah's house. Beulah stayed on East Duffy Street, three houses from East Broad Street. Across East Broad on the corner of Duffy was a store where a group of guys hung out. Most of the time they were standing in front of the store, but sometimes they would be inside. One of Beulah's sisters told me that these guys were always stealing from the owner when they would go into the store.

My daddy had gone to the store to learn more about who were the boys who had attacked me and why. Not looking for trouble, he took my sister's daughter, Angie, with him. She was almost one year old and he was very proud of her. As he was talking to the owner of the store outside, one of the guys who was standing outside of the store said something to him.

"What you doing here?" said someone named White. During the past Christmas I was sitting on Beulah's porch talking with her mother when I saw someone playfully pointing what appeared to be a gun at several boys. From their reaction I knew it was a real gun. He pointed the gun over at us on the porch, but none of us moved. Someone on the porch said that the guy pointing the gun was James White and that he tried to go for bad.

"I'm not talking to you," my daddy said. "I'm talking to this man."

"We kicked your boy's ass and we'll kicked yours."

22

My daddy began to get angry and fumed. "What did you say?" He was holding Angie in his right arm and shifted her to his left arm. When he did, White assumed that daddy was armed and was about to shoot him. White hauled ass down East Broad Street, and all the other boys ran too. In a few seconds, only he and the store owner were standing on the corner.

Beulah was watching the incident from her porch and ran to Daddy to get Angie. She took Angie into her house and tried to talk Daddy into coming into her house too. But he stayed, cussing profusely. He angrily shouted that he had not said anything to this guy. "Who in the hell does he think he is talking to me that way," uttered daddy. When he came home, he was still hot.

When it comes to trouble, Daddy was fearless, and he is even more fearless when he is drinking. He was 51 years old and had had his share of trouble in Crawfordville, Georgia, his hometown. His mother died when he was nine, and shortly afterwards, his father left him to move in with another woman. Daddy, his oldest brother Willie (whom my brother Willie Lee was named after), and Daddy's oldest sister Ella lived alone, far back in the woods. But they were really only children. My daddy, as a teenager, hired himself out to a white farmer and worked for 50 cents a day. He stated that there wasn't anything like welfare to feed them. Ella did the cooking. They were living mostly on a diet of bread cooked on top of the stove and syrup. They also got food, from time to time, from their aunt Annie, who had been a slave. At 19, my daddy couldn't write his name, but he later taught himself to write his name and to read.

On his time off, he began to drink at the moonshine house. He frequently fought with others who had been drinking. Occasionally, he would talk about the stab wounds on his body and that he was almost killed by two brothers. One had repeatedly stabbed him with an icepick, and the other brother hit him in the head with a pipe. When he got to the doctor's office, the icepick was planted deep in his back and the doctor's had a difficult time pulling it out. The doctor told him that had he been sober, he would have died. His drinking prevented him from bleeding to death. Besides the skirmishes, he would sometimes go to jail in Crawfordville. The sheriff of Taliferro County told Daddy's brother that if Roe (which was my daddy's nickname and what everyone called him) didn't leave that area that he was gonna kill him. With his sisters in Ohio, he left Crawfordville and moved to Savannah.

When I went back to work, Douglas told me that he didn't want any more trouble from me. I got angry and told him that neither what happened to me in January or this most recent incident was my fault. Douglas wasn't listening. He told me that if I got into any more trouble, he was gonna let me go. Fuck him, I thought to myself. My original plan was to join the Air Force in the latter part of 1967 after I turned 18 and I was not planning to spend my life putting up stock.

I didn't like Douglas. The summer before, we had a pair of white twins who were working part time. Both were planning to go to the University of North Carolina. Douglas was encouraging them to get an education and stating how important education was. At the same time, he encouraged Boot to skip school and work. He even asked me one day if I wouldn't go to school and come to work the next day. I told him no. Although I was not planning to go to college, I had planned at least to finish high school. It was plain by Douglas's attitude that school and education were important for white people, but not for Negroes.

In the next few days, several people, hearing about my attack, came into the store and asked me about it. One person was one of Beulah's friends who was at the party. She came up to me in one of the aisles as I was listlessly stamping prices on can goods and putting them on the shelf. She said that she was very sorry about what had happened to me. She told me that the reason why I got jumped was because of Thomas. She told me that he didn't like me and was angry because Beulah liked me and not him. Her version was similar to what Beulah had told me.

After I told Beulah what happened, she called Thomas. She asked Thomas why did he and the other boys do that to me. She told him that they almost cut me in my good eye. Rudolph never did anything to him or any of the other boys, she reminded Thomas. According to Beulah, Thomas told her that he hated me and he didn't care if I went blind.

Beulah's friend continued talking as I continued to put stock on the shelf. I wasn't looking at her very much, but I was listening. She told me that they had a gang on the east side called the Tornadoes and that Thomas was a member.

I didn't know Thomas very well and had only spoken to him two or three times. The first two times were very brief, and, as I recall, all I said was how is it going. The last time was when he approached me and asked my name. I had heard recently about a gang called the Tornadoes, but I didn't connect this gang to the guys standing on the corner of Duffy and East Broad Street.

I had heard that the Tornadoes had shot a guy I knew named Campbell who lived on 31st Street near Ogeechee Road. I heard that Campbell had an argument with a guy from the east side named Little Tony. It was just an argument between teenagers, and no one was hit. But Tony went on the east side and returned with some of his fellow gang members. They found Campbell near Florence Street School, and fired at him with a shotgun. Some of the buckshot hit Campbell in the back of the leg and butt.

I also remembered what Patricia, who I dated briefly in the summer of 1966, had told me. She was another girl at Richard Arnold who had a crush on me.

One day in the hall, Patrica asked me if she could sign my year book. I said yes and handed it to her. She wrote a very sweet note to me. A few weeks later, she came in Foodtown, and we began to talk. She invited me to her house in Liberty City and told me how to get there. Her house was next to a juke joint. She told me that the guys there did not like guys from town and then told me that her brother was almost killed on the east side. He said he was beaten so badly that when he came home, he was bleeding like a hog that had been butchered. She said the boys on the east side did that just because her brother didn't live on the east side.

I also spoke to Henry Beasley, one of my best friends since the third grade. Beasley and I went to Florence Street School together, Beach High, and transferred together to Richard Arnold where we both later graduated. We even double-dated and went to Johnson High School prom together. He took Jeannie, who was a student at Johnson, and I took Beulah, who also was a student at Johnson. So he and Beulah knew each other from this prom. Beasley worked at M & M Supermarket on Habersham and Gwinett, which was on the east side. Beulah, in addition to going to Foodtown on the west side, went to M & M Supermarket to buy small items. A few days after I was attacked, Beulah went to M & M and related to Beasley what happened. Beasley described their conservation to me.

"Beulah came into M & M and told me what happened," Beasley said. "She seemed like she was smiling when she said that you had gotten hurt. She said that you had been ganged by some boys and you got cut again. Then, she smiled."

"What are you saying?" I inquired further.

"I believe she caused those guys to jump you."

"I don't believe that. It doesn't make sense. How can she make someone jump me?"

"You don't know what she has said to these guys."

"These guys hurt people out of meanness and to impress each other how tough they are," I said. "They do it for a rep."

"Well all I know is that she didn't seem to be too concerned about you and smiled when she talked about you getting hurt. I don't trust her and you shouldn't either."

I dismissed Beasley's interpretation of Beulah's behavior. I knew that some girls get nervous and say and do things they do not mean. I recalled how she behaved when she visited me at Memorial Hospital in January. She was visibly shaken, and when she picked up my hand, she dugged in her fingernail. I had to pull my hand away. If she smiled when talking to Beasley, it was just nervous energy, I believed.

Swinton told me a more plausible reason for why I was jumped. Swinton lived on the east side at one time and had met someone named Alvin. He saw Alvin as his protector. I believed some of what Swinton was saying was coming from Alvin, but I knew that Swinton also knew other guys on the east side. He told me that these guys didn't like me because I thought I was bad, that I thought I was better than them. They would see me drive over and pick up Beulah and said I thought I was something. Swinton said that they wished that they had put out my eyes and that I deserved what happened to me.

I got pissed about this justification for hurting me. Even if this were true, who gave them the right to correct anyone's behavior? I never said or did a damn thing to any of them. Saying that someone thinks he is something or thinks he is better than others as justification for hurting and maiming someone is horse shit.

I recalled hearing how white people would attack Negroes for being up-pity or not acting docile enough. But they seemed to have stopped. Now, it was these nasty, silly Negroes who had taken over this job, who thought that they had the right to put other Negroes in their place. But I knew what the real problem was.

When people say that another person thinks he is something, what these people are really saying is that they are jealous. But they will never admit that they are jealous because someone dresses better than them, rides in a car when they are walking, or has more dollars in his pockets. Instead, they talk about someone thinking he is something as if this is offensive to them or a violation of their rights. They think they can read minds. Whenever these nasty Negroes say that someone else thinks he is something, then they are gonna come up with a Mickey Mouse reason to hurt this person. If there is no reason, they will make up one.

Swinton also told me that I was in serious trouble. He said that these guys were threatening to kill me and that White had said that he is gonna shoot me or my daddy on sight. He said that he was asked where did I work be-cause they were gonna get me after work. Swinton said that he told them that he didn't know where I worked. But I felt very uncomfortable after leaving work at night. I was constantly looking over my shoulder and was looking for anything that seemed menacing. I was terrified that I was gonna turn a cor-ner and meet several boys from the east side, and I wouldn't have a chance to get away. This was my major fear.

I told daddy what Swinton had said. He told me he was not worried one bit about himself, but he was concerned about me. He told me that we should swear out another warrant. In January, the police came to the hospital, but no one came back. We had to go to the police station a week later to file a com-plaint against Lawrence. This second time, I called the police and a unit came to the house, but no one came to the hospital and no one came back. I felt that pressing charges was okay, but that it was not gonna solve the problem. The po-lice were good at filling out reports, but they did not protect anyone. The police were not there to protect me from Lawrence and they were not there to protect me from the Tornadoes. It is very likely that the police wouldn't be there to protect me a third time, but I intended to protect myself because I was through going to the hospital.

Shortly after Swinton told me that the guys in the Tornadoes were trying to find out where I worked, I was on the way home one night and had a fright-ening experience. I was looking over my shoulder as usual, and I searched the darkness of each alley as I walked passed it. There is a row of six houses next to my house. The front of the houses didn't face 31st street, like ours and other houses on the street. Instead these houses faced each other, three on each side. The side of each house on the end faced the street and one must walked through an opening of about 12 to 14 feet to get to the front doors.

Some of the people have lights on near their front doors, but tonight it was dark. As I passed it, I saw a figure inside it that seemed out of place. Although I couldn't see the face, I knew this person didn't live there. I continued walking, afraid to say anything. A few seconds later, as I was near my house, which was only a few feet away, I heard footsteps behind me, and I immediately knew it was the person coming out of the shadows. My heart began to pound fiercely against my chest, and I could hear a roaring sound in my ears.

Shaking, I reached into my pocket and pulled out a 22 pistol. As the sound of the feet was closing in behind me, I quickly stepped off the sidewalk and was near the curb on the dirt between the sidewalk and curb. Simultaneously, I turned with the pistol in my hand and pointed it at the figure that was within a few feet of me.

"Rudolph, don't shoot," the figure said anxiously.

I quickly recognized that this was Larry Smith, who lived on 33rd street between Jefferson and Barnard. He and I were in the second grade together, and we both had lived on Grapevine Avenue, years ago. I liked going to his house after school because his daddy worked for Starland Diary, and they always had a refrigerator full of milk. Larry's sister would pour us a glass of milk, and I liked milk.

I lowered the gun, knowing that I was not in any danger from him. But my hands were still shaking, and my heart was still pounding.

"What the hell you mean by coming up behind me like that?" I said. "Dammit, I almost shot you. What were you doing back there anyway?"

"Nothing," he replied. "I was just hanging out tonight."

I knew then that he was looking to steal something.

"I heard you had some trouble with some dudes on the east side," he commented.

"Yeah, they're looking for me."

"Where did you get that gun?"

"That's none of your business." I put the gun back in my pocket and went into the house.

I was talking with Beulah now by telephone. I told her that my daddy and I had decided to swear out a warrant against Thomas. She told me all the names of the boys who had attacked me, and the other boys who were in the Tornado gang.

Saturday night, I received a telephone call, and the woman on the other end identified herself as Mrs. Ruby Wright. She told me that she was Thomas's mother and that she had heard that I was about to press charges against her son.

Immediately I knew that Sarah, who was always at Beulah's house and is related to Thomas, told her what had happened and what I was planning to do.

Mrs. Wright told me that she and her husband wanted to speak with me and my parents. She asked if they could come over to my house tomorrow. I told her to wait a second and cupped the telephone. I told momma who was on the telephone and what she wanted. Momma said it was okay. I told

Mrs. Wright that she could come, and she said that they would be there about 3 o'clock tomorrow. Momma was a little concerned. She stated that she hoped that daddy was not at home when they came because he cussed a lot when he was angry, and he was very likely to have a whole lot to say.

When they came, daddy was not there. I explained to her what happened and told her that I didn't do anything to her son or to the other boys. I also told her that I had heard that her son was in a gang called the Tornadoes. She and her husband looked at each other as if they didn't believe this.

Mrs. Wright did most of the talking. She said that she knew Thomas hung around some other boys, but she didn't know anything about a gang and wouldn't allow it.

She said, "Thomas told me that he saw you being attacked but he didn't have anything to do with it and didn't know the boys who were involved."

"That's not true," I interrupted. "He was very much involved. Thomas also took my watch."

"I didn't know anything about a watch. Thomas had a watch briefly, but he said he borrowed it from a friend and had returned it."

I described the watch to her. She and her husband again looked at each other.

"I don't know all that happened or why, but we all know boys will be boys," she said mostly to my momma. She further asked what would it take to satisfy us.

I told her I wanted my watch returned.

My momma told her that she wanted those boys to leave me alone and said, "My boy has lost his eyesight in one eye after being hurt in January, and he came close to being injured in the eye again. I do not want my boy to go blind."

"Well," she said, "we'll return your watch, and they will leave you alone."

After they left, I told momma that all they were concerned about was that I didn't press charges and name her son. She didn't care how badly I had been hurt and didn't believe what I said although she didn't say so. I was almost maimed, and she described it as boys will be boys.

Two days later, her husband came to my house and returned the watch.

Swinton continued to feed me information. I believed that some of the guys on the east side were telling Swinton what they were gonna do to me in the hope that he would tell me. It was a one-sided conflict in which I was guaranteed to lose. Basically, it was the Tornadoes against me. Swinton told me that I was virtually the talk of the corner. He said that he saw Bro, who held the gun on me and shot at me, talking with Thomas across from Beulah's house. Bro was teaching him or explaining to Thomas what to say and how to attack someone. He was schooling him on how to be a Tornado.

Swinton said that were discussing what they would do if I had actually gone into Beulah's house as they thought. During the previous night, one of the guys on the corner thought that he saw me going into Beulah's house. He ran into the store and told everyone that Rudolph had just walked into Beulah's house. Everyone spilled outside, as the store owner said, "Leave that boy alone. Watch my words, someone is gonna get killed."

"Yeah, someone is gonna get killed, and it is gonna be him," one of the boys said.

However, I was not at Beulah's house. I had stopped going to her house because it was too close to their hangout, and I felt that I would be at a disadvantage.

Swinton was over at my house a lot and he was over one Saturday night. We were all sitting in my living room. He asked about going to get a hamburger and some fries at Banton Chef, which was two blocks away. I thought about going, but said no. My brother Willie Lee said he was hungry and was gonna get something. So, he and Swinton left and I continued to watch television. After about 15 minutes, they returned, excited. My brother's eyes were as big as eggs and he was trembling.

"Man, it is a good thing that you didn't go," Swinton said excitedly. "Some of the Tornadoes were up at Banton Chef. White pulled a gun on Chimp" (the name most people called my brother Willie Lee). "He was gonna shoot. I told White that Chimp was not you. They asked about you and that they were gonna get you good."

Looking at my brother and how scared he was, I became scared for him. A lot of people have stated that my brother and I look like twins, and some people have been known to get our names mixed up. I couldn't live with myself if either he or daddy was hurt because of this situation. My mind began to race. After I went to bed, I couldn't sleep and didn't sleep the entire night.

I began to think about everything as I lay in bed. I thought about Lawrence and the situation with him. I thought about how this problem with the east side gang started. I thought about Beulah, and I thought what Beasley had said. I remembered when I first met her, and some of our early conversations as we were getting to know each other. I recalled that Beulah told me, to my surprise, that she was Catholic and that she went to St. Benedict Church on East Broad Street. She told me that she would like for me to go to Mass with her one Sunday. I told her I would, but I really didn't plan to go. This was back in December. I thought now that near St. Benedict would be a good place to see her and to see if there was anything that she could do since she knew all those guys. I would talk to Beulah and maybe walk with her a few blocks but not close to her house. I didn't expect to encounter any trouble, but I would be armed just in case. I didn't know all the guys in the gang or where they stayed. I thought it would be wise to be armed just in case I ran into someone on the way home. I tried to sleep, but I couldn't.

When I got near St. Benedict the next morning, I saw a guy on East Broad Street. He was dressed in slacks and had a clean white shirt.

"Is church out?" I asked. I started to mention Beulah's name and asked did he know her, but decided not to mention her name because I didn't know him. He could tell someone later that a guy was looking for Beulah and someone could figure out it was me.

"No," he said.

I went into a store on the corner and bought a coke. The person behind the counter asked if I was taking the bottle because if I did, I would have to pay a deposit. I told him that I would drink the coke there. Just as I was finishing the coke and had placed it into a crate, I heard voices outside the door. The voices were getting louder as they came closer to the store. I recognize Thomas's voice, and my heart began to pound. Thomas walked in and was headed to the counter when he turned towards me. He was dressed in the same clothes that he wore the last time I saw him. He had dark slacks on and a striped, white, long-sleeved shirt. He had rolled the end of his shirt sleeve under. He was standing about 5 feet from me, and the other boys were mostly in the doorway which was the only way out of the store. Thomas frowned when he saw me and said, "It's you."

I pulled out the gun. Unlike when I pulled it out on Larry Smith, I didn't point it at Thomas and had the gun pointed down at the floor. I said the first thing that came into my mind and posed a question to him that I didn't have an answer to.

"Why did you guys gang up on me?" I said.

"You wrong, I was helping you. I was trying to pull the guys off you. I was really on your side."

I thought that he was about to try something. He had to know that I knew better. My heart rate began to increase.

I quickly looked over at the door, but I didn't know anyone. I thought I saw Sarah's brother Willie in the back, but I wasn't sure. I heard someone say, "You're gonna get it now." At that time, I saw Thomas's hands, which were down at his side, begin to come up. When his hands moved, my hand instinctively moved too. His hands were about waist high as if he was gonna wrestle the gun from me when I fired without thinking about it. Everyone began to run from the store, and they were pushing each other to get out of the way. I heard someone said again, "You're gonna get it now." I continued to fire at the door as I was running out. The voice had become hysterical, and he was shouting louder and louder that I was gonna get it now. I knew, then, this was Sarah's brother who said that I was gonna get it. I also remembered what I got before and that I was not gonna get it again.

Chapter 5

I was running as hard as I could, trying to get back to the west side and try-ing to figure out what had just happened. I wasn't sure if I had hit anyone when I fired, although Thomas was standing only a few feet from me. As I crossed Forsyth Park, I was constantly looking over my shoulders, expecting to see members of the Tornado gang behind me. I saw no one and began try-ing to catch my breath as I walked across Whitaker Street. I was on Wald-burg Street and had just crossed Barnard Street, but I didn't know where I was going. I didn't know anyone on this street. I needed time to think, but my mind was racing so fast that I could not think. I looked back over my shoul-der, and I saw a police cruiser coming down Waldburg Street behind me. I continued to walk. Then, I saw a police car on Jefferson Street that was headed south. The police car that was headed south stopped directly in front of me, and the police cruiser turned north on Jefferson Street, sandwiching me between the two vehicles. I recognized both officers. Almost everyone in Savannah knows by names the Negro officers on the police force and I knew both by their names. The police officer in the car was Bush, and the officer in the cruiser was Nealy.

"Where are you coming from?" asked Bush.

"The park," I responded, trying to sound calm.

A third police car drove up, containing a white police officer.

"Is this him?" Bush asked the white officer.

"I don't know. They're giving out so many descriptions that I do not know if it is him or not," said the white officer.

"You can leave," said Bush.

I started to walk off in the direction of home. After I had walked 4 or 5 feet, Nealy told me to stop.

"Come back here for a second."

I walked back towards Nealy.

"I wanna search you," Nealy said as he got out of the cruiser.

Nealy patted my front pockets and then felt my back pockets. Then, he patted my mid-section in the back, bringing his hands around to the front. Nealy pulled up my shirt and pulled out the gun. Bush, then, got out of his police car and grabbed the back of my jeans. He had his hand just inside my jeans and was holding a fist full of my jeans. I knew that I could never pull away from him with this type of grip on me.

"Do you have a permit for this gun?" Nealy asked me.

"No, I don't."

"You are under arrest for carrying a pistol without a license and carrying it concealed," Nealy told me.

"Did you just do some shooting on the east side?" Nealy then asked me.

"Yeah," I answered.

Then, one of the officers began to read some rights to me as I was being put into the back of the police cruiser. On the way to the police station, I could hear someone telling Nealy not to let me near any water. I wasn't sure why he was being told that, but I assumed that someone wanted to run some tests on my hands. After a few minutes, I was inside the police station, sitting at a desk.

"You're lucky," the officer said at the station. "The boy you shot is gonna live. The bullet didn't hit any vital organs. What was this all about?"

"There was some trouble between me and a gang on the east side, and I thought they were about to attack me again," I said.

The officer walked out of the room for a few minutes and then came back. "That boy just died. You are being charged with murder."

I began to tremble a little, and my heart began to pound fiercely.

"Could I call my daddy?" I asked nervously.

The officer handed the telephone to me.

I called home, and Mildred, my oldest sister, answered the telephone.

"Let me speak to Daddy," I said to Mildred.

Her voice was quivering when she called for Daddy, and I could sense that they already knew some of what had happened.

When Daddy took the telephone, I told him that I had been arrested for shooting one of the guys on the east side.

"I know," he said nervously. "I have been talking to his parents over the telephone."

"The officer just told me that he died and I am being charged with murder."

There was a brief silence on the line.

"I want you know that I am with you one hundred percent, and I will do everything that I possibly can do. Will they let me see you?" Daddy asked.

"I don't know." I looked over at the officer and asked him could my daddy come down here now to see me.

The officer took the telephone from me and told Daddy that he could not come that day and tomorrow would be better.

He handed the telephone back to me.

"I will be there tomorrow to see you. Don't worry," Daddy said trying to reassure me.

"Okay," I said and hung up the telephone.

Another police officer came in and began to make menacing remarks to me. "You in big trouble," he snarled. "I saw that boy you shot and everybody said you shot him for nothing."

"You didn't have to kill him," the officer said as he charged me, bringing his face a few feet from me.

I thought that the officer was gonna hit me, but he didn't. The officer left the room angrily.

Then, an officer took me in the back to a cell. There were four beds in the cells, two on each side. I sat on the bottom bed on the right side, holding my head as I looked at the floor. I was still trembling from the entire incident this morning and the threatening police officer. After a few minutes, I surveyed my cell more closely. There were no sheets on the bed, but there were several blankets in there. The mattresses were dirty, and the blanket on my bed smelled of puke. There was a dirty commode in the middle of the cell.

I thought that being in the hospital was terrible, but I quickly learned that jail was terrible too.

I had sunk since the beginning of the year, and I was sinking further. Like I had done in the hospital in January, I began to wonder again why had this happened to me. Why me? I felt awful being in the hospital bed and not being able to get up. Similarly, I was now in a jail cell and was not able to leave. How could this all have happened, I wondered. In the beginning of the year, I felt as if I was on top of the world. Now, I felt as if the world was on top of me.

An officer came for me and took me into a room. He told me that he was gonna fingerprint and photograph me. I did everything he told me. I had to put my fingers in some black ink and the officer rolled my fingerprints onto a card. Then, I was told to stand against the wall with a sign around my neck, but I could not read it. I was told to turn sideways, and the officer took a side picture. After finishing, he took me back to my cell.

I was getting worried. It was later in the afternoon and I knew night was approaching. I was afraid of the night because I had heard once that if you kill someone, you have trouble sleeping. I was afraid to be in the cell by myself.

I heard someone coming. It was an officer carrying a paper bag with sandwiches in it. On Sunday, there was no supper and only bologna sandwiches were given to prisoners. He offered me one, but I said I didn't want any. I recognized him as Delores's husband. I didn't know if he had recognized me. Delores was one of the white cashiers at Foodtown. Sometimes, her husband would come to Foodtown in his uniform and he and Delores would get into arguments. But mostly it was Delores who was arguing with him. He was always very quiet and didn't raise his voice. I remembered one time, Delores shouted at him and told him not to walk away from her. He turned around and accepted her angry words.

Later, I heard more footsteps coming, and it was an officer and an old Negro man, who had been drinking. The officer put him in my cell, and he came in denying that he had done anything wrong.

"How you doing young fellow? They call me Pop."

"I am okay. My name is Rudolph."

"They accused me of shoplifting a jar of coffee. But I was gonna pay for it. They didn't give me a chance to pay for it," Pop continued.

He sat on the bed opposite of me and continued to talk about the shoplifting charge. Finally, he stopped talking about himself.

"What did they get you for?" Pop asked.

"I killed a guy."

"When?"

"This morning."

He became more attentive, sitting up straight. "You need a good lawyer. I have been in Savannah for a while and the lawyer you need is Aaron Kravitch. He has been around a long time, and he is Savannah's finest criminal lawyer."

I had read about Aaron Kravitch, having seen his name in the newspaper involving several murder trials. I didn't know if he was good or not, but he was well known. Seemingly, his name was always in the newspaper.

"I killed a man in Florida years ago," Pop said. "It was a white man. A lot of white men think that they can have any colored woman that they want and a lot of them mess around with colored women. Well, I was seeing a colored woman, and this white man came up to me and told me that he was going with this woman. He tried to beat me, and I pulled out my gun and shot him. But he didn't die right away. He lived for awhile before he kicked the bucket. The judge told me that if this white man died within 30 days that I would be brought back to court and tried for the electric chair. That son-of-a-bitch died 32 days later. Damn I was lucky. They gave me 20 years, and I did 13 years before they let me go.

"Do you have any help?" Pop asked. "Do you have any witnesses for you."

"I got my family," I said.

Pop continued to talk. I didn't have much to say but Pop did. He talked about his days in Florida and Savannah.

Listening to him made me forget temporally what had happened this morning. I also felt better about the approaching night and felt that the demons wouldn't attack me. Pop talked until about 10:30 P.M. When he went to sleep, I went to sleep. I didn't wake up once during the night.

When I woke up, it was morning, and the jail trusty was serving breakfast. I woke up Pop. The trusty put two trays under the door. They served us grits with red-eye gravy and white bread. The trusty also gave us two cups of coffee. We could hear noises and voices on the other side.

A police officer came to the door as he was putting on his shirt, and I recognized him as Officer Baker. People on the street called him Baker Black because he was somewhat dark skinned.

"Do you want me to go by your house and give a message to your parents?" Baker asked sympathetically. "I am about to go on duty, and I can easily go by your house."

"Thanks for the offer, but my daddy is coming this morning," I said.

About an hour and a half later, my daddy and momma came to visit me. I was taken to a cubicle that had a glass in the middle and a hole with a wire screen to talk to the person on the other side. My daddy looked very nervous, and he was talking rapidly. He told me that he didn't care what people would say and that he would always uphold what I had done. He turned to Momma and told her to talk to me. Momma asked some general questions and then they began to give me a little update on what had happened yesterday.

According to them, they received a telephone call from Thomas's father, and he told them that I had shot his son and that he was gonna kill me if he found me. Daddy and he then got into a heated argument over the telephone and Daddy told him if he saw me that he had better leave me alone. Daddy reminded him that when I had been hurt, he didn't threaten to kill anyone because of what had been done to me. Upon being reminded of that, Thomas's father told Daddy that he was right. He said further that if his boy lived that they wouldn't press charges against me. Shortly after this telephone conversation, I made my telephone call from jail.

Momma told me that later that morning, Swinton came by the house to talk about what had happened. She said that when Swinton was about to leave our house, he saw a group of boys across the street from our house, and Swinton hurriedly came back into our house. Swinton told them that those boys across the street from our house were members of the Tornado gang from the east side. Momma said that Swinton looked really scared and stayed in the house until they left.

My daddy talked next, and he told me that he had gone to the store where the shooting happened later that afternoon. He said that he didn't say anything at first and just walked in the store. Within seconds, the storeowner told him that there had been a shooting earlier that morning in his store, and a boy had been killed. Daddy said that he still didn't say anything and was letting him talk. According to Daddy, the store owner said that he heard some arguing between two boys and it seems that they were about to get into a fight. The storeowner told Daddy that he told both boys to get out of his store if they were gonna fight. When he said this, he heard a gunshot, but he didn't know which boy had the gun and didn't know if anyone had been shot. Continuing, he stated that everyone started running, and later he was told that someone had been shot and later died. He stated that for awhile he didn't know who shot who and who died. At this point, Daddy said he told him that his boy was the one who did the shooting. The storeowner then told Daddy that his boy probably will come out of it okay.

Two days later, my parents were back again and told me that they had hired Aaron Kravitch to represent me. Momma told me that when they went to his office to see if he would take my case that he told them that he had been contacted by the other side on Monday and had been asked to help prosecute me. Momma said that Kravitch showed them a telephone message with Thomas mother's name and telephone number on it. According to Momma, Kravitch said that he had told the dead boy's mother that he could not be hired to help prosecute me because he is a defense attorney and he only works for the defense.

"How much does he wants to represent me?" I asked.

"Don't worry about that," my daddy said.

"How much," I begged.

"A thousand dollars."

I was stunned. I knew how much my daddy made at Union Camp. I thought that this amount was too much. I had been in a lawyer's office last year, and I had overheard that the hourly amount that lawyers' charge was about 15 or 20 dollars an hour. I also knew that most murder trials in Savannah lasted less than a day and most only a few hours.

"Don't worry about the amount. Mr. Kravitch told me that he had to have some of the money this week and I told him that I would get it. I have called my sisters in Ohio, and they are gonna wire me some money. I'll get the rest of it from the credit union at Union Camp."

I had heard my Daddy talk about his four sisters in Ohio, but I had never seen them. He has always said that he could get money from his sisters and he wouldn't have to pay them back. This was due, in part, because he had hired himself out to a white man in the 1920s to help feed them. So, although none of his sisters had ever seen me, they would be willing to send him money for a lawyer because my Daddy asked.

The next day Aaron Kravitch came to see me at the city jail. He told me that he had been hired to represent me and he wanted to introduce himself. Also, he told me that the police might wanna put me in a line-up and that he didn't want me to go. He told me that if they forced me into the line-up to cover my face with my hands. He told me not to worry and that everything would be fine. He talked to me for between 5 and 10 minutes, and then he left.

Pop was pleased that I had Aaron Kravitch as my attorney and told me that I needed Kravitch arguing my case before a jury. Pop went to court that day and didn't return. I missed him because now I didn't have anybody to talk with. But that was okay because I felt stronger now. Although Pop didn't know it, he really helped me during my first day and night in jail.

I learned that I was supposed to have a preliminary hearing the following day. They took me to the holding cell by the side entrance to police court. A white officer was holding me the way that Bush had held me, except tighter.

They stick their hands inside your jeans and grab the back part of your jeans.

This officer was pulling up, pulling the crotch of my jeans tightly against my nuts. I believe he was doing this on purpose. I was as tall as this officer, but much lighter, and it was not as if he had to bend or stoop over to hold me.

While in the holding cell, I heard someone say that my case had been passed. I didn't know what this meant. So, I asked a person outside the door. He told me that my attorney had my case passed, that I would have a preliminary hearing later, and that it would probably be next week.

I was trying to figure out why my case was passed. I wondered if Kravitch wanted part of his money before making any court appearance for me. But I was not sure why it had been passed and didn't think anymore about it. As I waited to be taken back to my cell, I tried to think about other things, such as the first job that I had.

The first real job that I held was washing dishes a few years ago at a restaurant called Bon Air Restaurant, which was located about four miles south on Highway 17. I was in the 10th grade when I began working at Bon Air, and this was in 1965. I was making 21 dollars a week, which I thought was a lot of money for a 15-year-old. I was on the second shift, and we worked from 4 P.M. until early in the morning. The restaurant closed at midnight, and it took us about an hour and a half to clean up. So, I wouldn't get home until about 2. This was part of the reason that my grades were low, but this was not the only reason.

I recalled seeing a sign just across the highway one Saturday when I went to work, indicating that "A Meeting Will Be Held Tonight." I wondered what type of meeting and how would people know which meeting was being held. As night fell, I learned what type of meeting and understood how people would know.

It was a meeting of the Ku Klux Klan. As dark fell, two robed Klanmen stood on the side of the highway and were directing traffic down a dirt road that went right by the restaurant. Every Negro knows of the Klan, but this was the first time that I had seen some in person, fully dressed. I had to take some trash outside and I watched them for a few minutes. They were directing traffic and waving at those who were attending the meeting. Close to 11, the meeting was over. I started counting the cars that were leaving, which were all headed back to Savannah. There were so many cars that I got tired of counting them. I knew there were mean white people in Savannah, and many of these people were in the Klan but I didn't know it was a lot.

My next job was at Foodtown Supermarket. We were making minimum wage there and this allowed me to continue buying my own clothes and going places. I always had pocket money.

Then, an officer came to take me back to my cell. Like before, the white officer had a firm grip on my jeans and was pulling my nuts tightly against my body. It was hurting a little, but I believe that if I had said something, he would have pulled them even tighter.

The next time my parents came to see me, they related that Thomas's aunt and uncle came to the house following Thomas's funeral. His aunt and uncle wanted to know what happened because they could not believe what they were being told.

According to the reports on the east side, I had shot Thomas for no reason, that I had just wanted to kill someone out of meanness, and that I had picked Thomas. Further, they had been told that Thomas didn't know me and had not done anything.

Momma said that she told them that she was very sorry about what had happened, but there were some problems between me and a gang on the east side and their nephew was part of this gang. Momma said Thomas's aunt and uncle told her that they knew there had to be more to the story than what they had been told and that what they had been told didn't make any sense. Momma said that they told her to get me a good lawyer because if their nephew was involved in something that led to his death that I shouldn't be held responsible. Further, Momma told me that Thomas's aunt and uncle said that there was a lot of talk going on about how people were planning to get me when I went to trial and begged her to make sure that I had a good lawyer.

Later, I learned that a date had been reset for my preliminary hearing, September 21, 1967. I was taken to the holding cell. As I was waiting, Beulah came to the holding area. Like she had done when I was in the hospital in January, she nervously squeezed my hand so tightly that her nails were cutting into my hand. She was very nervous and asked how was I doing. I told her that I was doing okay under the circumstances. Momma came around to the holding cage. I asked her did she have a comb, and she said no. Another person who was in the holding cage handed me a comb and spoke to my Momma. They knew each other and talked some. While they were talking, I was combing my hair. This was the first time that I had combed my hair in the 11 days that I had been in jail. I only had one shower and that was earlier in the week. One of the Negro police officers who had been manning the jail moved me one day into the shower. He also had done another big favor for me in expressing sympathy for my situation.

My name was called, and I was let out of the holding cell and walked into the courtroom. As I was walking in the side door, my parents were walking to the front of the judge's bench. In police court, everyone stands in front of the judge's bench. Not particularly attentive, I was standing next to an elderly man, who I initially thought was Aaron Kravitch. But when he starting speaking, I knew that it was not Aaron Kravitch and the man I was standing next to was Andrew Ryan, Jr., the solicitor general for Chatham County. I moved away from him a little. Someone read that I was being charged with the murder of Thomas Wright Williams and the state witnesses were called. The first person to testify was one of the boys that was with Thomas. It became interesting when the police officers began to testify because Aaron Kravitch was very aggressive and combative with them.

"I don't have anything to add at this time," stuttered Bush.

"What do you mean that you do not have anything to say?" shouted Aaron Kravitch. "If you got something to say, I wanna hear it now, because I might wanna prove contradictory statements later."

"Well, all I did was make the stop," said Bush.

"Let's hear from Office Nealy," said Ryan.

Nealy went on to say that they had received a report of a shooting and someone called over the radio that he saw someone running across Forsyth Park. Nealy testified that I was stopped and a gun was found on me.

Aaron Kravitch wanted to know how was the gun discovered and got Nealy to admit that I was not under arrest when the gun was found. Nealy admitted that they were not sure that I was the one they were looking for and that they had prepared to let me go when he decided to search me.

Aaron Kravitch told the judge that the search was illegal and all the evidence that came about because of the search was tainted.

"I wanna ask you something else, Officer," said Aaron Kravitch. "Have you been having a problem on the east side with a gang?"

"Well, we have problems with gangs all over this city," Nealy testified.

"Do you know this boy?" Aaron Kravitch pointing to me.

"I do not know him, but I have seen around the city," said Nealy

The medical examiner testified that the deceased died of a single gunshot wound and the wound was parallel to the floor. Next the person that had done the ballistic test on the gun testified.

"Now we should hear from the defendant," someone said.

Quickly, Aaron Kravitch stated that I had nothing to say at this time.

The judge then stated that I was being bound over to the superior court, and I was taken back to the holding area. After about an hour, I was told that I wouldn't be returning to the jail cell and that I was gonna be walked over to the county jail, which was next to the police station. Several of us were being taken to the county jail, and all were handcuffed. Additionally, an officer held me by the back of the pants. I was the only one that was being held this way. As we approached the county jail, I didn't know that this would be my home for the next 2 years.

Chapter 6

After arriving at the county jail, we were taken to the third floor. As we passed the second floor, I noticed that it contained all white prisoners. As we reached the third floor, the jailer hollered, "Houseman, take three," and the door was opened for us to enter.

I scanned the faces of the people there and some I recognized but didn't know their names. I had seen them on the streets or at high school football games. Most of the guys looked to be in their early twenties, but there were a few teenagers being kept there, too.

I spotted Pop and shouted his name happily. Someone quickly told me to be quiet because they were trying to get the television back, which the jail guards had taken because there was too much noise on the floor. Pop discussed his case in hushed tones and told me what happened when he went to police court.

Pop also gave me a quick education about the county jail. Women prisoners were on the upper floor and on another upper floor was the "hole." We were standing in the bull pen and the jail guards were called Captain. The nastiest talking guard was Captain Oliver who worked the morning shift. The main guard during the afternoon shift was Captain Fields. The prisoners who worked outside the door were called "bridgeboys." They were dressed in white pants with a blue strip down the sides, and their shirts had blue stripes down the buttons and blue collars. These were the standard prison uniforms that prisoners all over the State of Georgia wore. I remembered seeing prisoners from the main prison at Reidsville dressed this way when our family visited Momma's cousin who lived on a farm near the prison.

A person approached me and told me that he was the "houseman" and gave me some linen and a towel. He told me that I was in Cell five and pointed to a cell on the left side with a five over the top. He told me that this was the west side. I walked over and peered through the flat bars. I saw two beds in it and a commode. I couldn't get in because the doors couldn't be opened because of a short bar keeping all the doors closed. There was a big lock on each door that was locked on the middle of the door and was used to lock a door latch to the wall. I looked down the wall and I could see that the long bar was connected to a round wheel outside the door in which we were let in. There was a wheel on the opposite side too that held the cells on the east side closed too.

I began to look around. There were five long wooden tables with wooden benches on each side of the table. The third table had a checker board painted on it. Also near the third table was a long sink on the east side. To the right of the sink was a door that led to the showers, and I peered in it. There seemed to be about four showerheads in it. On the left side of the sink was another door that contained a urinal and a couple of commodes.

After surveying the interior, I began to study the guys more closely. Many of the guys I had seen their faces on the streets at one time or another, but I didn't know them personally. I did recognize several persons.

Willie Joe Newton was there. I remembered him from Cuyler Junior High. We were in Mr. Harris's physical education class. One day, Mr. Harris said something to Willie Joe in class, and Willie Joe told Mr. Harris, "Fuck you." Upon hearing that, Mr. Harris threw his wooden paddle at Willie Joe so hard that the paddle knocked a hole in the door just as Willie Joe was running out of class. Later, Mr. Harris committed suicide after shooting his wife in Carver Village. Thinking that he had mortally wounded his wife, Mr. Harris shot himself but his wife recovered. He was the first Negro that I knew who had killed himself.

I recognized Horace Edwards because he used to come around Barnard Street. He told me that he was in jail for robbery, accused of snatching a woman's purse. He asked me what was I in for and I told him. He seemed surprised. A few guys had gathered around, and one asked who my lawyer was. I told him Aaron Kravitch. Then they began to debate Aaron Kravitch.

"He used to be good, but he's not worth a damn now," said one guy.

Another person said, "You need to watch Aaron Kravitch because he will sell you out."

I didn't ask him what he meant by this statement and didn't know what being "sold out" was.

Another guy related that he had once been a witness in a murder case, and Aaron Kravitch was the defense attorney. "He was good in this case. At first I thought the guy was gonna be convicted the way Ryan was talking. Two dudes got into a fight in a cafe and one left and got a gun and came back and killed the other dude. Ryan said that it was premeditated murder. But Aaron Kravitch turned that shit around, and the jury cut him loose."

"Well, I said he used to be good, but he ain't shit now," said this guy who first had something bad to say. "I know some people Aaron Kravitch fucked over."

I sat on one of the benches pondering what I had heard, but not really understanding or believing it. I heard Captain Fields call for the houseman. When the houseman came to the bars, the jailer opened the door and handed him a television. The houseman, with a group of smiling prisoners following him, took the television to the back of the bull-pen and placed it on a stand that was connected to the bars. He plugged the television in and turned it on. The volume was turned low. A group of prisoners took one of the benches and placed it in front of the television.

It was getting later in the afternoon and I heard someone say, "Cups on the tables." The guys began to put their cups on edges of the first table. The houseman gave me a cup, and I put it on the table too. I could see that the kitchen door was being opened, which was outside the third floor door. As the guys put their cups on the table, they began to line up on the west side against the cells. I stood in line too. After a few minutes, a bridgeboy was let in with a large pot. He began to pour tea into each person's cup. A few minutes later, two bridgeboys brought in food trays that were carried in a metal holder. The houseman gave each prisoner a tray. The prisoners circled around, picked up their cups, and sat on one of the benches at the tables. I took my tray and sat at a table. I could see the bridgeboys carrying some of the trays on the elevator. I assumed that they were taking some of the trays downstairs to the white guys.

When the meal was finished and after the tables and floor had been cleaned, the wheels outside the doors were turned. The bars, as a result, were pointing away from the cell doors instead of lying against them. We could open the cell doors. There was a little hole in the wall that was called a "Pigeon Hole." This was for toothpaste, toothbrushes, and deodorant. I made my bed and decided to take a shower. I watched television for a while. At 9 o'clock, Captain Fields called "Cell Doors," and this was the command for everyone to get in their cells. I got in and peered out of the bars. The wheels were turned and the short arms on the long bar pressed against the doors. The wheels were being chained to keep anyone from turning the wheels and letting everyone out. Then, Captain Field and one of the bridgeboys came in. The Bridgeboy was putting his foot against each door and Captain Fields was putting a lock on each door. I sat on the bed for a while and then lay down, with my head towards the door and away from the commode. I could hear someone walking outside the cells and sat up to see the head of a guard walking by. There was a passage around the cells that allowed the guard to see the prisoners on the second and third floors.

A little after 6 in the morning, a guard came inside the bull pen and began to take each lock off the door. The bar was still holding the doors closed. A little later, the wheels were turned and the prisoners began opening their doors. The guys came out and began to wash their faces at the long sink. Later, cups on the table was called and breakfast was served. When it was finished, we were put back into our cells while the houseman and several others cleaned the tables and mopped the floor.

The houseman shouted "Morning news," and came by my door. I gave him some money to buy a paper. I had not read the paper since I had been in jail and I missed reading it. I had been reading the newspaper daily since I was about 13 or 14 years old. I had read about some guys in Savannah and else-where who had been charged with crimes, but I had never paid it much at-tention. I read the articles just like I was reading other articles that caught my eye. In the past year and before, I had read about people who had been on trial in Georgia and elsewhere. For a number of years, I had been reading about Preston Cobb. Preston was a 15-year-old Negro who was given the elec-tric chair for killing a white man in some small Georgia town. Locally, I knew about Robert Manor and Eddie Simmons and that both were given the elec-tric chair for killing white people. I had heard that Joseph Bonaparte, who I had seen around Hog Shaw where my daddy played checkers, had been given the electric chair for raping a white waitress who worked at Porzio Restau-rant on 37th Street and Montgomery. I knew about a few other people, but I didn't realize that these people were in the county jail on the same floor that I was now on. In fact, I didn't know where these people were kept, but I was about to meet all of them.

As I read the first newspaper as a resident of the county jail, I came across the story of my preliminary hearing. It was entitled "Illegal Arrest Charged in ChoirBoy Slaying."

I had learned later that he was called the ChoirBoy because a Catholic Priest at St. Pius High School told the newspaper that Thomas was a good athlete and sang in the choir. Thus, he was dubbed the "Slain ChoirBoy." Noth-ing was mentioned yet about Thomas's involvement in the Tornado gang.

The story about the preliminary hearing went on to say that "the arrest of a teenager for allegedly murdering a choirboy following a Sunday morning church service was illegal, the defendant's attorney has contended. . . . Aaron Kravitch said Patrolmen James Nealy and W. J. Bush had no search warrant when they allegedly took a pistol from Rudolph Alexander following the shooting. . . . Officers Nealy and Bush testified that they arrested Alexander at Waldburg and Jefferson streets. Nealy said he touched Alexander on his shirt front and found he had a .22 caliber pistol tucked in his clothing. Nealy asked Alexander if he had shot anyone and the youth replied yes. . . . Officer Nealy, during his testimony, said police had trouble with gangs of Negro youths all over Savannah." Later, when I went to trial, I knew the focus would be on the Tornado gang and the so-called Choir Boy's involvement with it.

Visiting hours at the county jail were on Tuesdays from about 9:30 A.M. to 5:00 P.M., with a break during this time for lunch. We were only allotted about 15 or 20 minutes per visit. Some of the guys were grumbling because the white prisoners had visiting days everyday but Tuesday and sometimes they would have visits for more than an hour.

On Tuesday, I had my first visit. There was a small speaker just outside the door and a voice said that I had a visit. The visiting room was very small. You had to enter it from the bottom floor. As you reached the bottom floor, you could see the room where attorneys talked with their clients. But it really wasn't a room. It was a cell with a table and two chairs in it. There was little privacy because you could hear what a client was saying to his attorney and vice versa unless they were whispering. At the opposite end was a barber chair that had no back to it. The door leading to the visiting room was just under the stairs and you had to climb up the stairs to a little room that was about the size of a cell. It had a small bench in it and a thick wire mesh around it. It could seat about four or five people and one person had to stand. When I went down, my mom and dad were there.

They told me that Aaron Kravitch told them that he was gonna get me out of jail on bond until my trial started. So far, I had been held without bond. Daddy also told me that he was meeting with Aaron Kravitch soon to discuss the case. I asked about the family and they told me that everyone was holding up. Daddy told me that a lot of things were being said about me all over town, and they were damn lies.

He said that he was on his break at his job recently and went into the rest room. As he entered the door, one of his coworkers was discussing me and telling other people how I shot the dead boy. Daddy said the guy who was speaking didn't see him, and Daddy said he just stood and listened to his coworker. Daddy said finally he had to say something and told his coworker that what he said about me was a goddamn lie, and he didn't ever wanna hear him talking about me again. He said his coworker shut up then.

He also told me that my Aunt Bertha stopped a woman from talking about me on the bus. This woman was repeating some of the lies that were being told about this innocent church boy and said something about what needed to happen to me when I went to court. Daddy said that Aunt Bertha told her that she was talking about her nephew and that she had better shut her damn mouth.

Finally, he told me that Cora Lee's preacher got in on the act. Cora Lee went to a Baptist Church on Burrough Street, and I was the subject of the preacher's sermon. She said the preacher told the congregation that I was a very wicked person and needed to burn in hell. Cora Lee came home and told Momma that she was not going to that church again because the preacher had talked badly about me. She said further that she should ask for her money back, all the nickels and dimes that she had given to the church.

Daddy told me not to worry and that we all know how some Negroes are. He stated that he had confidence that Aaron Kravitch was gonna speak for me when the time came and expose the other side. They handed the guard some money to give me and left the visiting room.

Sometimes, a couple of guys got together and start talking about other guys, such as what they had been accused of doing and how much time they had. Simultaneously, some of the guys would be whispering about new guys whom they had read about and who had been arrested and later brought to the county jail. So, while someone was whispering to me about other guys, some guys were whispering about me.

Someone pointed Calvin Mitchell out to me and stated that he had "Miss Ann" trouble. I knew that "Miss Ann" was a slang for a white woman and was the female version of "Mr. Charlie," the universal name for a white man.

Calvin had been convicted of kidnapping, robbing, and raping a white woman. The story circulating on the floor was that Calvin was going with this woman. So, when they were seen together, he ran and she said that he had kidnapped her. I didn't know whether this was true or not, but I had heard of a few Negroes who had been seeing white women and got into serious trouble. I was warned once to be leery of all white women who were friendly and suddenly changed when white men came around. Whatever the truth was, Calvin was convicted of rape and given life imprisonment, although Solicitor General Ryan had asked for the death penalty. He was also given 7 years for kidnapping and 20 years for allegedly robbing the woman of 1 dollar. So, Calvin had life and 27 years and was appealing his case.

Calvin and Joseph Bonaparte talked a lot, and this may have been because they had something in common. Bonaparte was given the electric chair for raping a white woman. Unlike Calvin, the word whispered about Bonaparte was that he indeed was guilty. Both Calvin and Bonaparte played cards a lot and gambled. I was warned never to play cards with Calvin because he was slick with the cards.

Eddie Simmons was pointed out to me. Eddie was a very quiet short, muscular guy. They told me that he had recently became a Black Muslim but had not changed his name. Eddie, who had never been in any trouble, was given the electric chair for killing his white supervisor at the Coca-Cola plant on East Broad. I remembered reading about his case. He had an argument with a supervisor, and the supervisor told another supervisor that either Eddie or this supervisor had to leave. Since this supervisor was white, Eddie had to go and was fired. According to some people, when a person is fired from a job, that person is entitled to his money that day. Eddie, who had a permit to carry a gun, returned armed to the Coca-Cola plant for his money. Eddie contended that the supervisor threatened him with a long screwdriver, and he shot him. He also shot at someone else in the plant. He then went to the police station and gave himself up. At the trial, he pleaded self-defense, but his attorneys asked the jury for a manslaughter verdict. They did this because juries do not acquit Negroes when they are being tried for raping white women or killing white men. There are only two possible verdicts—the electric chair or life imprisonment and more times than not, it was the electric chair. The solicitor general ridiculed the defense and stated that if it were self-defense, he would recommend a not guilty verdict. But he said it was murder and pointed to the now empty life of the deceased's wife, whom Ryan had sit with him at the prosecution table. Killing a white man was bad enough, but causing pain and trauma to a white woman was doubly bad. Eddie was given the electric chair and 4 years for shooting at another person. His case was under appeal.

Henry Furman was pointed out to me, a man with crossed eyes who smoked a pipe. He had not yet gone on trial but was waiting to be tried for killing a white man. I had heard about Furman one day at work. I was working in the produce department at Foodtown when one of my coworkers was telling us about his cousin who was a police officer. Singleton, my coworker, told us that his cousin was searching for a suspect and was looking under a house. He found Furman hiding under the house and told him if he moved an inch, he would be a dead nigger. Supposedly, Henry Furman was looking for a house to break into and when a light came on inside the house and the back door was opened, he fired through a screen door and hit a man. I was told that Henry was awaiting to go to Milledgeville State Mental Hospital for psychiatric testing.

Being sent to Milledgeville was a precursor to getting the electric chair. Robert Manor was sent there before he went to trial and so was Eddie Simmons. Whenever someone has been accused of killing a white person, they were sent to Milledgeville before going to trial. It was almost as if they thought one had to be crazy to kill a white person given the history of lynching and crazed mob action that generally followed.

I was told about Marvin Lowe and John Foster. At first, I didn't recognize the names, but I remembered what they had done. They went on trial a few months ago for robbery, and Dunbar Harrison, the judge of Superior Court, found them guilty and gave both of them 20 years. Outraged at the conviction and sentence, they tried to attack Dunbar Harrison in the courtroom before they were wrestled down. I remembered reading the article about this incident in the newspaper, and the article explained that Dunbar Harrison was very stunned by this reaction. Dunbar stated that in all his years on the bench this was the first time that someone tried to attack him in the courtroom. When they returned to the jail, Foster said that he was gonna stomp Dunbar Harrison's fucking brain out for giving him 20 years for something he didn't do. Both Lowe and Foster had a special air about them because they were the first Negroes to stand up to a judge that many in the jail believed was a no-good white man.

Willie Robinson was pointed out. He tried to look mean and tough. He had recently stabbed a guy in the back inside the Eastside Theater and the guy died instantly. He had not been put on trial yet. No one liked him because of his attitude. His cell was near the television and he didn't want anyone sitting by his door. There was a paper on the bar near his cell and I picked it up to read it. He told me that was his paper and to put it back. I put it back, wondering what harm I had done. He used the paper to lay his washed clothes on instead of hanging them on the dirty metal bar. Willie Robinson liked to talk about when he was in Reidsville and bragged that he was sent there when he was 15 years old. He had a 4-year sentence and did all of it. He had an ugly, swollen scar on his arm and claimed that he got that in a fight when he was in Reidsville.

From him, I began to learn prison and jail slang. Willie Robinson liked to brag that he was "a real man" and others were "fuck boys" or "pussy boys." He talked about "sissies" and "fuck boys." "Swapping out" was two faggots taking turns fucking each other. He also talked about "running the boo," which was a prison intimidating tactic. He talked about who was and was not a "hog." From the days living in the country, I knew that the large "hog" always pushed aside the smaller pigs at the trough. In prison, the "hogs" were the heavyweights or really tough guys.

Willie Robinson was always talking about some of the "hogs" in Reidsville when he was doing his time and included himself as a hog. One name that Willie Robinson repeatedly brought up was a guy called Bill Bo, who was out of Atlanta. Bill Bo was a legend in Reidsville because he was the baddest nigger in the penitentiary. He wasn't mean, and would often help younger prisoners who were under pressure to fuck. Bill Bo just kicked asses and he would kick the asses of other convicts who supposedly had a reputation for being tough. Willie Robinson said that he would let sissies say anything to him and he would just laugh at them. One of Bill Bo's tactics was to make prisoners quit playing baseball on the yard. If some guys were playing baseball, he would yell, "You motherfuckers put those bats and ball down and stop playing that ball." The guys playing ball would have to stop playing. Bill Bo was the only person in the penitentiary who could do this. He was killed in Reidsville by a guy from Savannah named Robert Pryor. The white guards and warden were so happy that Bill Bo was killed that Pryor didn't go on trial. They convinced the authorities that Pryor shouldn't go on trial and that they were happy to get rid of Bill Bo because he was not an ordinary nigger. Willie Robinson tried to copy Bill Bo and live up to the reputation that Bill Bo had in Reidsville.

Willie Robinson and Horace got into a fight because Horace was sitting by Willie Robinson's cell, and he was choking Horace before someone broke it up. They said that Willie Robinson acted bad, but he really wasn't as tough as he pretended to be.

Then, there were the regular guys. One was Lucious Jackson. He was in jail for stealing a car. Jacob Argrow was in jail for murder, but everyone expected him to be cut loose when he went to trial. The story was that a man was threatening Jacob with a gun and somehow dropped the gun. Jacob picked it up. Jacob was backing up with the gun, saying that he didn't wanna shoot. But the guy kept coming and Jacob had to shoot him. Some people thought that he should have been acquitted in police court. The grand jury could have refused to indict him, but it didn't.

Jacob was familiar to me because he was related to Bubba Delegal, the biggest moonshine bootlegger in Savannah. People called Bubba Delegal the mayor of Grapevine Avenue. Bubba had several men working for him and would disciple them by beating them up. One time, he locked one of his workers in the trunk of his car. Most people were afraid of him and some talked about Bubba having killed a man years back. One day I read that he was arrested three times in one day for hauling moonshine. Jacob's sister lived on Grapevine too, and later on, I went to school with another sister, Alice.

Guys were leaving and coming all the time. Guys were being transferred from the city jail to the county jail after appearing in police court for their preliminary hearing. Some guys were coming to the county jail after receiving a misdemeanor sentence in state court. Then, guys who had been convicted and were not appealing were leaving the county jail.

I learned that some of the prisoners in the county jail were federal, and the federal government was paying the county jail to house and feed its prisoners. One federal prisoner told the guard that he wanted to write a letter to Vice President Hubert Humphrey, and he wanted to seal the envelope. There was some discussion between the guards whether he could send out a sealed letter, and they decided that he could write the letter and seal it. Within a matter of days, this federal prisoner received a response from the vice president in the form of a transfer. A guard came up to the bars and shouted that there will be no more sealed letters written to the vice president.

From this incident, I learned the power of putting the right words to the right person on paper.

One day, someone hollered for Bonaparte to pack his stuff and get ready for transfer. The wheel was turned and he was allowed to go into his cell. Calvin came over to talk to him. Everyone knew what his transfer meant. He was going to death row at Reidsville State Prison where the electric chair was.

Other guys were being transferred to the Chatham County work camp, which was located near the airport. Everyone referred to it as the chain gang. It was also called the Deuce.

Two guys came in from the east side after being arrested for several armed robberies. One name was Edgar Lonon and the other was Clarence Warren. I heard Clarence talk about a girl he used to see and this girl went to Richard Arnold. So, Clarence and I talked a little. Lonon didn't say much to me because the guy I had killed was his neighbor, but Clarence didn't have any problems with me. Clarence was telling me how they robbed people.

Clarence told me that he and Edgar had a deal that called for a 50/50 split on whatever they robbed. Clarence would go into the store with the gun, and Lonon would stand outside to watch. Clarence, however, renegotiated the arrangement without telling Lonon. Clarence would put money in two pockets, but when they left, he would only divide out of one pocket and not tell Lonon that he had money in another pocket. He told me that he felt this was fair because he was taking all the chances. He had the gun and was likely to get more time if they were caught. Also, he was exposing himself to being shot if the store owner had a weapon. He rationalized his behavior this way to me, but I concluded that it was thieves stealing from other thieves.

I was receiving visits each Tuesday. Beulah was coming every Tuesday and writing me almost weekly. She was having difficulties too. Sarah, who was related to Thomas, stopped coming to her house. Beulah also said that she had gotten into a fight with Thomas's girlfriend, and other people were blaming her for what happened. She said that one of her high school teachers from Johnson had come to her house and asked her about her role in what had happened. I told her that it was strange how people change. The boys in the Tornado gang said that I was attacked primarily because I thought I was something and suggested that they were gonna teach me that I was nothing. Then, when one of the gang members is killed, it was all her fault.

Daddy told me that he has been talking with Aaron Kravitch about the bond that Kravitch had promised to get for me. Daddy said that one day, Kravitch told him that his secretary had forgotten to type the bond application for Judge Dunbar Harrison. Another time he told Daddy to talk to Saseen, who operated the primary bonding company in Savannah. Daddy said that Saseen told him that he didn't understand why Aaron Kravitch was discussing a bond for me. Daddy said that Saseen told him that a bond will never be set for me in this case and Kravitch knows it. However, Daddy trusted Aaron Kravitch and believed what Kravitch was telling him. He said that Kravitch was working on something else involving a bond.

Hearing excuses about why I was not out on bond was disappointing to Daddy, but he and Momma were optimistic because Kravitch told them that he could beat my case and promised them that when I went to court, he was gonna "put my feet on the ground," which is a slang some lawyers use when they are able to get a defendant acquitted at trial. Kravitch said that he could convince a jury that my life was in jeopardy in that store by telling them about my eye injury, the threats on my life by this Tornado gang, the dead boy's involvement in this gang, the taking of my watch, and the dead boy's parents having to return the watch. They were feeling very positive and hopeful hearing Aaron Kravitch say that he was gonna win my case.

Daddy said that Kravitch was totally convinced that he could win the case and told Daddy not to be alarmed about another case he had defended. This case involved a white man who had shot and killed his wife. The man shot the woman once in the chest and three times in the back. The gun that the man used had belonged to the sister-in-law, and Aaron Kravitch blamed her for the trouble leading up to the killing and the bringing of a weapon into the conflict. The jury appeared to be a little accepting of the defense and convicted the man of manslaughter with a sentence of 15 years. Daddy said that Kravitch told him that if the man had not shot the woman in the back, he could have won the case.

Momma said that Kravitch asked her and Daddy about witnesses for me. So, Momma gave him a piece of paper with Beulah, Julia, and Swinton's names, addresses, and telephone numbers. Kravitch told her that he was gonna subpoena them as defense witnesses. Daddy said that Kravitch asked him for $50 more, and Daddy gave it to him but he was not sure what it was for. Kravitch also sent a letter, indicating that Daddy had not paid him his fee. Daddy said that he went to his office to straighten it out, and Kravitch told Daddy that the secretary had made a mistake and not to worry about it. Daddy said that Kravitch initially told him not to leave any money with anyone in his office and that if he, Kravitch, was not there to hold the money until he gets back in the office. Daddy said he didn't know what was going on down in Kravitch's office, but he had paid Kravitch in full within a month after hiring him.

Chapter 7

Willie Robinson was getting worse in some of his antics, trying to prove how tough he was. He has been pouring water on the floor by his cell so that the guys would not sit by his cell. He also had been making references about the guy that he had killed and was laughing and bragging about it. He tempered his attitude temporally in this respect when he went to court and was convicted. The jury gave him a life sentence. Willie Robinson decided to appeal his sentence and returned to his antics. Now, he was lamenting that he had a life sentence and was acting angry because of it.

For some reason, he started talking to me and mentioned that we had both killed someone on the east side. I did not respond to that, but we did discuss other aspect of the east side and Savannah. I did not think we were friends, but I was the only person that really talked to him.

Willie Robinson, trying to emulate Bill Bo, began to turn the television channels and dared guys to change the channel back. He would wait until something good was on that most people liked to watch, such as the "Wild Wild West." The guys always laughed when the character in the beginning of the program kissed the woman, and then knocked her down. Willie Robinson would wait until the "Wild Wild West" came on and then turned the television to "Lawrence Welk." He would then stand by the television and dared anyone to turn it back, declaring that he was bad and would kick anyone's ass. A few guys would get up and leave the area and, after no one stepped up to challenge him, he would turn it back to the "Wild Wild West" and laugh. One day, during a football game, Willie Robinson turned it, and Calvin Mitchell turned it back. Willie Robinson turned it again, but he did not hit Calvin. Calvin cursed and then walked away, calling Willie Robinson a foolish Negro.

I began to have a problem but did not talk with anyone about it. On two occasions, I saw what appeared to be heat waves in front of my eyes. It increased in intensity to the point that I couldn't see anything for about 5 minutes. I knew what the problem was and it had to be my abrupt stopping of the medication that I was putting in my eyes since January. I started to request to see a eye doctor, but I didn't think the jail would do it.

One Friday, Farmer Brown came in and told everyone that he had just been tried in Superior Court for burglary and was given 3 years.

I remembered him vividly from a high school football game when he repeatedly tried to sneak in without paying, and a police officer was determined to keep him out. It was a game of cat and mouse. Farmer Brown climbed up the wall of Grayson Stadium on Victory Drive. When the police officer saw him, he slowly started walking up to the top. Farmer Brown swung his leg over the wall, and as the police officer got closer, Farmer Brown climbed back down the wall. When the police officer got to the top, he peered over to the ground and said smilingly that there will be no free game watching that night.

The Houseman put Farmer Brown in my cell, and he talked more about his 3 years. He also talked about how his momma and girlfriend cried when Dunbar Harrison said 3 years. He and a friend broke into a clothing store on Broughton Street. His fingerprints were found on the store glass, but he did not think that this was enough evidence since the prints were on the outside of the glass. But he wasn't too disappointed since he did it, as well as numerous other burglaries. Once, he said that he and this guy named Pecker got high and decided to break into a store distributor on Barnard Street. He said that they got on the roof and took a hammer and a fifth of wine. One person used the hammer while the other drank, and then they switched. He said it took them about an hour to get a hole big enough for them to get into and by then they were good and drunk. He was talking so much that I was afraid that the guard would hear him. I told him to listen for the guard on the catwalk because he would leave the lock on the cell in the morning when he had caught someone talking after the doors were locked.

I read a story in the newspaper that caught my eye. A white man who managed a downtown motel shot and killed a Negro after a heated argument. The lawyer for the white man claimed that his client killed the man out of a fear of a reasonable man, and therefore, this was justifiable homicide. According to the testimony of the motel manager, the Negro was almost foaming at the mouth and this made him fearful for his life. The lawyer, attempting to discount that racial prejudice on the part of the manager set off the Negro, introduced evidence that the manager permitted an integrated football team from out of town to stay at his motel. Although the Negro was unarmed, the jury acquitted the white man based on fear of a reasonable man.

I suspected that fear of a reasonable man would be my defense when I went to trial because it is what lawyers cite whenever they plead someone not guilty because of self-defense.

By reading the newspaper and listening a little to guys in the jail, I began to learn more about the law. Besides learning that Georgia's law on justifiable homicide is called fear of a reasonable man, I learned that Georgia had a provision in the law whereby a defendant could make an unsworn statement to the jury. The difference between the sworn and unsworn is that if the defendant is sworn, then the prosecutor can cross-examine the defendant. But if the defendant is not sworn, the defendant can't be cross-examined by the prosecutor. Some defense attorneys, fearing that their clients might not hold up on cross-examination or might say something harmful to the defense, have their clients give unsworn testimony. Then, again some defendants do not testify at all, like Calvin Mitchell, who did not testify in his own defense to the rape, robbery, and kidnapping charges. At my preliminary hearing, I did not testify at all and did not know what I was gonna do when I went to trial.

I began to think more about these issues because my momma told me that my trial had been set for November.

While momma was telling me this, I couldn't help hearing Farmer Brown's sister talking to him because Farmer Brown was sitting next to me. She told Farmer Brown that Frog and Calvin Red had left town because they had robbed a Chinese man and beaten him to death. She said that she saw them do it.

I thought that what I had just overheard was interesting, but I returned to what my momma was saying. I also began to get worried about going on trial for murder. But what was worried me even more was that my daddy was the only person that Aaron Kravitch would talk to about the case. I had not been asked anything at all. Daddy was providing Aaron Kravitch with information about my case although Daddy did not know anyone's name in the Tornado gang, did not see me being attacked, and was not in the store when the shooting occurred. The only thing that Daddy could talk about was taking me to the hospital in January, going to court with me when Lawrence was put on trial, taking me to the hospital this last time, and his confrontation with one of the Tornadoes. At one point, Aaron Kravitch asked Daddy a question that Daddy couldn't answer. Daddy said he told Aaron Kravitch to ask me. Aaron Kravitch said he would later. But I had not heard anything from Kravitch, and I was getting nervous.

Arrests were later made in the robbing and beating of the Chinese man, but they were not the guilty parties. There were several robberies in the city and the Savannah Police Department was sending out police officers as decoys. In one of these decoys, five boys allegedly tried to rob an officer, who was posing as a drunk. The officer killed one of the boys and the others were arrested. They were charged with attempting to rob the officer as well as the murder of the Chinese man. The boys were 14 and 15 years old, and they were transferred to the county jail after their preliminary hearing.

Farmer Brown left after a while, but others continued to come. Tan came to jail, and he and I were kind of related. His girlfriend was Rita Williams, who was the sister of my brother-in-law, Louis Williams. Louis married my oldest sister, Mildred, who is Angie's Daddy. So, I knew of Tan through this connection, but I also had seen him around. He was always fighting with someone, and I remembered that he had once hit a county police officer in the mouth at a night club, causing extensive damage to the officer's teeth.

When Tan came to jail, he immediately got into a fight. Tan was playing cards when another new guy told Tan that when the game was over, he was gonna see what Tan knew. As soon as the game was over, Tan hit the guy and knocked him down. Then Tan began to kick him, saying that he was gonna stomp the guy's eyes out. The next day, Tan was in another fight with another inmate.

Rita came to visit Tan, and I had a visitor too. The guard hollered to Tan that his time was up and Tan got upset at the guard hollering at him. Rita was trying to calm him down. The guards decided to put Tan on the first floor in a cell by himself, but they knew that he was a problem. Tan had told the Bridgeboys that they better not touch him, and they were afraid of him.

I was looking at Tan's hands one day and I could see why he hurt people when he hit them. Not only were his hands big, but they were rough.

The guards told Tan that his lawyer wanted to see him. But when Tan got downstairs, they told him that he was gonna be put in a cell on the first floor, and his lawyer was not there. The guards felt that they had to trick him out of the cellblock in order to get him down on the first floor.

Red Roberts came to jail and was telling people that I had killed his half-brother. It seemed that they had the same father, but not the same mother. Also, I was told that the man that I thought was Thomas's father, the man who had returned my watch, was really Thomas's stepfather. Red Roberts had reportedly said that he had seen my brother several times and had thought about shooting him out of revenge against me. Although Red Robert was telling other people this, he didn't say anything directly to me. But he did try to give me hint during a checker game.

"You know, I'm gonna hurt you really bad," said Red Roberts, pretending like he was talking about the checker game.

"Do it, don't just talk about it," I said as I moved my checkers.

We both knew that we were not talking about the game.

I also knew that I was not gonna apologize to him and tell him that I was sorry. I didn't like him. Sometime ago, a former high school friend of mine had been shot after a March of Dimes program. I had heard from several people that Red Roberts had done this and had done so for fun. Someone challenged him to shoot into the crowd as people were coming out and handed Red Roberts a gun. Red Roberts fired and hit the guy in the side, but the wound was not fatal.

I was not about to apologize to someone like him. He probably knew that his half-brother was in a gang and probably knew that they had attacked me for no good reason. Now, he was upset because his half-brother was dead. Red Roberts probably encouraged his half-brother's behavior. He should have been telling his half-brother to leave other people alone.

I was upset further because he would tell someone that he started to shoot my brother, who had nothing to do with that mess. I had heard people say that the Tornado gang wanted to kill me and planned to do so if I got out. But they didn't act like they wanted to get me because they had threatened Swinton not to testify in my behalf. If they really wanted me as bad as they said, they should have been threatening the state witnesses. Then, I could get out and they could get all of me that they wanted. Now, Red Roberts had a chance to do something, but all he was making were veiled threats.

Someone came one day and everyone was calling him Honey. His real name was Edward Tyler, and he looked to be in his early twenties. The way some of the guys who knew him talked, you did not wanna get into a fight with him. I had seen him once at a football game. He had a group of guys following him, and they were all looking as if they were gonna fight someone. Honey told some guys that he was arrested for snatching a moneybag from a guard. He, also, when arrested, was charged with having a gun. He was convinced that he would beat the robbery because the guard said that all he saw was the back of Honey's head and the bottom of his feet.

One day Stacko, Vic, and Banlon were brought into the county jail. They were bound over to the superior court for burglarizing a downtown store. An officer chased them, and they had armloads of clothes as they tried to vanish in Yamacraw Village, one of the oldest projects in Savannah. Stacko I knew because I was messing around with his cousin Vida at one time, and he was there when I picked her up.

Stacko mentioned that when he spoke to his lawyer, a young Negro, his lawyer asked him the race of the officer who made the arrest. Stacko said he told him colored and the lawyer asked him again was the officer black or white. Stacko said colored, but the lawyer repeated, black or white. Stacko said he said exasperatedly that the officer was colored, and the lawyer went on to someone else. Stacko said he had apprehension about this lawyer who did not understand something as simple as being colored. Someone in the jail told Stacko that we were black and shouldn't be ashamed of it, and his lawyer was only trying to get him to say black. We were through being colored and Negroes. We were now black and proud to be black.

I thought that being black was a good idea because I really didn't like Negro although I knew that it was close to a Spanish word for black. Negro, now, is used as a step above nigger and connotes a less than favorable black person.

Other guys were going to court and sometimes there would be four or five guys going to court together. They would talk about wanting to be first to go before Dunbar Harrison, because if he got mad during one case, he would take it out on others. So, some guys cautioned each other not make Dunbar Harrison mad.

They also did superstitious things. For some reason, guys thought there was power in salt. They would try to get some salt from the kitchen before they went to trial. The word was that salt in each pocket would get you acquitted at trial.

One guy did not believe in salt. Instead, he had some dried-out chicken bones from Sunday's dinner. He put the bones on his bed, and this was supposed to help him when he went to court.

I was talking to another guy whose wife took his clothes he was gonna wear to court to the root doctor. This root doctor was a woman, and she sprinkled some dust onto his pants and shirt and ironed the dust in. The root doctor also instructed the woman to tell her husband to read a certain passage from the Bible each night until he went to the trial. For ironing the clothes and identifying the Bible passage, she charged 50 dollars. When the man went to court, Dunbar Harrison gave him 3 years on the chain gang. He was angry and threw away his Bible.

But I couldn't be amused with this incident because my parents went to a root doctor on my behalf. The root doctor stated that 1967 was a bad year for me because someone was working roots on me. According to the root doctor, I had been hurt and hospitalized in January, hurt again in August, and in jail now for murder because someone in Savannah had "fixed" me. The root doctor sold my parents an anecdote that was supposed to take the hex off me and to help me walk away a free person when I went to court.

If I had known that my parents were gonna see a root doctor, I would have tried to stop them because I did not believe in that nonsense. But I knew they, being born and raised in the country, believed in it. Momma was convinced that someone had her father "fixed" by putting something in his liquor. Momma had someone to take her to the root doctor's house to purchase some special water that was supposed to cure him. It did not cure him or make him better.

I knew that many black people attribute other black people's psychiatric problems to someone working roots when really it is because of stress. But I couldn't get Momma and Daddy to understand this.

A week before I was supposed to go on trial, my trial was postponed. Daddy said that Aaron Kravitch wanted the case to cool off more.

I wondered why the case needed to cool off since Aaron Kravitch vowed that he was gonna win the case. Smith, the white man who killed his wife by shooting her three times in the back, went to trial 2 months after he was initially arrested. I had been in jail for 2 months, but my trial was being postponed.

"Aaron Kravitch said that he is putting the trial off, and he is gonna get you out on bond by Christmas," said Daddy.

"If that's the way it is, then I can accept it," I said. "I am a little concerned about Swinton, Daddy. He told me that he has been threatened by the Tornado gang and they told him that he is gonna get hurt if he testified and tried to help me."

"Don't worry about that, I have all the confidence in the world in Aaron Kravitch and he is gonna straighten this all out," said Daddy.

After Daddy left, I couldn't help wondering about Aaron Kravitch. I had heard some bad things about him and did not have the level of confidence that Daddy had in him.

My lack of confidence in Aaron Kravitch loomed immensely when Christmas came. At one time, my parents told me that I would be out in a few days based on what Aaron Kravitch told them. The days passed and I was not out.

To me, this meant that Aaron Kravitch was lying and had been lying since September. More than the bad things that I had heard about Aaron Kravitch, it was the lying and talking exclusively with my Daddy about the case that prompted me to wanna fire him. So, I wrote Aaron Kravitch an angry letter telling him that I wanted another lawyer working on my case and wanted him to refund the fee that my Daddy had paid him.

"Rudolph Alexander, you have someone hear to see you," said the jailer.

It was not visiting day, so I knew that someone had come in response to my letter.

I was directed to the visiting room when I saw a large-headed man waiting on me on the other side of the screen.

"Sit down you little punk," snarled the man.

"My name is Lionel Drew and I work with Mr. Kravitch. You are waiting to go on trial for cold-blooded murder, and you are headed to the fifth floor in Reidsville where the electric chair is unless you put some confidence in Mr. Kravitch. Your father hired Mr. Kravitch and you can't fire him because you are a minor."

"You don't know what I did, you weren't there," I said.

"I know what you did. You got a gun, concealed it illegally, and you gunned down that boy in cold blood and did not give him a chance."

"He brought it on himself," I said.

"No, he did not," Drew charged.

"I lost my vision in one eye and he had deliberately tried to put out my sight."

"Well, you should have killed the first boy who put out your eye," charged Drew.

"How come no one has asked me anything and my daddy is being asked things that he doesn't know? I had a trial set for last month, and no one has asked me anything."

"Listen you, when the time comes for someone to come down and talk with you, someone will be here. Until then, you need to sit quiet. Mr. Kravitch has asked me to leave this information for you."

I got up and walked out. On the way back up the stairs, someone handed me the material Aaron Kravitch had sent to me. It was a write up about his career and that he was approaching 50 years of practicing criminal law. The write up discussed some of his big criminal and civil cases. It stated that in all his murder cases that he has only lost two clients to the electric chair. In one of those cases, the client, who had killed his wife, refused to authorize an appeal, believing that God would not allow the switch to be pulled. However, God, according to Aaron Kravitch, did not intercede and the accused died in the electric chair. There was no information about the other person who died in the electric chair.

Wyman Gordon told me that I was a fool for trying to fire Aaron Kravitch and that I couldn't talk to a white man the way that I had done in my letter.

The next day, I received a letter from Aaron Kravitch, telling me that the letter that I had written insulted him. He told me that it was my attitude that was gonna determine if I lived or died, and my attitude was very bad. At the bottom of the letter, the secretary indicated that she had sent a copy to Daddy.

Momma and Daddy went to see Aaron Kravitch, and he told them that in his 50 years of legal practice that he had never had someone to talk to him the way that I did in my letter. However, he said that he was still willing to represent me.

Momma and Daddy came to see me and told me that everything was okay with Aaron Kravitch, but they told me not to write to him anymore.

I thought that Daddy would be upset with me, but he wasn't. I told him what Drew said to me, and Daddy was upset about it.

As January 1, 1968 came, I couldn't help but compare it to January of last year. Last year, I was looking forward to the coming year, but not this year. I was not looking forward to anything really. I was not the same person that I was the year before.

Despite what Drew had said, I did not blame myself for what happened and all this talk that I had no business going on the east side. I always believed that I had the right to go wherever I wanted to go. I recalled going to the Weis Theater downtown in 1965. Many people believed that blacks should only go the Star Theater on West Broad or the Eastside Theater on East Broad. I started going to the Weis and two times that I was there, I was the only black person in the theater. I couldn't believe the differences in the black and white theaters. The Weis had cushioned seats, smelled clean, and most of all they put real butter on fresh popcorn. At the Star and Eastside, the seats were hard and ragged, the bathrooms were dirty, and the popcorn was stale if you bought some when the theater first opened for the day. I recalled seeing at the Weis, *The Guns of Navoronne*, *Nevada Smith*, and *Thunderball*. I would go to the concession stand two or three times at the Weis and always had a pleasant evening when I went. I did not bother anyone there, and no one bothered me.

Some of the guys were commenting about my case, repeating erroneous information that they had heard on the streets. A guy on the east side named Mel told these guys that they were wrong because he had spoken with one of the guys who had attacked me. Mel told them that the dead person wanted to fight me because he was jealous, but he was afraid that he couldn't beat me. So, he asked the guys in the Tornado gang to help him hurt me so badly that I would never come on the east side again. When they heard that I had not been hurt badly enough, they intended to hurt me worse the next time. Mel said it was a lie that Thomas was an innocent bystander and that, in his opinion, he never should have attacked me in the first place.

Joseph Bonaparte was in the news. The State Board of Pardons and Parole had decided to hear a request to commute his death sentence to life imprisonment. When the board heard his case, it commuted his sentence. Several people in Savannah were quite angry. Ryan, the prosecutor, was upset and asked what was this waitress supposed to tell her daughter, insinuating that only Bonaparte's execution would allow the waitress to save face.

Willie Robinson's attitude changed. He tried to be friendly with Honey, but it was obvious that Honey did not like Willie Robinson. Honey liked to gamble and he and Willie Robinson and others would play Skin.

Woodrow Ware came in and he became someone else that Willie Robinson tried to befriend. Woodrow grew up with Honey and people said that these two ran the "block," which was some area on West Broad Street.

Gary Nelson out of West Savannah came to jail. He swung at Willie Robinson with a mop, but Willie Robinson did not want any part of Gary. Willie Robinson stopped talking about how bad he was because there were guys in the county jail who wanted to stomp his ass and he knew it.

Gary and I talked a bit. I did not know him and did not ask him about his case or anything. But some guys liked to talk or socialize and some guys would talk to me. Why me, I did not know. Everyone also said that I was very quiet and this goes back to when I was very young. I did not talk very much.

Gary said that he had Aaron Kravitch on a rape case a few years back. He stated that he was found not guilty after Aaron Kravitch humiliated and embarrassed the girl in the courtroom. In the summation to the jury, Aaron Kravitch characterized the doctor's testimony as revealing that the girl had a gigantic hole and then demontrated to the jury how big with his two hands. Seeing this demonstration, the judge, jury, and prosecutors all laughed.

I knew that Aaron Kravitch would never say such a thing about a white woman, and a white woman who said that a black defendant had raped her was treated with velvet gloves.

Guys were still coming and going. Joe Gator, a huge awkwardly looking person, came in and was made the houseman. The fellows said that he was in for robbery and had dressed up like a woman. But Joe Gator being a woman could fool no one. This was an ugly dude.

My trial date had been set for April 23, 1968 and I was beginning to get nervous. My parents were convinced that I would be acquitted when I went to trial based on what Aaron Kravitch had told them. I was hopeful because they were, but I was nervous.

A few days before I went to trial, I was writing a letter to Beulah. Joe Gator opened my cell and handed me the broom to sweep out my cell. I told him to wait a few seconds, but Joe Gator said he was too busy to wait. But I did not move to his prompting and was trying to finish my thoughts in this letter.

"You know I can have your ass put in the hole," said Joe Gator. "You don't believe me," he said as he turned to leave.

I could hear him calling the fat guard and telling him that I did not wanna sweep my cell. Joe returned to my cell and told me that I was wanted on the bars.

I walked up to the bars, thinking I would have an opportunity to explain that I was just finishing a letter. Instead, the fat guard opened the door and told me to come outside. I did and he started walking to the elevator, saying that he heard that I had an attitude problem. So, he, two bridgeboys, and I got on the elevator up to the hole. On the floor where the hole is, we got off and they locked me in a cell that did not have a bed. All it had was toilet and a ragged blanket on a concrete floor.

I was surprised that he had put me in the hole and thought that I would only be there a day or two. However, I stayed there until I went to court, five days. I was not allowed to shower on the floor where I had a cell. Instead, I showered on the basement floor and got dressed. I needed a haircut because I had not had one since August. Haircuts were on Saturday, and I was planning to get my hair cut the Saturday before I went to trial. But I did not have a chance to get a haircut because I was in the hole. Now, I was going to court with very bushy hair, and looking in the mirror, I knew that I looked like a black militant. When my name was called, my heart began to pound fiercely as handcuffs were put on me to take me to court.

Chapter 8

At the courthouse, I was taken to a holding cell in the Sheriff's office. I did not have a watch, but I guessed that it was about 9 in the morning and my trial was supposed to start at 10 A.M. An elderly deputy began to ask me some questions that he was typing on a form. I saw Sheriff Griffin walk in and sit at a desk. A few minutes later, another elderly man came to the cage and was asking me did I have a juvenile record. I told him no. At that point, Sheriff Griffin looked up and said, "you better leave him alone until you get him in the courtroom." Then I realized that the man who asked me that question was Solicitor General Andrew Ryan, Jr. A few minutes later, I heard Drew come in and asked if they had brought in Alexander, and then someone said yes. Drew came to the cage.

"Tell me only what happened in the store," he snarled slightly.

I nervously told him that I was in the store when Thomas and the other boys came in. We started arguing and . . .

Before I could finish, Drew interrupted me angrily and said in a very loud voice, "And that's when you just shot him down."

I felt as if Drew had punched me in the stomach when I wasn't looking. I did not expect that type of attack minutes before walking in the courtroom. I was stunned and did not know what to say.

"Did you buy anything when you were in that store?" Drew asked.

"Yes," I stammered. "I bought a Coca-Cola."

Then Drew walked off without saying any more.

I was stunned by the exchange that had just occurred and did not know what to make of it. This was the first time that anyone had asked anything about what happened, and the nastiness with which it was done confused me. In December, Drew told me that when the time came for someone to talk to me, someone would be at the jail. But no one came and then I was asked basically two questions in the sheriff's office and I was not given an opportunity to finish one. I was stunned and did not know what to make of it. It caused my heart to start pounding more fiercely, and this exchange made me more nervous.

Then, a black man came for me and I was ushered into the courtroom. I had to walk by all the state witnesses, but I did not look at any. I was ushered to the defense table. Kravitch was not at the table, and there was only Drew. My heart was pounding so fiercely that I was having problems hearing. The judge was talking, but I initially couldn't hear him because I was hearing a roaring sound in my ears. I was really nervous and was trying hard to calm down. I started looking around and saw my momma, Daddy, and Willie Lee sitting on the right side of the room from where I was sitting. The prosecutor table was directly in front of the defense table, and it contained Andrew Ryan, Jr., his son Andrew Ryan, III, and Robert Barker.

When I walked in the courtroom, Daddy had to take out his handkerchief because he started crying. He felt responsible for me being in jail and believed that he did not do enough to keep the situation from coming to what it did. He had told me during one visit, that he should have been the one in jail and not me. I knew that he meant it. Now, he couldn't take that I was about to go on trial for murder.

Jury selection began. Before it did, Drew asked that jurors not be excluded because they were opposed to capital punishment, but Dunbar Harrison ignored him. People were called in panels and, among other questions, were asked if they were related to me. Drew asked some questions, such as people's ages. The prosecutors did not have many questions to ask, but they rejected some of the jurors. Drew rejected one juror and I heard a strange statement from one rejected jury that puzzled me. But really I was too nervous and tense to understand much of what was going on at my trial.

After Drew rejected a male juror, this male juror walked behind the defense table and between the court deputy that sat behind the defense table. Just as the juror was between Drew and me, he leaned over and said, "Lionel, you sure surprised me."

I looked at Drew, who heard the juror's statement, but did not look up to acknowledge it.

I immediately understood that this juror knew Drew personally and knew him well enough to call him by his first name. This juror was surprised that Drew had an opportunity to select him to sit on the jury, but did not.

I did not know what to make of it and really couldn't process what had just occurred. But my thinking was that many defense attorneys would want a friend or neighbor to sit on a jury in which they were trying a case, unless something was wrong with the juror. From the juror's reaction and Drew's reaction, this prospective juror was not biased against me. If this juror had told Drew that the boy who killed the so-called choirboy should have the book thrown at him, then this juror should have expected Drew's decision to reject him, and Drew could have faced him. Instead, there was a reason unknown to me that Drew did not want his friend on this jury.

When the jury was picked, it consisted of all men, 11 white and one black. However, having this one black juror did not thrill me. He was elderly and the way he held his hat in his hand suggested to me that he had never disagreed with a white man in his life and had never expressed an opinion that was different from a white man in the white man's presence. He would go along with whatever the 11 white men told him to do. I did not think that this black juror was any good, because if he were, the prosecutor would have excused him. I had learned from listening to some of the guys in the jail that many of these jurors repeatedly serve. A case could be tried on Monday and the same jurors come back on Thursday. So, the prosecutors are very familiar with the jurors and know a lot about their attitudes and views.

The jury left the room and the issue regarding the gun and whether it had been illegally seized was being reviewed. I was trying to follow what was being said and comparing it to what I heard 7 months ago at my preliminary hearing. I wasn't sure, but I believed that Officer Nealy and Bush lied and changed their testimony from what they said in police court at my preliminary hearing.

Officer Nealy testified first. I felt uneasy about what he was saying, but I did not know why. The most striking statement that he made was in response to one of Robert Barker's questions, Officer Nealy said, "I gotta tell the truth."

Immediately, I knew that Nealy had been asked before the start of the trial to change his testimony. I knew this because I had seen and heard state court prosecutors coerced and asked police officers to change their testimonies. When I prosecuted Lawrence for cutting me, I always had to go to court early and I was directed to report to the prosecutor's office. There, the prosecutor would be going over testimony and in one case he told a police officer that he had done wrong. The prosecutor then lowered his voice and leaned over to talk to the officer. Daddy told me that the prosecutor was telling the officer to change his story. When we got in court, this case was called before ours and sure enough, the officer lied. Daddy nudged me in the side and said, "I told you so."

There was something wrong with Nealy's testimony, but I couldn't say for sure what it was.

Drew asked Officer Nealy some general questions and seemed to concur that I had a bulge on my person that caused me to be searched. Drew was interested in whether Officer Nealy knew that he was gonna find a weapon when he touched this bulge and whether he had a search warrant.

I had an idea that this testimony was not correct, but I did not know why. I couldn't think. I had the same feelings about Officer Bush's testimony, but I did not know what was wrong with it. The highlight of Bush's testimony was that he said Officer Nealy stopped me and Dunbar Harrison interrupted him and said that they had just heard from Officer Nealy and Officer Nealy said Bush made the stop. Dunbar Harrison was angry about this contradiction. Bush repeated the story about the bulge and that I was standing at an angle at which he couldn't see it.

Drew then began to talk about the Fourth and Fourteenth Amendments to the United States Constitution, but I did not know what he was talking about. The issue was resolved, and the jury was returned for the start of the trial.

Drew's opening remarks to the jury were that there was bad blood between the deceased and me, that there was some type of conflict between myself and some boys, and that these boys had been harassing me. He asked the jury to listen closely and he knew that they would.

I disagreed with his description of bad blood and harassment. It sounded as if there was some type of feuding going on involving me, and I knew that was not the case. Also, using the word harassment was totally inaccurate. There was an attempt to maim me. Moreover, I was shot at, a gun was pulled on my brother whom someone thought was me, and my life and my Daddy's life were threatened. This is not harassment.

The prosecutor's first witness was someone named Charles Green who went to Saint Benedict and testified that the deceased went to Saint Benedict too. Green testified that he saw me in the store and I asked him was church out. He said further that I did not ask him any more questions.

The prosecutor knew that I had a girlfriend that went to Saint Benedict because the detectives who investigated the case were trying to get Beulah to testify against me. She told them that we were going together, and she was not gonna testify against me. So, the prosecutor was careful not to convey to the jury that I had a valid reason for being in that area, but I did not really expect him to convey it. That was Drew's job.

But Drew declined to ask Green any questions. I felt for some reason that Drew did not wanna get into that with Green and would do so when Beulah testified. The prosecutor was trying to lay the basis for premeditation, but I was sure that Drew could disprove this or at the least cast doubt on it.

The next witness was Willie Wright, the deceased's cousin. He testified that Thomas was about 3 or 4 feet from me when the shooting occurred. He testified further that no one in the group said or did anything to provoke me to shoot. He had his legs crossed and was trying to talk cool. When Drew asked him about the attack on me, he stated that he did not know anything about it and Thomas said that he was helping me when I was assaulted.

I thought to myself that Willie was a lying dog. Willie was at that party and was there when I was jumped. He, along with a few others, stood in the back about 10 or 15 yards, and the other three guys attacked me. He lied when he testified that there was nothing said because I heard him when he said that I was gonna get it now. Drew's questions were centered on trying to get Willie to admit that I was attacked, but Willie claimed he did not know anything about it. The problem was why try to prove that I was hurt by the testimony by the deceased's cousin. I was taken to Memorial Hospital and medical records would show that I was injured.

The next witness was William Cameron and he testified that no one did anything to put me in fear of my life. Drew again was trying to get this witness of the state, who was a friend of the deceased, to talk about a fight.

The storeowner testified and changed his testimony considerably from what he told my daddy on the day of the shooting. He lied about where I was standing and where the deceased was standing. He also lied about seeing a gun. According to Daddy, the storeowner told him that he never saw a gun and did not know who shot who. But I know the detectives and prosecutors helped him with his testimony.

Then, several police officers testified, including Bush and Nealy.

The prosecutor's last witness was the lab person who tested the gun, and then the prosecutor rested.

Immediately and without a recess, Drew began the defense and told me to take the witness stand as the first defense witness. I had no idea that I would be called as a witness, and I did not have any idea what questions he was gonna ask me. My heart was pounding fast as I walked to the witness stand. It began to pound harder when Drew told the bailiff to swear me in because I knew that this meant that I would be cross-examined by the prosecutor. I had no idea what to expect from the prosecutor and I had heard how defendants have been tricked on the witness stand.

Drew began by asking me some relatively easy questions like where did I live and how old I was. When he started asking about Thomas, I did not like how he was phrasing the question.

Q: Rudolph, prior to the time when Thomas was killed, did you and Thomas have a fight?

A: Well, he was with some—he-well, he was leading them. He led the boys that jumped on me.

I was trying as best as I could to correct what Drew told the jury in his opening statement about there being bad blood on my part and I had some fight with Thomas. The Tornado gang, of which Thomas was a member, attacked me without any warning and without me hitting anyone. In my mind, this is not a fight. I never hit any of them.

As I was trying to explain further Barker objected:

May it please the Court, I hate to object, but his line of questioning would be entirely immaterial and irrelevant to this case. If any conflict existed—we don't know that it existed except for his testimony—but if it existed prior to this it would certainly be no defense or mitigation for shooting and killing a person and we would object on the grounds that it's immaterial and irrelevant.

Dunbar Harrison said it is true that a defendant can't kill another person for a past wrong but he would let the jury decide its relevance. Drew told the judge that he was gonna connect it.

Q: Rudolph, were you hurt in this fight?

A: Yes, sir, I was.

Q: How were you—how did you get hurt?

A: Well, one of the boys cut me with a knife.

Q: Where did he cut you?

A: Right over my eye.

Q: Which eye?

A: My right eye.

Q: Did you have to have medical treatment for this?

A: Yes, sir.

Q: Rudolph, did you lose any of your property, your personal property, any of your belongings in this fight?

A: Yes, sir, I did.

Q: What did you lose?

A: A gold watch.

I was so nervous as I testified that I did not realize that Drew was changing to my disadvantage what happened to my watch and led me to convey that I simply lost it. Thomas took the watch off my wrist while a gun was being held on me.

Q: All right. Now, tell the jury, Rudolph, in your own words, exactly what happened when Thomas came into the store.

I paused a little and I thought about what Drew had said to me in the Sheriff's office when he asked me to tell him only what happened in the store and then cut me off, accusing me of just shooting the choirboy down. I tried to answer as best as I could.

A: Well, when he came into the store he saw me and he got kind of a frown on his face and I got kind of scared . . . I asked him why did he jump on me and he say "no man, you know that wasn't me." Say, "I was trying to help you," like that and he kept on talking. Then he made some kind of hand gesture, gesture, like he was trying to bring over a point—

Q: Like—like what now?

A: Hand gesture, you know, bring his hands up like this and when did that I became frightened and started shooting.

Drew asked me a few more questions, then he sat down. I knew that I had not conveyed accurately what happened, but had done the best that I could, given the circumstances.

Then, Barker, one of three prosecutors, got up to begin his cross-examination.

Q: You were scared? But at no time had he threatened you over there that morning, at no time did you see a weapon in his hand and at no time did he jump you that morning?

A: That morning?

Q: That's right.

A: No.

Q: And this is for something that you say took place some two weeks before?

A: It did.

Q: You really hated his guts because this other thing had happened, didn't you?

A: I didn't hate his guts.

Q: Well, didn't you hate him enough to pull that gun out and kill him?

A: No, I did not hate him.

Then, Barker told me that I could come down. On the way back to the defense table, I realized that Barker was trying to get me to say that the shooting in the store occurred because of something that happened two weeks earlier, and I responded that it did. However, I was not agreeing with Barker, but I was saying that it did happen and was responding to Barker saying "you say." The tricks that the guys in the jail had warned me about occurred, but I knew that this was all Drew's fault.

Beulah testified next, but her testimony was not particularly helpful. Before asking Beulah any questions, Drew looked at a note on the defense table, but I couldn't see what he was looking at. Drew failed to ask her specifically if she went to St. Benedict Church as a way of explaining to the jury why I was in that area. Instead, he established that she was my girlfriend. He never asked her about the many threats made on my life by that gang and Thomas.

Swinton, who shunned my parents around the courthouse and who refused to sit by them before the trial started, stunned me by testifying in a damaging manner. He said that I told him that I was not gonna stand for the way that I had been attacked, and on cross-examination the prosecutor asked him to repeat it to the jury.

I knew then that I was sunk and that I was gonna be convicted. Shortly afterwards, Dunbar Harrison told Drew that they had heard enough and the trial came to a close, a couple of hours after it started.

The witnesses were allowed to return to the courtroom. The State's witnesses sat opposite to my parents, including Swinton. He had not sat by my parents before the trial started or when it closed. Instead, he sat by some of the Tornado gang members who had sat in on my trial.

Drew's summation to the jury was terrible. He began by telling the jury that he was a law-abiding citizen and did not like to see someone take the law into his own hands like I had done. He said that he did not know anything about me and that I might be a hoodlum. But he knew that if I could bring the deceased back, I would. Then, he said that he knew that there was no one on the jury who opposed the death sentence because if they did they would not be on the jury. He told the jury that I shouldn't be given the death penalty and instead the jury should let me go so that I could do better.

I couldn't believe my ears.

When Andrew Ryan III stood before the jury, he told them that the deceased had held his hands up and demonstrated by stretching both of his hands to the ceiling. He was depicting a situation similar to one in which a person was committing an armed robbery and told everyone to reach for the ceiling. As Ryan held his hand up-stretch, he said that Thomas said, "I did not do it," and this was the moment that I shot him. As he parroted the last phrase, he had a dramatic sound in his voice. Picking up on Drew's discussion about the death penalty, he told the jury that the state did not care whether the jury gave me a life sentence or a death sentence. The State just wanted a murder conviction, the Ryan son said.

The judge charged the jury. The jury was read the definitions of murder and manslaughter and the penalties for each. They were also given the charge on justifiable homicide although Drew never mentioned it in either his opening or closing statements. At the end, the judge asked if there was any objection to the charge. Drew told the judge that the requested charge on admissions and confessions was not given. Dunbar Harrison told Drew that it was unnecessary, but Drew stated that I had admitted to the shooting. But Dunbar Harrison reminded Drew that came during my testimony.

It seemed odd that Drew told the jury a few minutes earlier that I had taken the law into my own hands and might be a hoodlum, and then quibble with the judge whether a charge should be given regarding confessions and admissions.

The jury then was allowed to go to lunch. Upon their return from lunch, they began to deliberate and returned to the courtroom to ask for the charge again on murder.

Dunbar Harrison read the charge again on murder and told them that they do not have to assign a reason to recommend mercy. He told them that if they said that they found me guilty and said no more, then that would mean the death penalty for me. If they said that they found me guilty with a recommendation of mercy, then that would mean a life sentence for me.

When I heard this exchange, the blood drained from me just like it did when I was staring down the barrel of the gun that was being held on me a few months ago. I was taken back to the holding area in the sheriff's office, and I went completely numb. I thought that I was looking at a life sentence for sure. After about 15 or 20 minutes, I was taken back into the courtroom.

On the way to the defense table, I looked over at my family. My parents looked dazed and my brother was shaking violently. A deputy walked over towards them and said, "There will be no outburst when the verdict is read."

The verdict was handed to a deputy. When the deputy took the card and looked at it, he flipped it over to see if there was something on the back of the card. This was an omen of what was to come! He read to the court, "We the jury find the defendant guilty." I knew that this meant that I had been given the death penalty and I was thunderstruck.

The three prosecutors had seemed to go after me hard and aggressive. However, they, in addressing the jury, never pressed the jury to give me a death sentence. I knew that in other cases, the prosecutors had asked the jury to bring back death sentences. Many times juries did, especially when the defendant was black and the victim was white. A few times, the prosecutors asked for death sentences and the jury rejected this demand, sentencing the defendants instead to life imprisonment. But I was getting a death sentence in a case in which the prosecutor had not asked for the death penalty.

Dunbar Harrison said that he was not gonna sentence me that day and that I would be returned to court the next day to be sentenced. Then, I was ushered out of the courtroom. The handcuffs were immediately put on me, and I was directed to the stairs. As I was walking towards the stair, I could hear celebration from people from the east side.

When I was returned to the jail, the jailer asked the deputy what sentence did I get. They did not say anything until I was let through the door to the jail floors. I was told that I was gonna be returned to the hole, and I was allowed to change my clothes. When I returned to the cells, I leaned against the wall and slid down the wall until I was on the floor. My head turned towards the floor, and tears started to stream down my face. After a few seconds, I began to lie on the floor. When supper was brought to me, I refused it. I wondered how did this all happened and began to replay everything that had happened as best I could. It took me several hours to replay everything and calm down. I tried to sleep. However, the concrete floor seemed to be much harder this night.

When I returned to court the next day, only Daddy, Beulah, and Julia were there. My heart was pounding so hard that I couldn't hear what Dunbar Harrison was saying. I knew that he said something about what the jury decided and then I heard him said something about June and I heard him say may God have mercy on my soul.

I asked Drew to ask my daddy to come around to the holding cell. Drew snapped, "You ask the deputy."

I did not ask the deputy and was ushered to the holding area in the sheriff's office. A few seconds later, my Daddy, Julia, and Beulah were standing at the door of the holding cell.

They had taken it upon themselves to come to the sheriff's office. Beulah and Julia were crying, and Daddy had his head down as he talked to me. He voice was so low that he seemed to be whispering. I thought that I heard him say something about Mrs. Pearson, whom my momma worked for, but I couldn't understand him.

I told Daddy that it was not over yet and was trying to raise his spirit. He kept his head down and one might have thought that he had been given the death sentence instead of me. I was still shaken, but I was beginning to recoup a little. I was taken back to the jail and allowed to return to the third floor. The guard who had put me in the hole decided to suspend my time in the hole.

The next day, when I read the paper I learned that my execution date was June 14, 1968, less than 2 months away. As in the beginning, Thomas was always referred to as the choir boy who was killed after he had attended mass. I wondered did he have mass or confession on the Friday before he hooked up with the Tornado gang to attack me.

Chapter 9

Later that week, I received a letter from Mildred. In the letter, she mentioned that momma had spoken with Mrs. Pearson, and Mrs. Pearson had talked to her brother-in-law about me, a lawyer named James Head. She said that Mr. Head agreed to meet with Daddy to talk about what happened at my trial. Mildred said that Momma and Daddy were perplexed and upset that the newspaper said that I had a court appointed attorney and that people were saying that my parents had failed to hire a good lawyer for me and this was the reason why I got the electric chair. She closed by telling me not to give up because no one at home had given up on me.

I also received a letter from someone in Atlanta. He told me that he had read about me getting the electric chair and wanted to save my soul before I was executed. I tore up the letter. One of the guys told me that I shouldn't have torn the letter up because I may need that man later if my appeals were unsuccessful. The last place to invalidate a death sentence is the State Board of Pardons and Paroles, and this is where condemned persons turned when their appeals have been unsuccessful. However, I felt that I did the right thing by tearing up the letter.

On Tuesday, I received several visits and heard an earful that made me extremely angry. Daddy told me that he did not know that Aaron Kravitch was not coming to my trial, and that Aaron Kravitch did not say anything about not coming the day before the trial. Expecting Aaron Kravitch to come to court and win the case as he had promised that he would do, Daddy said Drew came up to him and told him that Aaron Kravitch wasn't gonna be there and had sent him. According to Daddy, Drew said that he did not know that much about my case and I had to go to trial that day.

"After your trial ended, I had your sister Mildred call Aaron Kravitch at home and his wife said that he was down at his office," said Daddy.

I learned that Daddy and Momma were both crying when they returned home and couldn't talk. So, they asked Mildred to make the call. Moreover, they never told my other sisters and brother what happened to me at trial when they returned home. My youngest sister learned what had happened to me when she went to school the next day. She came home crying and found Momma crying as she was cooking dinner. Momma awkwardly told her that I had been given the electric chair.

Daddy said that he had met with Mr. Head, and Mr. Head couldn't believe what Drew had said to the jury. Daddy said that he had told Mr. Head that Drew had told the jury that I had taken the law into my own hands and that I was a hoodlum.

"Oh, no, he did not address the jury like that," said Mr. Head, according to Daddy.

Daddy said that Mr. Head told him that if Drew said that he did not know that much about my case that Drew never should have proceeded, and my trial should have been delayed if Aaron Kravitch truly couldn't come.

"Why did Drew go ahead with the case?" Daddy said Mr. Head asked him. Daddy said that Mr. Head told him not to tell Aaron Kravitch that he had spoken with another lawyer. Daddy said that Mr. Head told him that he was an official with the Savannah Bar Association, and the bar association has gotten a lot of complaints about Aaron Kravitch. He said that he couldn't understand why people continue to go to Aaron Kravitch because the last few years he has been doing nothing but taking money from people for legal work that is not done.

Daddy said that he told Mr. Head more about the case and what was told the jury by Drew. Daddy said that Mr. Head told him that my defense was not handled right.

"Mr. Head told me that me and Thelma both should have been defense witnesses in this case," said Daddy. "Also, the dead boy's parents should have been subpoenaed."

"That makes sense, Daddy," I said. "That would have taken a lot of responsibility and pressure off me in this case. That jury was probably wondering why, if I had some problems, didn't I tell my parents or call the police. So, it makes a lot of sense for you, Momma, and the dead person's parents to be called as defense witnesses. It also made sense for the jury to be told that I had pressed charges last year against Lawrence and had called the police when this gang attacked me. The jury was not told any of this because Drew was gonna tell them that I took the law into my own hands and Drew wanted the jury to believe this damaging statement."

Daddy said that Mr. Head asked why didn't Aaron Kravitch leave the case alone if he did not really want it. Instead, Aaron Kravitch took the case and had messed it up.

"Daddy, there are some lawyers who tell people that they are not gonna work hard to help you if you don't pay them. But there are some lawyers that you can pay and they still won't try to help you. All they are interested in is how they can flimflam you and how much they can make from selling you out. Aaron Kravitch had the parents of the dead person wanting to hire him to prosecute me and you wanting to hire him to defend me. This is ideal for a corrupt lawyer. He takes money from both sides and then sends Drew to do a hatchet job on me."

My brother came to see me and told me that I had been the subject of a call-in radio talk show. He said that a white woman called and stated that I had not been given a fair trial and it was wrong for the jury to have given me the electric chair.

Daddy said that he met with Aaron Kravitch a few days after my trial, and as soon as he walked into the office, Aaron Kravitch starting talking. He told Daddy that he was sorry and that he thought that Drew could handle the case. Continuing his lying, he stated that he had to go out of town and that he asked Judge Harrison to put off my trial, but Dunbar Harrison said no and I had to go to trial the next day. Daddy said that Aaron Kravitch closed by telling him that he had to have 500 more dollars to save my life.

"I told him that I did not have any more money, and I couldn't get any more," said Daddy. "I told Aaron Kravitch that he did not do me or my boy right," said Daddy.

Daddy said that Aaron Kravitch told him that he had always helped Negroes and to go to the NAACP, Mayfield, or Gadsen and asked them about him.

I knew that Mayfield and Gadsen were two of the three black lawyers in Savannah.

"Don't do that Daddy," I said. "He is working with both Mayfield and Gadsen now on cases, and they are not gonna say anything against him. Also, he represented an official with the NAACP in a case involving the sodomy of a boy and Kravitch got him off. All of them are gonna tell you can trust Aaron Kravitch. Aaron Kravitch is nothing but a crooked dog. He represents some people, and some people he steals and cheats. We don't need some Negroes to try and tell us differently."

Daddy also told me that he met one of the jury members in my case. According to him, a white man came up to him at work and told him that he heard that one of the employees at Union Camp had a son who had been given the electric chair. He realized that he had served on a jury in which a boy was given the electric chair. Daddy said that he and the white man starting talking and daddy told him things that were not brought up at trial. The white man told Daddy that he should fire the lawyer who represented me at the trial because if the jury knew that I had been having as much trouble as he heard and that the dead boy was part of a gang, the jury would have turned me loose. The white man said that the jury went mostly by what they heard in court, and that there was nothing good said about me. Everything that was said at the trial was against me, and even the lawyer who was representing me was talking against me.

Daddy said that this juror told him that I could easily get a new trial because another juror admitted in the jury room that he was on the grand jury that had indicted me. He said the jury decided not to say anything about it, and they all knew that he was not supposed to be on my trial jury. Also, this juror who served on the grand jury that indicted me told the jury things that were said about me during this grand jury process.

Daddy said he was talking to another white person about Aaron Kravitch and this white man told him that he should have gone down to Aaron Kravitch's office and blown Kravitch's brains out and he wouldn't blame him one bit. This white man told him that if he had hired and paid a lawyer to represent his son and the lawyer did what Kravitch and Drew did and his son got the electric chair that he would have killed both of them.

Before leaving Daddy told me that one of Mr. Head's associates was gonna come to the jail to interview me and that he had signed a paper for Mr. Head to take over the case.

Later that day, Beulah and Swinton came to me. Swinton couldn't look me in the eye and looked down at the floor. I told him that he hurt me in the trial, but I mostly wanted to know from both of them who did they talk to before coming to trial. Both Beulah and Swinton told me that they never spoke with Drew or Aaron Kravitch before the trial date. Both said that they just received subpoenas to come to court.

I knew this was gross malpractice. My momma gave Aaron Kravitch the names, addresses, and telephone numbers of possible defense witnesses in September, and no one attempted to contact either Beulah or Swinton to see if either had beneficial testimony to offer my defense. It was unconscionable for any lawyer, regardless of his experience, to subpoena people and not learn what they have to say until they get on the witness stand. I also remembered Drew looking at some notes just before Beulah began testifying. Drew was faking because no one had interviewed Beulah or Swinton. Drew was pretending like he had notes from a previous interview.

The next day, I received a visit from a lawyer who identified himself as Mr. Boney. He told me that he worked with Mr. Head and they had been asked to look into my case. We sat in the cell that was used for lawyers to meet their clients. This was the first time that I sat in this little room.

Mr. Boney told me that he had an appointment later that day and needed to leave shortly but he wanted to begin the interviewing process and would come back the next day to finish it. He told me that he had already done some investigation and pulled out a long yellow pad. He told me to begin at the beginning and tell him everything.

After a few minutes of writing, Mr. Boney asked, "Did anyone from Aaron Kravitch's office come down here and do what I am doing now with this yellow pad?"

"No, Sir. You are the first person to ask me questions about my case. I saw Mr. Kravitch in September for a few minutes when I was in the city jail, but he just introduced himself and told me that he had been hired to represent me. He told me that I might be put in a line-up, but he did not want me to go. Then he left. In December, I saw Mr. Drew after I tried to fire Mr. Kravitch and Mr. Drew told me that I couldn't fire Mr. Kravitch because I was a minor.

Minutes before the trial, Mr. Drew asked me to tell him what happened in the store, but he did not let me finish."

Mr. Boney paused, looked at me, and shook his head.

Mr. Boney asked me about my watch, how much I paid for it, and where I purchased it. He asked me exactly where was I attacked and wondered if there might have been someone looking out the window that saw me being attacked and saw the deceased participating in it.

Drew pretended that he couldn't prove that I had been attacked and was trying unsuccessfully and unwisely to get the friends of the deceased to testify that the deceased participated in an attack on me. The prosecutor was saying that there was no evidence of an attack except for my word. But Drew never intended to prove that the deceased attacked me or was a member of the Tornado gang.

But Mr. Boney was taking a different angle, which was the only correct angle for a honest lawyer.

Mr. Boney also asked me about the Tornado gang and who were some of the other boys in this gang. I told him the names of the boys who attacked me and the ones who were threatening my life and my daddy's life.

"There is one of them in the kitchen now," I told Mr. Boney.

"One of who?" said Mr. Boney.

"One of the Tornadoes and one of the boys who attacked me. "His name is Thomas Williams. He has the same name as the dead person and he is the one who actually cut me. I did not see who had the knife and never saw a weapon, but I knew a few seconds after I was hit that I had been cut and that it had come from one of the Williams. There was some talk that I shot someone who had helped me and who did not have anything to do with hurting me, but this was not true."

"I need to leave now, but I will return in the morning," said Mr. Boney.

The next morning he was back, and we picked up where we left off. He told me that he had checked the criminal records of the boys that I named and all had bad criminal records. He also told me that he had checked on the Thomas Williams who was in the jail and told me that he was there for carrying a .38 pistol.

I thought that this was another piece of evidence that could have been used in my trial. This Thomas Williams had been in jail a couple of weeks before I went to trial and if Drew or Kravitch had properly interviewed me and come to the jail before the trial like all lawyers did then, they would have had that information and could have used it in my trial.

Mr. Boney stayed for about 2 hours, and when he left, I had told him everything.

He wanted the names of possible character witnesses for me and this was something else that Drew and Kravitch did not want. Kravitch and Drew did not want any character witnesses because they had planned to tell the jury that I might be a hoodlum.

I began to process everything and came to the conclusion that what I had initially heard about Aaron Kravitch was true, and my fears when I tried to fire him were justified. Now, I knew what being sold down the river was.

I also remembered that being sold down the river was a term used during slavery. When a slave was deemed to be a bad nigger, the slave was threatened with being sold down the Mississippi River. They were doing it during slavery. Now, some crooked defense lawyers in the 1960s were doing it in the courtroom.

When my daddy hired Aaron Kravitch, he had no intention of actually representing me at the trial. He decided to represent the dead person and steal money from Daddy. Supposedly, he told my daddy that when he was asked to help prosecute me, he turned it down because he only worked for the defense. But this was a lie. Aaron Kravitch took money to sabotage and throw my case. He was not gonna represent me, and he was gonna send Drew. This was Drew's case from the beginning and no favorable evidence was gonna be presented to the jury in my behalf. Nothing. They did not need to interview me, Beulah, or Swinton because all Drew was gonna do was go through the motions at trial. I was not gonna be told that I would be put on the witness stand, and I was gonna be steered to give useless and bad testimony. I understood now why Drew approached me in the sheriff's office in the manner that he did and what the purpose of this tactic was. Although Aaron Kravitch asked about a gang at the preliminary hearing, this was not gonna be touched at the trial where it would have been more helpful. Nothing bad was gonna be said about the deceased and bad things were gonna be said about me to the jury. I was gonna be deliberately hurt at the trial and Aaron Kravitch's alibi was gonna be that he had to go out of town and Dunbar Harrison would not let him put off the case. Drew's alibi was gonna be that he did not know much about my case. The end result would be that they couldn't be blamed for the lack of favorable evidence at my trial. I thought that these were two low-life, back-stabbing dogs who deserved to be butchered.

My blood was boiling just as it does when one is put in the electric chair. I had heard guys talk about it and how the skin is burned. Willie Robinson said that he was in Reidsville when the last person was electrocuted. According to him, on the day of an execution, everyone is kept inside and they do not go out to work in the fields. At the moment the switch is pulled, the lights in the dormitory flicker, and everyone knows that in a minute or two the condemned person is dead.

Willie Robinson also talked about other executions. He said that Bully Wallace, one of the most infamous guards in Reidsville, participated in executions and would talk about it after they had executed someone. Willie Robinson said that they would turn down the power when they were executing a white person so that the body would not be burned too badly. But the guards talked about really frying niggers and laughed afterward. He said the guards and especially Bully Wallace would come down from the fifth floor after an execution and brag about how the nigger's skin burst open.

I knew that I was in for a wait with respect to my appeal, so I settled back. I began to pay more attention to the guys on the floor and what was going on in the county jail. I started playing checkers and cards more. I played cards for pennies, and I only did this to pass time. I refused to gamble seriously, but I stood and watched.

The guys were always playing Skin and that was a game that I refuse to play. In my opinion, winning was based on luck or cheating. Little skills were involved. The dealer would turn out cards and guys around the table would take a card. Everyone has a different card, and no two players can have an ace, for example. Everyone around the table bet each other. The dealer takes cards out one at a time, and when a player card comes up, he loses everything around the board. So, someone with a jack of hearts loses if another jack comes up. This player then takes a clean card and bets everyone again. As long as a player's card doesn't come up, he keeps winning. Some bets will be increased as the game continued. When most of the cards are turned out and no more clean cards are available, a new game begins.

I quickly learned that some guys try to cheat by "running the cub." They would palm or hide in the palm of their hand, perhaps, all the sixes and put three on the bottom of the deck and keep one. Thus, this person is guaranteed to win and all the other cards will fall before the sixes. Generally, only the weak guys are cheated. I knew statistically that something was wrong if a deck was shuffled and three kings were at the bottom of the desk and a player had the other king.

I started playing poker and did not know how to play until some of the guys taught me. I would only play for pennies. After I learned what hand beat what hand, I had to learn how to bet. One day, I had a guy beat but did not know it. We both had the same thing, and he said that we were supposed to split the pot. Someone was tapping me on the foot, but I did not know what to do. Later, the person who was tapping me on the foot told me that I was supposed to have the entire pot myself because I had hard cards and the other person had wild cards. I was told that hard cards beat wild cards when two players have the same thing.

In June, the U.S. Supreme Court ruled in an Illinois case that the a man named Witherspoon had been given an unfair trial because persons opposed to capital punishment were improperly excused. The newspaper article stated nine defendants in Chatham County might be affected by the Court's ruling, and my name was included as being one of the nine. This ruling gave me some confidence that I was not gonna be executed.

One day, I was playing cards and someone asked what time was it. Another person answered 10 o'clock. At this moment, I began to shudder a little. Today was my scheduled execution day, and I heard that the execution time in Georgia is between 10 A.M. and 2 P.M. Georgia does not execute at midnight like in some movies, but instead does it during the day. A few minutes after 10 o'clock, I knew that I could have been dead. But to ease my mind, I also thought that I could have been dead in Memorial Hospital. I knew that if I had continued to go to the hospital that I was gonna go one too many times and eventually would be dead.

Out of curiosity, I asked a couple of the young boys who were arrested for killing the Chinese man about their case. Generally, I did not ask people about what they had been accused of doing. But I knew that they didn't do this crime and believed what I overheard Farmer Brown's sister say several months back. What made this interesting was that some of the guys who actually committed this crime were in jail too.

Two of the four boys who had been falsely accused signed confessions admitting to robbing and killing the Chinese man and two did not. This is what interested me. Why would someone sign a confession for a crime that he didn't do? I heard that some people are beaten in jail and forced to confess.

"Why did you sign a confession to this crime?" I said to Joe Brown, who was about 14 years old.

"The detectives were buying us hamburgers and telling us that there was nothing to the case. That they were gonna talk to the judge and the case probably would be thrown out of court. I never read the paper I signed," said Joe.

The other boy who signed a confession was Alonza Grant, and I could understand how he would sign it after observing him for a while. Alonza wasn't too smart and seemed to be a little slow, like he was retarded. He could be easily tricked. I wasn't being critical of him and felt sorry for him. They both got life and Barker told the jury that the robbery netted only a few dollars, but Joe Brown didn't care. Joe Brown didn't care because he didn't do it. Alonza cried throughout his trial with his head on the table.

Another guy who was charged with rape appeared to be totally innocent and had no involvement in what he was accused of doing. This was a black guy who was accused of raping a white nurse who worked at Memorial Hospital. He claimed that he was visiting his wife who had just had a baby and had complained to the supervising nurse about the nurse's behavior. The next day he was accused of kidnapping and raping the nurse. At the trial, the solicitor general put on the witness stand another nurse who testified that she saw him watching the nurse in the hospital and this was the gist of her testimony. So, if a black man watched a white nurse in the hospital, it made sense that he would later rape her. The case was very weak, but the jury convicted him and gave him a life sentence. Later, he was saying that the nurse admitted that she lied and he was gonna get out. He left the jail one day, but there was nothing in the newspaper.

But not all the guys were innocent. "Do you see that little son-of-a-bitch there?" asked Wyman. "He is a raping little bastard. Don't let his size fool you. He will take a woman's drawers down in a minute. I saw him yoke a drunk woman and was dragging her into an alley to rape her. He hollered for me to come get some too, but I got the hell away from that alley. I can't do any serious time. When it comes to doing time, I'm a pussy. I can do 6 months here and there, but I can't do a lot of time. I'll leave that hard-doing time for these tough motherfuckers."

One day as I was reading the newspaper, an article caught my eye. Dunbar Harrison declared a mistrial in a murder case. The article stated that "the mistrial came after what Solicitor General Andrew Joe Ryan described as a one in a thousand possibility had occurred. The possibility was that one of the twelve men selected for the trial jury had served on the grand jury in January, which indicted Hakala on a charge of murdering his wife, Mrs. Kate Goodman Hakala. As Assistant Solicitor General Andrew J. Ryan, III started to outline what the state's case would be against Hakala, a juror asked to approach the bench. The juror, John L. Anchors, said that he did not recognize the name but the circumstances outlined sounded very familiar. He said that he thought he might have served on the grand jury that indicted Hakala on January 16. Judge Harrison scanned the indictment, which contains the names of the grand jurors and found Anchors's included on the list. . . . Solicitor General Ryan said that it was to Anchors's credit that he quickly let it be known that he had served on the grand jury. Had he not, and had the matter been discovered later, the outcome could have been overturned as a matter of law."

But this was not a one in a thousand possibility because it happened in my case and it certainly was to no one's credit because my jury initially decided not to tell anyone that one of my jurors had served on the grand jury that indicted me.

A few days later, another article caught my eye. It was about the Tornado gang on the east side of which Thomas William was a member, but his membership had been protected by Kravitch and Drew. The article was entitled "Tornadoes Down to Slight Breeze." The story said that a guy in Hitch Village was jumped, beaten, and shot at. The article went on to say that the gang "had terrorized the neighborhood and that following the arrests several weapons were confiscated, including two sawed-off shotguns and several pistols."

I knew that this information should have been presented at my trial. The Tornado gang should have been put on trial and connected, properly so, to the dead person. The jury could have been told why the gang called themselves the Tornadoes, and the jury could have been reminded how quickly a real Tornado can touch down and how quickly it can move. Therefore, I had a legitimate reason to be fearful in the store, especially since I had been robbed and attacked before. I recalled that when the white man downtown at the motel was on trial, evidence was presented that he allowed an integrated football team to stay at his motel. Surely, if this white man could present this type of evidence, evidence about the Tornado gang could have been presented in my behalf. I knew that if a white person was attacked by a gang called the Tornadoes, the defense attorney would have been talking about this gang until he was blue in the face and demonstrating to the jury how dangerous the Tornadoes were. In a white man's case, the Tornadoes would have been compared to the Mau Mau's in Africa.

During my next visit, Daddy told me that he saw the article and called Mr. Head to alert him. Mr. Head told Daddy that he had read it, and this gang should have been talked about in my trial.

Instead, the jury, as I vividly remembered, was told about the poor choir boy who was gunned down for no reason.

Chapter 10

The next person after me to get sentenced to the electric chair was William Henry Furman. Before I went to trial, there were two guys in the County Jail with death sentences, and I became the third. Now the fourth person was William Furman. He had gone for a while to be evaluated at Milledgeville. When he came back, he was very fat, having gained considerable weight. Everyone knew that he was gonna get the electric chair. He had been charged with killing a white man, and the solicitor general always asks for the death penalty in capital cases involving white people as victims. A few get lucky and walk out of court with life sentences, but not many. Also, the guys mentioned that he had Mayfield as his defense attorney, and no one spoke highly of his skills as a defense attorney. The word on Mayfield was he was okay in state court where misdemeanors were tried, but he was not worth a damn in superior court.

When Furman came inside the doors after returning from court, everyone looked at him as he slowly walked inside the bull pen. When he reached near the sink, someone asked him what happened.

"They gave me the chair," said Furman. "That damn Barker told the jury that I should get the chair because I did not say that I was sorry."

I remember Eddie Simmons telling me that one of the prosecutor's tactics was to stress to the jury in summation that they did not hear him say that he was sorry for what he had done. The implication given to the all-white jury was that the nigger was glad to have killed a white man.

When Furman got to the sink, he put some water on his face. His behavior was similar to what Harold Young did after he came back to the jail and told everyone that he had gotten a life sentence. Harold had three cases of armed robbery, and in one case he pistol-whipped the white manager. For this, he was given a life sentence. When Harold came back to the county jail, he was choked with emotion as he repeated what Dunbar Harrison said about him spending the rest of his natural life in prison. Harold took out his washcloth, which he carried around with him to wet his face occasionally. He put it to his eyes, and I suspected that he did so to mask the tears that were welling up in his eyes.

Not many guys were being acquitted when they went to court. A few were acquitted, but not many. Horace got 10 years for robbery by sudden snatching. Guys were teasing him before he went to court, telling him that he was gonna get the electric chair because he broke Miss Ann's arm when he snatched her purse. They would tell him that he was gonna get the chair for breaking that white woman's arm.

Some guys teased and joked one another about how much time they had to do. One Sunday, Horace said that he wanted to watch "Wild Kingdom" on television, and a guy named Mel told him that he was gonna see all the wild animals he wanted to see when he went to the chain gang to begin serving his 10 years.

After things settled down and boredom set in, it seemed that some guys' playfulness increased. Woodrow and Honey played a lot and would start teasing some guys. When they saw the person was getting mad, they just kept on. There was no where to go to escape their pranks. After awhile, they would pick someone else.

Honey was playing with a young guy near the door when Captain Oliver came up to the bars. He told the guy that Honey was playing with to come out and then took him to the hole.

"Why didn't he put you in the hole, too, Honey, since you were horse-playing," asked one guy.

"He knows better than to fuck with me," said Honey. "I did 3 years at Chatham County Camp, and Oliver was a guard there then. He knows that I will kick his ass. He comes here hollering and cussing and you sons-of-bitches run from him. But not me. I learned a long time ago that white folks do what you let them do, and if they think you're scared of them then, they are gonna be nasty. You let them know that you will kick their asses, they leave you alone. Once white folks know that you ain't scared of them and would kicked their asses, you get more respect from them."

This reminded me of hearing white people saying, "treat me like a white man." The implication was that white men had two ways of dealing with people—like a nigger, which entailed disrespect, degradation, and dishonesty, and like a white man, which entailed respect, honesty, and fairness. I have heard some white people complaining that they had been treated like a nigger in some situations and I knew what that meant. I also knew that Kravitch and Drew treated me and Daddy like niggers.

Besides the guards being scared of Honey, so was Willie Robinson. Willie Robinson was trying to be friendly with both Honey and Woodrow, but it was obvious that they did not like him. They had been told how Willie Robinson had acted, pouring water by his cell and turning the television for spite. They tried to get some of the younger guys to provoke Willie Robinson, and as soon as Willie tried to fight one of the guys, Honey or Woodrow would step in and kick Willie Robinson's ass. But Willie Robinson never took the bait. He was quite meek now. Woodrow told me that Willie Robinson was not a real man and was pussy when he was in Reidsville. Willie Robinson used to say that he was a sissy, but most guys thought he was joking. Woodrow and Honey certainly made Willie Robinson's tough act vanish.

Honey left for a few months to serve his sentence for having a gun when he was arrested. He was sent to Chatham County prison camp and would return to the County Jail to await trial for robbery. It seemed that Willie Robinson was partly relieved that Honey was gone.

One day Woodrow, Joe Gator, and Willie Robinson were playing cards. Joe Gator and Willie Robinson appeared to be partners because Willie Robinson was giving Joe Gator money to bet. Woodrow was losing, and as the game came to an end, it was obvious why. Joe Gator and Willie Robinson had run the "cub" on Woodrow. When Joe Gator turned out the deck, three jacks were on the bottom, and Joe Gator had the fourth Jack. Woodrow and Joe Gator started fighting, but they were mostly wrestling with a few punches being thrown. After they fought for a while and stopped, Woodrow asked for Willie Robinson.

Upon hearing this, Willie Robinson ran to the front bars screaming like a woman for the guards. "Captain! Captain! Captain!" he screamed like a woman. He was running and turning his head to see if Woodrow was behind him. Guys were looking at each in other in shock. Some guys, remembering the antics of Willie Robinson, were laughing at him, and some were mad. Some said that they outta kick his ass now because it was plainly obvious that he was a fake. Since then, Willie Robinson stayed close to the front. He would not come back by the television anymore and would watch television from around the checker board. If a fight broke out by the television, Willie Robinson headed for the front. He had been totally exposed.

Woodrow came up to me one day and told me that I needed to do something about Stacko, who was in my cell. Woodrow said that he had noticed that Stacko did not take showers and wondered how I could live in a cell with someone like that.

"Well, I noticed that he doesn't take a shower, but he doesn't smell," I said. "Maybe he is a person with little body odor, and I have seen him washing under his arms."

"Well, if you don't do something about it, I will," said Woodrow.

"Hey Stacko, I noticed that you haven't been taking a shower. Are you afraid someone is gonna fuck you in your ass?" Woodrow shouted to Stacko.

"Hell no, I'm a real man," Stacko answered.

"Then why won't you wash your ass? You can't stay on this floor without washing. You don't have to be afraid, ain't no one gonna take your ass."

"I've showered," Stacko said.

"Has anyone in here seen Stacko wash his rusty ass?" asked Woodrow.

No one said anything.

"I'll wash if it will satisfy you," Stacko said, embarrassed.

Stacko got his towel and headed for the shower. After he had taken his clothes off and stood under the water, he told Woodrow that he wasn't afraid, that this proves it.

Guys were laughing as Stacko washed and thanked Woodrow for embarrassing Stacko into washing. This was the first shower that Stacko had taken in the jail since he had been there, and he had been in jail over a year.

A blatant sissy was put in the cellblock, and Willie Robinson immediately had the sissy put in his cell. Woodrow told Willie Robinson, "You can get that sissy in your cell, but you're not gonna fuck him in here." Woodrow, then, turned to someone and said that Willie Robinson probably was gonna swap out with the sissy. Woodrow kept going to Willie Robinson's cell to see what they were doing. At one point, Willie Robinson and the sissy were in bed together, the sissy in front of Willie Robinson, and Willie Robinson trying to pull down the sissy's pants.

"I told you that you're not gonna fuck in here," said Woodrow. "Captain, Captain," Woodrow shouted loudly. "There is a sissy in here and they are trying to fuck." One of the guards came to the bars, and Woodrow said to the guard to get that sissy out of here because they were trying to fuck. A guard and a bridgeboy came in and went to Willie Robinson's cell. They took the sissy out of Willie Robinson's cell and put him on the first floor in a cell by himself. After everyone came out of their cells after lunch, Willie Robinson went into the bathroom to call downstairs to the sissy, reassuring him that they would be together. Later, Willie Robinson went to the back near the television set and was on his knees calling down to the sissy. I was sitting next to Calvin Mitchell, and we both looked at each other and shook our heads.

The end of 1968 was coming, and rumors were circulating that the jail had to be integrated by January 1, 1969 by orders of a federal judge. The rumors were correct. On the first of January, after breakfast, we were locked in our cells longer than usual. Sims, who operated the jail, came up with a clipboard and began telling specific guys to pack their gear. The guards were escorting guys out to the second floor and bringing white guys up and putting them in the vacated cells.

I did not wanna go downstairs although the set up was exactly the same. Sims did not call my name, so I stayed in my cell. After the reshuffling, the doors were opened and the County Jail was integrated. When the white guys came out, they seemed to accept their new homes and began making small talk like white people did.

Before long, the white guys were talking about how much pussy they had eaten and telling a few skeptical black guys that they should try it. For most black guys, eating pussy was taboo.

But the white guys looked a little scared, and one could easily see the change in their attitude. When they have the upper hand, they are quite nasty, but when they don't, they try to be friendly. However, it is obvious that the friendliness is not genuine. There was hardly any fighting between black and white prisoners. This was mostly because the white guys would back down quickly before a conflict escalated into a fight. On the other hand, two black guys would try and show that they are tough and unafraid. If one person said, "I oughta kick your ass," the other person would say, "And what will I be doing when you doing all this ass-kicking?" Then, the fight was on.

The only interracial conflict that I saw after integration of the jail involved Prayer, but it was not much of a conflict. Prayer, who lived on the west side and who used to come around Beach High to fight or attend football pep rallies although he had dropped out, was smoking some aspirins and pretending like he was getting high. He had a hat tilted on the side of his head and was strutting down the cellblock like he was on West Broad Street.

I could sense that he was gonna do something to someone and I had a suspicion that it would be a white guy. As he approached a white guy who was returning to his cell with a magazine, Prayer reached out for the magazine and gently pulled the magazine toward him and away from the white guy. Prayer did not pull the magazine hard enough to snatch the magazine. So, the white guy gently pulled the magazine towards himself and away from Prayer's tug. At this moment, Prayer slapped the white guy in the face so savagely that it could be heard throughout the cellblock. The white guy, his face brightly reddened from the vicious slap, went into his cell and slammed the door violently. Neither Prayer nor the white guy had said a word during this incident, and Prayer continued strutting down the cellblock, although he had to readjust his hat. I knew that Prayer didn't want the magazine, he just wanted to slap the piss out of a white guy.

On the streets, Prayer was always into some things. I had seen him fighting at Beach High School one day. Once, I heard that he went on the east side and really got the shit kicked out of him at St. Pius, where a dance had been held. This must have been true because I went to a basketball game one night at Beach High, and Prayer came over and sat next to a guy who was sitting just below me. Prayer told the guy, who lived on the east side, that he should hurt him really bad because of what happened to him when he was attacked on the east side.

"You know, I should really fuck you up because of how they did me," said Prayer. "About seven or eight guys jumped me and they were kicking the shit out of me. But I am not gonna do anything to you. I'm not gonna do you like they did me. I'm gonna let you go. But I am supposed to fuck you up really bad."

As Prayer was telling the guy this, this guy was crying softly. Prayer never raised his voice and was enjoying tormenting this guy. Prayer, who had some friends with him, got up and went to stand against the wall with others. I wondered if Prayer was gonna wait until the game was over and then tell the guy that he changed his mind. But I did not notice any commotion after the game, and I believed that Prayer let him return to the east side unharmed.

Honey returned from the prison camp much darker upon his return. It was obvious that he had been out in the sun.

One day I heard some rumbling and looked around. It was Honey. He had a guy named Lester, who was in his thirties and who bragged about all the asses he had kicked on the east side, stretched out over the table and was hitting him in the face. He was so terrified of Honey that he was whispering— "Okay Honey, Okay Honey, Okay Honey." After hitting him in the face a few times, he turned and asked where Harry was. Harry quickly stated that he did not do anything and was not involved. Honey stared at him but did not attack him.

I saw another incident involving Honey that made an impression on me. The guys on the floor decided to strike for better food and so they told the guys not to eat when the trays were brought in. One guy from the east side, who was called Yammy and who was in jail for stabbing his girlfriend to death, insisted defiantly that he was gonna eat and sat down at the table. A young boy whom Honey played with some times poured coffee in Yammy's tray to keep Yammy from eating. Yammy jumped up to hit the boy, but did not after Honey told him that he better not hit him.

The strike was ended when some of the believed ring leaders were put in cells on the first floor, and everyone was fed in the cells.

One day Lawrence Williams came to jail. He looked at me but said nothing, knowing that he might have been the one who was dead instead of the guy on the east side. I immediately remembered Drew angrily telling me that I should have killed Lawrence. Lawrence, I knew, did not sing part time for the white Catholics and would not have been publicly eulogized like Thomas was. But I knew that there was no choice, and even if there were, the right person was dead. Lawrence was a big enough person to apologize for hurting me, and he seemed sincere. More importantly, I did not think that he would try and hurt me again. But, according to Drew, I should have killed him anyway.

On the next visiting day, my name was called, but when I got downstairs, I did not immediately recognize the people sitting on the other side of the wire mesh. A lady said hello and reminded me that she was Lawrence's mother. She told me that she had requested to see me and that she wanted me to know that she had asked her church to pray for me. I thanked her and, in response to her question about how I was doing, told her that I was doing fine. Lawrence had come down, and I knew that she did not intend to talk long to me. She told me that she just wanted to speak to me and let me know that she was praying for me. I thanked her again, and as I got up to leave, she gave the guard some money to give to me.

As I was walking back up the stairs, I thought again what Drew had said about Lawrence, and I was convinced that I shouldn't have done anything to Lawrence. Lawrence was not a threat to me afterwards, but the so-called choirboy was. They knew that I had eye problems and intentionally attacked me around the eyes. Then, instead of being sorry for almost maiming me, they talked about finishing me. There was a big difference between when I saw Lawrence in the cafe after he attacked me and when I saw the choirboy in the store. The right person was dead. Drew told me that I should have killed Lawrence only because I killed Aaron Kravitch's true client, who was the choirboy, and there was never any intention to represent me vigorously in the courtroom. Additionally, the choir boy had white people working behind the scene to get me convicted, which Lawrence would not have had. But I knew that the right person died, despite Drew telling me that I should have killed Lawrence.

Honey was sent to court for robbery and was given seven years. He declined his lawyer's suggestion to appeal, declaring that he would do his time. He said further that because Dunbar Harrison sentenced his to the state penitentiary that he was not returning to Chatham County work camp.

Shortly afterwards, a jailer called Honey one day and told him to pack up and get ready for transfer. Honey had said that he was not going to the prison camp and was going to Reidsville because he had been sentenced by the judge to the state penitentiary. He said that he believed that he could get out quicker from Reidsville than a prison camp. He also bragged that he did not have to worry about going to Reidsville because he did not have to worry about someone trying to fuck him. There was a lot of talk about how some guys were turned out and made into fuckboys in Reidsville. There was also a lot of talk about how some guys were killed in Reidsville.

Honey packed up his belongings and headed downstairs with a guard and some of the bridgeboys. After a few minutes, we realized that there was a problem because more bridgeboys were called downstairs.

Realizing that the guards who had come from him were from Chatham prison camp, Honey refused to let them put shackle on him and told the bridgeboys that they better not touch him. After about thirty minutes, some of the bridgeboys came back upstairs saying that Honey was gone and wasn't as tough as he thought. A bridgeboy stated that the jail officials called for some county police officers and about seven came in with their night sticks. Seeing this, Honey allowed them to put the shackles on him and take him to the prison camp.

Three federal prisoners came in for bank robbery. What made them somewhat interesting was that they were black and in their thirties. One would talk about some of the banks that they had robbed and how easily they robbed one bank.

One morning as I was washing my face, I picked up a ring that had been left on the sink. No one else was around, and I did not know who had left it. But one of the bank robbers saw me pick it up and asked me could he have a look at it. I gave it to him to examine and continued to wash my face. Later that morning, I learned that the person who had left the ring had been discharged that morning. I asked the bank robber for the ring back.

"I left it in my cell," he said.

"Well, when the cells open, I want it back. I only showed it to you."

But my mind was on my case. Daddy and Momma had come to the jail and dropped a bomb on me. They told me that Mr. Head had decided not to take over my case after listening to the tape of my trial. They told me that the case had been messed up too badly and that one of the damaging aspects was my testimony. Daddy said that Mr. Head told him that he could have helped me if they had only come to him in the beginning.

Daddy repeated what Mr. Head said to him. "You never should have gone to Aaron Kravitch and should have come to me first. The next day after the shooting, you should have been in my office. I could have helped your boy, then."

Daddy said further, "Mr. Head said that he would have charged me less money and he would have gotten you out of this. He said also that Aaron Kravitch could have won this case if he had tried it and used the evidence that we had. He said that you are not gonna be executed, and that you are eventually gonna be given a life sentence. He said that this case has been messed up too badly and nothing could be done now."

I had been under the impression that we had finished with Kravitch and Drew. I had not had any contact with either of them in about a year and neither had my parents. I was cursing to myself as I returned to the third floor.

As I was thinking about my case, I asked the bank robber about the ring again. He decided to get nasty, however.

"I'm not gonna give you back a damn thing, and you best not ask me about it again young motherfucker," said the bank robber. As he was telling me this, he pulled out a sharpened toothbrush for me to see.

I did not say anything and walked away, but I did not intend to let it drop.

"Let it go, Rudolph. It's only gonna lead to trouble," said Eddie Simmons. "He has made up his mind that he is keeping that ring, and you can also get hurt with that toothbrush."

"He might have made up his mind, but I'm gonna change it," I said. This was not a good day to fuck with me.

When we came out of the cells after lunch, the bank robber went up to the bars. I got the lid from the trash can and went up to him. When I got within three feet, I swung at his head as hard as I could. I was holding one side of the lid and hit with the edge. When it hit him, he screamed. A nasty gash opened up on his forehead and he started bleeding.

I intended to hit him again, but the lid fell out of my hand and rattled as it hit the floor. Our eyes met and it was obvious that he was surprised at what I had done. He charged me and I met him half way. We both hit each other with our fists and then he slumped back. I did not hit him that hard with my fist, and I knew that he was feeling the effects of the lid.

The guards opened the door to let him out and someone threw him a towel for his bloodied head. They took him downstairs and came back for me. I voluntarily went. As we were on the elevator, the guard asked me why I hit him.

"He has something that belongs to me and wasn't sure if he should give it back. I was helping him make up his mind," I said.

They put me in the same cell that I was in when I returned from court with the electric chair. But this time, I felt different. In fact, I felt good.

A few hours later, they were bringing someone else up. He was pleading for an explanation for why he was being put in the hole. I knew that he was not on the third floor and had to be on the second floor.

"What did I do, Boss?" the man repeated over and over as the guard and bridge boys walked him to a cell.

Finally, the guard decided to answer.

"Sol, I heard that you have been agitating down on the floor," said the guard.

"Boss, I haven't done anything," the older man whined.

"Get in the cell, Sol," said the guard.

When they left, he began to talk about who he thought told the guards on him. He stated that it was because he was winning the money during the skin games and someone wanted him gone. Then, he changed the subject and began to talk about himself. He was in jail for manslaughter, resulting from hitting a guy during a dice game and causing the guy to hit his head on a brick. He also had just gotten out of Reidsville and had served 21 years of a life sentence for rape. He was worried about the manslaughter charge because he was still on parole for the rape.

After I had been in the hole for about 5 days, a guard came up and called my name. I thought they were gonna let me out and I got off the floor and hurriedly walked to the cell door. It was Lionel Drew accompanying the guard.

He came up to the door and asked if I remembered him.

"Yeah, I remember you," I said wearily and cautiously.

"I know you wanna get out of here where you can get some fresh air, Rudolph," said Drew with a disingenuous smile on his face.

I did not respond to this comment.

"The judge has asked me to come to see you to let you know that he is willing to do something for you that he will not do for anyone else with a death sentence. Now I don't want you to think that I have sold you out because I haven't. The judge has your appeal and he is willing to overturn your death sentence and sentence you to life imprisonment. But let me say Rudolph, a life sentence does not mean you will be in prison for the rest of your life. In fact, you can get out 5 years from now when you are about 24 or 25 years old. That's still young, and young enough for you to begin a new life. All you have to do is keep your nose clean, and I will get you out of prison. But the judge is not gonna overturn your death sentence unless you agree to the life sentence. You can trust Judge Harrison. He is not gonna trick you."

"I'm not gonna agree to a life sentence. In fact, I believe I should be given a whole new trial. You didn't handle my case right and you made a lot of mistakes," I said.

"I might have, but I did not make any as big as the one you did," Drew said looking down at the floor as he talked. He was beginning to sneer at me as he raised his head.

Undaunted by his sneer, I said, "You were the cause of me getting a death sentence and you helped got me convicted."

"Rudolph, I didn't know the jury was gonna be as tough on you as they were. I thought that they would give you a break, just based on your age, but they didn't. They held your feet to the fire."

"Why didn't you tell the jury that my girlfriend went to St. Benedict?" I asked.

"To protect you," Drew lied.

"How is that protecting me when the jury was told that I asked someone if church was out. That needed to be explained and you could have explained it but you didn't," I said. "Even if you didn't convincingly explain it, you could have raised doubts about what the prosecutor was suggesting. Raising doubts is supposed to be good for the defense."

"Why didn't you tell the jury that I had no criminal record?"

"I forgot."

"Why didn't you let the jury know that I was attacked in the beginning of 1967 and lost the sight in my left eye and also had the guy prosecuted?" But I knew why he didn't bring that up and it was because he long planned to say I took the law into my own hands and this contradicted what he wanted the jury to believe. An honest, competent lawyer could have used that in my favor. A few seconds ago, he stated that he didn't ask Beulah about St. Benedict to protect me but I wondered how he was protecting me when he put me on the witness stand with absolutely no preparation and no indication that I would testify and what I would be asked.

Drew looked down at the floor and did not say anything to my specific question. He acted like he was having a hard time looking me in the face.

"Well then tell me why you did not tell the jury that I was robbed of a watch by the dead person and there was an agreement not to press charges. You led the jury to believe that I simply lost my watch and his family returned it to me as a favor."

Drew was getting angry at my questions and comments.

"Listen, I don't give a goddamn if he took two watches from you. You shouldn't have killed him. When he came in the store, you should have run."

"How could I have run when there was only one way in and the door was blocked?" I asked.

"Well, you should have just shot him in the leg," said Drew.

"That's not for you to say," I said. "I am not agreeing to accept a life sentence and I want a whole new trial."

Sol Brown called Drew, who was representing Sol. Drew went over to talk to Sol and told Sol that he didn't have anything to worry about because his case was an accident.

Drew left and told me that he would see me later.

I pondered what Drew had just said, and I knew that he deserved to die what for he did to me. It was obvious who was the client and it certainly wasn't me. The more I thought about it, the madder I got. No one held a gun on Lionel Drew and made him sit next to me at the defense table. If Drew felt sorry for the dead person, fine, but he should have been sitting at the prosecution table. A lawyer's job is help someone, not hurt the person deliberately and talk about parole 7 years later. What I needed to do was to figure out what I was gonna do after I got a new trial. That was gonna be the hard part.

A few days later, I was allowed out of the hole. On the way back down, the guard asked me was there gonna be anymore trouble from me.

"I've not caused any trouble," I said.

"Well, the other fella says the ring is his and you saying it is yours."

"He and I both know who the ring belongs to."

When I got down on the floor, everyone was in the cells because lunch had just ended. I was put in my cell.

After a few minutes, the bank robber came up to my cell. He still had a bandage on his forehead.

"I wanna apologize and return your ring. I tried to take it and it wasn't right."

"Are you sure that it is mine?" I asked.

"Yeah, I'm sure."

He handed the ring to me and I took it. I didn't say anything as I took it from his hand. When the doors were opened, I went into the shower. I felt that I was vulnerable in the shower, but I didn't give a damn. I showered without incident and neither the bank robber nor his two friends said anything to me. Other guys were looking at me differently, and some told me that I had looked beaten from getting the death sentence and my looks may have led this guy to try and run over me. They said that they were happy that I split his head. But they blamed me for not having a lid for the trash can because the guards took the lid out to prevent it from being used as a weapon again. But I saw it as a defense weapon. The other guy had a sharpened toothbrush, and I had the lid.

I gave the ring to Snake. It had no significant meaning to me. I found it. I might have given to the bank robber if he had only asked me for it. It only became a big deal when he said that he was taking it from me, and I wasn't gonna let that happen.

But my daddy wasn't too happy. They had come to visit me and was told that I was in the hole for hurting someone.

"You don't need anymore trouble now. Your head is in the lion's mouth," Daddy stressed.

"I don't feel right Daddy. I have always treated people the way that I like to be treated. When I had gone out, I was out to have fun. But I never thought about hurting someone to make myself look good and I have never taken anything from anyone. Daddy, if I am supposed to be treated like I am dirt or a nobody, then I don't wanna live anymore and maybe I should be executed."

"Don't say that," Daddy said.

"I am not sorry for shooting him. I am only sorry that I dragged you into this and caused you to give money to a corrupt, backstabbing white lawyer," I said. "If I had known what I know now, I never would have allowed myself to be arrested."

I told him about my conversation with Drew.

A few weeks later, Drew returned to the jail. He told me that Dunbar Harrison had turned down my appeal after hearing my response to the life sentence deal, and they were now gonna appeal to the Georgia Supreme Court. He had a paper for me to sign. I scanned it quickly and learned that it was a pauper affidavit. I handed it back to him and told me that I was not gonna sign it.

"You have to sign this for us to appeal," said Drew. "It is not a confession or anything like that."

"I read it and I am not gonna sign it," I said.

"Well, if you don't sign it, we can't appeal your case," said Drew.

"Well, don't appeal it."

Drew left the county jail without me signing the pauper affidavit.

A few days later, I got a call that I had a visitor. I wondered who could it be since this was not the regular visiting day. When I got to the visiting room, it was my daddy. He told me that Drew had contacted the jail officials and requested that he be allowed to visit with me other than on a Tuesday.

Daddy told me to sign the paper and I told him I would.

A few days later, Drew returned and I signed the paper.

Signing it, however, confirmed what I initially thought about my right to fire Aaron Kravitch in December 1967. Drew told me that I couldn't fire Aaron Kravitch because I was a minor. I was 18 then and now I was 19. If I were legally a minor, my daddy could have signed the pauper affidavit for me just like he signed for me to be operated on in 1967 at Memorial Hospital. I was legally an adult because I had been tried as an adult, and I was legally an adult when I tried to fire Aaron Kravitch. Aaron Kravitch did not wanna relinquish the case in 1967 because he had not yet stabbed me in the back and helped secure my conviction.

There was another story in the newspaper about the gang on the east side. The article stated that three youths had been bound over for severely beating another youth. Police said there were at least four beatings in two days and the "gang which consisted of about 30 youths, had the area terrorized."

But I was scoffed at when I tried to discuss this gang, and I was told that I was in no danger. At trial, Drew said that I was being harassed.

One small article in the Savannah Morning News was that the Savannah Bar Association had passed a rule that a retained attorney couldn't give a case to another lawyer.

When I read this, I immediately suspected that Mr. Head had something to do with this rule change. I also knew immediately that this was directed at Aaron Kravitch. Kravitch was the only lawyer in Savannah who was giving away cases and not telling clients that he intended to do this. Shortly thereafter, I was shocked to see a notice in the newspaper that Aaron Kravitch and Lionel Drew had formed a law partnership. People assumed that they were already partners.

I also read a letter to the editor that was written by Drew. It was titled "Police on Campus Should Be Armed." He, like he had said at my trial, wrote that he was a law abiding citizen and law abiding citizens and students at Armstrong State College had nothing to fear about armed officers. What made this letter striking to me was the conservative tone to it. Drew wrote that "colleges and universities of this country are at present being disrupted daily by lawless minority groups who think nothing of destroying public property and threatening the lives and property of peaceful citizens." Drew made specific references to the Black Panthers and Students for a Democratic Society.

After I put down the newspaper, I thought that son of a bitch should have never tried my case. I later learned that Drew was a former state legislator in the Georgia legislature and had gone to high school at St. Benedictine in Savannah, a military school full of white Catholics.

Chapter 11

A huge guy came in one day, he looked to be about six-foot seven and weighed about 260 pounds. He had on traditional prison clothes, white pants with a blue strip down the sides and a white shirt with a blue collar. Willie Robinson went up to him and started talking to him. A few other guys knew him too and said that he was Robert Pryor, the person who killed Bill Bo down in Reidsville. Someone told him about me, and he started talking to me about his trial. Pryor initially was tried in Savannah for murder and hired Aaron Kravitch. However, Aaron Kravitch sent Drew to the trial, and Pryor did not know how to stop the trial from proceeding.

"That son of a bitch acted like he did not wanna speak up for me," said Pryor referring to Drew. "He was allowing the prosecutor to do all the talking. I was telling him what to say. I got 10 years, but I would have gotten more if I had not been pushing Drew to speak up in my behalf."

"They got me with that flimflam too," I said.

"There is a guy named Norris Hodges in Reidsville now and they did the same thing to him," said Pryor. "Kravitch even stole more money from Norris after Norris went to the prison camp. Kravitch went to Norris at Chatham County Prison Camp and told Norris that his case had a lot of appealable errors. Norris had his wife borrow money from a loan company and paid Kravitch to appeal his case. But after Kravitch got the money, he did not have any more contact with Norris again."

"Kravitch is a crooked, money-grubbing, backstabbing dog," I said. "Aaron Kravitch takes every case that comes in his office, and the cases that he doesn't want or the ones that he intends to sell out, he gives those cases to Drew," I said. "He will never tell someone that he doesn't want the case, but there are some cases that he doesn't want. He just wants people's money."

Pryor nodded his head and told me that he never should have allowed Drew to proceed as his attorney. He stated that he saw in the Savannah Morning News that Drew and Kravitch just became partners. I told him that

I saw that in the newspaper too. Because they worked in the same office, a lot of people assumed that they were law partners, but they were not.

That's all we talked about and he walked off.

I wondered about Pryor's other case when he killed Bill Bo in Reidsville. But I would not ask him about that.

Stacko had been transferred and for a while I was in the cell by myself. Lucious Jackson came up to me one day and asked could he move in my cell. Some of the guys on the floor were shunning him and calling him stupid.

Lucious had been given 3 years for stealing a car. While he was serving his 3 years at the prison camp, he escaped while the prison gang was working on Wilmington Island. He broke into a house and a woman was at home. He was charged with rape and the woman was white, which meant that the solicitor general was gonna be asking for the death penalty for him. When he went to court, he was given the death penalty.

I told Lucious that he could move in my cell. Before long, he was talking about his case and he told me what happened.

I heard one guy say that a lawyer, defending a Black guy for raping a white woman, told his client that he should have killed the woman because the penalty is no greater. Also, killing the woman eliminates her as a crying witness for the state.

Bobby Hill, a young Black lawyer, was Lucious Jackson's attorney. I did not ask what Bobby Hill told him, but I knew Lucious would have told me if I had asked.

For some reason, Lucious was upset with Eddie Simmons. I believe that Lucious suspected Eddie Simmons of talking about him.

"Eddie is supposed to be a Muslim now, but he ain't as right as he pretends," said Lucious. "Do you remember when that woman's drawers was on the floor?"

I recalled that one of the guys who was in the hole begged a woman prisoner, who was in the hole too, for her drawers, and she took them off and threw them to him. When the guy was let out of the hole, he was letting some guys sniff the drawers. I was asked if I wanted to smell them, but I said hell no. I was told that I might not ever smell pussy again since I had the electric chair over my head. But I still declined and thought that it was perverted. Later, I heard that Willie Robinson had the panties and had put them on.

"Yeah, I remember," I said.

"Well, Eddie was sniffing the drawers, and he is supposed to be a Muslim."

"I don't believe that."

"Well, he did."

I got down on the floor near the door so I could read. This was the signal for Lucious to stop talking. I could read a book by holding it so the light through the flat bars illuminated the page. The light was rather small and I had to move the book up to read the bottom of each page.

Beasley came to see me one day and told me that he was all torn up about me. He said that he and some guys that we went to school with were talking about me one day, and they talked about breaking me out of jail so the white folks would not execute me. I laughed at him, but Beasley insisted this was no joke. I thanked him for thinking enough of me that he would risk breaking the law so that I might live.

Earnest Robinson came to see me too and told me that everyone in the neighborhood was mad with Swinton for what he had done to me at the trial. I told him that Swinton came to see me the first visiting day after I was tried, but he had not been back. I guess he found it too hard looking at me.

I continued to buy a newspaper each day, attentive to the crime stories in the city and around the state. I had read earlier about a girl who was killed by a guy in Sylvania, Georgia. They were out on a date, and he stabbed her to death. What made this story catch my eye was that a lawyer from Savannah was hired by the parents of the dead girl to help prosecute the case. This lawyer was a defense attorney in Savannah but went to Sylvania as a prosecutor. The guy on trial received the electric chair and the lawyer from Savannah encouraged the jury to bring back a death sentence, saying that the defendant was just plain damn mean.

I thought that this lawyer did not do anything wrong as long as he knows what side he is supposed to be on when he has been retained and paid. I had more respect for this lawyer than I had for Aaron Kravitch. Kravitch wants to be only known as a defense attorney and told the parents of the person I killed that he couldn't work for the prosecution. But he had no problem with stabbing me in the back by planning to throw my case and then hide in his office. What he did was far worse than openingly working for the prosecution.

Although in 1967 my parents told me not to write to Aaron Kravitch anymore, the situation had radically changed. I decided to write to him and tell him that I was misrepresented, listing the evidence that should have been presented at my trial and the damaging statements that Drew had made about me. I also told him that one of the jurors who had been on the grand jury that indicted me was placed on the trial jury by Lionel Drew.

Kravitch wrote me back and "heartily" disagreed that I had been misrepresented. He stated that my case was properly presented to the jury and defended what Drew had done at the trial. He also told me that there was nothing wrong with a juror serving on the grand jury that indicted a person and then sitting on the trial jury, apparently unaware that I read the newspaper and had read about the Hakala case. I wrote to Kravitch again and told him that I know about the Hakala case and if what he told me was correct, then Hakala would not have been given a mistrial. Kravitch's response was that Hakala was eventually convicted and given a life sentence so the issue was meaningless.

I decided to write to Dunbar Harrison to tell him that I had a juror who had been on the grand jury that had indicted me. I did not get a response from him. I did not know what I would gain by writing Dunbar Harrison, but I did not think that it would hurt. I had observed Dunbar Harrison when I was on trial and he was giving me nasty looks at times.

I later wrote to Drew to tell him that he and Aaron Kravitch could stop with the pretending. I told him that I knew what they had done and that they had always wanted me to be convicted and had set me up for the prosecution. I told him that they never intended to present any favorable evidence for me at the trial and that he had deliberately hurt me during my trial.

The day Drew got my letter, he came to the county jail. When I reached the visiting room, he had the letter in his hand. I repeated to him what I had written and I could sense that he was trying to figure out what to say.

"You helped get me convicted and caused me to get the electric chair," I charged. I repeated to him that what he had done, no defense attorney would do. I also told him that I had observed lawyers come down and interview their clients. Everyone in jail was interviewed by their attorneys, and then the attorneys came back just before trial and told their clients what their defenses were gonna be.

"When I have come down on Saturdays to get a haircut, I have listened to lawyers tell their clients what to say. One guy was charged with murder and his lawyer told him where the State's case was weak, what he was gonna argue at the trial, and what to say on the witness stand. You never even told me that I would be put on the witness stand. No defense attorney would do that. You hurt me at the trial and you meant to do it."

"I know you feel like killing me," said Drew looking at me.

I did not say anything and just stared at him through the wire mesh. I knew he was asking me a question and that I shouldn't acknowledge what he asked. But I certainly believed that both he and Kravitch should die viciously for the treacherous manner in which they dealt with me and my daddy. Taking their lives would not be wrong and when I was killing Drew, I would repeat back to him what he told me, "I don't give a goddam."

Drew did not say much, but he left me a copy of my appeal to the Georgia Supreme Court.

I read it and what the legal issues Aaron Kravitch planned to argue. Kravitch put in the brief that I accosted the deceased after the deceased had left church. I wondered why he did not write that I went to see my girlfriend, and a group of boys, some who were members of a gang, accosted me. But I knew why Kravitch did not say the truth. He took money under the table to sabotage my defense. The only thing that went wrong was that the jury went one step further than what had been planned for me.

The legal brief that Drew left contained the address of the attorney general. I did not know who the attorney general was or what he did, but I decided to write to him and tell him about my trial containing a juror who served on the grand jury that had indicted me.

I received a letter from a deputy attorney general who told me that they represent the state and he couldn't advise me. He sent Aaron Kravitch a copy of the response to me. A few days later, Kravitch and Drew came to the county jail to see me. They were in the cell that was used for lawyers seeing their clients. Kravitch was sitting in the chair and Drew was standing.

"Is this him?" Kravitch asked Drew.

"Yeah, that's him."

"You wrote to Judge Harrison and the attorney general complaining about your trial," charged Kravitch angrily. "You act like we've given you the sham."

I sensed that he was trying to sound angry and he probably was to some extent, but I sensed that he was putting on an act and was trying to intimidate me. White people talk down to some Black people and are very aggressive when they are talking. Kravitch was doing this, and he was talking to me as if I was a nigger on his plantation. When white people are talking this way, they expect you to look down at the floor. To look them in the eyes and to challenge what they say is blasphemous.

"That's because you haven't been straight," I said looking him in the face.

"Look, I'm trying to save you from the electric chair. But your attitude has been bad from the very beginning. If I didn't feel sorry for you, I would get off your case and let the state give your behind a good burning. You had better stop listening to your boyfriends."

He really put some emotion on the word "boyfriends."

I stared at him, and tried to remain calm although he had implied that I was a homosexual.

"You told my daddy that you were gonna put my feet on the ground," I said. I wanted to hear him lie in person because this was the first time that I had seen him since my preliminary hearing in September of 1967.

"No, I did not."

"You never told my parents that you were gonna win my case?"

"No, I didn't."

"Well, did you tell them that you would get me out on bond after I was first arrested?" I asked.

"No, I didn't say that either," said Kravitch.

Kravitch, then, changed the subject.

"Your father told me that you were ready to get this case over and take a life sentence," charged Kravitch.

"I saw my daddy earlier this week and he never discussed that. I want a new trial."

"I'm gonna get this death sentence off you, and when you go to prison, you're gonna be beaten to death by the prison guards because of your bad attitude."

"You are not gonna be in prison long and all the time you have been in this jail will count," said Drew softly.

This was the old Mutt and Jeff approach. One person is angry and the other is nice. Before, Drew was the angry person. When they left, I knew that what Kravitch said was mostly an act and was trying to put me in my place. Talk down and nasty to a nigger and scare him.

The next day, I received a very nice letter from Kravitch, telling me that he was sorry about all the miscommunications. He told me that he would not act on my father's statement and would only act on what I say.

I was angry at what he had done. When my parents came during the next visiting day, I told them everything Aaron Kravitch said.

"Your daddy didn't lie. I was there when Mr. Kravitch said he would get you out on bond and would win this case," said Momma.

Daddy was nodding his head and said, "He told me."

"You don't have to defend yourselves to me. I know he told you those things," I said as tears began to swell in my eyes. "I'm sorry I brought this on you."

During my next visit, my Daddy told me that he had spoken with Drew, and during the conversation, money came up. Daddy said that Drew was shocked to hear that Aaron Kravitch was paid in full and told Daddy that he didn't know that.

"Drew told me that I didn't pay Kravitch, but I told him that was not right," Daddy said. "I told him that Kravitch charged me a thousand dollars and I paid him in a few weeks. I told Drew that Kravitch told me initially not to give anyone in that office any money if he was not in the office. And when I would take money to him, Kravitch would take out his billfold and put the money in it. When I told Drew that, Drew leaned back in his chair and told me that he was told something else. I also told Drew that Kravitch asked me for 50 dollars later for something that I didn't understand and I paid him that too.

"Daddy, these are nothing but crooks," I said. "Maybe Drew didn't know you paid Kravitch, but even if he did, Drew still would have done what he did."

"There were two guys here for armed robbery and they had agreed to split everything they stole 50/50. Clarence would go into a store with the gun and Edgar would stay outside to watch. Clarence told me that he would put money in two pockets, but would only divide out of one. Clarence said this was right because he was taking more chances. Aaron Kravitch is doing the same thing. Kravitch thinks that his name brings in clients and therefore he should get the most money. But he doesn't tell the other lawyers this. So, when a case comes along that he can flim-flam, he puts money in his wallet and indicates to the other lawyers that he wasn't paid very much, or even not at all. When Kravitch sent you that letter saying that you had not paid him, and when you went to the office, he told you it was a mistake. Well, it wasn't a mistake. He had that letter sent so that he could fool the other lawyers down there. It's nothing but crooks stealing from other crooks. Just like Clarence and Edgar."

"When Kravitch was supposedly robbed at this house, I don't believe it was the whole story. I believe he stole money from this guy or someone close to the guy, and this guy went to Kravitch's house to take back the money. Instead of pistol-whipping Kravitch, that guy should have shot him in the head."

Momma interrupted, "Kravitch did not do us right but don't say that."

"He is telling me now he is saving my life for free, but I don't accept it, and I will never say that he did anything for me. All con artists wanna trick people and then have people think that they had been helped. You are a really good con artist if you can hurt someone and then have the person believe that you were helping. They laugh about something like that. That is what the so-called choirboy had been taught. Do a person wrong and then look him in the eye and tell him that you were helping. Kravitch, using his 50 years of experience, told Drew how to really hurt me in the trial. It was all planned from the beginning. This was Drew's case from day one. Kravitch has bragged that his name will never get mixed up in a railroad, and the reason it won't is that he won't attend the trial. Kravitch will help to plan a fix, but he won't go in the courtroom when it is being done. He got Drew to really do his dirty work."

"Kravitch and Drew did me wrong. I didn't do anything wrong to them. Now, Kravitch came down here for the very first time and threatened my life because I did not believe his lies," I said. "They are supposed to be professionals. But they think that even if you hired them, they do not owe you anything. They can take money for a professional job and do whatever they wanna do. White people are just like that. After they have your money, they do not have to perform and do not want you to question their performance."

"I'll tell you something else, Daddy, about Kravitch. He steals from people after they leave the county jail and go to the work camp. If the jury had returned a verdict of life imprisonment for me and you believed his lie about him having to go out of town and the judge wouldn't let him put off the case, Kravitch would have called you shortly after I left the jail, promising to appeal. Kravitch would have taken money from you as long as you gave it to him, and there would not have been no appeal. Kravitch would have lied to you about an appeal just like he lied to you in the very beginning. These were his intentions from day one, but me getting the electric chair spoiled his plans."

"Also they are telling their other clients that I got the electric chair because I killed the wrong person. You remember him telling you about the case of the white man who shot his wife in the back three times and that he would have won the case if the man had not shot the woman in the back. When a client is convicted, they always say something to excuse themselves. With the white guy, he shot his wife in the back. With me, I killed the wrong person. With the guy who told me what they said about me, he let the police officers search his car, and if he had not done that, they would have won the case. They are always gonna have an excuse to shift blame from them as they are taking money from other people."

As I was returning upstairs, I repeated to myself that the man who pistol-whipped Aaron Kravitch should have shot him in the head, despite what momma had said. What they did was unforgivable. I would have been better off sitting at the defense table by myself, trying to put on my own defense. And the only thing better was not appearing at all in the courtroom and not allowing myself to be arrested.

I learned from my brother later that day that Momma and Daddy had sent some money down to Florida for one of our relatives to see a root doctor on my behalf. According to the report from the Florida root doctor, I was not gonna be executed. I would serve some time, but I would turn out all right.

If I had known Momma and Daddy were gonna give money to another root doctor, I would have tried to stop them. But I believe that they would have done so anyway. Uneducated black people believe in roots because they do not have much of anything else to believe in. They do not have white people to pull strings for them. Daddy told me that someone was working roots on me, but I didn't believe it. No supernatural forces were working against me. My trouble was first some silly, nasty Negroes, and then some corrupt, back-stabbing white lawyers. These white lawyers know that many black people are superstitious and believe in bad luck and roots. These lawyers do their dirty work and try to make people think that it was just bad luck.

The Georgia Supreme Court finally decided my case, and it turned down my appeal. It stated that a key part of my trial record was not included in my appeal. Kravitch quickly asked for a rehearing and the missing record was sent to the court. After several weeks, the Georgia Supreme Court overturned my death sentence. I saw it in the *Savannah Evening Press* one Saturday, and shortly after I read it, a guard told me that Aaron Kravitch had called the jail and asked someone to tell me.

On Monday there was a big article in the newspaper about my case. Kravitch characterized my case as a "mess" because I was not gonna be given a new trial. The Georgia Supreme Court had only overturned my death sentence and my conviction still stood. Kravitch stated that this was unfair and I was only being given half of a new trial. He also described some changes in the Georgia Code with respect to death sentences, which a jury must specifically say instead of just finding someone guilty of murder. There were some additional changes in federal law and Kravitch speculated that the combination of the two might spare my life.

I thought that he gave the *Savannah Morning News* a fraudulent story about this half-new trial being unfair when they sat on evidence that would have given me a new trial without question—the participation of an unqualified juror to sit on my trial.

Kravitch later sent a letter to me, saying that he wanted me to be resentenced by Dunbar Harrison, and Dunbar Harrison would impose a life sentence on me. The alternative was to be resentenced by the jury and this sentence could be anywhere from 1 year to the electric chair. Kravitch said that he would leave my case if I chose to go before a jury rather than Dunbar Harrison. Kravitch sent a copy of the letter to me to Dunbar Harrison.

I wrote to Aaron Kravitch and told him that I was not agreeing to a life sentence and repeated again that I was misrepresented and that my appeal was handled in a way as to prevent me from getting a new trial.

Kravitch responded that Dunbar Harrison had contacted him to tell him that his interpretation of the ruling from the Georgia Supreme Court was wrong. He said that the Georgia Supreme Court upheld my murder conviction so I could only get a life sentence or the electric chair from the jury. If I went before Dunbar Harrison I could only get a life sentence, but if I went before a jury that I could get only a life sentence or the electric chair again. He closed by saying that he would resign from my case if I wanted it.

I wrote him back and told him that he had never been on my case, and that he chose to hide when I went to trial, which was the critical phase. I told him that his threat to me to get off my case was fine with me and that I would have been better off if my daddy never went to him in the first place. I told him that he had not done anything special for me with the Georgia Supreme Court because I had read about another case in northern Georgia that had been reversed on the same legal issue. Moreover, this reversal and my part reversal came about because of a five-to-four U.S. Supreme Court decision that was handed down 2 months after my trial and that he did not have anything to do with this decision. I was lucky only because of an Illinois case.

I got a terse letter from him saying that he was resigning, and there was not any indication that he was sending a copy of the letter to my daddy. After a few days, I received a letter from Drew, saying that he had been appointed by Dunbar Harrison to finish my case.

I didn't believe Drew's letter, but there was no one to complain to. I had been severely abused by some corrupt white lawyers, and they had decided that they can do niggers anyway they wanna do them.

When I saw my daddy again, he told me that Dunbar Harrison called the house and told Daddy that he wanted to see him in his office to talk about me. Daddy said that Dunbar Harrison told him that if I did not come before him to be sentenced to life imprisonment that I was gonna die. Daddy said Dunbar Harrison said that I had to go to prison because my mind was made up to kill that boy. Dunbar also said that I was not gonna serve a long time in prison because I wasn't a hardened criminal, and the parole board would let me out early.

"Dunbar Harrison had a hand in what happened to me," I said. "I could tell how he looked at me at the trial and Kravitch sent him copies of letters to me so that he would know what was going on. The decision to convict me was made months before I went to trial, and my trial was fixed so that I would have no chance whatsoever. The statement that my mind was made up to kill is their excuse for railroading me. They didn't know a thing about me and what I was like prior to me being arrested. If Thomas had said to me in the store, or before, something similar to what Lawrence said, nothing would have happened. We would have passed each other in the store without saying a word. I didn't like what Lawrence did to me and I am still mad about it. But when he said that he was sorry for hurting me and seemed sincere, I accepted his apology. Thomas and the other members of the Tornado gang deliberately tried to maim me and were threatening to finish it. He was only a few feet from me. Barker thought he was making a point when he asked did I see a weapon and I said no. But I never saw a weapon the first two times and the jury should have been told this. That white man who was found not guilty almost 2 years ago never saw a weapon either because the guy never had a weapon. That did not stop the jury from believing that the white man's testimony that he feared for his life and then finding him not guilty. They haven't convinced me that I did anything wrong. If I were wrong, one prosecutor in a fair trial could have gotten me convicted. Instead, there were three prosecutors, and they were getting help in getting me convicted. This tells me that I did not do anything legally wrong. That jury rubber-stamped a decision made by some corrupt lawyers."

"They didn't do you right and they never intended to do you right," Daddy responded. "The judge talked nasty to me and talked nasty about you."

"What did he say?" I asked.

"I don't wanna get into it," Daddy said dejectedly. "I've talked to some other people too, and they told me that you will be able to get out of prison with a life sentence. I will always stick by you, and no one can ever make me turn against you. I just wish that I had done more to keep you out of jail in the first place. I need to be the one going to prison, not you, and if they want someone to send to the electric chair, they could have sent me."

Tears started welling up in my eyes.

Daddy continued after a pause, "I'm gonna change my life insurance policy at Union Camp so you will be my beneficiary. In case I die while you are in prison, you will get some money, and you might be able to buy your way out of prison later."

"Thank you," I said. "And I want you to know that if I ever get out, I will never let some crooked white lawyers lock me up again."

Having no option, I agreed to be sentenced by Dunbar Harrison but Daddy had already told Dunbar Harrison that he did not want me to die and that I would agree to be sentenced by him.

When I went to court, there were two other prisoners going to court with me. Sol Brown was being tried for manslaughter. During a break in his trial, I was brought into court to be resentenced by Dunbar Harrison.

I could hear Dunbar Harrison perfectly from the defense table, but he asked me to come and sit in the witness chair. I reluctantly did.

I knew that Dunbar Harrison was playing the role of a sympathetic judge and that this scene was a fraud. He asked me were my parents in court, and I told him yes.

My parents had come, along with my daddy's oldest sister, Ella, who lived in Cincinnati, Ohio and who had never seen me. Some of the money to pay Aaron Kravitch came from her. Although she had never seen me, she would try to help out because of her relationship with my daddy.

Dunbar Harrison asked my parents to come up to the witness stand, and they came up and stood by me.

Dunbar Harrison pretended that he was talking to my parents for the first time and was explaining to us what my options were. He then asked me what I wanted to do, and I told him that I would waive sentencing by a jury.

I felt that some corrupt white lawyers were humiliating us and we were being used by a judge who did not give a damn about my parents or me. Dunbar Harrison was trying to get a favorably written article about him in the newspaper the next day about how he was explaining this complex law to these poor dumb Negroes and the implication would be that he was kind to niggers. It was a pure sham.

Dunbar Harrison told me that I could return to the defense table and I was given a paper to sign, waiving jury sentencing. When I stood to be sentenced, my knees buckled at the pronouncement that I would serve the rest of my natural life in prison.

Barker and Ryan were in the courtroom, and Barker seemed to be gloating at my sentence. I thought that those two, along with the older Ryan, did not beat me at the trial. I was set up to lose.

I always thought that I was just an average teenager and sometimes, I felt less than average. But I knew now that I was special. It took a gang of so-called tough Negroes to attack me to defeat me. A gang against one person. Then, it took a gang of corrupt white lawyers to convict me. I knew then that one-on-one I was equal to any person, black or white, and it would take more than one person to beat me.

Shortly after getting back to the county jail, my parents and aunt visited me. I apologized to my aunt for having to meet for the first time like we were. Daddy was totally dejected, but he was trying to be brave. My Aunt Ella told me that I did not seem bothered by what had happened earlier in court. I told her that everything had been decided earlier and what she heard was just an act by the judge. Momma told me that Drew gave her a letter and told her to put the letter in a safe place. He told them that when I come up for parole to bring that letter to him and he would get me out of prison. Momma said that Drew had written that he would not charge them, and all they would have to pay would be his transportation to Atlanta to the parole board. I told Momma to tear up the letter and throw it away. It was another scheme, more flimflam. I did not want Drew to know anything about when I came up for parole.

The following week, my name was called to pack up and get ready for transfer. As I was packing up, Lucious was asking for some of my things, but I told him that I wanted to take all my magazines with me. I wished him luck as I left and said goodbye to the other guys.

Chapter 12

Lorenzo Stevens, who had a 3-year sentence for theft, left the county jail with me. We both were shackled around the waist and our handcuffs were fixed to the waist shackle.

As I walked outside, I was squinting my eyes because I was having difficulty seeing. The sunlight was too strong for me. I knew that I was reacting to not seeing the sun in a long time, but I also knew that part of the problem was the damage that had been done to my eyes.

We were led to a van that had two seats behind a wire mesh that separated the people in the back from the driver. As I climbed in the van, I was wondering if I would ever come back to Savannah. I was not sure if I would ever see Savannah again. I knew that I would be going up for parole in about 5 years because in Georgia a lifer must serve at least 7 years before going up for parole. However, I remembered Sol Brown telling me that he served almost 21 years on a life sentence. Sol stated that although a person serving a life sentence goes up for parole after 7 years, there is no guarantee that the person is gonna be paroled and most guys are not paroled after serving 7 years.

From what I was hearing in jail, the parole board begins to think about paroling a lifer after 11 years. I had heard that some guys serving life sentences were paroled after 11 years. I concluded that this was the benchmark, because on a 20-year sentence a person, with good time, must serve about 10 years and 8 months. Thus, I figured that the parole board won't start thinking about paroling a lifer until after 11 years and this made sense to me after hearing about a couple of guys who were paroled after serving 11 years. But I knew that I could serve as much time as Sol and perhaps more.

"Which one of you guys has been in jail for almost 2 years?" asked the guard just as he turned the corner leading away from the county jail.

"Me," I responded.

"Where are we going?" Lorenzo asked.

"You're going to the Georgia Diagnostic Center in Jackson, Georgia. But first, I have to stop at the prison in Reidsville for gas."

As we headed towards Reidsville, I began to recognize the route that we were taking. We were heading towards Claxton, Georgia, the fruitcake capital of the world. Claxton also is the home of two of my aunts, Aunt Doll and Aunt Cecilia. Both were retired schoolteachers who lived on a farm. I enjoyed spending the summer there for a while, but I got tired one day of picking butter beans. We drove through Claxton as I was thinking about all the summers that I spent there.

One summer I did not go to Claxton. Instead, my sister and I went to Crawfordville, Georgia and stayed with my daddy's brother. I remembered that the first time that I saw my Uncle Willie I was surprised that he and my daddy looked alike. They had the same type of cheekbones. Daddy told me that he took me up there when I was about 2 or 3 years old, his brother begged him repeatedly for me. My Uncle Willie wanted me to stay in Crawfordville with him and his wife, but my daddy told him no. This was a very difficult for my daddy since he had a lot of respect for his older brother, who had helped him numerous times out of trouble. When my daddy was stabbed in the back as a young man in Crawfordville, my Uncle Willie took his shotgun and went looking for the two brothers. He also frequently got my daddy out of jail. Despite their close relationship, my daddy told him that he couldn't give him his then only son. I remember Momma discussing this too and she hinted that she was never gonna agree to give me up. So, I remained in Savannah. As a consolation, Daddy named his second son after my Uncle Willie. But Uncle Willie never asked about my brother coming to stay with him. He just wanted me. As we drove through Claxton, Georgia, I knew that Reidsville was not too far away.

My momma had a cousin named Louise who stayed near the prison in Reidsville. Louise's husband was named Sylvester and he and Daddy really liked each other, and they enjoyed our coming up from Savannah. We would drive by the prison and see a group of prisoners dressed in white sometimes working near the prison. I recalled that there were two guards holding shotguns and wearing pistols on their hips guarding the prisoners. The guards had the prisoners between them and I knew that if one prisoner tried to escape that he would be cut down in a crossfire. I was thinking about several visits to Louise and Sylvester's house when I could see the top of the prison from a distance as we drove over some hills near the prison.

As we passed the front of the prison, I couldn't help but look up towards the fifth floor where the electric chair was located. I knew that I could have been taking the ride to death row if the U.S. Supreme Court had not ruled in a five to four decision that jurors couldn't be automatically excluded from juries in capital cases. I knew that if the decision had gone the other way, my ride to Reidsville would have been to death row.

We passed the front of the prison and turned down a road that was taking us by some houses on the left and the prison yard on the right. A few prisoners were out on the yard but not many.

"They know everything here. Those prisoners you see on the yard know where I'm going now," said the driver.

We drove around the back of the prison and I could see some large gates as well as several towers lining the perimeter of the prison. We drove up to a gas tank and the driver got out and began to fill up the tank.

I looked around and knew that prisoners come out the back gate in the morning to work on the prison farm. A few prisoners were walking around, wearing their traditional white pants and shirts with blue stripes on the pants or blue on the collars of their shirts. Some had on matching caps that were white with blue. I still had on my regular clothes. In the county jail, I refused to wear the prison clothes. Some guys wore the pants occasionally, but I believed that it was because they did not have anyone to bring them clothes from time to time. I had someone to bring me clothes, but I had decided early that I would not put on the prison pants. I would only put on prison clothes when I had absolutely no choice.

The guard got back in the van, and we headed out from the prison. The guard stated that he had to stop and pick up another prisoner, and before long, we were in a small country town that I had never heard of.

"Could I go in and use the bathroom?" I asked as we pulled into the jail.

"Sure, I need to go too," said the guard.

The guard took Lorenzo and me into the jail with him. It was a new jail and relatively small. It only had about ten cells in this jail and it was very clean. We were put in one cell and allowed to take a piss. There was an older black man in one cell and he was told to get ready to be transferred. We all climbed back into the van to continue our journey. Lorenzo decided to ask the other prisoner some questions.

"Hey, home, what are they sending you to prison for?"

"They gave me 3 years for stealing a hog"

"What? A real hog, an animal, or are you talking about a Cadillac?"

"A large pig."

"Hey, home, I didn't know people did that. I've heard of people rustling cattle years ago, but I didn't know that in 1969 people rustled hogs," Lorenzo said incredulously and mockingly.

I looked over at Lorenzo and tried to caution him not to laugh at this guy, although I thought it was funny too. He must have stolen a white man's hog, I concluded. Some white farmers had considerable power in some small towns, and they had a lot of say about some black people going or not going to prison.

I heard my daddy say many times that certain white people would get black people out of jail so these black people could return to the farm. Some of the offenses were serious but they were only serious if the offenses involved white people. Daddy said that one of the black guys in his hometown killed three Black people before he was finally sent to the chain gang. This man, after getting drunk, killed another black man, and his white boss was able to get him out of jail without bond and without going to trial. He then killed another black man and the white man got him out again. Feeling that he could do whatever he wanted, he killed a third black man, but this time the white folks decided that this was too much and sent him to the chain gang. A big part of the reason he went to the chain gang the third time was that another white man was upset that his best worker had been killed. Thus, this white man had some influence in determining the outcome.

We finally got to Jackson and the Diagnostic Center. It was very new and the guards had on new uniforms, a contrast to the Khaki outfits worn by the county jail guards in Savannah. We were taken to the showers, and our clothes were taken away including our underwear. After showering, we were issued new underwear and a white overall. Because it was late in the evening and after the other prisoners had eaten supper, we were taken to the cafeteria and given a food tray. The cafeteria was very nice and the food was good. Then we were taken down the hall. Lorenzo and I were put in a cellblock that was designated for first offenders. The cells had one bed in them and I was put in one cell. Looking around it as I walked it, I thought that it was not too bad. It had a wall outlet for three radio stations with some earphones on the bed. Frankly, this cell was much better than the cell that I had in Savannah. But I felt differently as I made my bed.

I had to reconcile being in prison now with a life sentence. I began to get angry because I knew that I had been grossly mistreated by the legal system in Savannah. I knew that I was gonna have to deal with some intense angry feelings and that it could consume me and make me worse. I could accept being in prison better if I, as a regular practice, was mistreating other people. But I hadn't. While it didn't make any difference to the white folks in Savannah, it made a difference to me. I didn't deserve to be attacked or hurt and tried to do the right thing. Despite Dunbar Harrison saying that I had to go to prison because my mind was made up to kill, he was wrong. I only wanted to be left alone and free to go anywhere that I wanted without the fear of being attacked for no reason. I felt that I had been forced to do what I did and then I was lied about in the trial. But the biggest hurt was the treachery by Aaron Kravitch and Lionel Drew. They planted a knife in my back, twisted it, and tried to beat me down to intimidate me. It really hurt and I knew that I would never forget what was done to me. The lesson that I had been shown was that might is right and white might is absolutely right. This was a lesson that I would never forget. I realized then that I was staring out of my cell and I needed to focus on where I was. I undressed and got into bed, but I couldn't clear my mind of how I actually got to this point.

The next morning we got up and were marched to breakfast. Lorenzo and I sat together with two other prisoners out of Atlanta. We talked about this Jackson place and someone stated that we were only brought here for testing. After breakfast, I was taken to have my picture and fingerprints taken. This was the third time that I had been fingerprinted. The first time was in the city jail and the second time was in the county jail. As my picture was about to be taken by a white prisoner, he said something that made me smile a little although I generally do not smile much at all. I was returned to my cell, but I was ushered back to the photographer. He told me that someone didn't like my picture and I had to take another one. Particularly, the half-smile on my face didn't make me look mean and they wanted a mean-looking picture of me. I thought that if I escaped that I would have to smile all the time to make it more difficult for someone to recognize me.

I received a copy of my sentence and it had that I had been given natural life. Below that, I saw that I was going up for parole in April 1975, which would be 7 years after my conviction. But I was troubled by the words "natural life." One of the guys out of Atlanta had a life sentence too, and I asked him to let me see his sentence. He showed it to me and it stated that he had life imprisonment. Someone who overheard the conversation stated that natural life means that you can't make parole and life means that you can. This prisoner also stated that there is a "concealed" life sentence and this is the same as natural life. I wondered if I had been tricked again down in Savannah. But someone assured me that if my sheet stated that I would go up for parole in 1975 that I indeed would go up for parole. I recalled further that I had been in the county jail for about 7 months before I went to trial, so I contacted the sheriff's office in Chatham County and requested that the office notify the parole board of the time that I had spent in the county jail. As a result, I received a new time sheet, indicating that I would come up for parole in September 1974.

Time was a big topic of prisoners and many of the guys with life or 20 years talked about getting their time cut in a few years and getting out early. I heard in the county jail that the parole board was quite corrupt at one time, and depending upon what you were convicted of doing, it was possible to get out early regardless of the sentence. It just took a little money.

The prison officials allowed us to go out on a yard. Some played softball and some guys just stood around. This prison appeared to have a considerable number of Muslims. The prison staff had decided to segregate all the Muslims in one unit. When they went out on the yard, they stood by themselves. Sometimes, they would have some guys standing at attention while someone preached to them about Allah and the white devil. I saw Willie Lee Robinson on the yard, and he was back trying to prove that he was tough. I knew him well now, but the other guys didn't. I didn't see him trying to bully anyone and he probably knew that he couldn't get away with some of the things that he was doing in the county jail back in Savannah. But he was trying to impress some guys by talking about when he was doing time in Reidsville.

I wrote home after I was able to get some envelopes and told my parents where I was. I also told them that they couldn't visit me because I was only gonna stay for about 30 or 45 days. I mentioned in the letter that Willie Lee Robinson was in Jackson, but he was in a cellblock for guys who had been in prison before. The letter was returned to me and I was told that it was against prison rules to discuss other prisoners in my letters. I rewrote my letter and mailed it.

The testing started. I was administered an IQ test and was given a test to see how fast I could work with my hands. We were given several screws with various washers and we had to put them together within a certain time. I wondered if they were testing us to predict how fast we might be able to pick beans if we were sent to Reidsville. My eyes were checked and the eye doctor extensively tested my left eye. I told him what had happened to me and he told me that it was a nasty cut. He told me that I could get some vision back in my left eye with a contact len, but that he couldn't prescribe it for me because it could cause a burden for the prison to which I was gonna be sent. He said that I would have to be taken periodically to an ophthalmologist and he couldn't prescribe the contact len for me for that reason.

Some flagrant sissies out of Atlanta were put in our cell block. Two were white and one was black. They walked with their arms folded like many women do and even sat like women with their ankles crossed. They sat as if they had on dresses and they were trying to keep guys from looking between their legs. All had adopted women's names to be called in the prison by other prisoners. Some of the guys were really going wild about them, but I stayed away from them. Lorenzo started talking to and playing with one of the white sissies.

"Lorenzo, you're doing wrong," I cautioned. "These guys are nothing but trouble."

"I don't wanna fuck him, but I might let him suck my dick," Lorenzo laughed.

"They're trouble and you are gonna invite trouble by some of these other guys."

Lorenzo did start having trouble with a black guy out of Atlanta who served food in the chow line. Whenever Lorenzo would extend his tray to the guy, the guy would throw the food on Lorenzo's tray, spreading whatever he was serving all over Lorenzo's tray and Lorenzo's overalls. When we got to the table, Lorenzo was talking about it. One of the guys said that it was because Lorenzo was playing with this sissy. Another guy said it was because Lorenzo had written "pimp" on the front of his overall. Lorenzo had decided to adopt a slick name and it may have offended this guy who thought that Lorenzo was just another nigger trying to impress someone. For whatever reason, this guy didn't like Lorenzo.

I was spending my time reading a lot. I began to buy the *Atlanta Constitution* and found that it was a much better newspaper than the Savannah newspaper. I really enjoyed the sport pages and the stories about the Atlanta Falcons. I also listened to the game on the outlet from the wall and began to learn the players. I knew that I was beginning increasingly to like sports and that this was gonna be one of the things I needed to keep my mind occupied in prison.

I continued to be tested by the diagnostic staff. One person was asking me questions about my brother and sisters. How old they were and how many did I have. I was puzzled why this information was needed. They were not in prison. Another person had me draw pictures of my family and asked me to draw a picture of God. I drew my family, using stick-like figures with frowns on everyone's faces. I drew God the same way. But I knew that he was trying to get a reading on me. The most puzzling aspect of this interview was that I was asked about specific names and did I know these people. One by one, the interviewer asked me if I knew some specific names. I thought this might be another IQ test, but the names were not names that I should know. The names were just ordinary-sounding and I became puzzled why he continued to ask me about these ordinary-sounding names. He asked about ten or eleven names. Each time, I told him that I did not know these people. When I returned to my cell, I wondered if he was ascertaining if I knew the people who had served on my jury. This was the only thing that I could think that someone might be concerned about. It might be that they wanted to alert members of the jury that gave me a death sentence if I escaped.

But I was not really angry with the jury that gave me a death sentence although it was a dishonest jury because they agreed not to disclose that one of the jury members was not qualified to serve and discussed information that was presented when the grand jury indicted me. I recalled that when Lucious Jackson was sentenced to die for raping that white woman, the newspaper said that he gave the jury a very scolding look. Perhaps some of the jury members in Savannah were frightened, and the officials instituted a policy to ascertain if a person who received a death sentence and had it commuted to life imprisonment knew members of the jury that returned the death sentence. In my case, I was not particularly upset with the jury members although I knew that they had been handpicked to convict me. I blamed Dunbar Harrison, Aaron Kravitch, and especially Lionel Drew. Drew provoked the jury into giving me the electric chair by telling them in summation that I had taken the law into my own hands, but they shouldn't give me the electric chair and instead should let me go free. This was a ridiculous statement to make to a jury. If a defense attorney, like Drew, tells a jury that a person is guilty of premeditated murder and asks the jury not to return with a death sentence, then the requested sentence should be a life sentence. But Drew never asked the jury to give me life. Instead, he asked them to let me go free, which he knew damn well that they wouldn't do after he told them I was guilty. Telling a jury that a person is guilty of murder and asking them to let the person go free is an insult to any jury. So, I was upset with Drew more than I was with the jury.

The same was true of Swinton. I blamed Drew and Kravitch for what Swinton said in court. Swinton was subpoenaed as a defense witness after my parents gave Aaron Kravitch his name, address, and telephone number. A competent and honest defense attorney would have contacted Swinton, Beulah, and Julia to learn if they had any information to help my defense. They should only be subpoenaed if they could help and if they couldn't, they shouldn't have been subpoenaed. I knew that no law school would tell a law student that it is proper in a capital case, or any case, to subpoena witnesses without interviewing them and find out when they are on the witness stand whether these witnesses have anything favorable to the defense. A lawyer fresh out of law school would not do what Kravitch and Drew did in how they subpoenaed witnesses to my trial. Also, Kravitch and Drew had about 75 years of combined legal experience, and no amount of experience can make up for subpoenaing witnesses the way it was done in my case. Thus, they were responsible for what Swinton said because if they had conducted a proper interview at the proper time, they would have learned that Swinton had been threatened and was scared. So, I knew who to blame.

I was sent to see a person who identified himself as a member of the clergy. He wasn't Catholic and I was glad. I didn't have positive feelings for Catholics. I began to discuss religion with him and told him that I had questioned the truthfulness of religion years ago when I began to doubt that hell existed.

"Why don't you believe in hell?" asked the white clergy man.

"When I was about 12 years old, a cousin was talking me how hot hell was and was pointing out it was 7 times hotter than the fire that was burning in her fireplace. It sounded like a bogey man story and I began to question it. But I really began to have doubts when a teacher, who was a Protestant, criticized Catholics' belief in purgatory. My girlfriend was Catholic and she told me that after death Catholics go to purgatory where their small sins are washed away. Then, they go to heaven. One of my teachers, who was white, told me that this was a bunch of nonsense and that sinners go to hell, period. A Baptist friend told me that all Jews are going to hell because the Jews haven't accepted Jesus as their Savior. Then, I heard that Jews have periods during the year where they have to atone for their sins committed during the last year. A few of the guys in the county jail had converted to Islam and they believed something else. I wondered how all these religions could be right."

"You are correct that people of different faiths have different beliefs, but they all believe in one Supreme Being."

"But why do they believe different things?" I pressed, although I knew he couldn't answer it.

"Well, it's like feeding a chicken. You throw out a piece of bread to a chicken and the chicken will peck at the bread, tearing a piece and running with it like it has the whole loaf."

"But each chicken has the same thing," I said with a puzzled look on my face.

"The chicken thinks it has all of it, though."

I continued to look disbelieving at him.

"Well, what do you believe?" he asked.

"I don't believe in heaven and hell. I think that telling people that they will go to hell for bad things and heaven for good things is a con game. I do understand why it is necessary to instill religion in people and that many people would run wild without a religious base. But I know that some religious people have done some awful things in the past, including killing other people who did not believe the right thing. I believe that one can be a good person and treat others humanely without religion. Most of all, I do not believe that God, if He exists, would get upset for someone believing differently.

People who live on the other side of the world who are not Christians and have not been exposed to Christian teaching can't be blamed for not having Christian beliefs. If Christianity is correct and hell does exist, I can't believe God would banish whole groups of people to an eternal hell, all because these people happened to be born in a different region where different beliefs were taught. If God is just, He would not allow this. This is why I believe that some people are lying about what God wants and what God has said. If God wants me to believe a certain thing, then I wanna hear it personally from God. I don't want someone interpreting to me what God said."

"Well, our time is up. Thank you for coming."

As I was returning to my cell, I wondered why he didn't get into my death sentence. I was sure that he knew that I had originally been sentenced to the electric chair. If he had asked me about my feelings concerning it, I would have told him. Of course, I was afraid for a few days after being given the electric chair, but I was also equally afraid of dying when I was stretched out on the table at Memorial Hospital. After I learned that my death sentence was the result of treachery and crookedness, I became less afraid of dying. If I had to walk the last mile to the electric chair, I would not want someone walking beside me telling me about what was awaiting me in the hereafter. I would have taken a deep breath and walked as best as I could, knowing that I had been unfairly outmanned by some corrupt white lawyers. If I did say a prayer, it would not be for me. It would be a prayer to God to cause some serious harm to all persons who helped me to get to this point. Give one cancer and a very painful death. Let lightning strike another one. Give one a heart attack. Let one be shot in the face. Let a truck run over another's head. If I knew these could really be done, I could die unafraid and content with my life.

Reality set in and I returned to the real environment. A fight between a white and black prisoner broke out in the cafeteria. The black prisoner was really whipping the white guy, but the black guy made a serious mistake. He, mimicking some wrestling he likely had seen on television, decided to drop-kick the white guy. Instead of kicking the white guy, the black guy hit his head when he fell to the floor. He grabbed his head with both hands and was rolling on the floor in considerable pain. The white guy stood back and watched, happy that the fight was over.

The fight was confusing to another guy who got up and began to walking aimlessly around the cafeteria. The guards looked at him but did not say anything to him as he slowly walked out of the cafeteria. One prisoner told the guard that this guy does not know that he is in prison and is crazy. The guard said that they are aware that this guy has some mental problems and they are trying to decide what to do with him.

I had a final meeting with a staff person after all the testing was completed. He was looking at my file and told me that he thought there was hope for me. He said that he was gonna recommend that I be sent to an institution for young, first offenders, but he explained that this decision was gonna be made by officials at the Georgia Department of Corrections, who may disregard his recommendation and send me somewhere else. About 2 weeks later, I was told to pack up and get ready to be transferred to Reidsville, the main, maximum-security prison. I knew that I could handle it. Most guys do not wanna go to Reidsville because guys are always getting killed there, and most young guys are forced to become fuckboys. But I knew that this was not gonna happen to me. One of the older guys in the county jail told me after I hit the guy in the head that I would make it at Reidsville because I was quiet and didn't talk much. He said that the less you talk, the more other guys wanna leave you alone because they do not know what you are thinking. He said my quietness was natural. But I really knew that some vultures need to be hurt before they get the message, and I was ready to do whatever I had to do even if I was giving up whatever small chance I had at making parole later. Because of my experience in Savannah, I developed an intense hatred for people who preyed on other people. As long as I was hurting a vulture who had done or was trying to do me wrong, I would never feel bad about it. Like in Savannah, I would not attempt to exploit, abuse, or mistreat any person, and when a situation required and demanded the shedding of blood, the other person's blood was gonna flow. Predatory people deserve whatever you do to them. With that frame of mind reinforced, I was ready to go to Reidsville.

Chapter 13

As I was walking through the double fences at the front of Reidsville, I was reminded of some movie scenes in which a person went into the front gate of a prison and the next scene said *10 years later.* Then, the person walks out the front door with bags in his hands. It only took a couple of seconds to do 10 years.

But I did not know when I would, or if I would, be walking out of the front gates of Reidsville a free man. I was thinking about this as I waited near the offices. I was taken into an office and fingerprinted again. After awhile, someone came for me and told me to follow him to quarantine. As I was following the guy, I realized that most of the prisoners I saw were white. Quarantine was E3 dormitory. When I walked in, a white prisoner came up to me and told me that he was the houseman. He asked me what my prison number was and I told him that I didn't have a prison number. He laughed and told me that as soon as I walked through the front gate, I automatically had a number and he would find out what it was. He looked on some papers and told me what my prison number was. He handed me some sheets and told me that my bed was on the right side and pointed to a bunk that was the third from the floor. I had seen double-stacked beds before, but this was the first time that I had seen triple-stacked beds.

I began to make the bed and had to stand on my toes to make it. I knew that I would have a difficult time sleeping in this bed because I would be afraid of rolling out of bed onto my head. I fell out of my bed at home once, but I did not have far to fall and was not hurt. But I knew that I could get seriously hurt if I fell out of this bed. After I made my bed, I began to look around. I noticed that from the way the guys were standing that this dormitory was segregated by beds. All the black prisoners were on the right side, and all the white prisoners were on the left. In all there were about 75 or 80 prisoners in this dormitory. I began to look the dormitory over and at some of the prisoners. None of the black prisoners said anything to me initially, and I preferred it that way. Looking around, I saw the bathroom facilities were small. There were four commodes and about the same number of showers. I took a piss and noticed that the bathroom had Dial soap in it which smelled good. In the county jail in Savannah we were always given Ivory soap. I liked the Dial soap. As I was walking out, I noticed a huge drum that served as a trash can. I looked into it and noticed that it had some sport pages in it. I reached in it and saw that it was a publication called *The Sporting News,* which contained nothing but sports, both college and professional. I had never seen a publication like this. I looked in the can and there was another paper that was dated a week earlier. I took both papers to my bed and climbed up to sit on it and read.

After awhile, someone called chow time and everyone began to walk out of the dormitory. I followed the group and went into the mess hall. This mess hall was not as nice as Jackson and the food was not as good. The mess hall was crowded, and I sat at a table with a black guy. I did not say anything to him, and just ate. I returned to the dormitory and went back to reading. There was a television on, and some guys had gathered around it to watch. Finally, someone sauntered over to me.

"Where're you from, man?" asked a somewhat young rotund guy.

"Savannah," I responded.

He began to ask me about certain guys that he knew from Savannah who were in Alto, a training school for boys.

I told him that I didn't know the guys he was asking about.

"I'm from Brunswick. Everybody calls me Iceman."

"My name is Rudolph."

Iceman chatted a little more and then he returned to talk to his other friends.

Night began to fall. I dreaded bedtime and climbing up on the third bed. When the houseman announced that lights would be going out shortly, I got ready for bed. I climbed up, trying to avoid stepping on the other two beds. I was trying to step on the metal part at the end of the bed. When I got up, I gingerly got under the sheet, moved to the middle of the bed and told myself to stay in the middle of the bed. I was lying on my back and staring at the ceiling. I fell asleep and was happy in the morning when the lights were turned on, and I realized that I had not fallen out of bed.

Besides being temporarily quarantined, newly admitted prisoners were given an orientation to the prison. I had learned some things in the county jail, and I had listened to conversations in the dormitory with guys who had been in Reidsville before and were there to serve a new sentence. We were taken to a church and various staff officials came to talk to us. One of the persons who spoke to us was a captain, who told us that why we were in prison was none of the guards' business, and they shouldn't be asking about what we had done.

I was told that guards in the past had some interest in whether someone had committed crimes against white people. I had heard too that some parole officers were interested in this area whenever they came to Reidsville to interview a black prisoner coming up for parole. The first question out of the parole officer's mouth was whether the victim was white or black. If the prisoner said white, the parole officer would close his book and get up and leave. There would be no early parole for these people.

He told us that we should address guards as Boss Whoever. Just like the old Georgia chain gang movies, I thought.

The captain told us that we would not have any cash money and should some cash money slip through in our mail that we should turn it in. He stated that the reason cash was contraband was to prevent guards from being bribed as there would be too much money in the institution. He told us that instead of cash, we would be issued a coupon book with our names on it, and if a person was caught with another person's coupon book, he goes to the hole.

He told us not to borrow money from other prisoners because this is the cause of a lot of trouble. Some guys borrow money, cannot pay it back, and then have to do what is called "catching-out." "Catching-out" is a term used when a prisoner comes to the control office and asks to be segregated because of death threats.

Someone came from the classification committee and told us that prisoners will meet with the classification committee to be assigned their work detail and dormitory or cellblock. Everyone, we were told, must work outdoors doing something on the prison farm or working around the prison. After 6 months of working outdoors, a prisoner can request an inside job, provided he has had 6 months without any disciplinary reports. If a person has 5 months of working outdoors and goes to the hole, he must begin to build his 6 months again and cannot start where he left off.

A doctor spoke to us to explain how the medical system worked. He stated that the doctors were good, but they may not exhibit good bedside manners. He explained that sick call is held every morning, but prisoners shouldn't come to sick call thinking that they can fool the doctor into giving them days in.

When I went before the classification committee, I was assigned to L2 dormitory and forty-three work detail. Shortly thereafter, I, along with several other prisoners, was taken to the clothing room. As we were waiting in line, a prisoner from Savannah who had attended Florence Street School with me and who had briefly been in jail stopped to talk to me. His last name was Jackson, but he went by the name of thirty-eight, not the number but the gun. Thirty-eight was smacking viciously on some chewing gum and was giving me a quick rundown on Reidsville. He told me that as soon as I hit the cellblock someone was gonna feel me out to see if I was weak and could be made into a fuckboy. He told me to tell them to go to hell. I was issued a pair of gloves, a hat, two changes of clothing, and a jacket with a thin lining in it.

With all my belongings and gear, I was taken to the L Building. A guard sitting at the desk was told that I had been assigned to L2 and the last door on the left was opened for me to enter. I walked in and stood looking up at three rows of cells. I was told that Charles was the houseman. Someone told me that there were five or six guys whose job is to keep the dormitory clean.

One guy took me to the third tier and showed me my cell. As I was hanging up my coat, someone stopped by and asked me how many guys left quarantine. I told him about nine or ten. Then, I was asked where I was from and I told him Savannah.

"Oh, you're a Geechee. We got a few guys in here from Savannah," said the tall dark-skinned guy, who identified himself as Nigger X. "We got Ervin and Giles in here. Crow is in here too, but he is in the hole. Do you know Crow?"

"No," I said slowly. "What's his real name?"

"Edgar Lonon."

"Yeah, I know Lonon."

Nigger X then left and I came out to look over the cellblock. I counted twenty cells on each tier and all the doors to the cells were open. Standing on the range, I could see another building that looked exactly like the L Building. Looking around, I could see several guys in the dormitory, but there were not many. I assumed that most of the guys were out working and would be in later.

Then, I saw a really grotesque-looking guy on the range. He had been burned fairly badly in the face and his hands were burned too. Part of his face was pink and so were his hands. As he swaggered down the tier, he stopped by me and asked me my name and where I was from. I told him.

"My name is Rudolph, too, Rudolph Heard. What a coincidence, two Rudolph's in the same cellblock. So, you're a Geechee."

I quickly learned that everyone from Savannah is called a Geechee.

Later, guys began coming into the cellblock. Most were dirty, holding their gloves in their hands. Some commented that they had a new guy in the cellblock, but most didn't say anything. Chow was called and I followed the group to the mess hall. However, we went to a different mess hall than the one that prisoners in quarantine go to. It was exactly the same, but it contained mostly black prisoners with a few whites. It was very noisy, produced by talking among prisoners eating and dirty metal trays being stacked and dirty spoons clanging as they were dropped into a metal pan as prisoners exited the mess hall.

After I returned to the cellblock, a tall guy walked by my cell as I was sitting on the bed and said something that I couldn't quite understand.

"Hey you, P. . . . wants you to come out on the yard," said the tall guy angrily.

I did not hear who he had said wanted me to come out on the yard and he didn't even stop so that I could ask him to repeat himself. Shortly afterward, the Boss outside the doors shouted yard call and began opening the doors to all four cellblocks in L building. I wondered if I should go out on the yard to meet someone that I didn't know, but something told me to go.

I following the group to the yard and was now standing on the same yard I saw when I was in the van headed to Jackson. Guys were coming out from other parts of the prison too. After a few minutes, there were hundreds of guys on the yard, both black and white. I slowly walked near the basketball court and just stood by the court.

Someone call my name.

"Rudolph, you got my message."

I quickly recognized Piggy whom I knew from the county jail and who hung out with my cousin Arthur. My daddy allowed one of his half-sister's children to stay with us for awhile in Savannah after he had left Crawfordville. Arthur was from the country and quite naive. Arthur drank a lot and was always broke 2 days after getting paid despite his working two jobs. Arthur would buy liquor for everyone and the women would take his money. One day he brought Piggy by our house, and my daddy told him not to bring Piggy back to the house again. Daddy told Arthur that Piggy steals a lot and he did not want him around. My daddy had a serious problem with anyone who steals. He told me that he would never try to help me if I went to jail for stealing, but he would spend his last nickel for me if I went to jail for fighting. To Daddy, stealing was inexcusable and he did not like being around people who did, such as Piggy.

"Come on and meet your homeboys," Piggy urged.

I walked over and Piggy introduced me to Flick, Rat, Sweetman, and Norris Hodges.

We all start walking around the perimeter of the yard, making a circle like a couple hundred of guys were doing too.

"We knew you were in quarantine, and we were watching out for you."

Flick, who I had never seen before, began to discuss L2 and told me to watch out for Blue. Blue was the burnt guy named Rudolph Heard. Flick told me that Blue was no good, and the guys from Savannah started to stomp Blue's ass. He told me that Blue raped Ervin James in L2, and he had gotten burned a few years ago because he took another boy's ass. After Blue raped the boy and began to gamble, the boy came up from behind Blue, threw gas on Blue, and set him on fire. Flick told me that Blue had a reputation for running over weak prisoners. Flick also mentioned some of Blue's friends in L2 that I shouldn't trust and that I should watch out for them.

"You're not here by yourself," said Flick. "You got homeboys all over this penitentiary and most of them don't just kick asses, they stomp asses. The Geechees here almost run this prison and the majority of the toughest motherfuckers here are from Savannah. If you need help, they'll help you. All you need to do is stand up and be a man. If you aren't gonna stand up for yourself, they ain't gonna do anything."

I nodded my head.

Some white sissies were walking in the opposite direction and I recognized them from Jackson.

"Hey baby," Sweetman said, looking at one of the white sissies.

The sissy who only associated with black guys in Jackson refused to look at Sweetman and had a frightened look on his face. Sweetman called out to the sissy again just as a white guy a few feet behind the Sissy looked menacingly at Sweetman.

"That's the sissy's War Daddy," Piggy said.

"Did you see how he looked at you, Sweetman?" Rat said.

"Fuck him. Shit. He acts like that's a real white woman with a real pussy. That is a stinking-ass punk. If he doesn't want me looking at the punk, make the punk stay in his cellblock."

"Some of these motherfuckers got shit on their brains," said Piggy. "There is a motherfucker in my dormitory who brags that he would run over ninety-nine pieces of pussy to get to one asshole."

Piggy and Flick continued to talk to me explaining things to me and pointing out other guys on the yard from Savannah.

The tall guy who told me to come out on the yard was from Savannah, and his name was Edward Giles. Giles spoke to Piggy and began to walk around the yard with us. A really dark guy Piggy called Sparky came over. Piggy stated that Sparky was the only outright sissy from Savannah and stated that a couple other guys from Savannah were fuckboys whom no one from Savannah talked to. He mentioned that Thirty-eight was a fuckboy and the guys from Savannah didn't talk to him.

"I know him as Jackson and he was a bully when we were going to Florence Street School," I said.

"He's is a bully here, too. It takes a bully to back up on a hard dick," said Rat.

Flick added that Thompson, the deputy warden, stated that guys from Savannah were unlike other prisoners. Guys from Savannah didn't fight each other in Reidsville, and Thompson said that he did not have the problems with Geechees that he had from guys from Atlanta. The guys from Atlanta were always trying to set each other up and outsmart each other. Then, he mentioned that the guys from Savannah who no one fucked with were Honey, Robert Pryor, Willie Gilyard, and another guy named Crow. Edgar Lonon's name was Crow, but there was another guy from Savannah named Crow. They called him Black-assed Crow because he was much darker than Lonon. This Crow was on segregation and had stabbed about three or four guys in Reidsville. His brother's name was Big Crow, and after getting out of Reidsville, Big Crow was killed in Savannah during a gambling game. Big Crow, when he was in Reidsville, was considered to be a hog.

Honey walked over and began to talk to me. He told me about what happened when he left the county jail and refused to go to Chatham County prison camp. He said that when they took him, they took him straight to the hole, and after a few days, he was transferred to another institution.

"I'll keep the weight off you if you're straight, but don't ask me to help you when you're not right," said Honey. "Be real careful who you pick to be your friends. Don't take anything from anyone. If you need something, come to me. Some of these motherfuckers here are not right in the head," said Honey.

"Thanks, but I feel that I will be okay," I said.

Honey left and walked over to where some guys were playing tag football.

As we were walking by the guys lifting weights, someone pointed out Ervin James to me. Ervin was a very muscular guy, but his large muscular physique did not prevent him from being forced to fuck. They said that after Blue raped Ervin almost everyone in the cellblock fucked Ervin too. One by one they went in the cell and fucked Ervin. I intuitively knew that size was irrelevant, and a big person is just as likely to be steamrolled as a small person. The size of the heart and what a person is willing to do is what is most important. This was confirmed even more when someone pointed out another muscular guy, who was more muscular than Ervin.

"Do you see that big motherfucker there? He ain't nothing but 250 pounds of pure pussy. He looks like Tarzan, but at night he becomes Jane."

I had already decided that I was gonna get me a knife although I knew that the penalty for getting caught with a knife was 14 days in the hole and 6 months on segregation. I thought that I might need it for my own protection, and this was the only reason why I needed it. When I got the gun, I did so only for my own protection, and the consequences of having a gun had not convinced me that it was a wrong decision. If I had not had it and continued to go the hospital like I was going then I was gonna go one time too many. Having a knife here wouldn't be wrong. If I used it on someone, it would only be in self-defense. I believed Honey and the other guys from Savannah were real and genuine in saying that they would look out for me, but I needed to be able to look out for myself. I was gonna be at Reidsville for awhile, and I did not wanna depend on anyone to keep someone from stomping on me. I knew I could put a stop to that myself.

Piggy pointed out the configuration of the prison to me. He pointed to the building on the end as A Building, which has A1, A2, A3, and A4. Next to it was the B Building with the same number of dormitories and then there was C Building. Except for a few white guys in the A Building, this entire side housed black prisoners. In addition, the L Building, which I was in, was all black. L1, behind my cellblock, was the designated cellblock for blatant black homosexuals. The other side of the prison housed white prisoners in E, F, and G Buildings. It had a cellblock for the blatant white homosexuals. The M Building, which I could see from my cellblock, was used as a segregation unit. Prisoners who assaulted other prisoners or prisoners who needed protection were housed in the M Building.

A voice came out over the loud speaker and told everyone that yard time was over. Guys started returning to their cellblocks and dormitories, including me. When I returned to my cellblock, I watched a little television for awhile. Several guys were staring at me. A few spoke and stated that they heard that I was from Savannah. One guy asked why Geechees like rice so much and asked if was true that the main meal among Geechees is rice and gator tails. I didn't say anything.

The dormitory began to darken and the music began blaring. Some guys were listening to radios and some were playing record players. I could hear the Supremes, Joe Simon, and Aretha Franklin. One guy on the second range was playing Aretha Franklin's "Ain't No Way." They called him Fat and he was parading around in some tight briefs. Someone whistled at him and I knew that he was a sissy. I was told that only sissies wear briefs and they do so because they fit like panties. So, almost everyone wore boxer shorts. Fat had his blanket hung up to prevent anyone from looking into his cell, and I noticed that others hung blankets too.

One of the guys who came to talk to me was someone that I had met in Jackson. He was partially paralyzed from a self-inflicted gunshot wound. He told me that he had killed his wife, mother-in-law, and his wife's boyfriend. He said that his wife was in their house with her boyfriend and his mother-in-law was watching out for her. So, he killed them all and then shot himself in the head. When he went to trial, he was given three life sentences. Because of his partial paralysis, his job was to help clean the cellblock.

At 9 o'clock, Charles blew a whistle for the count. Everyone came out of their cells and began lining up in pairs. The people in the showers did not have to come out as they were quite visible. A guard came in and began counting. When he went out, he went into L4 to count. At 10 o'clock, we were told to hit our cells. I went upstairs and got in my cell. After a few minutes, all the doors closed at once. For about 15 minutes, I just stared out of the cell, looking towards the M Building but mostly just looking. About an hour later, a guard came by with a flashlight and counted again. This was the third time today that a count was done. I got into bed and decided to sleep with my head towards the back of the cell. Before long, I was asleep.

At about 5:30 A.M., the doors opened. I got up and got dressed. I went down and washed my face. Charles told a guy named PeeWee to show me where forty-three detail met. We were let out for breakfast. After returning to the cellblock, I heard a loud whistle blowing. This was the signal to the community that prisoners are about to be sent out to work in the prison field. Then, a voice over the loudspeakers began calling details. When forty-three was called, I followed Peewee. We went outside toward the yard and walked to a spot near the canning plant. I saw Iceman, who told me that he was in this detail too. Peewee told me that Boss Ralph was in charge of this detail. Boss Ralph came and told forty-three to line up. Peewee said that we had to line up in pairs. So, I stood beside Peewee. Boss Ralph began calling guys by their last names from a a metal clipboard, and when he called my name, I said here. When he was finished, we began to march through two gates to a waiting prison bus. When we got in the empty bus, Boss Ralph came up and locked the gate separating us from the driver and the guards. The other guard came over with two shotguns and handed one to Boss Ralph. They also had pistols. We went somewhere back in the woods and unloaded.

A man in a pickup truck came up and someone stated that this was Bully Wallace, who I heard was actively and eagerly helping to execute prisoners. Bully Wallace in his younger days had a reputation for beating prisoners unmercifully. We were told to get shovels and begin digging near a bank. I believed that we were altering a waterway, but I was not sure. There were about forty prisoners on the detail. So there was a lot of dirt being moved. I looked over at Iceman and he was laughing. At 11:30, we stopped work for lunch.

Someone shouted, "P-Jack on the run," and a truck drove up with a white guy and four or five prisoners. It was pulling a trailer with three huge pots. We lined up and took a tray and a cup. The guards were sitting in chairs between us and had their shotguns on a table.

One detail moved chairs and tables around the prison farm depending upon where details were working. At 1:00, we went back to work. At 4:00, we stopped work and shortly thereafter, the bus returned to pick us up. As I got on the bus, I stated to myself that I had made it through the first day. Upon returning to the prison, we marched through one gate and then we were searched. I was told that we could eat now before returning to the cellblock, and we did.

I decided to wait until later to take a shower. So I kept on my work clothes when I went out to the yard. Laundry was once a week. So, one suit of clothes was designated for work and another relatively clean change of clothing was used to put on after getting off from work and showering. On laundry day, the work clothes were submitted for washing and they would be on your bed when you got off work. We could only get one washed and starched suit of clothing a week and most people kept this change for the visiting room.

On the yard, it was pretty much the same scenario as the day before. John Foster was walking with us. John lived in the cellblock across from me. I remembered John from the county jail and also remembered that he had tried to attack Dunbar Harrison in the courtroom. Someone mentioned it and John stated that if he had gotten to Dunbar Harrison, he would have put 20 years worth of ass whipping on him. Marvin Lowe, John's partner in the attempted attack on Dunbar Harrison, was also in Reidsville and was playing football today.

Someone pointed out Willie Gilyard, who was called Chick, to me. Although I had been in population only a day, I had heard a lot of talk about him, and many of the guys were afraid of him. I studied him and noticed that he was a short, somewhat stocky guy. He had an air about him that suggested that he was different from other guys on the yard.

Honey, I was told, lived in C1, and most people referred to this as the hog cell block. Prison officials put most of the black heavyweight guys in this cell block, and some guys wishfully aspired to be in this dormitory. On the work detail that day, one guy stated that he was gonna talk to Thompson about putting him in C1 with the rest of the hogs. In other words, since C1 was for hogs, he was being disrespected and demeaned by not being in there too. Someone retorted that he needed to be in L1 with his sisters because he was a pussy.

Willie Robinson, I was told, was in the M Building in segregation. When he was sent to Reidsville from Jackson, he was put in segregation and not in population. One guy speculated that Willie Robinson asked to be put in segregation because he feared that he might be killed because of the last time he was in Reidsville.

I also learned that the dominant discussion on work detail is who is a real man and who isn't. Pussy was a big topic, but it wasn't real pussy. It was chain gang pussy. Related to this topic was fuckboys. I couldn't count how many times I heard this word each day. They also discussed considerably who was bumping, which I learned was another term for swapping-out. So, I quickly learned that two guy who bumped were two guys who would took turns fucking each other in the ass. First, one would fuck the other in the ass and then they would trade places. Sometimes, guys agreed to bump or swap out and one insisted on going first. When finished, he would not reciprocate and sometimes fights broke out over this.

Another big topic was prisoners who were good at laying snares, which were traps for weak prisoners. So and so laid a snare for so and so. Like rabbits, they either were caught or got away until the next snare.

I learned that going out on the yard after work was a recent change in prison policy. In fact, I read about it in the *Atlanta Constitution* when I was in Jackson. The Board of Corrections had a meeting and decided that prisoners at Reidsville could go out on the yard during daylight savings time after supper during the weekdays. Prior to this decision, prisoners could only go out on the weekend. This change in policy was related to attempts at providing rehabilitation in Georgia's maximum-security prison. Other changes that were made were the expansion of athletics at the prison. A recreation director was hired and sports were expanded. Then, changes in the yard policy were made. I recalled that the director of the Georgia Department of Corrections stated that these changes were "enough rehabilitation."

I starting talking to Norris Hodges and was asking him about Drew and Kravitch. He immediately began telling me about how he was fucked over by Drew and Kravitch. He said that he hired Kravitch and Kravitch sent Drew to the trial. Norris said that after he was convicted and after he was sent to Chatham prison camp, Kravitch came to see him, promising to appeal. But he did not see or hear from Kravitch again after his wife took some money to him for an appeal. Norris said that he didn't know that he did not have to proceed at trial with Drew. Norris said he was pissed that Drew did not subpoena all the witnesses, but his biggest disappointment was Drew leaving him alone while the trial was going on. He said that Drew left him alone at the defense table, and according to Norris, this was a violation of his Sixth Amendment right to counsel. Norris stated that he filed last year a habeas corpus action, and Drew brought Barker to the habeas corpus hearing. Norris had his transcript with him and I asked if I could read it. He handed it to me.

I began reading Norris' habeas corpus transcript and came to the part when Drew was testifying.

Q: All right, sir. Now, of course, you made after your concluding argument, now, he has made a point in this petition that you left the courtroom, which I don't think is really material whether you did or not, but do you have any comment to make on that?

A: Uh, I probably left the Courtroom, uh, during the Solicitor's final argument. I, from time to time do, to get a glass of water or to smoke a cigarette or just to sit down and rest for a minute. I seldom, uh, stay out of the Courtroom more than three or four minutes. I'm always in the Courtroom when the Judge is charging the Jury. My recollection is that I left after Mr. Barker started his argument or just as I concluded mine, and came back within five minutes.

Q: Now, Mr. Barker was the Assistant Solicitor General who prosecuted the case for the State, is that right?

A: Yes, sir, that's correct.

Q: Have you had occasion to try other cases wherein Mr. Barker was prosecuting attorney?

A: Many of them.

Q: You are well familiar with Mr. Barker and his personality and character and in a general scope the type of argument that he would make. In other words, what I'm saying is, you didn't feel that he was making any statement to the Jury that would be unduly prejudicial or improper in his argument, and for that reason you didn't feel any necessity to stay and hear every word of his argument.

A: That's correct. I have never heard Mr. Barker make an improper argument or do anything improper in the Courtroom, and even if I didn't feel that way about Mr. Barker, I doubt if Judge Harrison would let him get away with it, if he did. I have confidence in both of these gentlemen. A lot of lawyers I wouldn't turn my back on. Mr. Barker, I will.

Then, it was Robert Barker's turn to say good things about Drew.

Q: All right, sir. Thank you, sir. Now, touching on the issue of Mr. Drew's competency as an attorney in representing particularly the petitioner in this case, how long have you known Mr. Drew?

A: I've known Mr. Drew, I would imagine fifteen years.

Q: Have you had occasions to have cases with him on the other side?

A: Oh, many cases.

Q: Many cases?

A: Many cases. As a matter of fact, I've probably tried more against Mr. Drew than any other lawyer in Chatham County.

Q: Would that be an indication of the volume of criminal work that Mr. Drew does?

A: I would say that the majority of his work is criminal work.

Q: An would you say that defense-wise, among the other lawyers in Chatham County, that he handles his share of criminal case?

A: I would say that he would probably, through that office, he handles I'd say ninety-five percent of the trial work for his firm. That they would handle the majority of the criminal cases in Chatham County.

Q: All right, sir. I forgot to ask Mr. Drew. About what age man would you say he is?

A: Forty-eight years old.

Q: All right, sir. Now, from your observation of his defense of petitioner during the trial of the case and prior thereto, if he, if any of his actions that you are aware of prior to that time, what would you say—What is your opinion and based on your participation in the trial, your observation of Mr. Drew's participation in the trial, your knowledge, past knowledge of Mr. Drew, and his ability as a trial lawyer, particularly in the field of criminal work, what is your opinion concerning the competency or incompetency of the way he represented the petitioner?

A: I'll put it this way. Uh, as the prosecutor, I know when I'm prosecuting a case when I can be lazy, and glide by, and then I know the lawyers that are going to come in the Courtroom and I'd better be on my toes constantly, and throughout my entire practice, I never get lazy with Mr. Drew. Mr. Drew is probably, I feel, is probably if not the finest criminal lawyer in Chatham County, one of the finest. I have prosecuted or tried, I would say, between five and ten thousand cases since I've been practicing law, and, uh, at no time will I be slack when Mr. Drew comes in the Courtroom. It actually is an enjoyment to try a case against him because you find out in the prosecuting business that if you have a defense attorney that isn't the most competent in the world, you have to soft-pedal a case so that the Jury doesn't develop too much sympathy for the defendant because of his attorney. I enjoy Mr. Drew coming into Court because no holds are barred. We can just go at it tooth and neck.

When I finished reading parts of Norris' transcript, I felt like vomiting.

After yard call had ended, I decided to take a shower when I returned to the cellblock. After I had showered, I realized that I had not taken clean pants to the shower, although I had clean underwear. What I had read in Norris' transcript was still on my mind. Rather than putting on my dirty work pants, I decided to return to my cell in my underwear. When I got almost to the third tier, I just happened to look down, and I saw that everyone was watching me. Although some guys return to their cells from the showers in their shorts, everyone was watching me because I was new. I knew that were all wondering whether I was a real man or not. I brushed it off.

I had written a letter home and told my parents where I was. I had not seen them since I left the county jail almost 2 months before. I was expecting one of my sisters to write me and convey when the family would come to see me.

On Saturday, movies were shown in the theater. The theater was relatively large and the screen was almost the size of the screen that one would see in the outside world. After about 30 minutes, a prisoner hall runner came into the theater and called my name and number. He told me that I had visitors.

I didn't know where the visiting room was and had to ask several people. The guard told me that I was not properly dressed for the visiting room and that he should write me up. I explained that I was new and wasn't expecting visitors today. When I got inside the visiting room, I saw my daddy and my brother, who were smiling broadly. Both of them shook my hand vigorously, inquiring how I was doing. I explained what happened in Jackson and discussed Reidsville a little. They told me that Momma had to work and asked Daddy to wait until Sunday. But Daddy said that he told her that he had to see his boy on Saturday, and the next time, they would come on Sunday. We visited for almost 2 hours and when they left they told me that they were gonna go by our cousins' home in Reidsville, Mary and Sylvester.

I had mentioned to one of the guys from Savannah that I had cousins who only lived about five or six miles from the prison. They told me that I should ask my cousin, who probably knows many of the guards, to talk to Boss Ralph about me. I didn't think that was a good idea because if the guard did something special for me, he would want something in return or other prisoners might think that I had been snitching or something. So, I rejected that idea.

Chapter 14

"I have two knives. If you want one, I will sell one to you," said one prisoner who called himself Wyatt Earp. "One bends, but it will draw blood. The other one is made of steel and will put a motherfucker away."

"I don't want the one that bends," I said.

"Oh, you wanna kill someone?" Wyatt queried.

"No, I did not say anything about killing anyone. You said that you have two knives and one bends. I said that I did not want the one that bends. That's all I said. Don't put words in my mouth. I heard enough of that when I went to court. As far as you know, I might want a knife to cut my toenails."

"Okay, toenail cutting."

Wyatt left my cell and came back with the knife to show me. I took it. It definitely was not a prison made knife and had a steel blade. A few days earlier I had seen another prisoner with a knife. This knife had to have been brought into the prison by a guard because it was hunting knife with a 12-inch blade.

"How much do you want for it?" I asked.

"Two packs."

"Okay."

I unlocked my footlocker and took out two packs of cigarettes and handed them to Wyatt. Wyatt took the cigarettes and gave me the knife.

After he left, I thought to myself that these motherfuckers here think that they are the smartest sons-of-bitches around. They sit around and do nothing but plot how to set someone up and how to lay a snare. Wyatt was a friend of Blue, and this selling me a knife was part of their snare. He was trying to befriend me and he didn't think that I would use this knife. But he was wrong. I told myself, if I need to use it, I will. What he originally said was actually right. When you moved on these types of vultures, you had to mean it and couldn't pussy around with them.

Another of Blue's comrades, whose name was Andrew, asked me if I wanted to play chess. I had just learned the pieces and couldn't play very well. However, I won the game and knew that Andrew had let me win. I guessed that Andrew thought that I would be so happy about winning that I would play him more often and thereby become more disarmed. So, I never played him again.

I developed a book on all the prisoners in the cellblock. According to my assessment, there were four really no good sons-of-bitches in the cellblock. Blue, Wyatt Earp, JB, and Cock-A-Red, who had recently been released from segregation for stabbing another prisoner. They scrutinized every person who came into the cellblock to determine if they could run over the person and perhaps turn the person into pussy.

JB tried a new guy named Larry Shank, who was relatively young but unafraid. Shank stomped JB's ass and JB quickly learned that he had tried the wrong person. Shank came by my cell one day and told me that Blue was no good and to watch out for him. I thanked him and told him that I was aware of what Blue was about.

Since my first day in the cellblock, Blue had been watching me relentlessly, and I could easily see that he was plotting how he was gonna approach me. Occasionally, he would stop by my cell to talk about football and to tell me how no good other guys were. Blue stated that someone had written a letter and signed his name. In the letter, Blue was supposedly bragging about how many white girls he was pimping in Atlanta. This letter was caught by the censors and Blue said that he was taken before the disciplinary court and told them that this letter was not written by him and offered a sample of his writing. Blue said the intent by someone was to have him put in the segregation unit in M Building. Another scheme that guys used to get rid of some prisoners for awhile was to put a knife under someone's pillow and then snitch to the guards. Because the rule in Reidsville is that anything in or by a person's bed belongs to that person, it is very easy to get rid of someone for 6 months. Blue concluded that the niggers in Reidsville were no good.

Despite Blue's warning, I knew that Blue was one of the no-good motherfuckers, but I wasn't afraid of him. I had stopped going out on the yard and started watching the evening news. Giles warned me that I might be putting myself in danger by staying in the cellblock. I told Giles that I was not gonna run from Blue. Blue had been telling some people that I was gonna be the next person that he was gonna turn out. He got Ervin and I was gonna be next. Upon hearing this, I thought to myself that instead of me being next on Blue's list, I was gonna make Blue next on my list. Blue epitomized the type of vulture that led me to being in prison in the first place. There are vultures on the streets, in the courtroom, and in the penitentiary. I now believed that you run from a fool, but you stand up to a vulture. Blue could watch me and talk behind my back, but if he gets wrong, I intended to kill him. Probably, then, someone will say that I killed poor burnt-up Blue for no reason and that Blue sang in the prison choir.

I didn't have much to say to anyone, but I did talk a little to some of the guys. I began to get a lot of magazines, subscribing to *Ebony, The Sporting*

News, Sport, Jet, and *Football News*. Additionally, I was buying Savannah and Atlanta newspapers. So, some guys were always asking to read some of my magazines or look at my newspapers. I became somewhat friendly with Lump Phillips from Columbus, Georgia, who wanted to read my black publications, as this was the beginning of black consciousness. Lump was getting a Columbus newspaper and I would read it, too. Lump told me that he had read about me. I didn't find this too surprising because my brother saw a former classmate of mine and she told him that in Los Angeles she had read about me getting the electric chair. Lump thought that I was intelligent and wanted to discuss social and political issues. He stated with pride that he convinced his sister to stop putting the hot comb in their mother's hair and to let it go natural. Lump said that he hated black people who were trying to act and look white, and when he returned to Columbus, he was gonna carry a bucket of white paint with him to paint all the Negroes who were trying to act and look white. That was his favorite saying, throwing some white paint on certain black people. "Ok, you wanna be white, here some white paint for your ass." Then, he would laugh.

Giles and I got to be pretty close too. Giles did not get any visitors or money from home. So, I would share whatever food I bought with him. My favorite nighttime snack was vanilla wafers and peanut butter, and I always had a jar of peanut butter in my footlocker. I would buy cigarettes too although I didn't smoke. Cigarettes are money in the penitentiary, as are stamps, cans of salmon, and loaves of bread. When guys gambled, they gambled with these items as well as new shoes.

Some guys were always trying to give younger and weaker guys food. A joke around the prison was that Jack Mackel salmon sandwiches have led to more guys getting turned out in Reidsville than any other thing. The game was to offer a weak or young person a sandwich, and after several sandwiches, the person was told that he had to give back the same sandwiches or fuck. It was done with cigarettes, too. A replacement pack would not be good enough: it had to be the exact same pack or else. But this game was just for weak prisoners, and predatory prisoners had a sense of how the person might react before they ran this game.

Cock-A-Red seemed to have targeted a guy named Gene in the cellblock. Gene was not thought of very highly by JB and Blue. Moreover, Gene and JB had gotten into a fight previously and JB went to the hole after Gene told the Boss that JB had a knife. I believed that Gene was viewed as a fuckboy by this group, and they were not gonna let him change his status.

As I was watching television, I noticed that Cock-A-Red went into Gene's cell, which had a blanket up. After a few minutes, there was a loud rumbling in the cell, and they were fighting. Gene screamed loudly, and one guy told Charles, the houseman, that Cock-A-Red was stabbing Gene.

Cock-A-Red was considered one of the bad guys in Reidsville, but Charles was more than a match for him. Charles ran to his cell, which was the first cell on the first tier, and ran back towards Gene's cell with a two-by-four. Just as Charles got to the cell, Gene ran out bloody from several stab wounds and called for the Boss to let him out. Charles held the two-by-four like a bat, and he was about to hit Cock-A-Red, who was holding a bloody knife. A guy named Genard begged Charles repeatedly not to hit Cock-A-Red. I was watching both of them and it was obvious that Cock-A-Red held Charles in high esteem. Cock-A-Red, without saying one word to Charles, started walking up to the front with Charles following him with the two-by-four. One had to walk through two doors to get outside of the cellblock and Cock-A-Red was let out by the Boss through the first door. The guard asked him for the knife, but Cock-A-Red refused, saying that he was not gonna give up his knife until he got to the control office.

What Cock-A-Red had done was not unusual. Another guy named Robert who was considered to be a fuckboy was told by another prisoner that he wanted Robert to be his boy. Robert said no. So, the next morning, while the details were lining up, the prisoner stabbed Robert in the chest. When he was asked why he stabbed Robert, he told them that he told Robert, who was pussy, that Robert was gonna be his boy.

This was the prison culture. Anyone who got fucked was considered to be less than a person and definitely not a real man. He couldn't say no to a real man. So, the view is that a pussyboy, one who is wanted by someone and not attached, can be stabbed or beaten into submission. It was the rule. Some guys, who are considered weak, may be stabbed to put pressure on them to fuck. The price to the person doing the stabbing is 14 days in the hole and 6 months in segregation. This wasn't long because a lot of guys were serving long sentences and didn't care about 6 months on segregation. When the prisoner returns from segregation, he would tell the weak person that he is either gonna fuck or die. The weak person generally gave in.

I was told that a young boy across the hall in L4 was being pressured to fuck by an older guy. The older guy stabbed him in the neck and the boy died. Everyone stated that this was a very sad situation, as the boy was begging the prisoners trying to help stop the bleeding not to let him die. But the knife hit his jugular. This was as an example of what made Reidsville a brutal prison.

Our detail, along with another detail, began working at the syrup mill. We rode there on a long trailer called the Fireball. I had seen livestock moved this way but not people. We had to climb up the sides and then ride standing up. The trailer would hold about eighty or ninety prisoners. In the cab of the tractor, one guard rode with the prisoner driver with just his pistol. Trailing closely behind the Fireball was a dump truck with three guards standing up with shotguns pointed at the back of the Fireball. If anyone jumped off the Fireball, they would be shot. Since the weather was getting cooler, most guys like to ride in the back to shield themselves from the wind, but none wanted to be the last, thinking that a shotgun could accidentally fire. I always got in the middle. When the truck came to pick us up, someone would shout, "Fireball on the run." That was both good and bad news.

I had no idea how syrup was made until we started working at the syrup mill. One detail was outside feeding sugar cane stalks into a machine that squeezed the juice out, which went into a large tank just outside of the cooking broilers. There were four large, rectangle, cooking vats, which had copper coils in the bottom. Juice would be poured into the vats from an overhead pipe and then heated up. My job, along with three others, was to skim the dirty foam that rose to the top. After about 3 or 4 hours of skimming, the broiler was turned on high and after an hour or so, someone would holler, "Syrup!" and the syrup would be drained from a spout at the bottom of the vat into containers. Then, we would make another batch. I thought that this was close to making moonshine. The syrup, like all things produced on the farm, was for the prison, but the guards had their wives and friends come by and get some of the syrup. The syrup was quite good, but I stopped eating it after one prisoner lost his hand in the machine. Visions of blood and ground-up bones turned my stomach whenever I looked at the syrup.

There was a list that came out every day that showed all the movement in the prison, guys going to the hole, guys moving from one cellblock to another, and new admissions and discharges. I saw one afternoon that Sol Brown had his parole revoked and had returned to Reidsville. All prisoners who had been convicted of rape, regardless of the sentence, had to do all their time in Reidsville under maximum security. Guys convicted of murder, attempted murder, or armed robbery could be transferred to any of the many prison camps located around the State, but not convicted rapists.

In my cellblock, most of the guys were serving life sentences or very long sentences. From what I heard, about fifteen of the twenty guys on the third tier had life sentences and this did not include me. Sylvester Martin was on the second floor and everyone called him eighty-eight because that was how many years he had. Eighty-eight liked to talk about doing some of his time at Chatham County work camp. He claimed that he escaped and a white woman, whom he did not know, put him in the truck of her car and drove him past roadblocks. I told him that she wasn't a Savannahian and probably was a Quaker, who had relatives involved in the Underground Railroad.

Jesse James, a reddish-looking black man, had been in Reidsville over 20 years. Jesse switched a little when he walked, indicating that he was homosexual. I saw him coming out of Eighty-eight's cell one night. He was sweating profusely and he stunk. I believed that Eighty-eight had fucked him in the cell. Despite knowing that Jesse was a homosexual, I made him my bridge partner. Jesse couldn't play and I was teaching him how. In the process, we were losing. Denard and his partner teased me and told me that I would never beat them because Jesse was pussy, and pussy boys are bad luck. When Jesse had the bid and my hand was the dummy, I would stand behind him and watch how he played. After he failed to make a bid that was achievable, I would offer constructive criticism. But he told me that I made him nervous when I stood behind him. So, I stayed in my seat and watched him fail to make enough bids. I didn't mind losing because I was only playing to pass the time. However, one time, I did get mad with Jesse for passing when I gave him a command bid. I told Jesse that I would have bid seven and would have made a Grand Slam double and redoubled if he had not passed. I told him that I could have felt good about achieving this for a long time and it would have helped me when I was feeling badly about being in prison and doing a life sentence. Jesse quit playing and told me that I was making him too nervous. So, I stopped playing bridge.

Afer Sol Brown was put in general population, I got a chance to talk to him. He was disappointed at being back, but he fit right in. I learned that many guys get out of prison and come back in a few months. It is as if they cannot make it in the free world and feel more at home in Reidsville, although they complain about it. Sol Brown had status in Reidsville and had been a houseman in the B Building for over 7 years. He was in the dormitory when Robert Pryor killed Bill Bo and said that he threw the knife Pryor used out of the window.

On the yard one day, Sol Brown told the story of how Bill Bo was killed, which a lot of guys wanted to hear. According to Sol, they were all gambling and a dispute erupted between Pryor and Bill Bo over a bet. They started to fight, and when the fight was over, Bill Bo continued to gamble but Pryor went to his bunk and got a knife. Upon returning, Pryor reached over Bill Bo's shoulder and stabbed Bill Bo in the chest one time. Sol said that prison officials were so glad that Bill Bo died that Pryor did not even go to court and no charges were filed against him. Sol said that he had the utmost respect for him, that Bill Bo was not an ordinary nigger. No prisoner could beat him and all the cracker guards were scared of Bill Bo. Sol said that he and Bill Bo got into a fight and that he knew he was good in a fight, but he couldn't do a thing with Bill Bo and Bill Bo beat him. For that, he would take his hat off to him.

Whenever the guys talk about tough motherfuckers in Reidsville, Bill Bo's name always came up even though he had been dead for 5 or 6 years. Some of the guys out of Atlanta hated guys from Savannah on account of Pryor killing Bill Bo. After Pryor got of Reidsville, other guys talked about how Pryor killed Bill Bo. Some of them stated that Bill Bo, who was not a very big man, was not afraid of Pryor, who was a giant, and this was why he had his back turned to Pryor. One stated that after Pryor stabbed Bill Bo, Bill Bo hit Pryor so hard that he knocked the knife out of Pryor's hand, and they started fighting again although Bill Bo had been mortally wounded. Bill Bo, the story goes, was beating Pryor and told him that if it wasn't for the fact that he was getting weak, he would beat him to death with his fists. Then, he collapsed and died. Some claimed that a doctor took Bill Bo's heart out and kept it in the jar on the hospital floor for a long time before throwing it away.

Now, a few prisoners aspired to achieve the status that Bill Bo had and the person that many prisoners talked about in the same breath as Bill Bo was Willie Gilyard from Savannah. Some called him by his full name and some called him Chick. By either name, he was the most feared prisoner there. Some guys were more afraid of him than Honey or Robert Pryor.

Blue told me that some guys from Savannah got mad with him for making Ervin James his wife, and he went out on the yard with two knives and the guys from Savannah backed off. But Frank told me a different story.

First, Frank said that he felt somewhat responsible for Ervin getting raped and told me that he roughly ordered Ervin to tell him about his case when Ervin was first put in the cellblock. Ervin, then, nervously started telling him about his case, and Blue observed that Ervin was scared. Seeing Ervin was an ideal young guy to have the boo run on him, Blue borrowed the big hunting knife with the twelve-inch blade and approached Ervin. Blue, with his grotesque burns, told Ervin if he did not let him fuck him that he was gonna kill him. Frank said that after the guys from Savannah heard about this, Willie Gilyard sent word to Blue to come out on the yard. Frank said that Blue was scared shitless because he knew Willie Gilyard would stomp Blue's ass. Blue asked Frank to go out on the yard with him, but Frank said that he wasn't involved and he did not want Chick down on him.

When Blue came out on the yard, Chick walked up to him and confronted him.

"You burnt-up motherfucker. You haven't gotten enough of raping people," Chick said to Blue shaking his finger in Blue's face.

"No, I didn't rape Ervin. He wanted to do it and gave me his ass," Blue pleaded.

Frank said that Blue was lying like a lawyer and managed to convince Chick that he did not force Ervin to fuck and Ervin did it on his own. Believing Blue, Chick walked away, but would have kicked Blue's ass if he didn't.

Blue was one happy, relieved nigger when he returned to the cellblock, and several guys told him that he was lucky and had talked his way out of a good ass stomping.

Frank said that Blue was scheming how he was gonna try me and had convinced himself that he could tell Chick the same type of thing about me, should Chick approach him. But Frank said that Blue had heard something about me and was afraid that I would hurt him. Knowing that I had a knife too, he was leery of approaching me with one of the prison games. Frank said that Blue often talked about me, and a bet had developed as to which of the two Rudolphs would prevail if conflict developed. Frank said that he had a carton of cigarettes on me.

I told Frank that I would do more than hurt Blue and intended to kill him if he tried anything with me. Blue didn't have to worry about Chick or anyone else from Savannah because I was gonna handle him myself and give him exactly what he deserved—a knife in the heart.

The word was out that anyone who killed Blue, JB, or Cock-A-Red would not get any more time. This was one of the prison's methods of getting rid of troublesome prisoners. The district attorney who had jurisdiction over the prison took his directions from the prison administration. So, if the prison administration said that the dead nigger was trouble, the person doing the killing would be rewarded with no prosecution, like Robert Pryor, who did not get a day for killing Bill Bo and didn't even go on trial.

But I wouldn't kill Blue because the white man said it was okay. Blue needed to die because he was a dirty, nasty vulture who deserved to die. All

Blue did was prey on young and weak prisoners, and if he made a mistake and misjudged me, that would be his last mistake. I was gonna be Blue's Waterloo. I heard him say that he was trying to stay out of the hole because he wanted to make parole, but I thought that I would parole his ass out of here in a box. One popular saying is, "speak softly and carry a big stick." But there is a part that was left out. One should speak softly, carry a big stick, and use the stick on a dirty motherfucker when it was necessary.

Although I had been telling my parents that I would try to stay out of trouble, I believed that they sensed that this was hard to do. My family was coming almost every 2 weeks. They would bring me some home-cooked food, which I had to eat in the visiting room. They were bringing some of my young nieces who were really too young to know that I was their uncle. After a few visits, they, as the family car pulled into the prison parking lot, would point to the prison and say that this was Junior's house. When my momma was getting ready to leave, she would always tell me to be good and I would say okay.

Momma's admonishments reminded me of one of Sidney Poiter's movies, *The Defiant One.* With Tony Curtis, Poiter played the part of an escapee from a chain gang and recounted that his wife always told him to be good. When the white man cheated him during tallying his share-cropping debts, his wife said to be good; when the white man came on his land and tried to beat him, his wife said to be good; and when the guards put him in the hole, she said be good. Now, my momma is telling me almost the same thing. The last thing she says is for me to be good.

I began to get worried about Lucious Jackson, who had been moved to death row. There was a story in the newspapers that his execution was scheduled for January 9, 1970, after the Georgia Supreme Court turned down his appeal. His attorney was requesting a stay of execution from Governor Lester Maddox and a commutation of the death sentence to life imprisonment by the Georgia Board of Pardon and Paroles. Bobby Hill, Jackson's attorney, stated also in a television interview that he was allowed to speak with Jackson by telephone, and Jackson was crying and begging Hill to save him. Hill said that it was a very tough situation for him as an attorney—to have someone's life in your hands.

I wasn't too optimistic for Lucious because of Governor Maddox, a segregationist without any political experience who was put in the Governor's Office because he threatened with a pickax handle Black people who tried to eat in his restaurant. Equally, I was not too optimistic about the Georgia Board of Pardon and Paroles, although it commuted Joseph Bonaparte's death sentence to life imprisonment after he was convicted of raping a white woman.

There had been a very disturbing article about one member of the parole board. According to a story in the newspaper, a former police officer who had been convicted of contracting to kill someone and who was in the M Building in a cell by himself had been writing to a parole board member to tell information on other prisoners. Although this ex-police officer was locked up, he was telling which prisoners in the general population were homosexual and which were involved in rule infractions. Although this information was unverified, the parole board member was putting this information in prisoners' files and using it to advocate against parole. A federal judge ordered the parole board member to stop this and to take this information out of the prisoners' files. This was the talk in the prison, for a number of people stated that this police officer needed to be killed viciously if he was ever put in the general population.

I was tracking new stories about Lucious Jackson, my former cell mate in Savannah. His execution day was coming up and a day before his scheduled execution, Governor Mattox granted him a 60-day stay, but Lucious' lawyer seemed to indicate that he was gonna ask Justice Hugo Black of the U.S. Supreme Court to give Lucious a longer stay. Lucious was the only person that I had read about from Savannah, and I hadn't read about the others who had death sentences, including Eddie Simmons, Henry Furman, James Thacker, or Robert Manor. I sure did not wanna hear any of the guards talk about how Lucious died.

A cell opened up on the second tier, and I asked Charles if I could move. I did not like the top range because of the height and it had a group of long-term prisoners who appeared to have been beaten down. It was too depressing. I liked the location of my new cell, which was near the stairs and a rail where some people sat and talked. I would be sitting on my bed and reading while guys would talk about prison life and memories of the outside world. But sometimes their conservation rang insincere and unreal. One conversation went this way:

"Damn, I'm tired of doing time. I've been in this motherfucker for 12 years and wanna be free," said Frank.

"I've been in here for almost 9 years and I am tired too," said Blue.

"Both of you sons-a-bitches are gonna be here a lot longer," said Wyatt.

"Frank, if the judge came to you now and told you that he would let you out of prison if you would suck his dick, would you do it?" asked Andrew.

"Goddamn right, I'd do it. I'd not only suck his dick but I would let him fuck me in the ass, if that would lead to me getting out of this motherfucker."

"Me too."

"I don't know if I could do that," said another person.

Someone on the range turned to me and asked me. "Rudolph, would you suck the judge's dick if he would let you off that life sentence you have?"

Putting my magazine down a little, I said, "This is your conversation, not mine, I don't have anything to say about what you're talking about."

"You're king of smart, and we just wanted to know what you think."

"I'm not involved in this conversation," I said again and raised my magazine to continue reading.

I knew that this conversation was for a foolish person and it was totally contrived to induce me to participate in the discussion. Those motherfuckers thought that they were the smartest people around. They were always plotting and laying snares, short and long. They had games that ran for months, befriending some people while planning their destruction 6 or 8 months later.

Someone advised me to lift weights to build more muscle, but I declined. A strong mind was worth much, much more than muscles. I had observed some guys on the yard lifting weights, and it was quite obvious that they were afraid and were thinking that muscles would keep them from being attacked. As a general rule, the guys whom most guys spoke of with reverence in their voices were not big people. You don't have to be big to be big in prison. There were only a few big guys that people feared and Honey was one of them. A guy from Atlanta called Big John was encouraged by a group of his friends to fight Honey and they were telling Big John that he could beat Honey easily. After surveying a few other people, the opinion was that Honey would stomp Big John's ass, and Big John decided not to try his luck.

A Muslim was put in our cellblock and he began stopping by my cell to talk and to recruit me.

"Brother, I've been watching you and know you are a strong, young brother. We need you. The Honorable Elijah Muhammad has been sent to bring the black man back from this lost wilderness in North America and to teach him about his history, which has been obscured by the white devil," said Samuel. "The only hope for the black man is for him to return to his true religion, which is Islam. Christianity is not our religion and was something forced upon us by the slavemaster to help keep us in chains. You know Christianity is no good because the white man was pushing it. The white man would not give black folks anything of value during slavery and the fact that they did shows that Christianity is the white devil's religion. We are in the shape we are in because we lost our true religion and the Honorable Elijah Muhammed has been sent to return us to our true religion. The Messenger has a program for black men and women in and out of prison. We need you, Brother Rudolph."

"Brother Samuel, I'm not fond of any religion, but I must admit that there are some things about Muslims that I like," I said.

"Let me send your name to Chicago so you can be put in the Book of Life and get your X," urged Brother Samuel.

"Although I like some things about the Muslims, this doesn't mean that I wanna be a practicing Muslim. For one thing, I can't change my name or insert a X after my first name. My parents wouldn't understand and might think that I am rejecting them. Also, the things that I like are the Muslim's beliefs about defending themselves and not waiting on the hereafter for a better life. There are some things that I have problems believing, such as that a black scientist made the white man in a laboratory," I said. "I find that hard to swallow."

"Brother, I don't have to tell you about the white man. You know how treacherous the devil is. All white folks are evil and the devils. The devil is not a cartoon character with a red suit and a pitchfork. It is the white man. I know, brother, that you know about the white man and how evil and treacherous he is. When you talk about the flimflam, the double-cross, and the trickeration, you are talking about the white man. This is his nature. He can't help being the way he is because that is his nature. Just like a poisonous snake cannot help it when it bites someone."

"Some white folks and some Negroes in Savannah have scarred my soul and I don't think anything is gonna ever change that," I said.

"Think about it, brother, and we can talk again later."

"Ok, we can talk, Brother Samuel, but I can't promise you that I will join the movement," I said.

I liked the Muslim prisoners. They did not bother anyone and they didn't believe in turning the other cheek. They had some extreme things to say about white people, but I knew that there were a lot more white people saying similar things about blacks. I knew that there were a lot of white prisoners who hated all black people and many of the prison guards. For that matter, there were a lot of white people back in Savannah who were no better than Brother Samuel.

The crew that thought they were so smart was back on the range talking about silly things. Instead of talking about whether they would suck a judge's dick, they were talking about the best way to kill someone.

"It's hard to kill a motherfucker when you are looking him in the eye. It easier to kill him from behind because you don't have to look at him," said Blue.

"No, you're supposed to kill a dirty motherfucker looking the motherfucker in the eye. You want the last thing the motherfucker sees to be you and to know why he's going to the other world," said JB.

"What do you think, Rudolph?" asked Blue.

"I'm not gonna get into this conversation," I said as I walked by.

I knew better than to get into a conversation like that. Some guys will repeat things like this back to the warden or write to the parole board, telling them that I had discussed the best way to kill someone. Although I had an opinion about what they had discussed, I would not share it with them and would keep it strictly to myself.

Someone came by my cell and asked me if I wanted any buck, which was prison-made whiskey. I wanted to know who made it because I couldn't drink some buck because of how it was made. One guy, who needed some sugar or other sweetener, filled up both of his rubber boots with syrup and poured it into a can when he got back to the cell block. I said no thanks to that buck. Another person made buck in his commode. Although he claimed that he cleaned the commode thoroughly and did not use his toilet at night, I told him that I couldn't drink anything that had been made in the commode and didn't care if he cleaned it with Spic and Span. I was assured that the buck that was being offered to me was made in a clean plastic bag and the ingredients came out of the kitchen. So, I was given a cup full and it was quite good. I felt mellow going to bed that night.

Chapter 15

"Rudolph, they're trying to escape from the M Building!" shouted Giles excitedly.

I came out of my cell and looked over at the M Building and I could see dust flying up as if the tower guard was shooting and I could also see a small fire. I made sure that I was not in the line of fire and continued to look. Someone said that some prisoners got out of their cells or had been let out to shower and got outside of M Building and tried to throw a molotov cocktail in the guard tower.

A few minutes later, I could see guards, some dressed in street clothes, going over to M Building. Then, we had an unscheduled count, and the guard who was doing the counting was in street clothes.

The next morning I had visitors and my daddy told me that he heard some of the guards discussing the attempted escape last night. I told him that it was in the building next to mine, and I saw parts of it. I told him also that I know now that I am really in the Big House.

The first killing that occurred since I had been in Reidsville occurred in one of the dormitories of B Building. Shep Dog, who was from Savannah and who also was put in my work detail, told us on the yard that he saw the stabbing. According to Shep Dog, one prisoner asked several guys who had thrown water on his bed. One person who was sitting on the toilet told the guy, "Fuck you." At that point, the guy on the toilet was stabbed in the neck. Shep Dog seemed a little scared as he told the story, and I guessed he, like many guys, was wondering if he could be next.

When someone was killed in prison, the killing prompted guys to discuss previous killings and compare them on occasion. I heard stories about other guys who had been killed in Reidsville and all the killings seemed really brutal. One guy, who was asleep in his cell during the afternoon, was hit in the head with a lead pipe and died instantly. In fact, this happened in my cellblock. Eighty-eight would say frequently that he would never go to sleep during the day because he knew that someone would try and kill him. That was one of the luxuries of living in a cellblock, you could at least get a good night of sleep although you could be killed somewhere else if someone really wanted to do you in.

Samson, a huge, slow-witted prisoner who reminded me of the character in Mice and Men, stabbed a guy to death. Samson was wrestling with a smaller guy and the guy threw Samson. After other guys in the dormitory began teasing Samson that he let a small man throw him, Samson got a very long knife and began stabbing the guy. One guy who said that he saw it said that the knife was so long that each time Samson stabbed the guy the knife went completely through him.

A prisoner was killed in the theater as he watched a movie. For this reason, some guys did not go the theater to watch movies because of their fear that someone would try to kill them when the lights were out. Wyatt Earp said that he wants his friends to be sitting behind him in the theater and that is the only way he would go.

But black prisoners were not the only prisoners killing. The white prisoners had their share on the other side. Someone pointed out a short white guy to me on the yard who was supposed to have stabbed a guy to death on the morning of being discharged from prison. He was mad with this other white prisoner and went into the other guy's cell, killed him, and then got dressed in his suit to be released. He was back in prison on another charge and the death was recorded as unsolved.

The other killing involving whites that guys talked about was the killing that happened on the walkway near the theater. Someone named Yank had killed another prisoner. As Yank was being taken from the hole to segregation by a guard, three friends of the dead prisoner were waiting for Yank. They told the guard to get out of the way or get killed, and the guard backed off. At that point, they began stabbing Yank and killed him.

These were all killings that occurred before I arrived, but another killing occurred when I was there. As I walked into the mess hall after work one day, I immediately felt that something was wrong. There was a significant decrease in the noise level and the mess hall seemed obviously different. As I looked around I noticed that there were not many people in the mess hall and this was quite unusual. After I got my food, Shep Dog, who was working now in the mess hall, came over to my table and told me that Palmer, who was from Savannah, and Will, who was from Atlanta, stabbed a guy to death in the mess hall during lunch. Palmer and Will were looking for this guy, and when they found him in the mess hall, both of them began stabbing him. Shep Dog said that the guy was screaming for help, but the guards in the mess hall only said to break it up. The guards did not really try to stop it. Shep Dog said that after the guy fell on the mess hall floor, Palmer jumped on the guy's chest and continued to stab him. Shep Dog said that this guy was dead before he was taken out of the mess hall and stressed that this was the second guy that he had personally seen killed in Reidsville. Now, I knew why some guys had stayed away from the mess hall today.

When I got to my cellblock, Frank remarked that a Geechee had killed someone and asked me why. I told him that I didn't know anything about it although I knew Palmer. The guys in the cellblock were trying to figure out why Palmer and Will killed this guy, and someone concluded that he didn't know what the dead guy had done, but knew that he would never do it again.

Brother Samuel continued to stop by my cell to tell me of the virtues of being a Muslim. Tears would come to his eyes as he related all the evils of the white man, and how Negro preachers helped the white man carry out his grand plans. Brother Samuel mockingly described how some Negroes act when they are told that they can't go to the white man's heaven, put on their white robes, and walk with the angels.

Some of Brother Samuel's comments I agreed with, but not all. He believed that all white people were evil. I had a somewhat different view. I believed that many white people were evil, but there were a handful who believed in doing right. Brother Samuel disagreed, insisting that no white man was any good, and no white man should ever be trusted. Brother Samuel went on to say that the Caucasians were the most evil race of people on this earth, and they were always scheming how to flimflam people. Brother Samuel said that when the white man first appeared on the continent of Africa proclaiming to be seeking trade, all of them should have been killed immediately. Further, Brother Samuel said that our red brothers should have killed the white man, too, when he first came to North America. Brother Samuel said instead of the Thanksgiving feast that is depicted with Indians and Pilgrims eating together, the Indians should have cut all the white men's throats because after the white man got a toehold on the continent, the white man committed genocide against the Indians. Brother Samuel said we should be celebrating the Thanksgiving massacre that should have occurred. The white man tries to get other races to trust him, and then the whites exploit and annihilate the other races.

Next Lump stopped by my cell. Lump talked about having to go to court, meaning the prison disciplinary committee earlier that day. According to him, the guard called him over yesterday and told him to write his name and number on the paper. After Lump told the guard that he couldn't read or write, the guard called him a dumb nigger. He called me dumb and the bastard couldn't write himself. But I got over on him because I can read and write, the stupid bastard.

Lump stated that as he was in line waiting to go in, he was standing in line with other prisoners. "I was in line with a lot of bad motherfuckers," said Lump. "One guy said that he was written up for unsatisfactory work. Another guy said that he was written up for talking back to the Boss. I asked this other guy what he was written up for and he told me that he had written a goat note—a love letter to a sissy."

We both started laughing.

"Can you imagine someone telling his family that he was in the hole for writing a goat note? Or the parole board discussing whether to parole someone based on a goat note?"

We both laughed some more.

Then, Lump started his harangue about throwing white paint on Negroes in Columbus who wanted to be white when he was released. He said that he was gonna have a gallon of paint with him and a brush, and whenever he saw Negroes trying to be white, he would paint their faces and tell them they wanted to be white so badly that he would help them be white.

Then Lump asked me what was I gonna do when I got out of prison.

"I really don't know. But I do know that this is gonna be the first and last time that I allow myself to be locked up by a corrupt legal system. There will be no more State of Georgia versus Alexander. I'll die before I submit to another arrest."

After we left the syrup mill, our next work detail was the stump field. The prison was clearing more land for farming and we had to dig up stumps that had been left after the cutting of some trees. We worked in groups of four. Four people to a stump was the requirement and two people had to be working at all times.

Iceman suggested that he and I, along with two others, work together. One guy wanted to volunteer to work with us but Iceman said no.

"You fuckass, pussy motherfucker. You're not gonna be in a hole with me. If you don't get away from me, I'll kick your ass."

Someone shouted laughingly at Iceman. "Ice, why you so hard on the sissy?"

"Sissies are bad luck and I don't want a motherfucker in a hole with me, especially *that* motherfucker. Do you know that stupid motherfucker has been bragging that he has a real pussy? Someone fucked him in the ass and told him that he had a real pussy, and this stupid, ugly motherfucker believed it."

We laughed about it and started digging around our stump, cutting the roots with an ax as we dug. Bully Wallace always stopped by the work details to see how things were going. One day, he saw some black prisoners lying on the ground and told Boss Ralph to not let the niggers lie down on the ground.

On our next day in the stump field, Boss Ralph said that anyone who laid on the ground would be written up. I was sitting on my shovel with the handle up in the air as my two other work partners were in the hole. The shovel was getting hard and I sat on the ground. Without realizing what I was doing, I started lying on the ground and was staring up at the sky. Iceman whispered to me that we were not supposed to be lying down and Boss Ralph was watching me. I sat up and looked over at the guard. He was staring at me and I was expecting him to take me to the hole after work. The jack-boy came over later and told me that Boss Ralph was gonna write me up, but changed his mind because he knew that I would go into court and tell the deputy warden that the white prisoners were lying on the ground, too. I hadn't thought of it, but I knew that white people don't like you telling on them.

Bully Wallace told Ralph not to allow the black prisoners to lie down but it was okay for the white prisoners. The white prisoners on the detail were lying all over the field with their shirts off and getting their tans. I guessed they decided that digging up stumps is really a job for niggers and not white people. In reality, black people were brought over to America to clear land in the South and this type of work is not for whites, even if they are prisoners.

This was not the only incident of racial discrimination that I had observed. The all-white prison staff was always trying to make it easy for white prisoners and more difficult for blacks. It was quite blatant. The L Building at one time was eating in the white mess hall because of the overcrowdedness of the mess hall on the black side. One morning, as the black prisoners went into the mess hall, they saw that the whites had cooked and served scrambled eggs. The regular way of cooking eggs was sunny side up and the yolk was running. I hated eggs that way and would only eat the white portion.

After the black prisoners saw that the white cooks stopped scrambling the eggs, some of them got belligerent.

"They were scrambling eggs before we came in, they can keep scrambling them," said one prisoner angrily.

Another prisoner said that he was not leaving the mess hall until after he had eaten scrambled eggs.

Another prisoner shouted that the prison was always trying to find ways to accommodate white prisoners and he was tired of it.

Someone whispered that the white cooks might spit in the eggs if we pressed them, but someone else responded loudly that if they spit in the eggs, he wouldn't eat them but they were gonna scramble them first.

The guard on duty got on the phone and called the control office. I speculated that he told the control office that the niggers were about to riot. Many of the black prisoners were sitting at tables without any food and stated that they were not gonna move until they had scrambled eggs. But some prisoners, after waiting in line and not moving, began to go through the line anyway. I decided to wait against the wall. After about 20 minutes, the cook was told to start scrambling eggs since they began that way that morning. The next morning the white prisoners did not get scrambled eggs.

The stump field wasn't really hard work, and I preferred it to a lot of other jobs we did. Once we had dug down to the bottom of a stump and had it ready to be hauled out of the hole. However, we decided not to pull it out of the hole yet. I told the guys not to pull it up and just play in the dirt and throw a shovelful up every now and then. We did this for a day until Boss Ralph said that we had been on this stump too long. Someone shouted that we almost had it, and two more of us jumped into the hole to push it over and help push it out. After we covered the hole, we went to another stump.

As we were digging around another stump, we began talking with some other prisoners who were on a nearby stump. One of the other prisoners was a guy named Joe Thomas. Some guys used to argue about who was the best basketball player in the prison, and some people liked the way Joe played, including me. Joe and I would talk sometimes. Joe was okay.

"Rudolph, how in the hell did someone like you wind up in a fucked-up place like this?" Joe asked.

"I guess I was unlucky," I said, less than serious.

"What would you have done if you had not got into trouble?"

"If my eyesight had not been affected in my senior year, I would have gone to the Air Force. My intentions were to join the Air Force and stay for a long time."

"I was in the service," Joe said. "With your intelligence, there is no telling what your rank would have been now if you had gone in the service."

"I'm not intelligent. If I were, I would not be here."

"A black man can be intelligent and still be put in the penitentiary," someone said. Continuing, "It is probably best that you came to prison instead of going into the Air Force. As of now, you have only killed one person, but if you had gone into the Air Force, you would have been helping the white man drop bombs on other colored people. You would have been killing people by the thousands for the white man. So, it might be a blessing that you came to prison."

The stump field was a place for some serious conversations.

We were taken out of the stump field and another detail was put there. Our job was changed to shoveling cow shit. Boss Ralph stated that it didn't seem right to him that our detail was taken out of the stump field and another detail was allowed to dig up stumps. It was clear that Boss Ralph did not like his job assignment and was trying to instigate trouble.

The guys started grumbling that it wasn't right. Boss Ralph then asked who didn't wanna shovel and to step over if they didn't wanna do it. Guys began stepping over, including me. Of about forty-plus prisoners on this detail about thirty-two indicated that they did not wanna shovel cow shit. In a few minutes, Bully Wallace drove up and began to shout that we were all going to the hole for refusing to work. A few minutes later, a bus came for us and took us back to the prison. Instead of going in the back, we went in the front and some of us were still smelling like cow shit. I heard one secretary ask why didn't they take us in the back. The elevator to the hole was closer to the front and we were taken upstairs, one small group at a time. We had to undress and put on some ragged pants and shirts. Our other clothes were put in individual bags, the regular practice when someone goes to the hole. Three of us were put in one cell with a guy in the hole from segregation. So there were four of us in one cell and I could see that there was just enough room for the four of us to sleep lengthwise. I decided that I wasn't gonna sleep in the middle.

This was my first time being in the hole since I had been in Reidsville. It was like the hole that was used in Chatham County jail, a concrete floor to sleep on. But instead of three meals a day, in Reidsville, we ate once a day at noon. We ate the same thing the prisoners ate in general population. But if something sweet was served in general population, we wouldn't get any. I was told that we would not have a chance to go to court and plead our case. Refusing to work was 14 days in the hole and no discussion was necessary.

The guy in our cell from segregation told me that Black-assed Crow was on the other side. I had never seen or met this Crow, but I had heard his name mentioned a lot. Some of the guys in C3 were talking about Crow on work detail and recounted an incident when Crow went into C3 because the houseman named Ben was giving someone Crow liked a hard time. Crow, who did not live in C3, came into the dormitory and went to Ben, who was taking a nap. Crow pulled out a knife and put it to Ben's throat, waking him and explaining that he was waking Ben up this time but if Ben continued to bother this guy and he came back into the dormitory and found Ben sleeping that he intended to let Ben sleep permanently. Ben left the guy alone and stopped taking naps during the day.

Hulbert, who was given a life sentence and who was on the case involving the last person from Savannah to be executed, stated that a relatively new guy slapped Crow one day and immediately realized that he had slapped the wrong person. For several days, the guy stayed off the yard and did not go the mess hall. Because Crow's work detail was called before this guy, this guy could see Crow and would wait until Crow's work detail had lined up and was ready to march out before coming out himself. But one morning Crow pretended like he was about to line up and slipped around the canning plant. Crow then came up from behind the guy and began stabbing him. He didn't kill the guy but he did stab him several times.

Hulbert also said that Chick and Crow did not like each other and they were about to get in a fight one day, but Hulbert begged them not to fight because a lot of prisoners would wanna see them cancel each other out. They didn't fight but some speculated that when they got back to Savannah, they would likely kill each other.

The days in the hole went slowly. There was nothing to do but sit and talk. We did mark the day by the whistle. When the whistle blew in the morning, we knew that the details were about to go out. A few hours later the doctor would walk by our cells hurriedly saying "doctor." One guy told the doctor that he got dizzy whenever he got up fast, and the doctor, without breaking his stride, told him not to get up so fast. Around noon, we would have lunch, and then we would wait for the whistle to blow, indicating that the last detail was in. Then, we would wait for night to fall.

Some guys are raped in the hole, but I wasn't worried about that. One guy in the hole with us was named Whitehead and some people said that he was a pussy boy. The guy from segregation knew Whitehead and told him to sleep next to him. This guy had one wall and I had the other. Shorty was sleeping next to me, but I wasn't worried about him. I got up during the night to piss but I didn't see anything going on with Whitehead, but he and the guy from segregation both were sleeping on their sides and Whitehead's back was to the guy.

Giles was in the hole for fighting when Will and Palmer went to the hole for killing the guy in the mess hall. They put Will in the cell with Giles, and after a short while, Will tried to rape Giles. Giles and Will fought for a long time before Will stopped and apologized to Giles. Will told Giles that he didn't know that Giles was a real man and shook his hand. Giles was extremely proud when he got out of the hole, asserting that he knew he was a real man.

The guys in the cellblock were teasing Giles about this incident. Giles went back to the hole for fighting a guy on the yard. This time he was put next to Bull, who was also in L2. A young guy was put in Bull's cell and Bull tried to rape this guy. When Bull and Giles got out of the hole, Giles told the other fellows in the cellblock what happened. As Giles told it, Bull fired up on this young boy and this young boy started fighting Bull back. Bull began to get tired and also realized that he had more than he could handle. So, Bull told the guy that he would give him a break and let him go. But Giles said that he started to tell the young guy to continue fighting Bull because if he did, he could have fucked Bull, who had gotten tired and couldn't overcome this young guy. Giles stressed that Bull almost lost his manhood and almost became pussy. Giles said that he regretted not telling the guy to keep fighting and would have if he didn't know and like Bull. All the guys, then, teased Bull about how he tried to take someone's ass and came damn close to losing his own.

When the last whistle blew indicating that this would be our last night in the hole, a loud cheer could be heard throughout the hole. Early the next morning, we were all let out of the hole and we were all very happy. We wouldn't have to go to work again until the next day, but I was sure that everyone would prefer to shovel cow shit if told again. But we were assigned to the field.

I wrote to my family and told them that I had been in the hole, but I was out now. The next weekend, they came to see me and told me that Daddy and Willie came to see me but they were turned away and told that I was in the hole. So, they went to our cousin's house and spent the day with him. Daddy told me that as he and Willie Lee were driving up, he told Willie Lee that he had a feeling that I was in the hole. When they left, Momma told me to be good and I told her I would try.

Things were beginning to happen in the prison. It began with an unusual occurrence in the mess hall, but I missed it. Double Ugl, a guard who was extremely ugly and the name prisoners privately called him, wanted to write up a prisoner named Marion for having a part of Marion's shirt out. Incensed that he was gonna be written up for what he considered a minor infraction, Marion put down his tray and attacked Double Ugl. He was hitting Double Ugl in the face, and Double Ugl was begging him to stop. This was the first time that I had heard of a prisoner attacking a guard. Generally, it was the other way around, and I could sense that times were changing.

I came close to my first serious altercation when our detail, along with several others, was working at the silo pit. We were unloading cut cornstalks into a huge hole. As we were waiting on a load, one guy on our detail was talking unusually loud as if to draw the guard's attention. Without thinking, I said something to him.

"Why don't you stop dry snitching," I said.

"Who're you saying is dry snitching?" he asked angrily.

I had seen this guy fight on detail and knew that I couldn't beat him. I had just written a check that my ass might not be able to cash. Nonetheless, I wasn't gonna back down.

"You."

The guy started walking towards me and I stood up to face him. When he got about 5 feet from me he stopped, stared at me for about 10 seconds, and walked away.

A few minutes later, someone came up to me and told me that this guy was hot. He said to others that he knew that he could beat me, but he did not wanna have to deal with Chick, who was at the silo pit with another detail.

I thought then that it pays to be from Savannah in Reidsville. I had never known Chick in Savannah and had never talked with him in Reidsville. One day as I was about to go into the mess hall, I was told to meet the Money Man, who required a signature on a money order that comes with a letter. The Money Man was just beyond C1. After I had signed my money order and was headed back to the mess hall, some guys in the door of C1 shouted to me.

"Hey boy, come here," one demanded.

I turned around to look at them and kept walking.

I could hear another person asking did they see how I looked at them. Someone else said that I was a Geechee and was from Savannah and wasn't gonna take any shit.

On the yard, a guy from Atlanta intended to stab Tommie Jones from Macon. Chick liked Tommie because Tommie played on the basketball team and Chick liked basketball. So, Chick decided to prevent Tommie from being stabbed. Chick ran to the athletic shack and picked up a board about 3 feet long and returned. The guy had his right hand in his pocket and everyone knew that he had a knife. Chick started hitting him in the face with the board, which made an extremely loud smack. Chick was screaming at him to pull it out. The guy wanted to pull out his knife, but he knew that he would lose it if he did. So, he kept his hand in his pocket. Chick continued to scream at him to pull it out, as he hit him in the face with the board. He was swinging the board like a baseball player trying to hit a home run. Other guys from Savannah were gathering around. Honey came rushing over and Norris came asking Chick almost hysterically what was the matter. Chick continued hitting the guy in the face and finally the guy backed off and walked away. I knew now why guys in Reidsville were so afraid of Chick, who believed that he ran the yard when he was out there.

On the work detail, Tommie Jones asked Boss Ralph if he could take five minutes with one of the white guys on the detail, which was a request to fight. Boss Ralph, believing that the white boy, who was a lot bigger, could beat Tommie Jones, said yes, and within a few seconds the white boy was on the ground with Tommie Jones kicking him.

"Tommie, do you think that's right to kick someone when he's down?" asked Boss Ralph.

"Yes, I do. He wanted to fight. So, I showed him," Tommie Jones responded.

"You ought to take that pitchfork and run it through that nigger," said another white guy who was on another detail.

The other guys from Macon immediately jumped up and told him to do it.

"Goddamn right, I'll run a pitchfork through you niggers," the white guy said.

The guards said that anyone who touched a pitchfork would be shot, leveling the shotgun at the detail.

When the Fireball came, our detail was told to get up front and this other detail was supposed to get in the back. The guards in the dump truck had their shotguns leveled at the back of the Fireball. After the detail got in, the guys from Macon caught up with the white boys behind the canning plant.

Booker T, who was from Macon too, asked the white boy who a few hours earlier urged his downed friend to run a pitchfolk through the nigger, if he wanted to fight too. The white boy said goddamn right, which was a big mistake. Booker T took off his shirt and asked the other guys to watch his back. Unknown to the white boy, Booker T was on the boxing team and was quite good. The white guy never laid a hand on Booker T, and Booker T quickly reddened the white boy's face. After repeatedly getting hit in the face, the white boy asked one of his white friends to give him a weapon. The other guys from Macon told them that they better not give him anything. Booker T continued to hit him and the white boy finally quit. The white boy didn't get one punch in. By then, a guard in the tower had called the control office and guards were headed in our direction. Everyone scrabbled to the cellblock.

The next day, Boss Ralph was told to come to the L Building and personally escort prisoners in his detail to the lineup area. He was cursing and upset after hearing about the fight. He probably heard too that another white boy got beat. They separated us from the other detail that day.

Bobby, who was in my cellblock, was stabbed out on the yard by Russell. He was warned to stop messing with Russell because this guy wasn't to be messed with.

Russell was a young guy but he had earned the respect of many prisoners. When Russell first came to Reidsville, a prisoner who had killed two people tried to make Russell his pussy. This prisoner, who was mean and big, beat Russell every day, repeatedly knocking him down and swelling Russell's face. Russell couldn't beat the guy and could only take the beatings. Some guys who witnessed this savagery stated that they felt sorry for Russell, but there was nothing they could do to help him. Russell was being unmercifully beaten, but he had decided in his mind that he was not to gonna be pussy. Finally, this prisoner got tired of beating Russell and stopped. Since then, Russell's stature had grown and most guys respected him, stating that many prisoners had submitted to being made fuckboys rather than take the beatings that Russell took.

Bobby, however, wasn't impressed with Russell, and some guys in the cellblock said Bobby was trying to regain his manhood which was taken away when he was in Reidsville before. I looked over and saw Bobby with some red stains on his shirt and Russell trying to stab him some more. Bobby starting running to get away, but Russell was right behind him, chasing Bobby off the yard into the area of C Building. After Russell was told in the hole that Bobby used to be a pussyboy, Russell really got mad, saying that if he had known that Bobby was not a real man he would have killed Bobby. Russell said that he was pissed that Bobby challenged him when Bobby was not a real man and was a former pussyboy trying to regain his manhood.

Shep Dog was having some trouble with one guy from Atlanta. He told me that he might need my knife because there was a guy from Atlanta who seemed to have targeted him for some unknown reason. I was out on the yard one day with Shep Dog and he and the guy almost got into it. I told Shep Dog that this guy was looking for someone to stomp so that he could look good. Because I sensed that I wasn't gonna need a knife, I gave the one I had to Shep Dog, who was somewhat afraid after witnessing two killings in Reidsville. He didn't wanna be the third.

The white folks really had us jumping now in the work fields. One Tuesday, we were cutting okra. Two days later we were back cutting okra and I was on the same row as last Tuesday. I knew that the okra couldn't have grown as fast as it did. Then, someone told me that the prison farm manager was putting something on the ground to make it grow faster.

Then, about five or six details were put in the bean field. As fast as we picked the beans, they were being canned. The next morning the guard told us that we were not picking enough, and they spent the entire day, cussing us and pressing us to pick them beans.

I was looking forward to getting my 6 months in so I could get out of the field.

Chapter 16

I read in the Savannah newspaper that Drew left Aaron Kravitch and began his own law firm. I knew that there were about five or six lawyers associated with Aaron Kravitch and it appeared they all had left except for Kravitch's daughter.

I wondered if Drew had gathered some additional evidence that Aaron Kravitch was pocketing money and then lying about what fee he had been given. Kravitch was keeping most of the money and then sending the other lawyers to do his dirty work.

I passed one guy in his cell and saw him bent over his footlocker writing seriously. I paused and asked him what was he writing.

"I'm writing a petition to have some charges against me in Alabama dismissed," said the guy. "I am alleging in my petition that the Alabama officials violated my rights by not giving me a speedy trial; therefore, I am arguing that the charges should be dropped. When I finish with my time here in Georgia, I don't want the Alabama authorities to have a hold on me."

"I thought you had to have a lawyer to do anything legal," I said.

"No; in fact, sometimes it is best to leave the lawyers alone," said the guy.

His comments rang true because the parole board had been sending memoranda to prisoners, warning them about paying lawyers to contact the board. The chair of the parole board stated it had come to the board's attention that some lawyers were taking money to get the board to consider parole for some prisoners. The memorandum stated that most prisoners automatically come up for parole after serving one-third of their sentences, and prisoners serving a life sentence automatically come up for parole after 7 years.

Some lawyers were exploiting some ignorant prisoners by taking money for something that was set out in law. They were charging some people to get the parole board to consider some prisoners' cases.

But seeing this guy preparing a petition for dismissal of charges against him caused me to consider for the first time instituting habeas corpus action in my case. I had heard the words "habeas corpus" in prison, but I didn't know what it meant and didn't know anything about it. But I would keep my ears open and try to learn more about it.

More guys were coming to Reidsville all the time. Some were in Reidsville only a few months ago and now they were back with considerably more time. But some of them were in Reidsville for the first time and some of them were from Savannah. On the yard one day, someone stated that Stump was in quarantine and he had been busted for selling drugs in Savannah. Over a short period of time, Mike Furman came, as well as Benny Maxwell, Glenn Jenkins, Dristain, and Tub. I knew all of them except Tub.

Mike Furman had a life sentence for a robbery and murder in West Savannah. I also knew about Mike because in 1967, he was arrested for killing another person at Singleton Beach in South Carolina. I knew Benny Maxwell quite well because Benny used to stay on 34th Street when I was living on Grapevine Avenue. Benny had been convicted of stabbing a man to death outside of Ben Spot on West Broad Street. I knew Glenn Jenkins from Richard Arnold High School when we were both students. Dristain I met in the county jail.

I thought that Dristain was gonna be the first black defendant in Savannah to be acquitted for killing a white person. The case against Dristain was very, very weak. There was no eyewitness, no weapon was found on him or near him, and the authorities had no confession. All they had was that Dristain was found running near Forsythe Park and he had a red substance on his hand, which the prosecutor claimed was blood. Dristain contended that the red substance was dye from a hat that had come off during the rain. Yet, the all-white jury couldn't bring itself to acquit him and gave him a life sentence. If the evidence had been there, they would have given him a death sentence.

I didn't know Tub in jail or on the street. One day after I came in someone told me that one of my homeboys had come in and pointed to Tub. I stared at him momentarily and said that I didn't know him.

"Yeah, man, you know me, I'm Tub."

"I don't think that I know you," I said.

"Yeah, man, you know me. I know your Daddy, Momma, your sister Betty, and your brother Willie."

I looked at him again, but I knew that I didn't know him despite him knowing some of my family. I was about to invite him to my cell, but he was following me anyway. I sat on my bed and he sat on my footlocker.

He told me that he stayed a few doors from my family on Florence Street and began to talk about himself and his wife.

My family had moved to Florence Street after I was in jail. So, I really didn't know Tub, but he was talking to me like we were old friends.

He told me that he knew the real father of the guy that I had killed.

Tub said that the real father was at my trial, and he told everyone after I got a death sentence that he was not satisfied and he wanted to kill me himself. I remarked that a lot of people reportedly stated that they wanted to kill me, especially members of the Tornadoes, but everyone wanted me to be convicted and threatened some people not to help me. I stated that they should have threatened the people who were witnesses for the state, so that I would be acquitted and then all the people who wanted to kill me would have had an opportunity.

Tub talked a lot and told me that his wife had killed another woman during a fight. During a visit to the lawyer whom he had hired to defend his wife, the lawyer received a telephone call and was talking about me. According to Tub, the lawyer, who had been a judge in Savannah, told the person on the other end that the church people at St. Benedict couldn't really hurt me in a trial and that all they could talk about was their views of the deceased when the deceased was around them. Tub said this lawyer told the caller that it would have been better for me if the shooting happened on the west side, instead of the east side.

I suspected that the person on the other end of the telephone was Mr. Head, who had initially indicated that he was taking over my case and then decided against it.

After a few weeks, Tub told me that I did not act like what he had heard about me on the streets and that I was okay. He told me that he felt sorry for me and planned to help me get out of prison when he got out.

In the mess hall, I sat with other guys from Savannah. One day, I saw Benny Maxwell putting salt in an empty Prince Albert pack. After he left the table, I queried Mike about it, who lived in the same dormitory as Benny.

"Why was Benny taking salt back to the dormitory? Are you guys cooking something in the dormitory?" I asked.

"No," Mike said, laughing. "We're not cooking anything. Benny uses the salt to sprinkle around his bed to keep the haints from bothering him at night. Benny doesn't sleep well because of that guy he killed. I have to wake Benny up almost every night because the haints are riding him."

"Shit, I should have known. Black people use salt for everything," I said.

"Have you ever had bad dreams about the guy you killed?" Mike asked.

"No," I said. "And I never will. What about you?"

"Hell no."

Mike and I use to talk a lot and he told me everything about himself and what he did. Some guys talked a lot and some didn't. I never discussed my case or my situation. Most people thought they knew everything about my case anyway from what they had heard on the streets.

There was a rumor that my daddy bought the gun for me and told me to kill some of those guys. There was talk that I had prepared a list of gang members to kill and the dead person was at the top of the list. There was a story that the person came into the store with a Bible in his hand and I shot his Bible out of his hand. It flew up and then I shot it again, like a sharpshooter in a western movie. There was also a story that he came into the store with his mother holding his hand, and I tried to shoot her too. There was a story that Beulah manipulated everything and told me to shoot Thomas to prove that I loved her. Then, there was the story that Thomas was the good Samaritan whom I killed out of meanness. I believed that some of these stories were told to the grand jury and the person on the grand jury who later served on my trial jury repeated some of these false stories during their deliberations.

One day we were peeling tomatoes for canning and Mike was talking to me. He told me that Lionel Drew had recently visited him at Reidsville.

I turned to look at him without saying anything.

"Rudolph, I'm getting out of prison next year," Mike said excitedly and confidently.

I still didn't say anything. I knew that some guys, for psychological reasons, needed to believe that they are gonna get out of prison soon and can't accept that they might spend their entire youth in prison or die in prison. I knew that it was wise not to burst some guys' bubbles and dash their hopes. So I said nothing to Mike.

"I know you don't believe me but I'm gonna be back in Savannah next year."

I knew the game that Drew was running on Mike and that he was playing on Mike's desire to get out. The game consisted of visiting convicted persons and convincing them that they could be out of prison shortly. These prisoners then contact their families, who would borrow money to take to the lawyers and then the prisoners would not hear from the lawyers again. The only expense for the lawyer is transportation to the prison and the payoff is several hundred dollars. Meanwhile, the guy stays in prison.

I knew that Mike was not getting out of prison next year. He had only served a year on a life sentence. He was convicted as the triggerman in a robbery/murder of a white man. Additionally, he was convicted, I learned, of manslaughter for killing the guy at Singleton Beach and was out on appeal bond when his latest offense occurred. Mike didn't have a snowball's chance in hell of getting out of prison next year and he would likely be in prison for a very long time. Drew knew this, but Drew told Mike differently just to get more money. I wanted to tell Mike what game was being run, but I knew that he wouldn't believe me and it would only affect our friendship if I told him. Mike might have to serve over 30 years before the parole board began seriously to think about paroling him.

On detail one day in the fields, Granddaddy, a young prisoner from Atlanta who looked about forty, came up to me and told me that he was in Alto with Stacko and had heard all about me. Granddaddy said that Stacko and another guy from Savannah used to talk about me almost everyday.

"They were talking about you and some gang. I believe it was the Hurricanes or something like that. They talked about how you had killed someone and were given the electric chair. They talk about you like you were some type of god. Now that I have seen you, you're just an ordinary, bowlegged nigger."

I laughed at him and asked what was I.

"An ordinary, bowlegged nigger."

I laughed some more and continued picking peas.

Granddaddy started talking to me everyday on work detail and sometimes during lunch, he would sit by me. He began to tell me about his love affair with a homosexual prisoner and how much he was in love.

I didn't wanna hear anything about homosexual love. Like the Muslim, I believed involvement with a man wasn't kosher. The guys in the cellblock told me that I should get some of Fat's ass, but I declined. That didn't interest me and I also knew that some guys are tricked and used by homosexual prisoners. Sometimes, they are paid to seduce other prisoners, and many prisoners are not necessarily forced to become homosexual but become so after some involvement with sissies. One of the star sissies in Reidsville was Kenny Jackson, and one of Honey's friends, Jim Brown, said that he wanted to fuck Kenny but was afraid that he would lose his manhood. Kenny stated that of all the guys that he had gone with in Reidsville, he had fucked all of them but one. The guys on the yard were teasing Jim Brown about his dilemma and joked to him that he was not sure of his manhood.

Granddaddy started telling me how much he loved this sissy and that he had given this sissy all his towels and had even given this sissy his manhood.

I looked at Granddaddy and I could see that he was not joking and was quite serious.

I continued to work as Granddaddy kept talking.

Granddaddy stated that the sissy now wanted to quit him and go with someone else and he was thinking about killing him.

I didn't say anything at all and decided to stay out of it.

Later on the yard that day, some guys were teasing Iceman. He had been moved from the C Building to a dormitory in the A Building.

"Hey, Ice, they got you in the dorm with the chronics," which was the dorm for mostly old prisoners.

"Yeah, they got me in the dorm with those old cripples," Iceman responded. "One of them is even trying to fuck me. Everyday when I come in an old motherfucker that can hardly walk has got some sandwiches for me or some candy."

"Did you eat 'em?" asked Sweetman.

"Damn right I ate 'em. He even offered me a smoke. I don't smoke, but I smoked it."

"That old guy is fattening Iceman up, just like you fatten a hog."

"That old dude don't want a boney ass, he wants some meat on that ass."

"Damn, Iceman, you got a lot of nerve, eating that guy's shit."

"I know I'm a real man. A real man don't have to worry about those weak-assed chain gang games. If he gets wrong, I'll whip his ass out of the A Building. Shit, the last time I kicked a motherfucker's ass, he told the guard that he had been beaten by a gang. I was hitting the motherfucker so hard and fast, that he thought it was about five or six," Iceman bragged. "I'll kick this motherfucker's ass for even thinking that I am that weak."

"Well, if that old dude gets behind you, don't call me."

The next day I didn't go on the yard, preferring to watch the evening news. Someone from Savannah asked about me and wondered why I watched the news so much when I had a life sentence and wasn't gonna be free for a long time.

I was told that there was an incident on the yard that day. Several guys in their late twenties from Atlanta wanted to gang a teenager. Honey began asking the young guy where he was from and he told Honey that he was from a small town between Savannah and Brunswick. Honey asked the guy if he had ever been to Savannah and the guy said not really. Honey told him that if he rode through Savannah on Highway 17 or 80 that was good enough. When the guys from Atlanta saw that the Savannah guys were backing the young guy, they decided to leave him alone.

Iceman was on the yard when this incident happened and he laughed about this for more than an hour the next day at work. Honey and some of the guys from Savannah were looking to fight. Iceman said that he heard some guys say that they would be glad when Honey left the prison because there were some young guys from Savannah that they wanted to fuck, but they couldn't do it as long as Honey was there.

I continued to get visitors on Sunday. After one visit, Charles, who was also in the visiting room, told other guys that I had a twin brother. One guy told me that I should change clothes with my brother in the visiting restroom and walk out. I responded that I couldn't do that and put my brother in such a place so that I could go free. I thought that would be very selfish of me. But I imagined that some of the guys in my cellblock would have tried to pull off such a stunt.

Later that day, Lump had a visit from his family. The guard refused to let Lump into the visiting room, contending that Lump's mustache was too thick and long. So, Lump returned to the cellblock and shaved off his entire mustache. When he returned to the visiting room, the guard told Lump not to tell his visitors that Lump was told to cut off his entire mustache.

I told Lump that white folks don't like people telling on them, and sometimes they can be backed off when you have something on them and suggest that you are gonna make trouble for them.

This incident caused Lump to begin talking about white folks and the legal system. He stated that when he went to court in Columbus, he told the judge that he, as a black man, didn't have any rights and the judge was gonna do whatever the judge wanted to do. Lump said that the judge tried to convince him that all U.S. citizens have rights, including colored people. Then, Lump shifted topics and beginning talking about Negroes who wanna be white and that he was gonna paint all these Negroes white when he returned to Columbus.

I told him if I read about someone doing that in Columbus, I'd know it was him.

On work detail the next day, one guy was telling me about his criminal history and how he committed some crimes for which he hadn't been caught. He told me that he considered himself a professional robber and he knew how to rob and take money. During one crime, he and a buddy approached a parked car with a white woman and a white man inside. He and his buddy approached the car and told the white couple to give it up.

"That bitch just started taking off her blouse. When I said give it up, I meant give up the money, not the pussy. But I didn't try to stop her from taking off her clothes. My buddy and me fucked her and then we took their money too."

"We were picked up later that night and put in a lineup. The white guy identified us, but she refused, saying we were not the two guys that raped her."

"If she had said you two were the ones, both of you would have been on death row," I explained.

"I was lucky then and I have been lucky in some other situations. Generally, I do not rob stores or businesses near where I live. I go to the opposite side of town. Once, I robbed a liquor store on one part of town. A week later, I needed some liquor to take to a party. So, I walked into this liquor store. I was buying then and wasn't robbing. As soon as I walked into the store, I looked at the clerk and the clerk looked at me. It was the same motherfucker that I had robbed the last week, but he was at this liquor store. I found out later that the person who owned this liquor store owned several liquor stores and moved this guy to this store. Well, getting back to the story, the clerk thought that I was in the liquor store to rob him again and the clerk pulled out a gun and fired three shots at me. I didn't see how he missed, but he did. He probably was nervous and his hand was shaking. I was armed too, and I pulled out my gun and fired back. I never said anything to the guy, and he immediately started firing."

"That sounds like an interesting legal situation," I remarked. "On one hand, the guy was right to fire, thinking you intended to rob him again. On the other hand, it seems to me that you had a right to fire back if you truly never intended to rob this guy that time," I observed.

"I could never have told the jury the truth because they wouldn't have believed me and I didn't tell my lawyer the truth either. My story was that I walked into the liquor store to buy some beverages, and this clerk, without me saying anything to him, started shooting at me. I said that I didn't know why he started shooting at me and I didn't do anything to him in the store to cause him to start shooting at me. If the guy had lived long enough, he probably would have told the police that I robbed him last week, but since he didn't, my version of what happened became the official story. But it really didn't do me much good because the jury convicted me and gave me a life sentence."

Dristain was put in L2, and he turned out to be a big disappointment. Immediately, he got involved with one of the sissies in L1, and called himself going with the sissy. L1 was directly behind L2 and one could talk through the vent located near the commode at the bottom of the back wall of the cell. Dristain was down on his knees in one cell, begging a sissy not to quit him. Apparently, the sissy had told Dristain if Dristain did not give him more money that he was gonna quit Dristain. So, Dristain was begging the sissy to give him more time and told the Sissy that he was gonna write to his mother in Philadelphia and ask her to send him some money immediately.

"What's wrong with that Geechee?" Eighty-eight asked me.

"I don't know and I don't care," I told Eighty-eight.

"Damn, Dristain is a weak Geechee. Most Geechees here are pretty strong," said Eighty-eight.

"Hey, Dristain!" Eighty-eight shouted. "You are one of the sorriest Geechees that I have seen in Reidsville. You know this dumb motherfucker has written his momma, telling her that he owes some guys some money and they are gonna kill him unless he pays up. Dristain is pimping his momma for a stinking-ass sissy. I know what's going to happen. That sissy is gonna fuck you, Dristain, because you are weak. The sissy is gonna demand that you give him some ass and you are gonna do it. When that happens, I am gonna fuck you, too," Eighty-eight maintained.

Eighty-eight was the preacher in the cellblock. He would come out on the range and talk. One day, he was upset with a guy named Country, who liked to watch *Tarzan* on television.

"Someone needs to turn that goddamn channel. Look at that Country motherfucker. He's rooting for Tarzan to whip a whole tribe of Africans. Dumb motherfucker. Look at that. One white man controls all the animals in the jungle and then beats two or three tribes. White folks put on this propaganda and this silly motherfucker sitting in front of the television is jumping up and down and rooting for Tarzan."

After preaching for several minutes, Eighty-eight would go back into his cell.

One of the more talked about events occurred with one of the trusties, who was working at one of the prison official's house. Supposedly, this trusty took some guns from the house, kidnapped the prison official's wife, who was pregnant, and made her drive him away from the prison grounds. At some point, he let her go and was subsequently cornered in a school. They had a fierce gun battle and the prisoner was killed but not before he killed one of the prison officials. When the trusty's body was returned to the prison, the word was that he had been shot to hell. One leg was shot off and he had been hit everywhere but in the face.

However, the talk around the prison was that there was much more than what was reported in the newspaper. First, the talk, overheard from one of the prison doctors, was that the trusty did not really kidnap the prison official's wife. Also, the trusty, who had been in prison for 11 years, was on the way to kill some of the authorities that he claimed framed him and sent him to prison.

I heard the guards outside my cellblock talking about this incident. One said that he told his wife that whenever the prison calls for him to help search for an escapee, she should tell the person calling that he just left and that she isn't sure when he will return.

A new guy came into the cellblock and one could see that he was serious.

"Hey man, you sitting in front of me and I can't see the television," stated Blue.

"If you can't see, you move," said the new guy.

"You heard what Brand-new said, Blue. Move if you can't see because Brand-new is not moving."

Blue liked to try and use new prisoners who he thinks are afraid, but it was quite obvious that this new guy was not afraid and Blue didn't want anything to do with him.

The new guy, after working one day, said upon his return that he wasn't gonna work anymore on the white's man plantation. So, the next day, the new guy didn't go to work and had to go to court the following day. The disciplinary committee gave the new guy 14 days in the hole. When he got out, he stated that he still didn't intend to work anymore. He wouldn't go to work the next day and he got 14 more days in the hole. Upon getting out the second time, he still maintained that he was not gonna work on the white folks' plantation. He was sent back to the hole for 14 more days, and at the end of this 14 days, he was put on segregation. The prison officials realized that he meant what he said. He was not gonna work on the plantation.

I had to admit that this guy had guts and he had more than me. I was anxious to complete my 6 months so that I could get an inside job and get out of the field. I was getting close, and it would take something major for me to go to the hole and lose it.

Eighty-eight was back on the range talking about a guy from Atlanta named Asa, who was supposed to be a snitch for the prosecutor. Asa supposedly was allowed to get away with relatively minor crimes by telling on others. His value may have declined because he was in Reidsville.

"All right, all you sons-of-bitches from Atlanta who said that Asa was a snitch on the street, here he is," said Eighty-eight.

Asa was standing by Eighty-eight with a stern look on his face and his hands on his hips as if inviting someone to call him a snitch. It was obvious, though, that he was scared as this was a serious thing that Eighty-eight was doing. Nobody confronted Asa, but I noticed that Asa didn't go on the yard very much and did not go to the movies.

Eighty-eight, like most guys in Reidsville, liked western movies on television or the theater. When a western came on television, someone would shout for Eighty-eight that they had horseshit and gun smoke on television, and Eighty-eight would come running.

The guys also liked movies with a lot of gunplay in it. *Bullitt* was shown at the theater, and guys talked about this movie all week. The movie had two professional hit men in it, and one used a pump shotgun to kill another guy. They talked about this pump shotgun and how it was similar to one they had used on the street, or one they intended to use when they got back on the street.

The cellblock was fairly mellow, and most guys got along okay. There was a lot of joking and teasing, especially around the shower. Some guys would sit on the bench in front of the shower and make fun of some guys taking a shower.

"Stovall, you know, you didn't wash your hair yesterday," said one guy on the bench.

"Why are you concerned about me washing my hair?" Stovall queried.

"I like to watch the soapsuds run down your back into the crack of your ass."

Everyone on the bench said amen.

Someone else came to the shower, and one guy on the bench said that he was waiting on this guy to take a shower because this guy had the best looking ass in the cellblock.

"You're not watching my ass. That's your camouflage. What you really watching is my dick because you looking for someone to swap ass with you. But you have to look for another swap ass, buddy."

One night, Stovall came down near the showers and announced excitedly that he intended to fuck one guy and he was close to getting him. About 10 minutes later, the guy came down and said he was close to fucking Stovall.

The guys on the bench looked at each other. After the other guy left, one guy on the bench commented that Stovall and this guy were gonna be swapping out.

Finally, my sixth month came and that night I wrote to the classification committee for an inside job. After a few days, I, along with several other guys on forty-three detail, was assigned to the tag plant, which was heated and located in the back of the prison.

I had been at Reidsville for about a year. In that time, I had dug ditches, dug up stumps, cut grass, peeled tomatoes, cut okra, picked beans, and skimmed syrup. Now, I was ready to make tags for the state of Georgia.

I was assigned to the press. Caghead showed me what my job was. I paid particular attention to the safety issues, hearing that some guys had gotten their hands caught in this machine. My initial job was to slide the blank tags into the machine one at a time. This job involved sitting down, like the other two main jobs. One person was on the other side changing the numbers and letters. The other person took the pressed tags out of a tray after fifty had been done. Other guys were responsible for painting the tags. My job was just to push a blank into the slot, and after the machine had taken the blank, to put in another. This was an easy job.

It was even better because we could take a nap in the corner because there were more people assigned to a machine than necessary. Pushmouth, a guard who twisted his mouth whenever he talked, didn't care about us taking a nap as long as the supervisor was not around.

One day we were asked to make some extra tags for tractor trailers and a man came to pick them up. I was told that they were stealing these tags and were planning to sell them to truckers. I knew this was probably true because the tags we made all had the same number.

I met one guy in the tag plant and he and I started talking about the law. He explained habeas corpus to me and gave me a sample habeas corpus petition. I looked at it and felt that I could file a petition myself if I had more knowledge of the law. There was a sparse library at Reidsville, but it didn't contain any law books. I would have to buy my own books before I could do anything.

I was getting somewhat relaxed in Reidsville and felt it was just about as good a place to do time as any other prison. The movies were something good to look forward to, and the person who was doing the movie selection was doing a good job. I didn't have any problems with any other prisoner. At first, I thought that I might have a problem with Blue, but he gave up trying for me. I felt comfortable enough to give my knife to Shep Dog and did not get another one as I didn't think that I would need it.

I didn't gamble, and I didn't mess with any of the sissies or fuckboys. This significantly decreased my chances of having altercations with other prisoners. Equally important, I did not talk much and only talked to a few people. So, I felt that I could do all my time in Reidsville, although I had heard that some prison camps afford prisoners more latitude. Some guys who were in Reidsville and had been at one of the county prison camps claimed that they had opportunities to get real pussy and real liquor. But these were not goals of mine.

One day at the tag plant, Pushmouth woke me up from a nap and told me that I was being transferred and some people were waiting on me. I returned to L2 and began packing my property. As I was packing, I wasn't too thrilled and really didn't wanna go. I had been in Reidsville almost a year-and-a-half and was getting comfortable, but now it was time to go somewhere else.

Chapter 17

Two white officers with "Wayne County Correctional Institution" printed on their dark green sleeves walked me out of Reidsville into a van. I wasn't sure where I was going, and I didn't know where Wayne County was.

I thought that I might be in Reidsville much longer. I was not walking out 20 years later like I had at one time envisioned. I didn't wanna be transferred from Reidsville because I was afraid of being transferred to Northern Georgia, which might cause a hardship on my family visiting me. At the same time, I didn't wanna go to the prison near Savannah, fearing that it would make me angrier to be out on a work detail and see either people that I did not care to see or family members. So, as far as being in prison, I was content being in Reidsville and had decided that I would not request a transfer to a county institution.

Georgia operated a number of smaller institutions in several counties in addition to its major institutions in Reidsville and Jackson. The prison system seemed to be undergoing additional changes since Governor Carter brought Ellis MacDougall from Connecticut to head the Georgia Department of Corrections. MacDougall was supposed to be an expert in prisons and was interested in rehabilitation. Under the old regime, rehabilitation was defined in Reidsville as the creation of expanded athletic programs under the supervision of a director and a change in yard policy where prisoners during daylight savings time could go on the yard after supper. But MacDougall was talking about going much further. One of the things MacDougall proposed was to change the name of the department to include the word "rehabilitation."

The guard who was not driving was reading my file. He discovered that I had been initially given a death sentence.

"Hey, they were gonna burn your ass in 1968?" the guard commented, half turning to me behind the wire screen.

I didn't say anything.

"What do you mean?" the driver asked.

"He was given the electric chair."

"Do you mean that he is gonna be executed?" the driver asked with a shocked look as he turned to look at the other guard.

"My sentence was changed to life," I volunteered.

I thought that he must be pretty dumb to think that someone with a pending death sentence would be sent to a institution that did not have the mechanisms to impose death in the electric chair.

I noticed that the driver had turned on Highway 341 and had gone through a small town called Surrency. Before long, we turned left onto a dirt road and I began to imagine that this institution must be very outdated. But I was wrong. I saw a very modern-looking institution on the left, and the driver pulled up in front of a gate locked with a chain and padlock. The other guard got out and went into the front.

I began to look around. Directly across the prison was a field and at the far end of the field was a house, which I guessed was the warden's. The institution had a fence around it, but the fence did not go completely around the prison. A person could walk into the front of the prison without going through a fence. There was a structure to the left of the prison that I knew was a treatment plant and I could see a pond of water. I could also see some structures in the back of the prison that looked like garages and toolsheds.

After a few minutes the guard returned with a key, unlocked the gate, and swung it open. We drove through it and around the back of the prison. The guard opened the back of the prison and I was ushered through the showers to a table.

Several guards began going through my personal belongings. I had some legal information about habeas corpus and the beginning of a draft of a habeas corpus petition that one guard thought I shouldn't have.

"What are you doing with this? Did you write this?"

"Yes."

"Listen, when an officer asks you a question you say No Sir or Yes Sir," bellowed one guard.

"Have you been suing anyone?" the guard asked.

"No," I said.

The guard who bellowed at me looked at me. So, I added "Sir."

"Can he have all of this?"

"Yes, give it back to him," the supervisor said.

My belongings were checked, and I was issued some additional clothing. Then I was escorted through two gates and into the dining room, which was very new. Each table had a number of condiments on it, which stood in contrast to Reidsville. I could see a door straight ahead with a glass window in it and I knew that this door went to the administrative offices. The dining area, shaped like a square, had something on all sides. On the right were the kitchen and the counter where food was served. Facing the kitchen on the other side was a library and a classroom. Two dormitories, I could see, were on each side, with a short hall between each dormitory and each dormitory with a barred door. One could see inside each dormitory from the dining area. I was ushered to one door on the left and to the dormitory on the right side. Only a few prisoners were in the dormitory and I knew that the prisoners were out working.

There were about twenty-five double bunk beds in the dormitory. At the far end was a one person shower on the right, three sinks, urinals, and three commodes. There were no barriers in front of the commodes. A television, located about 8 or 9 feet from the urinals, sat on a shelf that was suspended from the ceiling. So, a prisoner who sat on the commode could be viewed by the entire dormitory, especially if prisoners were watching television.

I was assigned a top bunk and began to put my belongings into one of the two drawers at the bottom of the bunk beds. I began to look around more, and I saw a guard walking on a catwalk at the far end of the prison. He was elevated and could see all the dormitories, the classroom, and library as he walked around the building. I walked to the glass at the end and could see prisoners walking in the dormitory on the other side. All in all, this place wasn't too bad. It was modern and it was air-conditioned. The only thing I wondered was what the guards and warden were like.

Later that day, guys started coming in. Most had their hair wet, having taken a shower before coming into the dormitory. Some prisoners were going into the dormitory just across the narrow hall from me. A few prisoners were going in the dormitories across from the dining area, which was primarily for trusties, drivers, and others who worked around the prison. I quickly learned that there were two guys in the dormitory that I was living in from Savannah—Point Jackson and Larry Hunter.

I had heard Point Jackson's name on the street and had seen him at a burger place. I also vaguely knew of Point's brother. Larry Hunter I didn't know, but later when he began talking about himself, I quickly realized I knew of him. Larry, who was convicted of murder and was serving life, mentioned that when the jury returned with its verdict blood spurted from his nose all over the defense table.

"So you were on the case with Mike Furman," I commented.

"Yeah, where do you know Mike?" Larry asked.

"Reidsville; I just left him there."

I told Point and Larry about all the guys from Savannah that were in Reidsville.

Point and Larry gave me their assessment of the prison and the guys there. They told me that the Warden's name was Harry Yawn, and the guards, following the warden's philosophy, tried to be tough. They told me that one of the guards slapped a prisoner named Cecil and another guard kicked another prisoner. But they both believed that the prison was okay to do time. Unlike many institutions, this institution was air-conditioned. The only negative that they had to say was that the television's antenna was controlled outside the dormitory and the guards would not activate the antenna until late in the evening.

Later other guys came in. Someone called to me from the other dormitory.

"Rudolph, how you doing?" said someone through the dormitory bars that I didn't recognize.

"I'm doing okay," I said somewhat quizzically. "Who are you?"

"You don't recognize me?" asked the guy.

I was staring at him very hard, trying to recognize him.

"I'm George Wilson. I used to live around the corner from you on Jefferson Street when you were living on 31st street."

"Damn, George. I didn't recognize you. I'm sorry. How are you doing?"

"I'm doing okay," said George. "I'll talk to you at supper. We can sit together."

At supper, George and I were sitting together. I immediately noticed after a few minutes that he acted differently from when I had seen him last, which had been 4 or 5 years before.

"The way you fell, man, was a shock to everybody. You would have been the last person in the neighborhood that I would have said would have gone to prison. Those white devils really fucked you over. The white man is no good."

This was one change in George. He was much more militant, like a lot of black guys had become, including myself.

"The crooked lawyers there decided that I was gonna be convicted shortly after I was arrested and the trial was a joke. They got me because I was young, under pressure, and didn't know how the system operated. Now, I know how they operate. This will be the last time for me."

"Goddamn right. I'm not coming back to this motherfucker again myself."

The next day, we had to go on the back porch to be assigned to a work detail. Prisoners in groups of about ten were put in the back of three yellow trucks, which were locked from the back. It had vents at the sides at the top, with a canvass rolled up that could be unrolled to keep rain from coming through the vents. I was put on a small detail that dug up small roots in the field. Some of the guys were digging up tree roots with a pickax and others were walking behind, picking up the roots and putting them in a pile to be burned. We did this all morning, broke for lunch, which was brought to us in the field, and then did the same thing all afternoon.

The prison purchased four Savannah newspapers and put one in each dormitory each day. It took almost several hours for this one newspaper to go around to about 50 people. I tried to spot the guard when he put the paper inside the dormitory so that I could read it early and would not be at the end of the line. On Sunday mornings, I never slept late, wanting to read the newspaper early.

After awaiting my turn to read the newspaper one day, I read that Aaron Kravitch had died. There were two articles in the newspaper about him. In one it said that "even with a sure loser, he could face up to a jury with all the confidence of a sure winner. Guts he had, and guts he used when everything appeared stacked against his client. . . . Many regarded Kravitch as a showman, and he was, indeed, highly capable of disarming a jury, as well as an opposing attorney or prosecutor, with the most unexpected histrionics. . . . Kravitch seldom made a distinction between big and little cases. A penniless client got the same consideration as a mighty corporation involved in a land-mark case. . . . He was a lawyer first and then a politician, the latter side of him emerging during an era of Chatham politics in which everything went and everyone played the game that way. If he put more into the game than most, it might explain some of the less enthusiastic comments you were likely to hear from some of his old enemies. . . . His ethics were largely his own, and he was one of the few lawyers who could afford this luxury."

The other article was mostly a testimonial from a federal judge who dis-cussed Kravitch in open court the day of Kravitch's funeral. It stated that Kravitch "will be evaluated as a legendary figure of the Savannah Bar. . . . On his 50th anniversary at the bar, Kravitch said he had tried to follow the advice of the late Judge Peter Meldrim, who told him never to refuse to rep-resent anybody. . . . Judge Lawrence . . . praised Kravitch as having pos-sessed talents of a high and unusual order . . . In his many years in the courtroom, he represented both the mighty and the meek; however, the record of which I am sure he was the proudest was his representation of the meek. . . . The University of Pennsylvania cited him in 1966 as a lawyer whose able and courageous representation of a person in an unpopular case exemplifies notable and inspiring accomplishment and the highest state of the conscience of the bar."

After reading these articles, I was amazed at how dead people are eulo-gized in a manner that hides their dirty side. Aaron Kravitch was a very cor-rupt lawyer. The things that the article discussed were not done for me even though I had been one of Aaron Kravitch's clients. Kravitch never appeared in the courtroom with me or used the skills that the article illuminated. I needed him and his 50 years of criminal experience at my trial when the jury was deciding my case. I needed him to disarm that jury and use some of those lawyers' tricks he was famous for. My daddy paid for it, but Kravitch did not give it to me. Instead, he sent Drew to do a hatchet job on me—a man who went to a Catholic high school and who sympathized with and protected the choir boy. Perhaps this was his political side that the newspaper article dis-cussed and how well he played the political game.

I was preparing to file a habeas corpus action and was gathering infor-mation about my case. I had received my trial transcript and indictment. As I was reading the transcript of my trial, it became very obvious that Patrol-man Bush, and Neely to some extent, told major lies during the motion to suppress. I had an impression during my trial that something was amiss when these two were first testifying. I knew then that the motion to suppress, like the trial itself, was a sham. Both Bush and Neely gave sworn testimony at my preliminary hearing, and there was absolutely no discussion about a bulge on my midsection. One of the prosecutors told Bush and Neely to lie and say that I had a bulge on me. The prosecutors were not worried about im-peachment because they knew that nothing would be said by Drew to chal-lenge the lies the police officers were telling. To prove this, I needed the transcript of the preliminary hearing and wrote to the clerk office in Savannah requesting it.

I read other parts of my transcript. A portion of Eddie Simmons's trial was made part of my transcript and this part took up most of my transcript. My trial transcript was about an inch-and-a-half thick, but about three-fourths of it was Simmons's. In Simmon's case, a challenge was made to how jurors were selected. One of the witnesses admitted that in Savannah, many Negroes who have college degrees and owned homes were working as porters because of the segregated structure of Savannah society. Several of the jurors admitted that they had served on another jury during the previous week.

But the part that struck me the most was that when the clerk voir dired the panel of potential jurors, the clerk asked, "Have you, from having seen the crime committed or having heard any of the testimony delivered on oath, formed and expressed any opinion in regard to the guilt or innocence of the prisoner at the bar?" The transcript of Eddie Simmons's case showed a note that no one made an audible response and the clerk went on to the next question. I recalled that this same type of question was posed in my case with the same results. So, the juror in my case who served on the grand jury that indicted me violated this oath. He heard supposedly sworn testimony in the grand jury room and voted to indict me. That was forming an opinion about my guilt. My transcript only had a line saying that the jury was selected, and the questions and responses that were posed to them were omitted from my transcript, unlike Eddie Simmons's case.

Another statement that caught my eye in Eddie Simmons's case was a comment by Dunbar Harrison. Someone from the jury commission was testifying and Dunbar said "Well, well, we have someone here now who we can assume is familiar with the Negro element in the community." The word *element* jumped out at me and I knew this was consistent with Dunbar Harrison's attitude. I had heard the term "criminal element" but I had never heard "Negro element." Dunbar Harrison did not consider black people to be human. They were elements, things, criminals, and niggers.

On the weekend, we went out on the yard. There was a guard walking outside the fence with a shotgun. Most of the guys were playing football and an argument developed between Point and a guy out of Atlanta who called himself Psycho.

I was convinced that he named himself Psycho in the hope that he would make an impression on other prisoners.

After Point and Psycho returned to the dormitory, they continued to argue and then began fighting. One guy wanted to break it up, but I told him not to hold Point while Psycho hit him. So, several guys broke them up, and by then, the guards were coming. Both of them were taken to the hole.

Other guys were being transferred to Wayne Correctional Institution. Honey came and immediately began gambling. I had seen him playing Skin in the county jail, but now he was playing mostly poker. He was playing a lot with a prisoner from Columbus named Doc Hodges and someone from some small town named Cecil. Honey told me that he was a very good poker player and that someone had taught him how to play much better. I would watch him play but only out of curiosity.

I saw Honey talking with a white guy named Charles from Atlanta, and Honey told me later that he knew this white guy from a camp he was in a few years back. Charles did not talk much at all, and he seemed to talk less than me.

"He ain't no ordinary white guy. He is into some heavy things. I overheard him talking to some bitches. A couple of them were black. Charles was cussing them out and telling them to go certain places and pick up his money. Those bitches were saying "Okay Charles, Okay Charles." You could tell that they were afraid of him and also that whoever owed Charles money was gonna pay even though he was in prison. I asked him about the women and Charles told me that he takes the bitches as they come. Once, the warden took all of my money and put it in the office. I borrowed $10.00 from Charles and within a few minutes, I had about $50.00 and paid Charles back. He won't talk much at all," related Honey.

"It sounds as if he is pimping or controls some prostitutes," someone commented.

Another Piggy from Savannah came to Wayne County. This Piggy was rather large, but he was a very young guy. I remembered when Piggy went to trial that the article stated that Piggy was about 14 or 15. His lawyer pleaded with the jury to go easy on Piggy because of Piggy's age. Despite his age, he was given 20 years for armed robbery.

George Wilson was moved into the dormitory that I was in and we continued to talk. The more we talked, the more I realized that something was wrong with George. Most black people in prison have some harsh statements to make about the white folks that run the legal system and many white folks in general. But George seemed more intense about it. He continued to wanna talk about me and my situation.

One day as we were watching television, George was on his back and lying on the floor.

"Homeboy, won't you get off the floor," urged Honey.

"I like it better on the floor," George responded.

"There is something wrong with him," I whispered. "I grew up with George, and we played basketball in my backyard many times. He acts much differently now than he used to act," I explained.

Some other guys were whispering about George's behavior too.

I concluded that George was losing it mentally.

One white guy that black guys talked a lot about was someone called Bo-Tee, who moved into the dormitory across the dining area. Bo-Tee would get extremely upset when he saw on the television a white woman and a black man together. He was particularly upset with the movie *My Sweet Charlie*, although the two characters never kissed, had sex, or were romantically involved in the picture. They just happened to be staying in the same vacant house due to unique circumstances. Bo-Tee said that he would kill any nigger he finds with a white woman.

So, some of the guys, both Black and white, started messing with him. A white prisoner, in Bo-Tee's hearing, would ask a black prisoner what is the first thing he, the black prisoner, is gonna do upon getting out. Most guys always mentioned getting something to drink and some pussy. However, in this ploy at Bo-Tee, the black guy would say a long-haired white woman. Upon hearing this, Bo-Tee would get red in the face and start spouting, with spit flying from his mouth, what he would do if he found a black son-of-a-bitch with a white woman. Then, everyone would laugh at him. In the institution, Bo-Tee was a joke and most people provoked him for laughter, but some said that he actually would do something in the street.

I continued having problems with my eyes. This problem had been going on since I was in the county jail almost 4 years ago. I would see intense waves in front of my face for about 5 minutes and then the waves would slowly go away and my vision would return. I had never told anyone that this was happening to me since it only happened about once every 4 or 5 months. I finally decided to request seeing a doctor about my eyes. The next time the doctor came, I told the guard that I needed to see the doctor.

"Your eye has been completely destroyed," the doctor said in amazement as he looked into my left eye with a small light. "You don't have a lens in your eye. I can see you had an injury. What happened to you?"

"Someone cut me with a box cutter and I got a cataract on it and the doctor took out the lens in that eye."

"You need to see a specialist about this. I'm just a general practitioner."

The guard told me later that I would be transferred temporarily to Reidsville to see a ophthalmologist that came to Reidsville periodically.

My parents continued to come to see me. My daddy told me that he did not have any problem finding the institution. Although he didn't say anything, I believed that he preferred that I stayed in Reidsville.

My brother came to see me. This was the first time that he had come without my daddy, this time bringing his girlfriend with him.

"Willie, he looks like you," said Joanne.

"No, I don't look like him, he looks like me. I'm older than he is. Therefore, I'm the original and he's a copy," I said jokingly.

"It seems that everywhere I go, I see guys who come up to me and ask me about you."

"What about the girls? I know some of my old girlfriends have been asking about me too," I said, joking some more.

"A few girls have asked me about you," my brother stated. "Sometimes, I will go places and I will see people staring at me. At one time, I would see some of the guys in the Tornado gang and they would just stare at me. They wouldn't say anything to me, but they would really stare at me. The other people, people that you went to school with, would stare at me and finally come up to me and ask if my name is Rudolph. I would tell them no, I'm Rudolph's brother Willie, and that you were still in prison. Almost everyone would tell me the same thing. They would all say that they have never known you to bother anyone or try to take advantage of anyone and that it was a shame that you got messed up the way that you did."

I was studying my brother's new girlfriend, who was cute. Before I came to prison, he was not into girls. Mostly, he played basketball all the time. I could see that he really liked her and could see that my brother was growing up.

One Saturday night, a dispute developed over the television. The white guys wanted to see *Porter Wagner,* a country and western show, but the black guys wanted to see something else. Larry Hunter turned the station away from *Porter Wagner,* and a white guy turned it back to *Porter Wagner.* At that point, Larry grabbed the white guy's collar and hit him in the face.

"I'm not gonna fight you," said the white guy.

The white guy walked off with his face reddened and his eye beginning to swell. The other white guys got up and left too.

In an integrated dormitory, the black guys always controlled the television. The white guys watched what the black guys wanted to watch. If they did not like what was on, they left the television area. It was democracy at work. The white guys were outnumbered and there was no need to vote.

The next day, as usual, I got up relatively early to read the Sunday newspaper. Later that afternoon, I looked over at the white guy Larry had hit the previous night. He was lying on his bed, but something seemed amiss. He had cleared his headboard of all his personal possessions. All of us had a headboard that some guys kept books, magazines, or pictures of their girlfriends or wives on. The next morning, it came to me and everyone else why he had cleared his headboard. He was planning to leave the dormitory.

At Monday morning breakfast, Larry was sitting two tables from me with his back to the serving area. I saw Larry jump and thought that he had spilled hot coffee on himself. But I saw the white guy Larry had hit looking at Larry and walking back towards the dormitory. As Larry turned, I could see that he had a knife sticking in his back and he began walking to the door that led to the offices. Larry had his hand at his back, feeling for the knife. He told someone to pull it out and one guy tried to pull it out, but couldn't. The guy put his knee in Larry's back to brace himself and pulled the knife out. By then, the guard had opened the door, ushering Larry out toward the front offices.

In the meantime, the guard had the white guy and was escorting him toward the back of the prison where the hole was.

"You low-life son-of-a-bitch, you stabbed that guy in the back like that," someone shouted to the white guy.

"I saw him do it and he is gonna be punished," said the guard.

"No, we're gonna punish this motherfucker ourselves."

At that point, about five or six guys, including Honey, swooped down on the white guy and pummelled him from all directions.

The guard was trying to stop them, insisting that the white guy was gonna be punished.

But they continued to beat the white guy. As the white guy fell to the floor, some of them began kicking him. The guard grabbed Honey's arm to pull him back and Honey snatched his arm back, raising his fist to the guard, and telling the guard to get his goddamn hands off him.

The guard looked like he was gonna let the guys have the white guy, indicating that he was afraid that the group would turn on him.

Someone shouted that he saw who gave the white guy the knife and stated that it was O'Neil. Upon hearing this, the group stopped beating the white guy and went to O'Neil's table. Someone threw the table aside and O'Neil broke toward the door that Larry had gone out. Someone threw a ketchup bottle at O'Neil and others began throwing bottles at O'Neil too. The dining area quickly divided along racial lines. The white guys, who were throwing bottles back, were huddled against the door leading to the warden's office, and the black guys had retreated inside the hallway leading back to the dormitory.

Piggy wanted to go back out but Honey told him to come back inside the door.

The whole incident occurred so fast that it was difficult to determine who did what. The dining area was a mess with ketchup and other condiments spattered against the walls and floor. One wall looked like one of those weird paintings when an artist throws different colors of paint on a canvass. The glass on the door and the windows was cracked from being hit with the condiment bottles. Only black guys were in the dormitory and all the white guys refused to come back.

A few seconds after the bottles stopped, only one white guy returned to the dormitory. It was Charles, who was plainly displeased with the bottle-throwing and totally unafraid. He had a look on his face that said, "Fuck this shit." All the other white guys were shaking and still huddled by the door, seeking the protection of the guards from these crazy niggers. Charles came back into the dormitory and went to his bed. He was the most fearless white guy that I had seen since I been in prison. It wasn't that he was an arrogant white guy who believed that he was superior to black people and no black person would dare touch him. He just was simply not afraid of anything.

The warden, Harry Yawn, was not at the prison. So, someone called Ellis MacDougall in Atlanta, who indicated that he was coming to the prison. A few hours later, MacDougall and a black man entered the prison. MacDougall identified the black man as a minister from Brunswick whom Governor Carter called at MacDougall's request to help restore order at the prison.

The prisoners began to make complaints to MacDougall about the prison. One prisoner claimed that he tried to write MacDougall, but the warden tore up the letter and told this prisoner not to write to MacDougall. Other prisoners complained about the medical situation and the guards. MacDougall assured the black prisoners that Larry was okay, that Larry was taken to the hospital in Jesup and the doctors determined that the knife did no damage. They made Larry, who was walking hunched over, walk back toward the medical area to show all the black guys that he was all right.

MacDougall and the black minster spoke with the black prisoners alone and then the white prisoners alone. Then, he spoke with all of them together. When he spoke with the black prisoners, MacDougall told them that he would transfer any five white prisoners the black prisoners wanted. When MacDougall spoke with the white prisoners, he told them the same, that they could name five black prisoners that they wanted to be transferred. Honey was at the top of the white guys' list and Bo-Tee the black guys' list.

MacDougall also announced that he had decided to dismiss the warden and told the prisoners not to applaud because it had nothing to do with the disturbance earlier that morning. Instead, he stated that something else caused him to dismiss the warden and that an acting warden named High-smith was on the way from Waycross and would be there in an hour or so. MacDougall then left and told everyone that they had to stop with these types of disturbances and assured everyone that he was gonna be making changes in the prison system in Georgia.

The next day, we were working in the field picking up roots. The radio and newspaper stated that a riot, which had racial overtones, had occurred at the Wayne Correctional Institution.

A few days later, I was told to pack up because I was being transferred to Reidsville because of the medical problem with my eye.

Chapter 18

For medical reasons, Larry Hunter was sent to Reidsville along with me. We were put in quarantine, but unlike the first time I came to Reidsville, quarantine was on the hospital floor and it was quite packed. The beds were about a foot-and-a-half apart and they were triple-bunked. Larry immediately voiced his displeasure with Reidsville, but I assured him that these quarters were temporary.

For perhaps understandable reasons, there was tension between Larry and Mike Furman. Larry was doing time essentially because of Mike. Mike did the shooting, and Larry happened to be with the wrong person. Then, at the trial, there appeared to be a split between them in how they presented their defenses, and Larry indicated that Mike was upset with him. So, this was the first time that Larry had a chance to see Mike after leaving the county jail, and Larry seemed a bit concerned. Perhaps, for this reason, as well as his newness at Reidsville, Larry seemed to be following me everywhere.

Mike and Larry, Lonon and Clarence, and to some extent, Kravitch and Drew, taught me to never do anything with another person. I had heard a number of times about partners turning on each other and one betraying the other.

When I went into the mess hall, I saw Eighty-eight and some of the guys from my old cellblock. They were teasing me and telling me that I requested to come back to Reidsville because of the recent racial trouble at Wayne Correctional Institution. Eighty-eight said that he heard that I was hiding under the table and went to the warden begging him to return me to Reidsville and to get me away from those crazy white people. I told Eighty-eight that I was only in Reidsville temporarily for medical reasons and that I would be returning to Wayne. However, they wanted their laugh and every time Eighty-eight would see me in the mess hall, he would crouch, cowering with his hands over his head, and everyone would laugh. Charles, the houseman in L2, came up to me and told me that I probably could get back in L2, but I told him that I would be alright anywhere the classification committee put me.

When I went before the classification committee, I was assigned to C4, which was an integrated dormitory. Thompson, the deputy warden, told me that it was a very quiet dormitory and people got along. Thompson also told the committee that I had a good attitude and I should be made an orderly. Thus, I was assigned to the MDTA building in the back of the prison near the tag plant and the sewing machine plant. The MDTA was a vocational training program that had been started recently.

The dormitory was quiet, but I didn't like my bed assignment. Initially, I was out in the middle of the dormitory where several beds were positioned. I did not have anyone over me, but I preferred a bed by a window, where I could play my radio. But all the beds against the wall were taken for now and the dormitory was quite crowded. There were almost 100 prisoners in the dormitory and they were continuing to bring in more beds to double bunk the beds in the middle of the dormitory.

A bottom bed opened up against the wall. I knew that the houseman was gonna try and sell it to a prisoner. I wanted it but I didn't intend to pay for it. I went to the houseman to talk to him.

"I would like to have the bed against the wall," I said to the houseman who was sitting on his bed.

I waited for him to respond, but I believed that he was waiting on me to offer him a carton or two of cigarettes. But I didn't make any such offer, I just stood by him waiting, and he waited on me. After about 3 or 4 minutes of silence, he said that I could take the wall bed. I guessed that he wore down before I did; I had no intention of paying him for this bed.

Housemen tended to have a lot of power in Reidsville. They were allowed to keep weapons, like Charles's two-by-four, and when they have shakedowns in the cellblocks or dormitories, the Houseman's footlocker is not searched. Sol told me that a new guard, who was helping to search Sol's dormitory, came over to Sol's footlocker to open it, but an older guard told the new guard that the Houseman's footlocker is not searched. Thus, Sol could keep contraband for himself and his friends. Housemen, as a result, were expected to help keep order but they did not do a lot of strong-arm tactics with prisoners. But there were some exceptions.

One prisoner in Sol's dormitory went to the control office to complain about how Sol was running the dormitory and how unfair he was to him. The captain turned his back to the complaining prisoner, telling Sol that he, the captain, was not looking. This was a signal for Sol to beat the prisoner, and Sol said that he kicked the prisoner's ass all the way back down to the dormitory. If the prisoner complained to the deputy warden, the captain would say that he did not see the prisoner get hit. But the prisoner was not likely to complain to the deputy warden, knowing what happened the last time he complained.

My job was very easy. In the MDTA building, I cleaned the toilets in the morning and swept the floors. There was a guard assigned to the MDTA building, and my job was to run errands for him too. But since there weren't too many errands to run, both of us sat down for most of the day. We read the newspaper and talked about how the prison had changed. Boss Cowins thought that the prison was going to hell and he did not have good things to say about Ellis MacDougall.

Ellis MacDougall, I was told, made a surprise visit to Reidsville. He came to the back of the prison very early one morning, and no one at the prison knew he was coming. He stopped prisoners from being driven to the fields in the Fireball, declaring that the prisoners were human beings and not animals to be herded up and down the highway, to and from the fields. Now all prisoners were to go to work in the prison buses. MacDougall also visited a detail in the field and sampled the food that was brought to prisoners by the P-Jack truck. Those who were there said that he didn't say anything about the food, but he put a stop to the P-Jack truck. Now, prisoners were brought back to the prison for lunch.

The prisoners reported that he went down in the B Building and asked a guard what his job was, and the guard responded that it was opening and closing the door. MacDougall told the guard to get off his ass and start opening and closing the door. Finally, he commented that the guards' uniforms looked like hell and he was gonna change them. They said also that he wanted to do away with the *Boss* title and *guards* would be called *officers*.

I hooked up with Mike Furman on the yard and he gave me the scoop on what had been going on in Reidsville in my absence.

Mike said that Willie Lee Robinson, who now went by the name of Rob, had a standoff with guards near L Building. Mike said that Willie Robinson had two bricks, cocking them and threatening to bust-out the guards' brains. Mike said that one of the guards left and returned with a shotgun, which they never bring inside the prison grounds, and told Willie Robinson to drop the bricks or he was gonna cut him in half. So, Willie Robinson dropped his two bricks.

I knew that Willie Robinson liked to put on a show like that, but I had seen the real Willie Robinson in the county jail. Mike had not, however.

Mike said that all the guys from Savannah were upset with Dristain and were shying away from him because of Dristain's weakness. He told me why.

"A sissy cut Dristain across the ass," Mike recounted incredulously.

"Damn, that son-of-a-bitch is weak," I said. "If you are gonna be stabbed in Reidsville, at least you should be stabbed by a real man. And then to be cut across the ass. That sissy was making a statement about Dristain."

"Also, Crow stabbed Eddie Ruffin out of Atlanta. Eddie was trying to run over Crow," said Mike.

I had a near run-in with Eddie Ruffin myself. I had a lot of magazines in my cell and gave a football magazine to a guy and he gave it to Eddie. Eddie had it on detail one day, and I commented that the magazine had been mine but I gave it away. Eddie said that even if I had not given it away, I wouldn't get it back because he had it now. This was totally unnecessary. If I had not given it away, I would have made that son-of-a-bitch give it back as a matter of principle or I was gonna make him very sorry. Eddie tried to act like a bully, and he needed the wind taken out of his sails.

"Well, after Eddie tried to take something from Crow, Crow decided to stab Eddie in the mess hall. We told him not to worry about his back and that no one else would get involved. Crow went up to Eddie and stabbed Eddie in the chest, but I was so afraid for Crow, although Crow had the knife. Crow's eyes were as big as saucers, and I was afraid that Eddie was gonna take the knife from Crow and kill Crow with it."

"Wait a minute. That doesn't sound like Crow," I said astonished.

"I'm not talking about Black-assed Crow. I'm talking about Edgar Lonon. If it had been Black-assed Crow, Eddie might have been dead. It was good that Lonon had a big knife with a big blade because Eddie quickly faded after throwing a chair at Crow. But I can't forget how Crow looked."

"It's not good for too many people to have that killer instinct, like you," I said, joking somewhat.

Then we talked about some other things. Mike was on the baseball team and he related that the team went outside the prison to play a game. Mike said that each player had a guard assigned to watch him, but he had two guards standing behind him in the outfield.

I thought that this incident should tell Mike that he wouldn't be getting out of prison soon. I didn't remind him of what he told me last year when Drew visited him. Supposedly, this was gonna be the summer that Mike was gonna get out of prison. I knew that if someone in Mike's family had contacted Drew, Drew would have an explanation ready for them and would tell them that Mike would be out the first part of the following year, stringing them along.

From my window, I could see the parking lot in the front of the prison. I had written to my daddy and told him that I was back in Reidsville to have my eye checked by a specialist. That following Sunday, I saw my daddy get out of a car and I recognized the car as belonging to Percy, one of my daddy's friends who grew up with him in Crawfordville. I went to the showers and washed quickly. As I returned to my bed to finish dressing, my family was walking in the front gate. I waited for my name to be called.

As soon as I walked in, I noticed a difference in my daddy. This was the first time that I had been in prison that he had visited me after he had been drinking. All the other times he had come, he had been sober. When I was in the county jail, he did come once after he had been drinking. This was just before Christmas in 1967 and I knew he didn't have to work. My senses told me that he wasn't doing too good.

I had always suspected that when Daddy and the family visited me and they decided to go by Sylvester and Mary's house in Reidsville, that Daddy would get a drink. But I didn't know and didn't find out until later that when Daddy visited me, he had some whiskey with him in the car. My momma had convinced him that he shouldn't go into the prison when he had been drinking because the prison officials might stop him from visiting. After walking out of the prison, he would be nervous and shaking. It was eating him up to see me in a prison uniform in Reidsville, but he had to come. On the way back to Savannah, his driving would be erratic due to his mental state and the family was afraid that he was gonna wreck the car. My Momma couldn't drive and so they were pressing for one of my brothers or sisters to get a driver's license so someone other than my daddy could drive back to Savannah.

I also learned that he had repeatedly said when I had the death sentence over my head that should I be executed, he did not wanna live anymore. On the weekend, he would drink and cry, blaming himself for not doing more when I had been attacked. Compounding and exacerbating this guilt was Mr. Head's admonishment that Daddy shouldn't have initially gone to Aaron Kravitch.

Daddy told me that his car was not running and Percy had brought them up and was waiting in the car. As always, they brought me some home-cooked food and my favorite dessert, German chocolate cake. They were giving me the rundown on everybody in general and the people who wanted them to relay a message to me. After I finished eating, Daddy asked if he could talk to me privately in the restroom. This was something else he had done for the first time. I would imagine that my daddy had visited me about twenty times in Reidsville in the year-and-a-half that I was initially in Reidsville, and this was the first time that he had asked to speak with me privately. I knew that if he had not been drinking, he would not have made this request. This made the visit hard for me and had me upset and concerned for awhile. I accompanied him to the restroom and he was crying as he related some things about one of my sisters. As he was wiping his eyes, I put my hand on his shoulder and tried to reassure him.

In the bed next to me was a white guy. He had a legal casebook that he would read sometimes. I wanted very much to see this book, but I knew that most prisoners with legal books do not let other prisoners borrow their books. Also, I had never spoken to this white guy, and he had never spoken to me although my bed was next to his. We were about 2 feet apart and never said one word to each other. But I decided to ask him to see his book anyway. At most, he would say no and I would say okay.

"Could I look at your law book?" I asked.

"Yes, you can. I have been noticing you since you have been here and you seem all right. You don't talk much and you don't bother anyone," said the white guy as he handed me his law book. "I like the way you carry yourself."

The book had a lot of brief statements about the law in Georgia and what was and was not a violation of the law. I turned to the section on justifiable homicides and began to read cases that the Georgia Supreme Court had decided since the late 1800s.

In an earlier case, the court said that "where it is claimed that a homicide was committed under the fears of a reasonable man, it is for the jury, and not for the judge, to decide whether or not the circumstances were sufficient to justify the existence of such fears." Later, the court held that "where, on a trial for assault with intent to murder by shooting, the defense was that the shot was fired under the fear that the person assaulted was about to inflict on the accused an injury amounting to a felony, defendant was entitled to have the existence and reasonableness of his fears determined by the jury in the light of all the circumstances, and it was error to withdraw from the jury the effect of any words or threats which may have accompanied the act of the prosecuting witness." Still later, the court held that "in homicide prosecution, whether words, threats, menaces, or contemptuous gestures together with other circumstances were sufficient to excite the fears of a reasonable man is a question for the jury." Finally, the court ruled that "where killing is claimed to have been done because of reasonable fear in the mind of slayer, threats accompanied by menaces, though not amounting to actual assault, may be sufficient to arouse fears of a reasonable mind that his life is in danger or a felony is about to be perpetrated upon him and motive with which slayer acted is for the jury." Also in this legal casebook was a case which stated that a previous felony against a person may give rise to a reasonable fear and whether a homicide was justified or not was for the jury to decide.

After reading these cases and others, I knew why Kravitch had Drew do what he did. In the very opening statement to the jury, Drew characterized threats on my life as not threats but harassment. That's a big difference. The incident with respect to my watch was characterized as me losing it, not that it was taken from me by gunpoint, which was a felony. No attempt was made to depict actually the scenario in the store, which amounted to menaces and a verbal threat. I was trapped in that store and the door was blocked. A consistent theme in the Georgia decisions was that the jury decides whether certain events could arouse the fear of a reasonable man, but information in my favor was never presented to the jury and the jury was misled and manipulated into a guilty verdict.

On Saturday, as we were getting ready to go to the movie, a prisoner we called Slim whispered to me to be careful where I sat because he heard that there was gonna be a stabbing in the theater. I went, but nothing happened and the movie was okay. But the next day, something did happen. As I was heading out to the yard and was on the walkway, I saw a young guy with a knife partially hidden behind his back. By looking at his face and his eyes, I knew that he was waiting to stab someone. I walked by him, knowing that I had not done anything to him and that he was not waiting on me. Just as I had walked about 5 feet from the guy, I happened to look back because I sensed that the person that he was waiting on was coming. The guy with the knife sprang quickly, pulled the other guy to the floor, stabbed the guy in the back three times very quickly, and walked away without saying a word. It happened so fast that the guy who had been stabbed couldn't do anything to prevent it. He had pleaded for the guy not to stab him anymore. Later, I heard that he had died from some other complications.

Sol Brown was still in Reidsville. On the yard one day, he was teasing a guy named Eddie about Eddie's underwear as Eddie was refereeing a basketball game.

"Eddie is the only person here who is not a sissy that wears briefs," stated Sol. "In Reidsville, only sissies wear briefs."

"Goddamn right I wear briefs. I been wearing them all my life and I don't intend to stop because you motherfuckers laugh about it," responded Eddie. "I know what I am and I'm not gonna let you guys change me."

"Man, the guys use to ride Eddie so hard about those drawers that my side would hurt from laughing," said Sol.

After laughing some more, Sol said that Eddie was lucky to be alive. Like Joseph Bonaparte, Eddie had received the electric chair for raping a white woman. Eddie's head had been shaved in preparation for the execution when the Parole Board commuted his sentence to life imprisonment. Sol said that Eddie was just an hour or two from being executed when the commutation came.

Hulbert was hanging out with Sol, too. Hulbert was another lucky person. Hulbert and someone called Ghost robbed and killed a black pharmacist in Savannah. Actually, it was Ghost who supposedly did the stabbing and the jury gave him the electric chair while giving Hulbert life. One guy told me that he saw Ghost in the funeral home after Ghost had been executed in Reidsville. He had burn marks on his forehead where the contacts had been. This was the last person from Savannah to be executed at Reidsville, but there had been others.

In the 1950s, one black person from Savannah was executed for raping a white woman on Bay Street. Another black person was executed for stabbing a white man to death at a gas station on West Broad Street. The story was that this black guy asked the white man about using the bathroom, but the white man refused. They started arguing and the black man stabbed the white man to death. At most, this was manslaughter, not murder. The black did not leave the scene and come back and he didn't plan it. The white guy probably provoked him, by telling him, "Nigger, pee in your pants."

For some reason, death was on my mind, but I couldn't say exactly why. Perhaps it was hearing Sol talk about Eddie and my thinking about what I had heard about some of the persons from Savannah who had been executed.

Guys from Atlanta talked about their former homeboys who had been executed in Reidsville. One guy killed someone in Atlanta with a hammer and was given the death sentence. When the guards came to get the guy at 10A.M., he refused to go and was fighting the guards. The story was that it took more than 3 hours to get the guy in the chair. This was one of the most talked about executions in Reidsville, and it was ingrained in Reidsville's folklore.

I had a tooth problem and went to the dentist. The dentist told me that the tooth was a wisdom tooth, and I would have to have a specialist from Atlanta pull it. I was told that the dentist comes late in the evening, about seven or eight. The day before the specialist came, I was put in the hospital. Just before going down, I was told that I had to have a shot, which a guard was gonna give me. I was hesitant about a guard giving me a shot in the arm, but I was told that the shot would be given to me in the butt. I took the shot and almost immediately felt like I was floating. I was feeling so good that I paid no attention to the dentist's assistant, an extremely attractive white woman in a white uniform. I had my eyes closed most of the time enjoying the relaxed state I was in. She was putting her finger in my mouth. I was afraid that I might bite her because her finger had a sweet taste. Finally, the dentist came over. He put his hand in, took it out, put it in again, took it out, and put it in again. When he took his hand out the last time, he told me that he was putting gauze in my mouth and for me to bite down. I never felt the tooth being pulled. He also told me that I would get another shot when I returned upstairs to the hospital. I welcomed the shot and slept very well that night.

The eye doctor was not as helpful. There was an extremely long line waiting to see the ophthalmologist. Larry Shank and Brother Samuel were in line waiting, too. We talked about Blue, Cock-A-Red, and JB. Shank stated that he had heard too that anyone who killed either of the three would not be given any more time. Shank said that he had kicked JB's ass once and he might have to do it again.

"Brother, if you have to kill another brother for your own protection, Allah is with you," said Brother Samuel. "I can't understand some of these young brothers. A lot of them come to Reidsville for murder and then they let these guys make them into homosexuals and use them like women. I don't understand it. I also don't understand why the brothers have to prey on the younger brothers. There are plenty of old sissies here. Why don't they use them? Why do they have to destroy the young brothers here?"

"They're predators and vultures," I said.

Changing the subject, Brother Samuel asked what was wrong with my eyes.

"My vision leaves sometimes," I responded.

This was the first time that I had told another prisoner that I had been having eye problems.

"My eyes burn sometimes. I don't want the doctor to do anything but give me some drops," said Brother Samuel. "Do you see that young guy over there?" pointing to a guy about six people over. "They sent him to Augusta for an eye operation, and when he woke up, he found out that they had taken out his eye. The doctor was supposed to operate on the boy's eye, not take it out. The boy happened to get out of bed and was looking under his bandage in the mirror when he found an empty socket. He went into a rage and had to be sedated. Brother Rudolph, don't let them operate on you. Put your faith in Allah."

After waiting about 4 hours in line, a guard came out and said that the eye doctor was leaving. The prisoners who had not been seen would have to come back when the doctor came back in a month and two.

About a week later, I was notified that I was returning to Wayne Correctional Institution. I protested that I had come just to see the eye specialist and had not seen him. After thinking about it a little, I decided to let it go. As Brother Samuel said, I needed to put my faith in Allah.

Chapter 19

As soon as I returned to Wayne Correctional Institution, I could sense the changes in the prison and the atmosphere. I noticed that there was a wooden partition in front of the commodes. Now, prisoners could take a shit without people staring at them. Although it was in the morning, the television was on and there were more prisoners in the dormitory.

With respect to the prison atmosphere, both the prisoners and the guards acted differently. Under the old warden, the guards were more aggressive with prisoners and prisoners were intimidated somewhat. But now, the prisoners acted as if they had more power. They had a more belligerent attitude. The prisoners whom I spoke with were happy with the recent changes in the prison.

I learned that the new warden was Robert Luzier, whom I recognized as a former supervisor at Jackson. His deputy was Brumbelow, and I also remembered him from Jackson. There was another deputy, who looked very effeminate and whom prisoners called Superchicken. He walked with his butt in the air and indeed he looked like a chicken in the face. I was told that one prisoner asked Superchicken if he was a homosexual, but Superchicken refused to answer, appearing shocked at such a question.

After supper, the guards opened the doors and prisoners started walking out.

"Where are they going?" I asked.

"This is free time, another change the warden made. We can go out and play cards in the dining room with other prisoners and go across on the other side to talk in the hall, although we can't go into the other dormitories. We can also use the library," Point explained.

I walked around the mess hall, observing some prisoners playing chess and cards. Many were just sitting and talking.

After a few minutes, I went back to my bed and took out my law book. I had purchased a rather huge legal casebook and had begun to read it. It contained cases in several areas dealing with the Constitution, and I had begun to understand some of the theoretical principles of the law. I also had some other materials that I ordered from the U.S. Government Printing Office. I found all of it to be very interesting reading.

I had decided to file a habeas corpus action in my behalf, although I wasn't confident that I could effect any changes in my situation. I knew that I had a case, but I had learned that right and wrong mean nothing in the legal system. Lawyers, including judges and prosecutors, do not care about what is right, and they protect each other. I knew not to expect anything from the Georgia courts, where I had to file first. A superior court of one county is not likely to disturb a conviction that occurred in another area of Georgia. Also, I didn't expect anything from the Georgia Supreme Court because Aaron Kravitch had campaigned on behalf of one of the chief judge's reelection. I also wasn't confident about the U.S. District Court for the southern district, where I had to file after exhausting my state remedies, because this federal court is based in Savannah and Judge Alexander Lawrence had eulogized Aaron Kravitch in open court after Kravitch's death. If I had any chance, it would occur in the Fifth Circuit Court of Appeals. But I wasn't confident about it either. But I felt that I had to try, and even if I didn't gain any victories in the courts, my emergence in the legal process would help me to do something more positive with my time than involvement in prison activities, most of which were inane and corrosive mentally.

"Damn, Rudolph, you reading again. If you are not writing, something, you reading something. What're you reading anyway?" asked Point.

"I am reading up on the law," I responded.

"You are gonna write your way out of prison, I bet. I have never seen anyone that reads and writes as much as you."

"It keeps me out of trouble and it helps my mind."

I had a lot of time to read because I wasn't working. We would go out on the porch each morning, but not all prisoners went to work. The names of prisoners who were called got on the trucks, and the people who were not called could go back to the dormitory and go to sleep.

I was still trying to get some additional information from the clerk's office in Savannah. I was also sent an order signed by Dunbar Harrison that declared that after my conviction I was a pauper and that my appeal was to be paid for by the county. I immediately recalled Aaron Kravitch telling me that he had appealed my case for free and had not been paid anything. But this was not true. The county paid him. The clerk refused to send me the transcript of my preliminary hearing, which was critical because I could show that the police officers lied in superior court and use it to show that Drew permitted these officers to lie.

I had read that the federal habeas corpus law stated that one condition for receiving a hearing in federal court is that the factual issues were not fully developed in the state courts. Thus, I decided to illuminate in my habeas corpus petition what the testimony was at the preliminary hearing and what it was in superior court. Then, I was gonna allege that the Savannah officials refused to give me a copy of this transcript and that I could show with it that there were outright lies told about the events surrounding my arrest.

After several weeks indoors, my name was called as part of a work detail. I got on the yellow, metal truck with nine other prisoners. After about 30 or 45 minutes of riding on the highway, we came to Blackshear, Georgia. I looked out the top of the truck and could see various billboards.

I learned that riding through towns was a major event. Most of the guys were looking at the women walking down the street. The rule was that we could look, but not holler at them from the vents at the top of the truck. The best part of the ride through town was stopping at a stoplight. Because the truck was higher than cars, we could look down inside cars that were beside the truck. Because many women drove with their dresses or skirts pulled up, seeing women's thighs was a major event for the day. You could hear guys sucking in wind. Anything pleasant to look at involving women was called "scoops." So, guys would talk about catching some scoops on detail. For this reason, most guys didn't mind the work detail.

Someone told me that we were going to the barn first, which was a county maintenance building. I could hear the prisoner driver pouring water into the water can over the ice that had been put in the large empty can as the trucks were being loaded. The driver told the guys on the truck that we were gonna be bumping curbs.

"What is bumping curbs?" I asked.

"You'll see. It is not hard work and you will be able to catch some scoops."

We went in the downtown area of Blackshear and unloaded. The tools were in a bin on the side of the truck and prisoners began taking them out. Some guys were sharping the end of their shovels and others were taking brooms. Looking around I could see some people looking at us, but mostly they were going about their business. The guard was about 15 feet behind us with his shotgun perched on his shoulder and his pistol at his side. When it was time to start, I learned what bumping curbs is. Some guys were using their shovels to pull up grass that had grown between cracks in the side walk and others were sweeping the grass pulled up on the sidewalks and the car curbs. Riding slowly behind us was a dump truck where two people threw the piles of dirt and grass into the back of the truck. The yellow, metal truck that we rode in was further back and the prisoner driver was either sitting in the truck and then driving it to keep behind us as we went down the side-walks or he would stand by the front of the truck and get in periodically to start it and keep up. When we hollered for some water, he would drive it up to the detail.

Some people avoided the detail, but most people didn't. They would walk through the detail as the prisoners stopped working to allow them to pass. This was a big contrast from Reidsville. At noon, we loaded up to go back to the barn for lunch. That meant looking out the windows because other people would be going to lunch too, especially women. At the barn, we would sit under a tree and eat the lunch that was prepared by the prison. Following lunch, we returned to bumping curbs. At about 3:30P.M. or 4P.M., we would stop for the day. Someone asked the guard to tell the driver to ride through the black part of Jesup, Georgia. I was told that if the guard was in a good mood and he thought that we had worked well that day, then we could be rewarded with a ride through Jesup before returning to the prison. As the yellow truck slowly went down certain streets, the guys would be looking for women in hot pants. As we pulled back into the prison, I felt that bumping curbs wasn't too bad, and I was anxious to go back.

We went back the next day to Blackshear and did the same thing. After this job, we began to cut grass along one of the county roads. I learned to use the sling blade, which everyone called a yo-yo. I had seen scenes from the movie, *Cool Hand Luke,* and I remembered the chain gang Paul Newman was on using yo-yo's. We were doing the same thing. Sometimes the rhythm of the work would be interrupted by the spotting of a snake; some guys took pleasure in cutting off its head. One day, instead of cutting grass, we were cleaning out ditches with shovels.

The only good thing about these jobs was that we were out and some guys could beg people that were riding down these roads. Sometime, they would beg for cigarettes and the drivers would throw his pack of cigarettes on the ground. Some guys asked for a cold drink, and one driver, hollering that he had once worked on a road gang, drove to a store and returned with a bag of cold drinks. Sometimes, we would ask the guard to stop at a store and the guys who had money would ask the driver to buy items for them.

Sidewinder, the name that prisoners gave one guard because he walked partly sideways, was very good to work under. He didn't like to walk much. So, we did not have to work very much. Sometimes, we would work only a few hours a day. The warden had indicated that if the guards are too hot, then the prisoners who are working are too hot and should be brought back to the prison. Sidewinder took advantage of this changed policy.

Sidewinder also looked the other way regarding alcohol. One day, a prisoner asked someone he saw on the road to go to the package shop. The guy returned with a bag full of beer and some liquor. The prisoner offered Sidewinder a beer, but Sidewinder refused it. The driver was given one beer, and the rest went on the back of the truck. After we had finished everything, the empty bottle and cans were given to the driver for disposal. Then, we headed back to the prison. Everyone had a buzz going, but we were admonished sternly that we should act normally when we went in the back of the prison for showers. No loud talking and no laughing. Moreover, everyone was instructed to act cool in the dormitory. Everyone did exactly that, and the officials in the prison never knew what occurred that day.

I was not involved in any of the prison programs. A boxing team was started, but I didn't consider myself to be a boxer. There was an AA group, but I didn't think that I needed it. All I did with my spare time was read my law materials and watch television. I was taken off detail for awhile, and I spent all of my time reading. After repeatedly reading cases and the Constitution, I thought that I understood criminal law a little. Although I never received the transcript of my preliminary hearing, I decided to go ahead with my habeas corpus action.

I knew that one of my grounds would be ineffective assistance of counsel, but I was searching for other grounds that might make my petition stronger. After reading about defective indictments in my casebook, I concluded that my indictment was defective. I had learned that an indictment must notify a defendant of what he is being charged with, and the indictment must charge all the essential elements of a crime. Because murder was defined in Georgia as the killing of a human being with malice aforethought, I thought that my indictment was defective because it failed to specify that I had killed a human being.

I tried to explain this point to Larry who had asked me what I was writing.

"I'm gonna allege that my indictment is defective because it didn't charge all the essential elements of the alleged crime. Specifically, it didn't accuse me of killing a human being. It just has a name in the indictment and I am alleging that this is insufficient," I explained.

"Who told you this?" Larry asked.

"No one. This is my conclusion based on what I read. A name is not necessarily a person. Some people name their pets human-like names, like Roy Rogers. In fact, I have read about a race horse that was named Riva Ridge. If an indictment accused someone of killing Riva Ridge, it could be a horse or woman named Riva Ridge. It is a crime to kill animals and people, and the indictment must put you on notice exactly what you are being with committing."

"Damn, you're cold. You are calling the person you killed a horse."

"That's not what I said. I'm not being cold. I'm just arguing the law," I said. "It may not get me anywhere, but it is something to argue."

Larry left, and I continue to draft out my petition in writing. My sister, at my request, had sent me some legal size paper. Because I didn't have access to a typewriter or a copier, I would have to print six copies of everything. But that was okay; I had the time.

I also decided to reargue that I had been searched illegally and the pistol that I had was illegally seized. I remembered that Aaron Kravitch had alleged this in my original appeal to the Georgia Supreme Court, but I was gonna assert that the testimony about a bulge was totally false and this was not a frisk for the officer's protection as the court found. I could prove that there was no bulge with the transcript of the preliminary hearing and the stop-and-frisk decision out of Ohio did not apply. In addition, I was gonna use this issue to attack the job that Drew did. He filed a motion to suppress and then permitted the officers to make up a story about a bulge without any challenge or at attempt at impeachment. This was a sham motion and would definitely be ineffective assistance of counsel.

A young guy out of Atlanta who everyone called Little Larry began talking to me. I had gained a reputation as someone who knew something about the law, and some guys would drift around me and start asking questions or want to talk about their cases. Little Larry had seen me reading my law books and began to ask me some questions.

"The fuckers in Atlanta messed me around. I killed a guy who came at me with a rubber hose that had tape around one end. Those fuckers stated that this was not an offensive weapon, but the dude had it taped for a reason. They convicted me of manslaughter and gave me 20 years. Shit, I shouldn't have gotten that on account of the dude having the rubber hose," Little Larry lamented. "I had someone helping me with a writ in Jackson, and I wondered if you could look at some of my papers that I had filed in Jackson and help me out."

"Sure, go get your stuff," I said.

After Little Larry returned, I immediately looked at his indictment to see if my ideas about my indictment appearing to be invalid was plausible. Little Larry's indictment was worded almost like mine except after the name of the dead person, there was a comma and "a human being" followed by another comma. This buttressed my beliefs that I had uncovered a valid argument in my case.

"I was just looking at your indictment, and it appears to charge all the essential elements of a murder charge," I remarked. "I see that you have already filed a petition. The thing you wanna do is to get into federal court. The state courts are not gonna do a thing. I believe that state court judges have an understanding that they are not gonna disturb the work of another superior court. Also, in this respect, the Georgia Supreme Court is not any better. But you have a good situation in that you are from Atlanta. The federal judges in Atlanta, from what I have read about them, are different and some of them have a sense about right and wrong. I only wished that I could have a federal judge in Atlanta to consider my arguments when I present them, but I have to go the federal court from the southern district. Let me work on this tonight."

I drafted out a petition to the U.S. District Court for the northern district of Georgia and cautioned Little Larry that I wasn't promising that a federal judge would act on it. Later, I was shocked to hear from Little Larry that a federal judge had acted on the petition and had appointed an attorney to file a more formal petition on Little Larry's behalf.

But I never learned if Little Larry eventually received any positive relief. I came in from work one day and was told that Little Larry was in the hole for trying to hit the Deputy Warden. A few days later, he was transferred to another prison.

Some of the white prisoners in the dormitory were shooting drugs. They had a syringe hidden in the dormitory and were mixing water and drugs in the syringe. Shooting up would be done behind the partition that was located in front of the commodes. The warden had put up the partition to allow a measure of privacy and the prisoners were taking advantage of his humanitarianism.

I couldn't figure out why the white guys would shoot up drugs during the time that they did. They would do it early in the morning before going to work or they would do it just before bedtime. After getting hit, they would start spitting up. It seemed to me that these were not the ideal times to get high.

I had decided that I could do without drugs and would not partake in this activity. Only one black guy would shoot up with the white guys, and as a result, he was being shunned by the other black guys.

"Look at that weak excuse for a black man," angrily said Horace, a Muslim. "He's letting those honkies put a needle in his arm. Those are some nasty honkies and he is sharing a needle with them."

I was asked by another guy if I wanted to get high.

"What you have? I don't do anything. If you have some Buck that was made cleanly or some beer or wine, I might be interested," I said.

"I got some Right Guard and Coke," said the guy.

"I beg your pardon," I said in astonishment.

"Right Guard and Coca-Cola."

"No fucking thanks. I have heard of rum and coke, but I have never heard of Right Guard and Coke. Man, that stuff will kill you."

I had learned that some of the guys were buying Right Guard spray in a can from the prison store. They would open the can, pour the contents in a cup, and mixed it with the Coca-Cola. They said that when you pour in the Coke, the cup would shake. One guy was hollering how good it was and I couldn't tell whether he was being frank or exaggerating and putting on a show for the other guys. At one point, he was howling like a dog.

"They must have not heard of Fat Hardy," I said.

"Who is he?" asked one guy.

"He was the guy who made some bad moonshine. It killed a bunch of people and made a lot of other people blind. It was pure poison," I told the guys. "These guys might go blind from drinking this stuff."

The prison clerk who operated the store was remarking how he couldn't keep Right Guard on the shelf and how hygienic some of the prisoners were. However, someone told the warden what the Right Guard was for and it wasn't sold anymore. Instead, the Right Guard was replaced with a roll-on deodorant of another brand that didn't have alcohol in it.

Some of the guys were encouraged to join the Alcoholics Anonymous group in the prison. A few did, but a lot of them joined just for the opportunity to take trips away from the prison. The group returned one night very excited. Apparently, the Alcoholics Anonymous group went to a meeting with a group of female prisoners from another institution. According to reports from the prisoners, the supervision was very lax and the female prisoners gave them some pussy. They said that the women wanted to fuck more than the guys. One black guy said that a white female prisoner offered him some pussy, but he turned her down. He told her that he wanted a black woman. So, the white female fucked another black guy who didn't care about her race.

I finally put together my habeas corpus petition, but I knew that it was not well crafted. I decided to stress repeatedly in it that the law has stated that petitions by prisoner should be construed with unusual liberality so that the spirit of habeas corpus would be upheld. All I had hoped to do was to lay out the facts and hope that someone later on would say that something was amiss. I wasn't expecting anything positive to happen in the state courts, and my only goal was to build a record. Then in federal courts I was gonna request a full hearing.

My case was gonna be heard by Judge Gordon Knox and the person that was gonna represent the state of Georgia was an attorney in Jesup called Jim Zorn. In addition to the habeas corpus petition, I filed two motions. One was for the appointment of counsel, which I knew the judge was gonna deny, and the other was for a subpoena from the judge to order the sending of the transcript of my preliminary hearing. I gave the reasons why this transcript was important and indicated that the officials in Savannah would not send it to me.

The deputy warden took me in handcuffs to the hearing, which was being held in Jesup. The actual hearing was held in an office. There was no court reporter, and the hearing was being taped for subsequent transcription by the court reporter. At first, I was very nervous, but I had read so much that I was citing my grounds and legal support without looking at my petition. Even as I was trying to get comfortable in the chair that was too low (and the back of the chair was too far away), I continued to talk without pausing, except for a few stumbles over some words. I began with the indictment and argued why it was defective. The judge was smiling, but he was denying all my claims. Even after, he said that he was gonna deny my contention, I continued to go back because I wanted to say everything that I had written and build the record as best as I could. At one point, the judge wanted to know if I had done the shooting, but I refused to answer, telling him that I didn't think I should have to answer a question like that. Zorn, then, told the judge that I admitted to the shooting at the trial and that I had pleaded that it was self-defense, but the evidence was that I just walked up to the guy and shot him. I tried to steer them back to the issues in my petition.

I told the judge that the arresting officers radically changed their testimonies at my trial so that the motion to suppress would not be granted and Drew failed to challenge or impeach these officers although the officers gave sworn testimony at my preliminary hearing. Specifically, I told the judge that testimony about a bulge was totally false and was presented for the first time at trial. At the preliminary hearing there was no testimony about a bulge on my person. Also, I told the judge that other details surrounding my arrest were added at the trial and had not been testified to during the preliminary hearing. Zorn, who admitted that he knew Lionel Drew, stated that the issue of what the facts were was decided by the judge and jury. Additionally, Zorn stated that if there was anything in my preliminary hearing transcript that would have helped my motion to suppress, Lionel Drew would have brought it up, and because nothing was said, this proves that the transcript of my preliminary hearing was valueless. I insisted that this was incorrect, and we should have the transcript to see whether my version is correct or whether the state is correct. Zorn stated that this issue was raised in my original appeal and it was decided adversely to me. I responded that this ruling was based on the false testimony by the arresting officers presented at my trial and this testimony was not challenged and allowed to stand.

The only concern from the judge came about when I was testifying about Drew's behavior. The judge was grimacing as I talked about Drew.

I told the judge, but mainly I was speaking for the record, that my parents hired Aaron Kravitch on September 12, 1967 and the next day, he came to introduce himself and to tell me not to appear in a lineup. I stated that I tried to dismiss Aaron Kravitch on December 28, 1967, and saw Lionel Drew for the first time a day later. Drew told me that I couldn't fire Aaron Kravitch because I was a minor. Responding to my complaint that no one had asked me any questions about this case in 3 months, Drew stated that when the time came, someone would be down to talk to me. But no one came. On April 23, 1968, I went to trial and Drew asked me two questions prior to the trial starting. I told the judge that I had two defense witnesses, and no one interviewed these witnesses before subpoenaing them. I told the judge that I didn't know that I was gonna testify at my trial, that Drew never told me. So, I did not know what to expect on cross-examination. I reminded the judge that many defense attorneys advise their clients when the clients are put on the witness stand and are told to wear a suit and tie and advised to watch the jury when testifying. Good defense attorneys also advise clients to answer yes or no to questions and not expand on any questions. But Drew told me nothing. The exchange between us went this way:

The Court: How old is Mr. Drew?

I knew the judge was trying to assess how experienced Drew was.

Mr. Alexander: He is—oh, I don't know. But he has been practicing law a long time.

The Court: He has been practicing law for a long time.

Mr. Alexander: Yea, he wasn't no . . .

Mr. Zorn: He's in the legislature now, or was.

The Court: What age would you say he was? 20, 30, 40?

Mr. Alexander: Sir?

The Court: I say what age would you say he was, approximately?

Mr. Alexander: I would say he was in his late forties.

The Court: Late forties.

I expected Zorn to ask me questions about my contention that I was not interviewed about my case and try to show that I had nothing to say.

Mr. Zorn: I would ask you, Alexander, if he had interviewed you as you say he did not . . .

Mr. Alexander: He did not.

Mr. Zorn: . . . what information could you have given him that he didn't have?

Mr. Alexander: He didn't have anything. How could he have anything if I didn't tell him anything?

Mr. Zorn: Well, what would you have told him?

Mr. Alexander: What had I told him?

Mr. Zorn: What would you have told him had he come down there to the jail to see you?

Mr. Alexander: I would have told him all about the case.

Mr. Zorn: Specifically, what would you tell him?

Mr. Alexander: I would have told him who was in the store at the time and who wasn't. And I would have told him—I could have told him lots of things, potential character witnesses. I could have told him, I could have told him about the time that I was attacked before.

Mr. Zorn: By the same party?

Mr. Alexander: No, not by the same party. But I believe this would have been, it would have had some bearing on the case, because I had been attacked before and I lost sight in one of my eyes because of it, and I pressed charges against the guy. And I think the jury would have been interested in hearing that. I'm not saying that it justified anything, but they should have heard everything that was involved.

I had heard that some state lawyers ask those types of questions and then argue that even if a defense attorney never interviewed a client, that the client couldn't say how he was harmed. But that burden should never be put on a client. A client may have information that he doesn't know is important and it is up to the defense attorney to conduct a proper interview. A lawyer that has a criminal case for 8 months and then waits until the morning of the trial to ask what happened should be disbarred and shot. Zorn acted like I didn't have anything to tell Drew if Drew had interviewed me.

When defense attorneys are representing white clients, almost everything in the clients' backgrounds are gone into. I had read about white adults on trial testifying about events that happened to them in childhood. But my losing an eye was treated as irrelevant even though my eye injury and the subsequent deliberate attempt to maim me further was a major factor in what happened in the store. Georgia law says that the jury is the ultimate decider if events give rise to reasonable fears, which would justify a homicide, but the jury was not allowed to consider everything fully.

I raised the issue of Lionel Drew and Aaron Kravitch lying to me by telling me that I was a minor and couldn't fire Aaron Kravitch. I told the judge that I was legally being tried as an adult, and therefore, I had the right to dismiss an attorney even if my father wanted the attorney. The judge asked me if I contacted Dunbar Harrison to tell Dunbar Harrison that I did not want Aaron Kravitch. When I said I did not contact Dunbar Harrison because I didn't know that I had been lied to, the judge stated that I did not follow the correct procedure.

But I wondered how I could be blamed for not knowing the correct procedures when lawyers are lying to me. I had the right to dismiss Aaron Kravitch, but he and Drew lied and said I couldn't because I was a minor. I believed them. I'm blamed for not knowing, but Drew and Kravitch are not blamed for lying.

I raised the issue of how Drew asked me the question about my watch and that Drew had misled everyone to believe that I simply lost the watch instead of it being taken by the deceased. Zorn told the judge, in effect, that this was my fault because I had testified about the watch, and I didn't say that it was taken for me. The problem was how Drew presented the question to me, and he asked it in a manner that was disadvantageous to me and protective of the dead person. But Zorn and the judge were indicating to me that this was my fault. I guessed it was my fault for not knowing in advance that Drew intended to deliberately hurt me and my fault for not knowing that a defendant is supposed to be distrustful of the defense attorney, in addition to the prosecutors.

White lawyers, and white people, can do niggers any way they want. That's their rule.

I was also amazed that lawyers are always looking for doctors to sue for malpractice and businesses for negligence, but there is much more malpractice and negligence by lawyers than any other group. Lawyers protect each other and their malpractice is hidden.

The judge was denying everything in the hearing and was not indicating that he was gonna take anything under advisement, including my contention of ineffective assistance of counsel. The judge initially stated that he knew Aaron Kravitch. But after grimacing so much as I talked about Drew, he seemed to reverse himself and stated that he was gonna take my petition under advisement and read my trial record. I told the judge that he should read the trial transcript and that he should read the transcript of the preliminary hearing. The judge promised to read the trial transcript, and if he thought it was necessary, he would request the transcript of the preliminary hearing from the Savannah officials and read it too. But I didn't believe him.

The judge was a former prosecutor and went up against Kravitch in a capital case. He was going for the electric chair, but Kravitch convinced the jury not to send his clients to their deaths.

Zorn tried to suggest that I lied about not being interviewed about my case. But they all knew that the jail records would back me up. Visitors, including lawyers, have to sign in and out when they visited someone in jail. There were no attorney visits for me, just as I said. But someone like me can't get those types of records.

On the way back to the prison, the deputy warden, who sat in the office and heard everything, told me that the judge might act in my behalf.

"No, I don't expect him to do anything," I said.

"Don't be so sure. I can't tell you who said this, but after the hearing, someone said that you were quoting the law better than a lot of lawyers," the deputy warden said.

"Thank you for telling me, but I don't expect the judge to do anything," I persisted.

In fact, I began drafting my appeal to the Georgia Supreme Court that same night.

As expected, in a few weeks, the judge denied my application for a writ of habeas corpus. I received a terse one-page order from the Judge Knox that read, in part, "the Court having carefully received the record in said case and determined that the claim of insufficient counsel is without merit and that the claim of illegal search and seizure has been previously determined adversely to petitioner." Judge Knox said nothing in his order about my claim of defective indictment and the little he did write did not elaborate on his finding of facts. That is, what did Drew do that made his representation adequate and how could he find that it was adequate when Drew did not appear and there was no affidavit rebutting my contentions?

I filed a notice of appeal. I asked for a copy of the transcript of my habeas corpus hearing to base my appeal, but I did not get a copy. I expected that too.

Chapter 20

I was summoned to the Deputy Warden Brumbelow's office one Friday after work. As I was walking through the door to the offices, I was wondering what I had done or been accused of doing.

"I've called you to let you know that the department has made you a state-wide trusty. We didn't have anything to do with it and I didn't recommend you for it. This decision was made totally in Atlanta. So, as long as you are in prison, you will be a trusty, unless, of course, it is taken away from you for violating a rule. But as long as you don't violate any rules, you will be a trusty until you get out of prison," Brumbelow explained. "For now you will continue to go out on the regular detail, but shortly you may be driving one of the detail trucks.

"Thank you for letting me know," I said.

As I was returning to the dormitory, I felt this might be the beginning of my luck changing. I calculated that the trustyship would take about 10 years off my life sentence. I had dreaded at one time that I may be in prison for 20 years, despite what the officials down in Savannah said about me getting out of prison in 7 or 8 years. I didn't believe Dunbar Harrison, Aaron Kravitch, or Lionel Drew. I had more confidence now in what the trustyship would do for me.

My brother had given my address to one of my friends from high school and she had begun to write to me. She told me that she had been praying for me for years, every since I was arrested. She said that she had prayed even harder when I was given the electric chair, telling God not to let me die. She said that she was still continuing to pray for me and wanted me to pray too. I had told her that I didn't believe in prayer and had a serious problem with some religious teachings. She told me that she would still continue to pray for me and pray to God for him to help me see the light.

Floyd Green had been transferred to Wayne Correctional Institution too. One day after he had returned from the visiting room, he had some hairs in a paper towel that he claimed came from his girlfriend's pussy. He was allowing some of the guys to smell the hairs and had given one of the guys one of the hairs. I told Floyd that he could sell hairs to the sick prisoners, but I knew that Floyd wanted most of the hairs for himself. When he asked me if I wanted one of the hairs, I politely declined.

In June of 1972, the U.S. Supreme Court made a major ruling in the area of capital punishment. It ruled that the manner in which the death penalty was being implemented was cruel and unusual punishment. The ruling was based on three cases—one from Texas and two from Georgia. The two cases from Georgia were from Savannah, involving William Henry Furman and Lucius Jackson. I mentioned to a couple of guys that I knew that I knew William Henry Furman and he was in the county jail with me and Lucious Jackson was a former cellmate. Later that day, I heard a radio interview with both Furman and Lucious Jackson. Both of them sounded well and I was happy for both of them.

I filed my appeal with the Georgia Supreme Court and its ruling was not a surprise in September 1972 when it came. It stated that the indictment didn't have to state that I killed a human being. With respect to the search and seizure, it stated that the court had already ruled on this issue on direct appeal. Then, it turned to my contention of ineffective assistance of counsel, holding that I was interviewed by counsel, that counsel filed motions on my behalf, that counsel subpoenaed witnesses on my behalf, and that my counsel had successfully appealed my case so that the death penalty was not imposed on me. Thus, in the Georgia Supreme Court's opinion, I couldn't complain about my counsel.

I thought that it was a fraudulent and dishonest opinion. It was not gonna rule in my favor and manufactured reasons to justify its decision. The record clearly didn't indicate that I was properly interviewed about the case. I stressed at the hearing that I was not asked any questions about the case until the morning of the trial and then I was only asked two questions. There was no contradiction to my testimony at the habeas corpus hearing. Yet, the Georgia Supreme Court stated that I had been interviewed. I knew that the court didn't want the official opinion to reflect what I had actually said. If the judges on the court were being honest, they would have said that asking only two questions minutes before a trial is inadequate preparation in a murder defense.

The court did the same thing with respect to my contention that the defense witnesses were not interviewed. The judges said only that defense witnesses were subpoenaed, but my contention was that they were not interviewed and this was improper. I knew that there wasn't one law school in the country that taught law students that it is proper to subpoena witnesses without interviewing them. It is malpractice to subpoena witnesses and wait until they testify to learn if they have anything useful to offer the defense. The judges on the Georgia Supreme Court, as well as Judge Knox, knew this was improper. But the court didn't state in its opinion that I had contended that defense witnesses were not interviewed. If they were being honest, they would have said that there was nothing wrong or improper about subpoenaing witnesses without talking to them first. That was my argument. Their discussion was misleading. It suggested that I made a vague, unspecific complaint about a lawyer, and they were creating a record that cited all these wonderful things Drew did for me.

Finally, the court stated that a successful death penalty appeal can't be viewed unfavorably towards the defense attorney. But the judges knew and I knew that preparation for trial is the key to effective assistance of counsel. A lawyer who sits on his ass and does nothing in a trial can't be said to have done a good job when the U.S. Supreme Court makes a five-to-four decision a month after the trial which resulted in the eventual reversal of the death sentence.

Three months before the Georgia Supreme Court ruled, the U.S. Supreme Court invalidated all death sentences in the United States in the Furman case. What the court was telling me was that if a defense lawyer in a capital case in Augusta, Georgia engaged in malpractice, this lawyer would be shielded because of what the U.S. Supreme Court had done in a Savannah case involving Furman. If the Augusta prisoner filed a habeas corpus action complaining of ineffective assistance of counsel, the Georgia Supreme Court would tell him that because he was not executed, he can't complain about his counsel, although the Augusta counsel had nothing to do with the Furman case. But I really didn't expect anything fair and rational from this court.

I became unhappy when Warden Luzier was demoted and transferred to another prison because some prisoners who were out on a trip escaped and kidnapped a soldier and the soldier's wife. Some of the prisoners, including me, were taken to the warden's house to move his furniture on a truck. When we were directed to take the furniture out of the Warden daughter's bedroom, the Warden directed his daughter to follow us to the truck as we carried out a chest. I whispered to the guy that the wardens daughter had followed us to ensure that we didn't go into the chest to steal some of her underwear.

Unknown to the prisoners, Warden Luzier had instructed the guards not to shoot any prisoner that tried to escape. The guards could shoot over the prisoners' head, but not shoot to hit them. He said that he preferred to catch them rather than for them to get shot. The warden was particularly concerned with a guard transferred to the prison from Northern Georgia. This guard had shot a prisoner during an escape attempt from a detail. The word among the prisoners was that the guard had killed the prisoner, but I knew from reading the Atlanta newspaper that the prisoner didn't die. He used his own shotgun, rather than the state's gun, and his gun had a longer barrel. Most prisoners were afraid of this guy and called him Crazy Jack.

I didn't think that the prisoners knew that they were losing a very humane guy in Luzier, and they were the cause of him leaving. Here was a man who treated prisoners like human beings and was as fair as fair could be. But the prisoners didn't appreciate it and took advantage of his humanitarianism.

Luzier's replacement was a warden from Waycross. Some of the staff were talking about the new warden extolling his deeply religious views. They also said that he had a master's degree.

I knew immediately that I wouldn't like the new warden because people kept talking about how religious he was. This didn't mean anything to me because I knew some religious people that were no damn good. But I wasn't the only one. No prisoner liked the new warden. The new warden was afraid of prisoners and never walked around prisoners in the mess area, like Luzier frequently did. The new warden stayed in his office. In the evenings, he would ride his bicycle with a pistol in his pocket. If he saw a car riding down the road, he would immediately turn back home. No prisoner respected him. The new warden reversed Luzier's policy about not shooting escaping prisoners. He told the guards to shoot any prisoner that tried to escape. On top of that, his wife was ugly. That was one awful-looking white woman. Her eyes were crossed and all the prisoners talked about her looks. No one said anything about wanting to fuck her. That's bad when prisoners don't want to fuck a woman.

During church one night, a black preacher came and told the prisoners that if they accepted the Lord, they could leave prison that night. The guard who was standing in the doorway was laughing at the preacher and later told the new warden what the preacher had said.

I told the guys that this preacher wouldn't be back for saying such a blasphemous thing. Everyone knows that the white folks control the prison. They decide who goes to prison and for how long. The Lord doesn't have any say in who gets out. That is the white man's decision, not the Lord's.

I was working mostly around the prison now with some other trusties. We decided one day to make some buck. We couldn't get any yeast. So we used bread. We had some peaches and put them and the bread in a gallon container and punched holes in the lid. Then, we put it in some bushes, but made sure that the sun could hit it. After 3 days, it was ready. We poured off the mixture, being careful to keep out the peaches and bread. Then, we began to drink it. It was quite tasty and gave a nice mellow buzz.

We were around the front of the prison, near a barrow on the side of the prison in which trash was burned. I happened to look inside the barrow and saw some letters that were partially burned. One was a letter that a prisoner had written to officials in Atlanta and had mailed it secretly without sending it through the front office. The letter had been stamped in Atlanta and sent back to the prison, so that the new Warden would know who sent it. The letter complained about things going on in the prison and promised to tell everything. I called some of the guys over to read this snitch letter and told them to watch out for this guy. One of the games that some prisoners play is to call someone else a snitch or proclaim how black they are and how much they hate white people, while they are trying to tell everything they know to white people. As a result, I have always been suspicious of some guys who project an image of militancy or who continuously talk about snitches. Sometimes, it's a front.

I was told one Friday that I would be driving a truck on Monday. I spent the whole weekend thinking about the gears in the truck. I had learned to drive an automatic and had never driven a stick shift. On Monday, I, along with the other drivers, were called out. I was given the keys to a truck that had a wooden body and a door in the back for prisoners to climb in. It looked just like the truck in the Paul Newman's movie, *Cool Hand Luke*. Another driver had to show me how to start the truck. It had a starter in the floor. When I got it started, I started driving it to the back of the prison. As I changed from second to third gear, I could handle it. I backed up the truck and filled the large can in the back with ice and put the lunch in the cab of the truck. Ten prisoners were put in the truck and I locked them in with three locks on the back. When the guard, who had only been at the prison for a few weeks, got in, he immediately told me what my job was.

"Your job is to open the back door when I say so," said the guard, holding his shotgun straight up.

The guard was sweating already and he had a strong body odor. I knew that he was nervous.

"I can handle that," I said.

We went to the barn in Jesup, and I filled up the can with water from a hose. We left after a few minutes and the guard told me where to drive. He told me that we would be cutting grass. When we got to the spot, I stood and waited as he went to the back of the truck and then began to back up about 15 yards. The guard hollered for me to open the door. After unlocking the three locks, I let the men out and locked the locks on the door. The guys got their sling blades and went to work. As they went down the highway, I followed them in the truck. When they got their first break that morning, I drove the truck up so that they could get a drink. When they started working again, I sat on the hood of the truck watching them work. We had lunch, and after lunch, they went back to work. At about 4 o'clock, the guard called me to tell me to load them up. I unlocked the locks and then locked the men in.

"Well, we done well. You didn't wreck and I didn't lose any of the men."

I thought that this was a pretty good job and I knew that this was much better than cutting grass.

I had my first problem with the new warden over my subscription to *Jet* magazine. He had the guard tear out the centerfold picture of the woman in a bathing suit, which was a regular feature.

"That son-of-a-bitch is tearing out the picture of the woman in the bathing suit," I said in astonishment.

"The warden knows how oversexed you niggers are and a picture of a woman in a bathing suit is trouble," someone said laughing.

"You're not looking at a white woman. Damn, he doesn't even want you to look at your own black woman," someone else commented.

"Why would he do that?"

"The warden is trying to lay his hang-ups about sex and women on us," someone else said. "Rudolph, don't let him get away with this. Fight him about this," another prisoner urged.

"No, I'm not gonna fight him about this. One has to pick issues to fight at times and I don't feel this is a good enough issue. If he and I tangle, I want it to be over something substantial. I'll just write to *Jet* and change the address to my parents' house. I'll stop getting them," I said. The fellows were more upset about it than me. I shared my magazines with them and they liked the woman in the bathing suit. I liked her too but I wasn't gonna fight with the warden over them.

I began taking books out on detail to read. While the prisoners were working, I was sitting in the truck reading. I was reading the *Godfather,* and it made an impression on me. But unlike most prisoners who liked the gangsterism in the *Godfather,* I was impressed by the discussion of them trying to keep drugs only in the black community. I had never used any drugs. They were in the prison but I didn't use any of them.

"Hey you, the guard up there wants you to drive the truck up," said a man in a pickup truck.

I was so into reading the *Godfather* that I had forgotten about the work detail. Putting the book down, I looked up and couldn't see the detail at all. I started the old truck and drove it up to the detail, which was about half a mile away around a curve. When I got there, the guard didn't say anything, but some of the prisoners were staring at me. There was only one prisoner on the detail who would joke with me. His name was Alonzo and he was out of Atlanta. I knew him from Reidsville. Everyone called him "Big Man." I just called him Alonzo.

"Rudolph, I need to teach you about your job. We out here working in the hot sun. You are supposed to make sure we have a cold drink of water when we want it," said Alonzo.

"I didn't know that was my job. When I first drove this truck, I was told that my job was to only open the locks when I was told to open them. The guard asked me if I could do that. After thinking about it for several seconds, I told him that I thought I could handle that job," I said.

Later that day back in the prison, Alonzo came over to continue complaining about how I was doing my job.

"Rudolph, the boys want me to talk to you about your driving. You are driving backwards. You leave this prison headed for the barn like a bat out of hell. You have that old truck wide open. You do this because you're trying to get us to work as quickly as possible. Then, on the way back to the prison, you slow poke, going 25 miles per hour. Everything on the road is passing us. This is backward. You are supposed to go 25 miles per hour in the morning and on the way back to the prison, put the peddle to the floor," Alonzo charged.

I knew that he was joking but he was a little serious.

"You know good and well that the guard tells me how fast or how slow to drive," I said. "I drive slowly in the afternoon because he lets you guys stop work early and he doesn't wanna get back to the prison too early."

"I also wanna talk to you about how you turn the truck around. When you turning around, you are turning wrong. You pull the front of the truck off the highway and the back of the truck is exposed on the highway. What if a tractor-trailer comes along and hits us? You are supposed to back up the truck in a way that we are off the highway," Alonzo charged.

"If I did that, I would be putting myself in danger. If this truck is gonna be hit, I rather the back is hit than the front," I said jokingly.

"I knew you don't care about us," Alonzo said.

"If you keep messing with me, I am gonna tell the guard what you and Dirty Red are doing on the detail," I said. "I know what game you two are playing. You and Dirty Red worked extremely hard, trying to impress the guard. There is no sense in someone working that hard. You sweat so profusely that your pants look like you took a piss in them. I believe that you have trained your body to sweat like that in order to impress the white man that you are a hard working nigger. The white man likes to see a hard working nigger. You and Dirty Red are ingratiating yourself to the white man by putting on this act that you are hard working. I know goddamn well what you two are doing," I said.

Alonzo starting laughing.

"I want a break like you. I have been in prison three times and I have never had a break like you have. I wanna be a trusty. I believe that you have made a deal with the white man. He doesn't give any nigger a break, unless you tell something to him."

"I don't have anything to tell," I said. "I have a friend from high school who is writing to me and she has been telling me that she has been praying for me every since I was arrested. Maybe it's working. They say that when you are carrying a heavy burden that the Lord can lighten your burden. Maybe that's it. Maybe the Lord has lightened my burden," I speculated.

"Shit, you have done something to lighten your own burden and I believe that you have told something," Alonzo charged.

"I ought not to tell you this, but the guard talks about you and Dirty Red all the time. He says that you two are his best workers and sometimes, he would say, 'Look at Big Man and how hard he is working.' If you keep messing with me, I'm gonna tell him that it is a game. If I see you fall out tomorrow and they are calling for some water for you, I'm gonna pretend like I can't start the truck," I joked. "I tell you what, when I leave here, I am gonna recommend that you take my place. Would that make you happy?"

"Damn right."

We both laughed.

Besides Alonzo and Dirty Red working to impress the guard, they also solicited the guard's opinion about issues that were being argued on detail. The guard would act like the U.S. Supreme Court. They would ask him who was right and the guard would decide the issue and say who was right. But the guard was always wrong. He had less than a high school education and didn't know shit. Once the guard told the guys that the government sets the price on everything sold in this country. I told the guys on the detail that was illegal to sell something below cost, but merchants can sell their goods for whatever price they wanted. The guys on the detail said I was wrong and asked the U.S. Supreme Court to decide who was right. I was overruled and told that everything in America that is sold is priced by the U.S. Government and it has always been this way. I shut up after this ruling, knowing that the guard would become an enemy if I insisted. After another day of a ridiculous ruling from the U.S. Supreme Court, I asked Alonzo why he continued to ask this son-of-a-bitch questions that brought ridiculous answers. Alonzo told me that was another part of his game—make the white man think that he knows everything, and you really needed his wisdom.

As a group of us were sitting around a table talking one evening, someone asked why it was that all the truck drivers, except one, had life sentences for murder. I decided to listen and not participate in this discussion.

"The reason why is that you thieving motherfuckers can't be trusted. The prison authorities know that there are some motherfuckers on the street that deserve to be blown away. There are some dirty motherfuckers out there, and some people understand why these people are killed. All they do is fuck other people over until they fuck the wrong person. A lot of free people will tell you that if their families were harmed and they got a chance to kill the motherfuckers who did it, they would do it. Some people have gone out to kill a dirty motherfucker but didn't find him. That is the only reason why some of them are not in prison. They simply couldn't find the low-life. Then, there are some backstabbing motherfuckers that deserve to die too. So, just because someone is in for murder doesn't mean that he is a bad person. Killing some people is righteous. You thieves and rapists can't be trusted and that is why there are few of you who are trusties," explained one of the trusties.

"Do you agree with that, Rudolph?" another person asked.

"I have a rule of not commenting on topics like this. You never know who is listening and who is waiting to go tell the warden something," I said.

Later, an issue came up in which I was willing to challenge the new warden. I had ceased my subscription to *Jet* over the bathing suit without a word, but the warden was now going too far.

I had submitted my federal habeas corpus petition to the U.S. District Court. While waiting on a decision, my sister mailed me a box containing some legal paper and other items. They gave me the other items but not the paper. I wanted to know why the office kept my paper.

"I would like to talk to the warden. Is he still here?" I asked the guard at the door.

"Yeah, he's still here. Wait a second."

I waited at the door that separated the mess hall from the offices. After a few seconds, the guard returned to the door."

"The warden wants to know what you want."

"Tell him that I need to talk to him about the legal paper that my sister sent me and that he is refusing to give to me."

I waited a few more seconds as the guard went back to the warden to relay my message.

"The warden said that you can't have the legal paper. You don't have a typewriter. So, you don't need to have lineless paper."

"Please tell the Warden that I need that paper to prepare legal petitions."

I waited some more as the guard went back to the warden.

"The warden said you still can't have it."

I didn't say anything and just walked back to my dormitory. I told some of the prisoners back in the dormitory about what had just happened.

"The warden ain't no damn good. That shit-eating motherfucker," one of the prisoner said.

"The warden has a master's degree. He knows that if he lets you have paper without lines, the next thing you are gonna want is pencils with no erasers. Then, you become confident and think that you are as good as a white man when you are writing on paper with no lines and using pencils with no erasers," someone else said.

"What are you gonna do?"

I didn't say anything, but I knew what I was gonna do. I let the issue of *Jet* go. Now, he is pulling this kind of shit. I know how to deal with dirty, arrogant white folks like him.

I told the guard that I was going to be writing a letter to a federal judge and I intended to seal the letter. I hinted to him that anyone in the office who opened the letter would be in serious trouble.

After I wrote the letter, I sealed it and gave it to a guard to mail. A few days later, a guard called me to the bars and handed me the paper.

I heard that that the federal judge had called the warden. I knew the warden would be angry, but it was all his fault. I tried to talk to him about it. In the letter, I tried to be nice. I told the judge what the problem was and to please contact the warden to tell the warden that he can't interfere with what I was doing and that I was within my rights.

Later, the deputy warden said something to me that I didn't like. In a letter home, I casually mentioned how some people don't know how to talk to other people or treat other people. As an example, I alluded to an incident with the deputy warden that was unnecessary. The Warden asked me to come to his office to discuss this letter.

"What do you mean by writing to your family and getting them upset?" the Warden asked.

I knew he didn't give a damn about my family.

"I didn't think that I had said anything bad. I just mentioned in passing that I was verbally attacked when it wasn't justified," I responded.

"You know, you have been given a break," the warden said, staring at me intensely.

"What do you mean?" I asked.

"You know what I mean. I'm gonna mail your letter, but I don't want you upsetting your parents and having them calling the department in Atlanta and saying that we are mistreating you."

"Is that all?"

"Yes, you can go."

On the way back to the dormitory, I pondered what he meant by the break that I have. First, I had a death sentence and the good white people spared my life. Moreover, the good white people have made me a trusty, and I don't have to work in the ditch anymore.

They had made me a house nigger and I was no longer a field nigger. So, I should smile all the time, be happy all the time, and accept whatever happens to me.

Then, I started considering all the people who had given me breaks and how I was so ungrateful. First, Lawrence Williams gave me a break. He only caused me to lose the sight in one eye and not both. Furthermore, he gave me a break by not cutting my jugular vein. Second, the Tornadoes stated that they had given me a break. They only fucked me up a little and left me breathing the first time. Third, Kravitch, Dunbar Harrison, and Lionel Drew gave me a break too. Fourth, the prison system had given me a break, which the warden was administering. All these breaks I have been given but I was an unappreciative nigger.

The warden, as I knew he would, finally struck back at me. As I was walking out the gate with the other trusties to work around the prison, a guard told me that I had a new job and for me to come back.

"The warden wants you to work inside the fence. Your job is to wash out these four trashcans every morning. You go in for lunch when the other guys go in and then you come back out until the first road detail comes in. Then, you can go back into the dormitory," explained the guard.

I washed out the cans, which took me about ten minutes, and then I sat down on the edge of concrete porch. After a couple days of this, one of the guys on the detail asked me why was I always inside the fence.

"The warden changed my job."

"I told you to leave that law alone. The white man don't want a nigger studying the law. The law is for white people, not niggers. You're are trying to act intelligent, and intelligence is for white people. Then, on top of that, you go over the warden's head and made him give you your legal paper. Now, he is paying you back. He got you in jail now. You're already in prison and now you are in jail. What are you gonna do?" said Alonzo.

"Nothing, this isn't an issue that I need to fight and I don't think that I could win it anyway. A prison warden is not supposed to interfere with a person filing a legal case and certainly is not supposed to retaliate against someone. I tried to talk to him about that paper, but he refused to even discuss it with me. After the federal judge told him to give me that paper, instead of admitting that he was wrong, he is trying to make me wrong. In his mind, I did something wrong to him. White people get mad when you don't let them fuck you over. They believe that they have the right to fuck over any nigger, any day of the week and any time of the day. If you say no, treat me fairly, white folks think you are doing something wrong. They want you to lay down and take everything, all the time. I saw that in Savannah and now I see here."

Alonzo took this as a another opportunity to joke with me.

"I had always wondered how someone like you got in prison. Now I know. You got a hard head. Those boys told you not to come on their side of town, but you went anyway, saying you had a right. The warden told you off the record to leave that law alone, but you wouldn't, saying again that you have some rights. I bet your parents tell you all the time, not to let your head be hard," Alonzo speculated.

In a way he was right.

A new state-wide furlough program was started for trusties. Trusties that had served a certain portion of their time were eligible for a 36-hour pass. Prisoners with life sentences were eligible after they had served 5 years, and I qualified. The first furlough had been set for Thanksgiving, and there was one planned for Christmas. Believing that it was an either/or proposition, I decided to apply for the Christmas furlough.

In November 1972, the federal judge denied my writ and rejected my request for a hearing. In addition, the judge ruled that I was not entitled to a certificate of probable cause to appeal to the Fifth Circuit Court of Appeals. The federal judge, newly appointed to the Southern District, used a case that I cited justifying a hearing for me to rule that I was not entitled to a hearing. I was surprised by the judge's misunderstanding or misreading of the case that I cited.

In *Townsend v. Sain* (1963), the U.S. Supreme Court formulated a set of definitive standards for federal judges to follow in deciding whether to grant a prisoner a hearing in federal court after the prisoner had exhausted state remedies. Particularly, *Townsend* said that federal courts must grant evidentiary hearing under the following circumstances: (1) if the merits of the factual dispute were not resolved in the state hearing. Thus, if the trial court believed facts which showed a deprivation of constitutional rights and yet erroneously concluded, that relief should be denied, a hearing must be held; (2) if the state's factual determination is not fairly supported by the record as a whole; (3) if the fact finding procedure of the state court was not adequate to afford a full and fair hearing and to ascertain the truth; (4) if there is a substantial allegation of newly discovered evidence; (5) if the material facts were not adequately developed at the state hearing for any reason not attributable to the inexcusable neglect of the petitioner; and (6) if for any reason it appears that the state trier of fact didn't afford the habeas corpus applicant a full and fair hearing.

In the attorney general's response to my petition, the person filing was reaching for any and everything to persuade the federal judge to reject holding a hearing for me. He talked about federal and state's relations requiring that the federal court not interfere. This person even stated that my rehabilitation was being hindered by my refusal to stop fighting this case. What a joke! To the contrary, it was helping me.

I filed an appeal to the Fifth Circuit Court of Appeals, seeking to overturn the federal judge's refusal to grant a certificate of probable cause.

I had been inside the fence for almost 2 months now, washing out my three or four cans. The weather was getting cooler and I couldn't read or sleep. I had seen the warden a few times looking over at me inside the fence when he was driving his pickup truck to the back of the prison. I knew that he was probably saying to himself how he had fixed this smart-ass nigger. But I wasn't bothered by him. I had him pegged the first day. I knew that he was not any good. One of the prisoners who was in the hole was cussing the warden out, calling him a Klanman and telling him any and everything. The warden was just staring at the prisoner and was keeping a good distance. I told some guys that the warden was trying to use his master's degree to assess what was wrong with this criminal nigger. I looked over at the warden as he drove his truck from around the back. I sensed that he was trying to provoke me into something that would permit the Department of Corrections to take away my trustyship. But putting me inside the fence wouldn't provoke me. He had to do more than that.

Chapter 21

My furlough for Christmas was approved. Actually, the furlough was a few days before Christmas, but I was not about to quarrel with it. I contacted my family and told my dad to bring me some clothes and what time to pick me up.

There were about four of us going on furlough. One guy had been rejected because he came back late from his Thanksgiving furlough. The warden called the group that was leaving the next day into the office and told us that we had to notify the sheriff in our county when we arrived.

Larry Hunter, although he was now a trusty, could not go because he did not have the minimum of 5 years that a lifer must have and he was quite despondent about it. We tried to cheer him up and told him that he would go later.

Later that evening during free time in the mess hall, Glenn Jenkins was hanging around me trying to tell me something but not knowing what to say. Glenn and I went to Richard Arnold High School together. In Reidsville, Glenn was pussy and he was being fucked here in Wayne Correctional Institution. Although Glenn knew that I knew what he was doing, I never mentioned it or brought it up. We would play bridge against each other and talk about high school basketball back in Savannah. Sometimes, we would argue over sports, but I never held it against him what he was doing, although I didn't approve of it.

Some of the guys in Wayne who knew Glenn often asked me about him. I always said that it was Glenn's business. I was asked if it was true that Glenn had been sold in Reidsville. I told them that I heard that he had. At one time, Glenn's War Daddy had bet Glenn's ass to cover a two-pack-cigarettes bet during a gambling game. When the War Daddy lost, he sent the winner to Glenn and instructed Glenn to give the guy some ass. Glenn did. Later, I heard that Glenn's War Daddy sold Glenn for two cartons of cigarettes. One of the guys said that if all he was worth was two cartons of cigarettes that he would cut his own throat. One day I recalled that at Reidsville some of the guys were talking about how well Glenn played basketball, but Honey said that anyone who was as weak as Glenn wasn't worth a damn regardless of how well Glenn could play ball.

Now, Glenn was staring at me and wanting to ask me not to tell anyone in Savannah that he had been fucked in the ass in Reidsville and was being fucked here now. I could clearly sense what he wanted. But Glenn couldn't bring himself to start that conversation because I had never discussed his personal business with him. I didn't reject him and I talked with him. All I liked to do with him is discuss sports, including high school basketball in Savannah. For sure, he knew that I didn't want any of his ass.

I decided that I was not going to help him bring up this subject. I suspected that if I had told him that he seemed like he wanted to ask me something but he didn't seem like he knew how to bring it up, that he would bring it up. But I wasn't going to help him. He had to bring it up first before I would say anything. When free time was over, Glenn had not touched that topic.

I could leave at 6 A.M. and had to be back by 6 P.M. the next day. My dad was early. I changed clothes and followed him outside. It was a good feeling to be temporarily free, even if it was just 36 hours.

My parents had moved back on 31st Street and moved in the house downstairs. When I was arrested we were living upstairs; now my parents were living downstairs. The house had been bought by a relative of one of my daddy's friends and this friend was managing the property as well as some others.

When we got home, I hugged my mom tightly, who had just finished cooking breakfast. So, my daddy and I sat at the table and began to eat. My mom kept wanting to give me food. She wanted to make sure that I had enough, and she was standing over me like a protective mother. As we were drinking coffee, I could not help but remember the anguish they had experienced 5 years ago. I had to reach deep inside to keep from crying.

"I could have come home during Thanksgiving, but I thought that it was either one or the other," I said.

"We just happy to have you here," Mom said as she put her hand on my shoulder. "A lot of people have asked about you and they always said how terrible it was what happened to you. I hope you can see some of them before you have to go back."

"I hope so. I need to go and call the sheriff's office," I said.

I got the telephone book and got the sheriff's number. I told the person who answered the telephone who I was and how long I would be in Savannah.

I talked to Momma some and then Daddy was ready to leave. Daddy told me that he was going to take me to see my brother, Willie, who lived on the east side with his wife. He had married his girlfriend.

As we were riding on the east side, Daddy began to tell me about my brother.

"Your brother has really changed. He is not the same person that you remembered," Daddy said.

I didn't say anything. I just listened to him. Within a few minutes, he parked the car on Habersham street. As I followed him to a house, I was looking around to see if everything looked the same to me. Savannah had not changed much since I was gone. After knocking on the door for awhile with no one answering, we left.

Daddy continued to grumble about Willie and that he should have been home, knowing that I was coming home and knowing that I was only going to be in Savannah for a day.

"Since we are on the east side, we are going to stop at Mrs. Caldwell's house," Daddy said.

I looked over towards Daddy's pocket, and I could see that he had an outline of a gun in his pocket. Within a few minutes, we were on East Duffy. I was trying to remember the last time that I was at this house. I looked over at the corner of East Duffy and East Broad Street and recalled that many of the Tornadoes used to hang out there, including the dead person.

My Daddy had always continued to go over to Mrs. Caldwell's house. He would stop by and talk. When he visited me in prison, he would tell me sometimes that Mrs. Caldwell asked about me and asked how I was doing.

"Who is that young man you have with you, Roe?" Mrs. Caldwell asked. "You'll have a seat."

"You don't know him. I just stopped by to see how old folks like you are doing. Why you keep looking at him? You don't know him, I told you."

"I was just looking at him. Most of the time when you stop by, you come by yourself. You don't generally have anybody with you. That why I was looking at this man," Mrs. Caldwell stated. "He isn't saying very much."

"Well, today, I have somebody with me," Daddy said. "And he don't have to say much. I can do the talking for both of us."

I finally decided to say something, sensing that Daddy had had his fun with Mrs. Caldwell.

"Mrs. Caldwell, this is me, Rudolph," I said.

"Oh my God," Mrs. Caldwell said standing up and coming towards me. "I didn't recognize you. Thank God! Praise the Lord!" she shouted at she began to hug me.

She kept hugging me and praising the Lord so loudly that her other children were coming up front to see what the commotion was. I recognized Brenda and Liz. Mrs. Caldwell acted as if she wasn't going to let me go. After a few minutes, which seemed much longer, she let me go.

I sat back down and explained to her that I was on a furlough and would be in Savannah a day and I would be gone tomorrow. I asked about her other children, including Beulah and Julia. I asked about Blue.

After a few more minutes, Daddy told her that we had to go because we had some more people to see.

Mrs. Caldwell hugged me again and I told her that I may be back in Savannah for another furlough during the Easter holiday.

Next, we stopped by Percy and Francis' house. They looked the same as before. Before I left, Percy took out his wallet and gave me 20 dollars. We went by my Aunt Bertha's house and she hugged me too. Then, we went out to Willie Rhodes and Manda's house. He also gave me some money.

I knew that Daddy was taking me by all the people who had been supportive of me and who were friends of the family.

I could sense too that this was a happy moment for Daddy because he had thought that he might die while I was in prison.

When we got back home, my brother Willie had called and left a number for me. I called him back and talked with him for awhile. He told me that he would be over shortly.

Momma told me that she wanted me to meet Pearl, who lived upstairs. Momma went to the door and asked me to come to the door. Momma introduced me as her big baby to Mrs. Pearl. I told her I was glad to meet her and Mrs. Pearl reached in her pocketbook and handed me a few dollars.

My brother Willie Lee came over and I accompanied him to his house on Habersham. As we were riding over, he was telling me about Daddy and how differently Daddy acted now. He told me how he had come to leave home.

I just listened and didn't say anything. I discovered that they were just barely speaking to each other, and I needed to do something about it before I left.

Willie Lee showed me a suit that Joanne had made for him and then told me that they thought that she was pregnant but she wasn't. After talking a little, he and I went back to my parents' house.

I spoke with Momma some more, trying to converse with her as much as possible. My sister Cora was there and they were telling me about people in the neighborhood and what they were now doing. Connie, who used to live next door to us, dropped by. When I saw her last, she was living a very sheltered life. But now she seemed to be a little fast. Later, my oldest sister Mildred and her husband Louis dropped by. My brother had told me that he and Louis were going to take me out later that night.

My brother wanted me to meet his in-laws, who lived in Frazier Homes. So, my brother, Daddy, and I went over to Frazier Homes. As we approached Joanne's parents house, I immediately recognized the house directly across the court because Pam used to live there.

I had taken Pam to the drive-in and when I went to pick her up, her mother wanted to see my driver's license, declaring that my voice was too deep to be a 16-year-old. It felt good reminiscing because this happened my senior year in high school, and at that time everything was going well until Lawrence cut me 3 months later in January and started my descent into the legal system.

"Look at Willie's brother, they look like twins," said one of Joanne's sisters.

"Oh, they sure look just alike," said a woman who was introduced to me as Joanne's mother. She reached for her purse and gave me 3 dollars.

We talked some more and then we went back to the house. I went over to Mildred's house and waited for Louis to wash and change clothes. When I went back to my parents' house, my momma had dinner ready and had cooked all of my favorite foods.

After awhile, my brother Willie, Louis, and I went out. I told them that I didn't want to go any place where there might be trouble. The first place they took me was a place that was called the Purple Plum on Ogeechee Road. When I walked in, it seemed that all the guys were dressed like Superfly. In the background playing was Stevie Wonder's "Superstitious." I recognized Esteen Myers, who looked the same as always. A guy came up to me and hugged me.

"Oh man, it so good to see you, Rudolph. I thought that we had lost you."

"At one time, I thought that I was gone too," I said.

I looked at the guy, trying to recognize him, but I could not place him. I turned to my brother and asked him who that guy was.

He laughed at me and told me that it was Joe Dobbs, who used to live on the corner of Anderson and Barnard Street. I looked at him again, trying to reconcile the picture of him now with what I remembered from years ago. I realized that some people that I knew would look the same to me and some wouldn't. I knew that I was much bigger now than I used to be: I weighed about 200 pounds. When I was arrested, I believed that I had weighed about 165 pounds.

I had a few beers at the Purple Plum and then we left. My brother told me that he was looking out for some of his old girlfriends because one of them might give me some pussy before I had to go back.

Then, we went on the east side to a bar near Oglethorpe Street. As soon as I walked in, I saw Point Jackson, who came up to me to shake my hand.

"Goddamn it, I knew it. I knew you were going to get out. I kept saying that Rudolph is going to get out because he was always writing something or reading something. How you doing? How are the fellas doing in Wayne Correctional?" asked Point.

"Well, I'm not out yet. I have a 36-hour furlough, and I have about 16 more hours before I have to return. Wayne is a little different now that the warden is the warden. Larry was rejected for a furlough and probably will not be eligible for 2 more years."

As Point and I were talking, Point went into his pocket and pulled out a roll of bills. He pulled off a 20 dollar bill and gave it to me.

I introduced Point to my brother and my brother-in-law.

"You just missed Honey. He was here a few minutes before you walked in. You should see Honey. All he wears now is suits."

A few minutes later, Honey walked up. He was high and we began to talk. He told me to tell Larry that he stomped that white guy for Larry. Honey took 20 dollars out of his pocket and gave it to me.

I introduced my brother to Honey. We talked awhile outside the bar and finally we left. It was close to midnight, and I was feeling a little high. I told my brother to take me home, but he was a little apologetic that he had not found any girls for me. I told him that was okay, and I had enjoyed myself anyway. On the way home, I told him about Honey down in Reidsville and

Wayne Correctional Institution. I told him about some of the stories about Honey. Honey was one of the few guys who had a reputation on the streets and in the penitentiary. Most guys who some people think are tough on the streets are not so tough in prison. It was different with Honey.

The next day, I told Daddy that we could leave to go back to the prison about 3:30p.m.. I had heard that Connie lived on Habersham and Gwinett Street. So, at about 10:30a.m., I got into the car and went over to her house. She got in the car and we talked awhile. Then, she got serious.

"I came over to your house yesterday to see if you wanted go out later and fuck, but I heard you say that you were going out with your brother. When I was growing up next door to you, I always thought about giving you some. I used to see you dressing up and going out in your Daddy's car. I wanted you to take me out, but I was too young and couldn't go out then."

"Well, I think I do remember where a motel is," I said as we drove off.

At about 2:30, I returned home with Connie. She told me that she and Joanne didn't get along because Joanne thought that there was something between my brother and her. I ate dinner and sat around and talked with the family some. Cora Lee called me back in a room and asked me to talk with Daddy. She told me that the family was concerned about Daddy since he bought that gun. She reminded me how Daddy is when he is drinking and sometimes he talks about shooting people, especially when he brings up my name. Then, it was time to return to the prison. I kissed Momma who was going to stay home and not ride back with us. Connie, Joanne, and Willie Lee were in the back. Daddy and I were in the front. I decided to wait until we got back to the prison before talking with Daddy privately. I was concerned about Daddy's relationship with Willie Lee and decided that I was going to write more to the both of them. At about 5:30, we drove up to the prison. I hugged the women and shook my brother's and Daddy's hands. I called Daddy over in the parking lot and talked to him for awhile. He assured me that he would be careful.

When I got back to the prison, a lot of guys wanted to know what I had done and who I saw. I filled them in and told them that I saw Point and Honey.

Glenn didn't say much and I sensed that he was hoping that I didn't bring up his name.

When it was time to go back to work, I continued to wash the cans inside the fence. It was cold now and my light jacket was not enough. There was a barrel near the far corner of the fence and I began to burn some wood that was lying around to keep warm. Shorty worked on top of the treatment plant and he had a small fire on the ground, too. Every now and then, Shorty would come down from the treatment plant and warm his hands. After awhile, I was out of wood, but Shorty threw me some wood over the fence, saying that he could see me trembling.

I heard some bad news out of Reidsville. Someone went to the dentist at Reidsville and returned to tell me that Larry Shank had been killed in the mess hall. Upon hearing this, I felt tremendously saddened. I then got angry when I heard that Larry's killing came about after another fight with JB. According to the story, Larry Shank and JB got into another fight and Shank kicked JB's ass a second time. One of JB's homeboys from Brunswick, who did not know the history between JB and Shank, told JB that he didn't want JB to mess up because JB was coming up for parole. At that point, JB had been in prison about 13 or 14 years, and his homeboy thought that JB should not stab Shank. Instead, JB's homeboy would do it. So, Shank was only looking out for JB and didn't see JB's homeboy come up to him in the mess hall. I was told that Shank was stabbed in the neck and died because of it.

I felt very bad that Larry Shank died because he stood up to a guy who was trying to run over him. Shank was a good person. He was decent, helpful, and honest. He was also a tough individual and died because of it. Shank should have killed JB, and I was wishing that someone would kill JB in Reidsville. JB didn't deserve to be free and neither did Rudolph Heard. I thought about Shank for days, and it was hard to get him out of my mind.

I heard on the news that there was also some racial trouble in Reidsville and then we heard the story from One-eyed Tony, who was down in Reidsville when the trouble happened and who had been transferred to Wayne.

I knew One-eyed Tony because he was in C4 with me. He looked a little creepy because he frequently had to wipe his bad eye with a handkerchief.

One-eyed Tony stated that three white prisoners ganged a black prisoner by the theater and this was the spark for the trouble. Tired of the arrogance of the white prisoners and the favoritism shown toward them by the guards, the black prisoners decided to retaliate. Tony said that Pork Taylor dropped a bag of knives out of a window, and the knives were distributed on the yard. Tony said that the black prisoners were stabbing anything that was white on the yard. One-eyed Tony said it was beautiful because not one brother was scratched. But One-eyed Tony did not tell the whole story.

A group of guys went to the dentist at Reidsville and related what One-eyed Tony had said. The Reidsville prisoners said that One-eyed Tony should be killed immediately and the guys in Wayne should not allow One-eyed Tony to live through the night because it was him that gave the names of the guys participating in the attack to the guards. So many Reidsville guys were planning to kill One-eyed Tony that the prison officials didn't think that they could even protect him by putting him in M Building, which was segregation. So, he was transferred immediately.

Some of the guys in Wayne started looking around for One-eyed Tony, but he was gone. The warden had transferred him after only being at Wayne a couple of days. I guessed that One-eyed Tony suspected that the guys who went to the dentist would find out about him.

I had mixed emotions about what had happened in Reidsville. I certainly understood the anger down there over the favoritism shown to white prisoners and the white prisoners sensed that they could do nigger prisoners anyway they wanted, just like the white guards. But on the other hand, I didn't like the idea of stabbing white prisoners for what some other white prisoners did. I was willing to bet that the white prisoners who actually attacked the black prisoner were not hurt and may not have even been on the yard. If just the three white prisoners who initiated the attack were stabbed, then I would have felt differently about it.

The winter was coming close to ending and I was quite happy about it. I had been inside the fence since October and now it was almost March. Although we didn't work outside when it was below 32 degrees, we did go out when the temperature got above 32. So, we sometimes did not leave for work during the winter until about 10 or 10:30 as opposed to about 7 o'clock. The guys waiting in the dormitory would say that the warden would be praying as he looked at the temperature, exhorting God to raise the temperature so he could put the prisoners to work. As soon as the thermometer said 33 degrees, prisoners were called out to work.

One morning after waiting for the temperature to go up, we were called out. The temperature may have been up a little, but the wind was blowing hard. I was huddled inside the fence and there was nowhere to go to hide from the wind. It seemed that the wind was following me to make sure that I was cold.

On the detail during days like this, working increases the body temperature. So, there was a little warmth from that. Also, during lunch, the prisoners were allowed to build a small fire. I didn't have this luxury inside the fence. I just had to tough it out. Even when I was the coldest, I never regretted writing the letters that made the warden upset with me. Fuck him and his ugly, cross-eyed wife.

Some new regulations were posted on the furlough program. Any trusty who had originally been sentenced to death was excluded from receiving a furlough. I applied for the Easter furlough anyway and was told that I could not go anymore because I once had a death sentence.

I wondered if this was the warden's doing or that of an official in Savannah. No one would tell me but likely it was both the warden and someone from Savannah.

I felt better when I saw the warden cut down to his true size. There was another problem in Reidsville. Some prisoners had taken some guards as hostages and were threatening to kill them. Ellis MacDougall came from Atlanta to negotiate their release.

As a result of the problem in Reidsville, some guys in Wayne decided to cash in on this trouble and refused to eat breakfast that morning. The prisoners wanted to see MacDougall to complain about how the warden was running the prison. A delegation of prisoners, including Larry Hunter, was selected to talk to the warden. Prisoners in all four dormitories were standing in front of their glasses watching the group and the warden, who had come inside the mess hall. The warden wanted the prisoners to follow him to his office, but in a gutsy move, the prisoners refused to follow the warden through the door and insisted that the warden sit down and talk at one of the mess hall tables. The warden reluctantly sat down and was trembling so badly that everyone in the dormitories could see it.

"Look at that scared motherfucker. Look at how he's shaking. This motherfucker is scared to death. He fucks over prisoners, but now he thinks he is about to get his and he is scared," said one prisoner standing next to me.

After talking for a few minutes, the negotiating prisoners returned to their dormitories and the warden returned to his office. He had a guard come inside and announce that the warden had called MacDougall in Atlanta and MacDougall would not come to the prison.

Safely in his office now, the warden sent four officers with riot gear inside the mess hall, and they sat with their riot helmets at a table for all the prisoners to see. I told one guy that this was a psychological move by the warden. We stayed in that day, and the next day, the spark was gone. The warden decided to move quickly and began transferring the perceived ring leaders. All the guys who made the warden tremble at the mess hall table were transferred, including Larry Hunter.

I knew Peacock was purging the prison of perceived troublemakers, and I knew I would be transferred too although I had no role in his humiliation.

One morning, I was told that I was going to be put on a detail that was going to do some light work around Jesup. Glenn was on this detail too and we continued to talk like always. However, I had witnessed a situation with Glenn that confirmed what I already knew about him.

One Saturday night during free time, I saw a prisoner from Reidsville named Jimmy slap Glenn. Glenn was backing up rubbing his face as Jimmy approached him. They were in the passage that separated the two dormitories. Although I could not hear them, I immediately knew what this was about. Jimmy had hit on Glenn and told Glenn that he wanted to fuck him.

The next morning, I got up to eat breakfast and to be the first in line for the Sunday paper. Most of the guys in the dormitory were still in bed and a few were having breakfast. Jimmy was in the dormitory that I was in and Glenn was in the dormitory across the hall. I saw Jimmy go into the one person shower and pull the curtain closed. As I was reading the newspaper, Glenn slowly meandered into my dormitory, stopping briefly by some beds. I continued to read the newspaper on my bed, but decided to look up. Glenn had disappeared and I saw his clothes near the shower. He had slipped into the shower with Jimmy. When the water was turned down, I knew Jimmy was fucking Glenn. After awhile, Jimmy came out of the shower and toweled off. A few minutes later, Glenn came out. I went back to reading the newspaper. Glenn, after getting dressed, walked out of the dormitory and went back to his dormitory. He didn't say a word to me and I never brought it up to him.

On the detail, he and I talked about what we generally talked about—sports.

After coming in one day, I was told to pack my gear because I was being transferred. As I was packing, I could see a Georgia state trooper walking on the catwalk inspecting the dormitories and all the other parts of the prison from above, but I didn't think that this trooper had anything to do with me. I was expecting one or two guards from another prison to be waiting for me at the back of the prison. When I walked out the dormitory saying good-bye to those prisoners that I was friendly with, I was shepherded towards the door leading to the front. The state trooper was waiting for me.

"You don't have to put handcuffs on him," said one guard named Henley. "He is a statewide trusty."

I walked out of the prison, glad that I was leaving. The trooper opened the back door for me to put my belongings and told me to ride up front with him. He told me that he was Corporal Evans, and he was taking me to Sylvania, Georgia.

Chapter 22

Corporal Evans was continuously talking as we rode down the highway. He told me that I would be working at the state patrol barrack and staying at the prison camp, which was run by Captain Gus. He began to tell me about Captain Gus and the state patrol barracks. I decided to listen closely because I knew he was giving me an orientation.

"Captain Gus is a really good man, and you will find him to be very fair-minded. The post is run by Sergeant Kicklighter. I'm one of two corporals and Corporal Wilson is the other commander when Sergeant Kicklighter is gone. We have about seven or eight troopers working out of Post 21. You will find everyone at the post to be fair and good people; however, I suggest that you don't get too close to the staff."

I took this mean that Corporal Evans was saying that we are in law enforcement and you are a felon, and there is a line that shouldn't be crossed. I also thought that it had a tinge of racial implications. I understood.

I had noticed when I got in the patrol car that Corporal Evans had a small Bible in his car, and I began to wonder if he was religious. I didn't have to wonder too long.

"Are you a Christian, Rudolph?" asked Corporal Evans.

I wasn't sure how to answer him.

"I used to be a long time ago," I responded wearily.

"Well, you should come back because it is not gonna be long before Jesus returns. All you have to do is look at what's happening in the Middle East. Yeah, it won't be long now before Jesus returns and a lot of people are not gonna be ready."

Then, Corporal Evans switched topic to politics and what was wrong with this country.

"It is really a blessing for this country that President Nixon won the last election. George McGovern might not be a communist, but he studied under that communist doctrine. So did Edward Kennedy. They might not be card-carrying communists, but they have been indoctrinated with those communistic beliefs. If George McGovern had won, he would have implemented communism in his social policies."

I began to have some serious doubts about Corporal Evans.

"I'm going to stop in Claxton, Georgia and pick up some fruit-cake."

"I have relatives here in Claxton and also I used to live here during the summer when I was 12 and 13. I used to work in the tobacco fields until it was time for school to start back."

"You don't say."

As we got to the bakery in Claxton, Corporal Evans told me to come in with him. Some people were looking at me in my prison uniform, but they saw that I was with a state trooper so that meant they were safe. I was looking around to see if I recognized anyone who was walking the streets, but it had been a very long time since I was last in Claxton. We got back in the patrol car and continued to Sylvania. Corporal Evans said that when we got to the patrol barrack, he would cut me a piece of the cake he had purchased. I thought then that he might not be as bad as he indicated when he was talking about Jesus returning and George McGovern.

Before long, we were at the state patrol barrack. As we pulled in the back, I saw several patrol cars under a carport that held about eight spaces for cars. We went in the back door and to the right was a kitchen. Corporal Evans got a knife and cut me a piece of his fruitcake as promised.

He also started talking specifically about the job that I would be doing at the barracks. In general, I would be doing janitorial work. I had to keep the barracks clean, change the linen on the beds in the barracks, wash the patrol cars, cut grass when it was warm, and rake the leaves in the winter. I was particularly concerned when Corporal Evans said that I would be at the barracks every day. I was wondering about visitation day, but Corporal Evans assured me that I would have a half day off on Sunday. Then, he took me to the prison camp, which was down the road from the barracks across Highway 301.

He pulled into a place that had brushes and benches in the front. Corporal Evans said that prisoners have their visits in front of the prison on the benches. He escorted me in and I was taken into a small office, where two staff persons were telling me about the camp and what a good man Captain Gus is. As I was walking in, I could see some beds behind the bars. The person was going through my prison file and commented that there was an unopened letter in my file from the clerk's office of the Fifth Circuit Court of Appeals. He took out the letter and stated that it had my first name and someone's else last name. I told him that the letter was mine and there was a mistake in the name. The letter was opened and then given to me.

I was given some new prison uniforms and let in the dormitory. Someone showed me my bed. I looked around and saw only about twenty beds. In the back was a shower for about three people, some sinks, and a couple of toilets. A prisoner named Hightower introduced himself and I asked him if this was the only dormitory. He laughed and told me that there were a few beds on the other side of the mess hall for the cooks, but what I saw was it. Hightower explained that visitation was on Sundays from 1 P.M. to 4 P.M. outside.

As I sat on the bed, I had a sense that this place was much better than that modern air-conditioned prison. The warden knew that the letter, though misaddressed, belonged to me and would not give it to me. He could have called me into the office, told me that there was a letter with my first name and his last name and then open it with me in the office. The warden had to think the letter was mine and not his because he wouldn't have put it in my file. I read the order again, which stated that a judge on the Fifth Circuit Court of Appeals had overruled the U.S. District Court and ruled that I did have probable cause to appeal. In effect, the Fifth Circuit Court judge issued a certificate to appeal, which had been denied by the district court. I began thinking about my appeal to the Fifth Circuit and my explanation for not filing a timely appeal. Damn the warden.

Most of the guys were already in the dormitory. I learned that a few of them were from Savannah. Stump, who had been given 10 years for selling drugs in Savannah, was there and was working at the county jail, which was next to the patrol barracks. A guy named Skeeter was there and I learned that I went to Beach High School with Skeeter's brother Earl. Grant, who lived in West Savannah, was there. At one time, Grant was the houseman in the county jail. Doyle Phillips was there and I remembered Doyle from Barnard Street, where he was seeing a woman near 31st. Yammy was there. I immediately thought about Honey making Yammy back down several years ago in the county jail. Herman was there and I remembered that he was good friends with Tony Scott.

We got up at about 6 A.M., and shortly thereafter, the side door was opened for breakfast. Through the door to the left was a window where the cook stated what he had prepared. You could tell him what you wanted, and he would fix your plate. I learned that the cook's name was Bruce.

The two people who worked at the courthouse were picked up by a guy in a pickup truck. I was told that this was my ride, too, and Stump's. I got into the back of the pickup truck. The truck turned right and circled in front of the barracks. In front of the barrack was a round area of grass that had a flag pole in the middle. Stump and I got off the truck, and Stump began walking over to the county jail. I tried to go into the front, but the door was locked. I went around to the back and walked in. A trooper was coming out from the back where the bedrooms were. I spoke to him and told him that I was gonna be working there. I was told to begin emptying the trash cans and cleaning the bathrooms. As I was doing it, I was looking around the barracks.

There was a lobby area with a floor model television and some furniture. The lobby had a picture window that had two glasses so that the person behind the glass could slide open the glass and talk to whoever had come into the front door. In this area behind the glass was the radio in which the dispatcher talked with the troopers in their cars. I emptied the trash can in a room that looked like some type of control room. It had the troopers' schedule on the wall. At the far end of the building on the right was an office, and I knew immediately that it was Sergeant Kicklighter's, the post commander. Opposite of it was a room in which driver's licenses were issued.

At about 8 o'clock, Sergeant Kicklighter came in and asked me to come to his office. He shook my hand and asked me my name. I sensed that he was gonna give me an orientation.

"How much time do you have, Rudolph?" Sergeant Kicklighter asked.

"I have life, but I am supposed to go up for parole next year," I said.

"Well, this is a good place for a prisoner to work. There are only two jobs at the camp that can help someone make parole: the courthouse and here because you are in the public. If you do well here, it suggests to some people that you can do well when you are free. Now, this isn't a hard job and you don't have to get the barracks spic and span, but it needs to be clean and the grass needs to be cut regularly. Also, the cars need to be kept clean. You are not really supposed to clean the shotguns in the cars, but you can. Just be careful when you are handling them. Also, some of the troopers might ask you to clean their sidearms. We have inspection once a month and you need to make sure everything is covered," explained Sergeant Kicklighter.

I was nodding my head and not saying very much.

"We used to have a prisoner here named Robert, but I had to get rid of Robert. Robert was a damn good worker, but he was doing something that I can't have. Robert had a woman meeting him in the woods across the far side of the barracks, and he was screwing her. I understand that. If I were locked up, I would be in those woods everyday too. But I can't have that here because we have to be very careful being out in the public like we are. I caught Robert once coming out of the woods and had a talk with him about it. Later, I caught him again. As he was coming out of the woods and saw me, he picked up a brick and held it for awhile before putting it down. I was pissed that he did that and I had to get rid of him."

"When I spoke to Captain Gus about a new prisoner, he told me that he didn't have anyone he could recommend. So, Captain Gus suggested that I contact the Board of Correction to request a trusty to work at the post, and Captain Gus said that he would keep the trusty at the camp. This is how you got here."

I suspected that the warden at Wayne Correctional Institution told the Board of Rehabilitation and Correction that he wanted me transferred, and it so happened that a trusty was needed in Sylvania. That was good for me.

"If you do a good job here, I will do everything that I can to help you make parole and will write a letter to the parole board in your behalf," Sergeant Kicklighter said.

"I'll do the best job that I can, Sergeant."

"I may ask you to do something specific, but I generally won't tell you what to do. You need to develop your own schedule. If you want to cut grass in the morning and wash cars in the afternoon, that is up to you. What day you cut the grass is up to you. All I expect is that the grass will be cut basically when it is needed, which is about twice a week," Sergeant Kicklighter said.

"Ok, that sounds good to me."

"Let's go outside and I'll show you how to keep records when you put gas and oil in the cars."

I got up and followed the Sergeant. He showed me a small concrete building where old tires were kept on one side. On the other side were some boxes. Sergeant Kicklighter told me that it was a sweatbox where prisoners were kept years ago. Looking at it more closely, I could see that it was. It looked almost like the sweatbox in a prison movie that I had seen.

I learned that I would have lunch back at the prison and the pickup truck would pick me up at 11:30. We would leave the prison camp at 1:00 to return to the post and the courthouse. On Saturdays and Sundays, a trooper would pick me up and return me to the prison.

I had quickly learned some of the troopers' names. Charlie Parker was the most active ticket giver on the highway. He prided himself in leading the post in the number of tickets given by a trooper. One day, Charlie Parker was working the afternoon shift. As he was coming to work, he learned that another trooper who had been working the morning shift had given eleven tickets. Charlie Parker hurried into the barracks to check in and came out almost running to his car. He sped off, burning rubber as he left. A few minutes later, he had called in that he had stopped a speeder.

Thompson was another trooper, and I really liked him. He had a cool air about him. He was supposed to be the roughest on cars. One day, he passed the prison going over a hundred miles per hour. He had a daughter who was just barely walking. She came up to me one day in the kitchen and was reaching up towards me to kiss me. I had seen very small children encouraged to kiss relatives and she thought that I was a relative. I leaned over and let her kiss me on the cheek, and then she walked off looking for her daddy. No one was around when she kissed me and I was glad. It was hard to reject a child stretching out her little arms.

The post had a young, female dispatcher named Janet. During my first week, she bought me a coke from the machine that was in the license office after I had cut the grass. She told me that the next time I could buy her one. Concerned about how this might look to someone, I told Janet that I knew she was being nice, but Corporal Evans had warned me about getting too close to the post personnel. Therefore, while I appreciated her kindness, I'd rather she didn't buy me any cokes. She told me that she understood. That was all I needed in addition to what I already had—Miss Ann trouble, which is in trouble involving a black man and a white woman.

Bohannan was another dispatcher. He was relatively young and gave me the keys to his Dodge Charger to wash. Bohannan's wife, Mickey, would bring his lunch or dinner every day and sit with him as he ate in the kitchen.

One day as I was returning to the camp with Hightower, he told me that other prisoners at the camp were mad with me for being assigned to the state patrol barracks.

"They talked about you and they were mad about it," Hightower said laughing. "A lot of guys wanted that job. After they got rid of Robert, no one was working at the barracks, except one day, about several guys were taken up there to clean up. A lot of them wanted the job. Then, they were told that the barracks was gonna get its own man, and a few days later, you came. When you got to the camp, someone was pointing you out as the one that was gonna be working at the barracks. Man, there was some Negroes mad with you. The first few days you were here, they continued to talk about you. I told them that you hadn't done anything and they should stop talking about you. But those were some mad Negroes for awhile."

"They say that many are called, but few are chosen," I said joking with Hightower as we headed back to the camp.

I was working on my appeal to the Fifth Circuit Court of Appeals when Skeeter came up to me.

"I see that you got a law book. Are you working on your case?" Skeeter asked.

"Well, it's mostly working on me," I responded. "I have learned a lot about habeas corpus, the Constitution, and how judges ignore the law and obscure legal issues to keep from giving someone a favorable decision. I am not confident about it, but I am doing it anyway. I learned that Congress has put a racist, segregationist, former Governor of Mississippi on the Fifth Circuit Court of Appeals. Many of these judges are hostile towards prisoners. So, I am not optimistic."

"I got a habeas corpus writ in Effingham County but the judge hasn't ruled on it and has had it for over 6 months. I just want him to rule on it so I can go to the next level. Can you help me?" Skeeter asked.

"I might. I have been reading up on mandamus"

"What is that?"

"Mandamus is a legal action that can be sought when a public official is not doing his job. It is an order compelling a public official to do his job. I would suggest writing a petition for a writ of mandamus in the federal court against the state judge. You send the petition to the federal court and serve a copy to the state judge. I will guarantee you that the state judge will respond. If you want, I will write it for you."

I began to write the petition, and in it I stated that it was axiomatic that 90 days is the limit for responding to a habeas corpus petition and the writ of mandamus should be granted.

"Is that true?"

"No, but the state judge is not gonna know that. All the judge is gonna think is that I need to move on this nigger's petition because a federal judge might say that I am not doing my job, and this could hurt me politically. I have learned that sometimes when you want something done from one person, you go to someone else," I explained. "But that's not always true. It's true here, though."

I finished my petition and mailed it to the Fifth Circuit. The petition that I had written for Skeeter got prompt attention. The state judge immediately dismissed Skeeter's habeas corpus petition. A few weeks later, the federal judge rejected the petition for a writ of mandamus and scoffed at this idea that "it is axiomatic that 90 days is the limit for responding to a state habeas corpus petition." But Skeeter got what he wanted.

One day after I was caught up on my work at the barracks, I began to look through the boxes in the cell next to the part in the concrete building where the old tires were kept. I saw that these were old Georgia Bureau of Investigation criminal files from the 1950s and early 1960s. I decided that I was gonna read them all. I only had time to read one that day and read one about an escape from the old prison camp. Two white prisoners escaped and drowned as they were trying to swim across a river. The file had the pictures of the two dead prisoners as they were found in the water. This was the first time that I had seen photographs of a person who had drowned and these prisoners were swollen as if they had been in the water for several days. It looked a little gruesome.

I was receiving regular visits on Sundays from my family. Daddy stated that he liked Sylvania much better than Wayne Correctional Institution. We were outside visiting at a picnic table and my family liked that much better than the visiting room at Wayne.

I told my family that I liked Sylvania a hundred percent better than Wayne Correctional Institution. The camp atmosphere was much better, and I liked working at the state patrol barracks. Most importantly, I told them that my chances of making parole were much better in Sylvania than in Wayne Correctional Institution. The warden thought that he was getting rid of me, but what he really had done was to help me.

I cautioned my family that although my chances of making parole were better, I might not make it the first time or the second.

"A prisoner serving life that makes parole the first time is like someone finding gold. Everybody is gonna hear about it. Since I have been in prison, I have only known, firsthand, one prisoner serving life to make parole the first time he went up. I heard rumors about another prisoner. The parole board doesn't like to do that because it doesn't make them look good to have a lot of guys making parole the first time. The board can defend its decision much better for paroling someone after 20 years than someone after 7 years. Generally, if the board paroles someone early, it means that there is something wrong with the case or someone on the outside is helping the person. There are some guys in prison with life sentences who shouldn't be serving a lot of time despite what the jury gave them. Some cases are truly manslaughter cases, but the person was given life for murder because of the defense lawyer or some other factor. So, don't get your hopes up too much. I want to leave now, but I know how these things work."

"I was talking to Bevins, where I buy my gas, and he told me that he has a mechanic working for him who is on parole. Bevins told me not do anything unless I talk with you first, and you know now how white folks operate," Daddy said.

I nodded my head.

"I also spoke with the mechanic. He served his time at Chatham County prison camp and told me that he had seen Aaron Kravitch come to the camp and take all the money that prisoners would give him. He said that Kravitch would tell them, "Boy, you've been in prison too long, give me five hundred dollars and I will get you out.' The mechanic said that some prisoners had that kind of money in the prison office and Kravitch would get it and they wouldn't hear from Kravitch anymore," Daddy said angrily. "For a long time, I had people, and some of them have been white, tell me that I should gone down to Aaron Kravitch's office and blown his brains out. Kravitch told me how juries listen when he talks to them and he was gonna talk about this gang on the east side and what had been happening to you. Kravitch said he was gonna put your feet on free ground and guaranteed that it would happen. But he never intended to fight your case, and I know he took money off the east side not to come to court."

"He did more than take money not to come to court. He helped plan the sabotaging of my case to ensure that I would be absolutely convicted," I said.

Sensing that things were about to get heated, Momma changed the subject and we began to talk about something else. I told them that one of my friends from Beach High had been writing me, and she was planning to visit me soon. Her name was Deborah. The following Sunday, Deborah did.

I was walking out the front door of the prison as she was walking up. We immediately recognized each other although it had been more than 7 years since I had last seen her.

"Can I hug you?"

"Of course, it's not against the rules."

We went outside and found an empty bench and reminisced about the good 'ole days. I was very happy to see her and didn't mind when she went into her religious bag. She told me that she knew that the Lord was gonna deliver me from this situation and return me to my family and friends.

But I knew the Lord was not gonna deliver me. White folks put people in prison and white folks let them go when they feel like it. The Lord has nothing to do with it. When white folks appear to be doing something good, it isn't the Lord compelling them.

However, I smiled as she continued to talk about how much the Lord had done for her and how much he was gonna do for me.

I was spending more time at the barracks. In fact, I was spending more time there than the prison. On Saturdays and Mondays, I would stay at the barracks until 10 or 11P.M. at night to watch football games. When I was ready to return to the camp, the dispatcher would call the patrol car that was patrolling Screven County to come get me. The other guys would be in bed when I returned to the camp. I joked once that I only sleep at the prison.

Many times during the day and night, only the dispatcher and I would be at the barracks. I would talk to Janet sometimes. She was telling me once about her wedding to Pete and told me that Pete stumbled a bit over "I do" and it made her a little concerned. She would talk about her father who operated a service station in Sylvania and who would come get the patrol cars to change the tires. He also drove a tow truck, and Janet would try to funnel some of the towing business to him when a tow truck needed to be called.

One day just Janet and I were there, and we were just talking. I decided to ask her a question, which caused the blood to drain from her face.

"Did you know Suggs?" I asked.

"No," she said as the color left her face and her smile disappeared.

I decided not to explore it any further, given that she was uncomfortable thinking about Suggs. I overheard the troopers in the kitchen discussing him and had remembered reading about him in the county jail. Suggs had taken a girl out on a date and stabbed her to death after she refused to have sex with him. According to troopers, Suggs had sex with the girl after he had killed her.

I had followed Suggs' case like I followed other capital cases. But Suggs had a special interest to me because he was prosecuted with the assistance of a defense attorney from Savannah who had been hired by the dead girl's family. I recalled reading that Suggs was sent to Millegeville to be evaluated and the psychiatrist testified at his trial and gave a clinical diagnosis for Suggs. The defense attorney told the jury that the diagnosis meant that Suggs was plain, damn mean. I thought that Janet might have known him, but she definitely had heard about him. Every town has its bad boy and Suggs was Sylvania's.

I went back to reading the old files. I found one striking difference in black people's behavior in the 1950s compared to the 1970s. In Screven County, black people gave up a lot. If they shot or stabbed someone on Saturday, they would be in the sheriff's office on Monday morning explaining what they had done and why they had done it. The sheriff didn't need to go out and make an arrest often. All they had to do was get ready on Monday morning to receive the reports.

I read one file involving a 16-year-old black youth who had been killed at a juke joint. The 16-year-old and his cousin were at this juke joint, and someone wanted to fight the cousin outside. The three went outside, and the 16-year-old threatened the other guy, putting his hand in his pocket. The other guy then pulled out a gun and shot the 16-year-old. Pictures were taken of the 16-year-old on the ground with his hand still in his pocket and blood on the ground beside him. Upon reading the notes on the case, there was some disagreement about whether this was self-defense. The boy didn't really have a weapon and had been bluffing, but the agent from the Georgia

Bureau of Investigation indicated that the defendant initiated talks about a fistfight, and he, therefore, couldn't claim self-defense. I disagreed but there was no indication of what happened in court.

I was particularly interested in all the murder cases. One guy had been stabbed in the chest with a butcher knife by his girlfriend. The file had a picture of him at the morgue, showing his stab wound in the chest. I noticed that he had nice hair. Some people may have wondered how he let the woman stab him, but I knew how fast these kind of things happened.

There was another case of a woman who had been killed by her husband in their country shack. He shot her with a shotgun and she was sprawled on the living room floor, which had little furniture in it. The picture of her was daunting because she had her eyes halfway opened and her hair was disheveled as she lay on the floor. They had another picture of her at the morgue, and she was nude, but only her upper torso was shown.

One guy had been killed and then was put on the railroad tracks, where a train cut him in two. Two guys were convicted of this crime and the theory was that they had done it for insurance purposes. Both of them were given life sentences and the file had an article from the newspaper about the resolution of the case.

The most interesting murder case had a beginning in Sylvania and an ending in Savannah. A guy had eaten something in Sylvania and gotten sick. The investigator concluded that someone had tried to poison him, but they couldn't find anything in the Sylvania home that had poison in it. He was transferred to Memorial Hospital in Savannah. While the man was recuperating in the hospital in Savannah, he was given some more poison and died. The authorities suspected that a family member had done it and wanted a specific family member to take a lie detector test. But she refused. The file indicated that the suspect was a teacher in Savannah and taught home economics. The case was not solved as there was no evidence. The authorities didn't even know how the guy got the poison and didn't find any traces of poison except what was in his body. I knew this teacher and had seen her in the halls almost every day when I was at Beach High. The files also indicated that Aaron Kravitch was her lawyer.

There were a few rape cases. I was extremely surprised to read that two white guys from Savannah were convicted of raping a retarded black teenager in the late 1950s. They only got a few years, but I was surprised that they had been given that. I wondered if the judge was concerned if this black teenager had gotten pregnant that she might have had a retarded child and this played into his decision.

Another person accused of rape was acquitted by the jury. He had taken a teenage girl out, and she claimed that he raped her in the car. The girl stated that she had never had sex before and her grandmother had put some Vaseline on her vagina when she returned home. The guy claimed that she agreed to have sex with him and that he had not raped her. The defense attorney called the boy's pastor as a character witness, and the jury acquitted the boy.

A white woman reported that her companion had beaten and raped her. Someone took a picture of her face, which was swollen. There was nothing in the file about the outcome of this case.

One day the sergeant saw these boxes with the files in it. He looked at one and told me to throw them out. I did and was happy that I had read all of them. I never told the sergeant that I had been reading these files. I didn't want him to know.

In reading the files, I compared the type of crimes that were occurring in the 1950s and the 1960s, especially among black people. A lot of it was the same except for some voluntarily giving themselves up and confessing to the sheriff.

But I had heard in Reidsville why black people would voluntarily confess when they suspected that they were gonna be accused of something. Even some of the prisoners in Reidsville would race to get to the deputy warden first. The word was that white folks believe the first story that they hear. So, if you had a problem, tell your story first. Then, when white folks hear something different from the other side, they think it is a lie.

I wondered if this was what happened to me in Savannah. For sure, the Williams' family got to Kravitch first and the white Catholics put out in the newspapers that Williams sang in the choir.

Chapter 23

Because I was coming up for parole soon, parole was very much on my mind. There had been some changes in the procedures of the parole board since I first came into the prison system.

When I first went to Reidsville, the parole board only considered a prisoner every year once he was eligible. Now, the parole board may deny someone parole and reconsider the prisoner again in 6 months or whenever the board wanted to consider the case again. Another change in the parole board's procedures was that it now gave reasons for its decision. The two dominant reasons for denial were that the serious nature of someone's case precluded parole at that time or that a person was a danger to society. Although the board may say that a prisoner had not engaged in rehabilitative programs, participation in such programs didn't help someone to make parole. A final change in the board procedure was that it now interviewed prisoners if the prisoners didn't make parole the first time. So, a prisoner who was denied parole when he was initially eligible saw the board before he came up a second time.

My reading of the parole board was that the main criterion for someone making parole was whether it is politically feasible to parole someone. This is the main question and my theory about how parole decisions are made. A person who is serving 10 years goes up initially for parole in 3 years and 4 months, but it may not be politically feasible for that person to be paroled. He might have to do more time. If the person has unusual support, however, it becomes politically feasible.

I remembered reading in the *Atlanta Constitution* that two prisoners—one black and the other white—were convicted as co-defendants for selling drugs. The white prisoner, who had a criminal record, came from a wealthy family, and his family arranged for him to go up for parole earlier than the normal one-third of the sentence. Although a prisoner must serve one-third of his sentence before coming up for parole, the parole board can suspend this criterion and can consider a prisoner at any time, even a month after someone went to prison. This is what happened to the white prisoner and he was paroled. To the prosecutor's credit, he stated that because the white prisoner was released early, the board should release the black co-defendant, who had no previous record. The board considered the black prisoner and turned him down, saying that it was wrong in hindsight to release the white prisoner and two wrongs didn't make a right. Thus, it was politically feasible to parole the white prisoner early, but not the black prisoner.

Since I had become a trusty, I had been thinking that I had a good chance at making parole early. I suspected that the problem with me making early parole was that I was originally given a death sentence and this might hurt me. Being a trusty refuted the view that I was dangerous to society and the only issue for me was the serious nature of my case. But I had several months to go before I was considered, and I tried to keep it off my mind, but it was tough.

My brother came to visit me and I marveled at him. He and Joanne had had their first child, and they named her Tamara. Willie Lee brought her for me to see. I could see that he was immensely proud of her as he gingerly changed her diaper. His relationship with Daddy was much better now than it was when I went on furlough. Daddy co-signed for Willie Lee to buy his first car. Daddy always bragged how he was never called by the finance company because Willie Lee was late with a payment.

I got a denial from the Fifth Circuit Court of Appeals and decided that this would be the end of my legal activities. My only victory was getting one of the judges to overrule the District Court's denial of a certificate of probable cause. I just wished that I had this judge and another judge like him on the three-judge panel that considered my case. Instead, I had the former Mississippi governor and a former attorney general of the United States. Also, the attorney general's son was a practicing attorney in Savannah. Despite the many denials, I knew that I had a valid case and I had learned a lot. Now, it was time to move on. I decided to trade my huge legal casebook to Skeeter for a small English book, entitled *Harbrace College Handbook*. I wanted to improve my writing and began reading this book like I read the law books.

When I initially became a trusty and began to think about getting out of prison, I wondered what I could do when I got out, knowing that convicted felons have few good job opportunities. I had thought about learning to drive a tractor-trailer, traveling all over the country pulling loads.

But I began to think differently because of my sister and my religious friend Deborah. My youngest sister told me that she had enrolled at Armstrong State College in Savannah and had decided to major in criminal justice. She discussed some of her classes and how interesting and challenging they were. Her recitations about Armstrong made me think about going to college when I got out of prison. Supporting my educational interests was Deborah who had a master's degree. I applied to take the SAT. When the examination was scheduled at Georgia Southern College, I was allowed to go. A staff member took me and read a book in the truck while I took the test. I was not dressed in the typical prison uniform. So, the students who were taking the test with me didn't know that I was a prisoner.

I believe that Captain Gus may have thought that I had a little too much freedom and wondered if I was doing something at the state patrol barracks that I shouldn't be doing. One night after I had come in after 9 P.M. Captain Gus was at the camp. He generally goes home at about 5 P.M. and this was unusual for him. He came up to me so closely that he could have kissed me, asking me how things were going for me at the patrol barracks. I knew that was not what he was interested in knowing. He was trying to smell my breath. So, I didn't back away. Instead, I told him that I was doing very well and this was the best job that I had ever had, as I blew my breath in his face.

Captain Gus was suspicious because some of the guys were smoking marijuana in the dormitory. It was Skeeter, Stump, and Grant. Stump would put up a huge, green towel on the side of his bed, and the three of them would light up as they sat on the bed behind the towel. They invited me to come behind the green door, but I declined. I told them that I only do a little alcohol.

On visiting day, some of the visitors would bring alcohol, but my family never did. One Sunday when I didn't have visitors, Stump called me over and his wife poured me a drink from a bottle in her big purse. He also shared some of his food. His wife had brought some greens and smoked neck bones, and they were good. Stump may have felt an obligation to pay me back because I had given him some bourbon that I got from one of the bedrooms at the barracks.

The license examiner would stay at the barracks sometimes and he would have a bottle in the back. Because he invited me to eat the food that he left in the refrigerator, I decided that this included his alcohol, too. So, I would pour a small drink for myself, but I would only drink it about a couple of minutes before the truck came by to pick me up to take me back to the camp. I also would make sure that I knew where the sergeant was. I knew that the sergeant would be upset if he caught me drinking, but he never told me not to drink at the post. He just told me to stay out of the woods.

Troopers had nighttime responsibilities to man the post after 11 P.M. and they would sleep in the back in one of four bedrooms. One trooper had a huge bottle of bourbon. I poured me a drink into a jar and poured some for Stump. The next day the trooper called me into a storeroom, closed the door, and confronted me.

"Rudolph, did you get some of my bourbon?" asked the Trooper.

I decided that I wasn't gonna lie.

"Yeah, I did," I said.

"I'm not gonna tell the sergeant on you this time, but don't ever do that again," said the Trooper.

"OK."

However, a few weeks later, this same trooper gave me some bourbon. I had walked in on him and a new female dispatcher and found them hugging in one of the offices. I immediately left without saying anything and he searched me out and asked if I wanted a drink. I told him yes and he poured me one. He didn't ask me not to tell on him and I wouldn't, but I knew that the drink was meant to say, "please don't tell you saw me." I wouldn't tell the sergeant and I, for sure, wouldn't tell his wife. He had some more bourbon in the bedroom, but I didn't bother it this time.

Another trooper offered me a drink that he had in his personal car. This was the post's playboy. He liked to chase women, and I saw a pair of women's drawers in the back seat of his personal car. I didn't touch them, but I knew that I probably could have sold them to one of the prisoners at camp. Instead of handing the bottle to me, this trooper put the bottle, which was in a paper bag, in the trash. I was to get it out of the trash so that he could say that he never gave me any alcohol.

Because I was at the barracks so much, some of the troopers would talk to me like I was just a person. One trooper told me that he and his wife wanted a child, but they were having a hard time.

"Maybe you should change your underwear. I was just reading an article about the effects of the type of underwear that a man wears on conception. Briefs hold the scrotum too close to the body and the heat hurts the production of sperm. So, some doctors recommend that a man stop wearing briefs and wear boxer shorts," I said.

"You gotta be kidding," said the trooper.

"No, I wouldn't kid you about this. I read it and it makes sense to me. I had read a long time ago that the reason why men have scrotums hanging outside their bodies was because nature did it that way, because the natural body heat is too high. This is why you have balls."

One day as I was hurriedly washing Trooper Charlie Parker's patrol car as he was waiting for it, Parker was talking about his gun, a .357 Magnum.

"I've never seen bullets like you have in your belt," I said as I washed the car.

The bullets were unusual in that they had a sharp point.

"These are special. They are supposed to go through a car engine. So, if I was shooting at someone crouched behind a car, I am supposed to be able to hit him with these," explained Parker.

Trooper Charlie Parker almost got a chance to test out his statement.

One day, I learned that Charlie Parker had a serious encounter while on patrol. He passed a car containing a prisoner and some deputies just as the prisoner was trying to escape. The prisoner had smuggled to him a gun into the county jail, and the deputies were notified by radio that the prisoner had a gun. Just as this was broadcasted, the prisoner pulled out the gun and starting shooting the deputies. Just as he started shooting, Charlie Parker rode by.

The prisoner kicked out the glass and tried to run, but Charlie Parker fired on him and captured him. One of the deputies died after being shot in the back of the head. The sergeant gave Charlie the day off to recuperate emotionally. According to Parker, some of the other troopers were mad with him for not killing the prisoner.

"They're mad with me for not killing Spencer. I didn't shoot him because I didn't have to shoot him. I saw where he had dropped the gun and I wasn't in any danger. But they told me that I should have killed Spencer anyway. That was the first time that I have come across anything like that and I never really had to draw my gun before," Charlie Parker said in a frank manner.

"Well, you are the one who would have to live with it and if you felt that it was not right to shoot, then you made the right decision," I said.

I wondered how Charlie Parker would react the next time he came across a similar situation. Would he shoot, thinking that the other troopers would criticize him for not shooting?

I also talked with the new license examiner. One day as we were in the kitchen drinking coffee, he asked me what was I convicted of and how much time I had. I told him.

"Well, in Vietnam I put a lot of those little fellas in the ground, but it was all legal. I guess that I probably killed about fifty over there," said the license examiner.

If things had been different, I could have gone to Vietnam too, and I probably could have killed fifty or more myself. I wondered which was worse: killing fifty or more for the United States or killing one for myself because I was forced to do it.

Because Stump worked next to me at the jail and because he was from Savannah, he and I would talk a lot. I was curious why he had Mayfield for his defense attorney, given that he had money to hire any defense attorney in Savannah.

"I contacted all the top criminal lawyers in Savannah, and none of them would take my case, even Black-assed Bobby Hill. I had done favors for Bobby Hill and that son-of-a-bitch wouldn't defend me. I saw him speaking to another client in the county jail and he tried to talk to me, but I told him to get the fuck away from me. I was told that the officials in Savannah wanted me in the penitentiary and they got me here," explained Stump.

"There is only one person that has the juice to make a lawyer turn down a case and that is Dunbar Harrison," I said. "They have two ways to get people in prison who they really want. The first is to fix the trial by having the defense attorney throw the case and all of them on the same side. The other way is to tell certain lawyers not to take cases. So, you are left with lawyers who cannot convince a jury what day of the week it is and who don't know shit about the law. If some of these lawyers tried to convince twelve people what day of the week it was, they would get a hung jury. Man, Savannah operates the most corrupt legal system in the country. The so-called defense attorney gets in bed with the prosecutor and then they put on this show. They all, including the judge, are swapping-out with each other. It's a rotten place, through and through, from the top to the bottom. On 31st Street, I lived behind a moonshine runner named Joe Kelly, and he was paying off the police to leave him alone. The patrol cars would come through the lane and blow their horns. Then, Joe or his wife would come out of the house and hand the police officer a roll of bills big enough to choke a horse. This went on from morning to night, 7 days a week. The only person who would bust Joe or his workers was a federal agent in an unmarked car. They would openly take moonshine out of their cars and take it into the house sometimes. The federal agent would catch them putting moonshine in their cars and chase them down. Man, this was a fast white man. After the agent caught the person, he would call for backup, and then the Savannah police would come. These would be some of the same officers who were taking bribes from Joe," I said.

"Shit, one of the detectives in my case had people selling drugs for him," said Stump.

"They get you off the street so that they can make more money," I said.

Stump explained a little bit about the drug trade to me and some people he knew on the east coast. Stump said that he was on the way to becoming a multimillionaire, but the white folks and the Negroes in Savannah derailed him.

"I bought a new car and my wife was upset when I drove it home. She told me that I knew that the Negroes in Savannah didn't want me in a brand new car and this was gonna start these Negroes telling the white folks things," Stump said. "The white folks took a lot of my stuff, saying that I couldn't show how I bought it."

"Some blacks cannot stand for another black person to do better than themselves. I could understand some of them calling the police because they have a problem with drugs, but that's not their reason. The reason is that you have money and more than what they have. If you were in a legitimate, legal business, these folks still would be upset. It is the crab thing. Crabs pull other crabs down who are trying to get out of the basket. I bet some of the black folks were happy you were busted and happy that you lost everything you had," I said.

Stump was upset about his repeated rejections for parole. The parole board was considering Stump for parole every 6 months, and every time the board would turn him down. He told me that the sheriff's wife had written a letter on his behalf, but it wasn't helpful. Stump said that he had someone to check into why the parole board was being hard on him, and he learned that one of the county commissioners had written a letter to the parole board urging the board to keep him in prison. I told him that it was not politically feasible for him to make parole.

But Stump was still making plans for what he was gonna do when he got out. He was talking about creating a gambling scheme involving taking bets on professional sports and suggested that I consider it since I knew so much about sports. But I told him no.

"It isn't because the white folks have rehabilitated me. But I have decided that this is gonna be my first and last time in prison. If I am faced with a situation and it gets nasty and ugly, I won't go on trial for it. When they come for me, I'll just tell them, 'I'm not going. Do what you have to do right here.'"

I had read in the newspaper that Red Roberts, the half-brother of the guy that I had killed, had stabbed a guy to death in a dispute over a girl. The jury gave him 1 year for manslaughter and he had just completed his sentence at the camp before I came. So, we had just missed each other.

Stump's wife had been on the east side the morning of my killing and had come home to tell him that someone had gotten killed and people said that it was because of a girl that both of them were seeing. Stump believed this version. I told him what he had heard was not wholly true. My primary concern was that I was having eye problems, they knew it, and attacked me with the stated purpose of putting out my other eye. All because I acted like I was something, they said. Beulah's name never came up initially. Their reason for jumping me was I thought that I was tough and something because I would pick Beulah up in a car. The real reason was that they had just started this Tornado gang and they were looking for people to hurt to enhance their reputations. They picked me and they picked the wrong person. What they tried to do to me was vicious and nasty. Some people say that nasty brings nasty.

It was interesting how some people leave out the dead person's involvement in the Tornado gang and say that I had a fight with him when I didn't hit him one time. The newspaper said while I was in the county jail that this gang was terrorizing the east side. Later, one of them, or rather another one of them, was killed. The guy who had done the shooting told the police that the gang had attacked him and was about to attack him again. This guy didn't come to prison for this shooting. The difference between him and me was that he had someone defending him and talking about this gang. I had no one speaking for me.

Back in the dormitory, I had been trying to mediate some brewing trouble between Stump and Yammy. I suspected that both of them had knives, and they were always arguing about the card game that went on in the back by the toilets. Sometimes, the arguing would get so loud that it would interrupt my reading.

"Come here, Yammy. How come you and Stump are always arguing about that card game?" I asked.

"Stump is mad because I won't let him cheat me. He cheats the young boys back there because they don't know how to gamble. I know how to gamble and I don't intend to let him cheat me," Yammy explained.

"How is he cheating?"

"He is hitting the cards and that's how he marks up the deck. Let me show you how. See whenever he is picking up the cards and shuffling them, he hits certain cards with his fingernails. So, what he is doing is marking the deck," Yammy explained further.

"Yammy, if that's what Stump is doing, don't play in the game. You can start a game and not let Stump play in the game. All I would like is for you and Stump to not argue so much. It is not necessary," I said.

But I was more concerned with them fighting and cutting up each other.

A parole investigator came by the barracks to interview me. He asked me what happened, that led me to coming to prison, insisting that I keep it brief because he had to put the story in a 2-inch section of a report. He further told me that I had positive evaluations from the warden and the Sergeant Kicklighter.

In my next visit, momma told me that a woman investigator came by the house to ask questions. She also mentioned that she had kept the letter that Drew gave her, ignoring my instruction to tear it up and throw it away.

"I might be able to use it if I don't make parole the first time. But I don't intend to contact Drew and I don't want anyone in the family to do it. Besides, Drew is in the prosecutor's office now and is officially prosecuting cases now. Even if he was still in private practice, I wouldn't want him to know I was being considered for parole. The parole board has warned prisoners about lawyers and that the presence of lawyers at a parole hearing does not increase the chances that the prisoner will be favorably reviewed. But really I don't trust Drew. I always felt that his giving you that letter was another opportunity to get money, not help me. Drew went to see a guy in Reidsville to tell this guy that he was gonna get him out of prison the following year. This guy is still in prison. This was just a crooked lawyer scheme. But send me the letter, and I will hold on to it until the parole board acts," I said.

As I feared, the parole board subsequently rejected me for parole, writing that the serious nature of my case precluded the board from releasing me. The board indicated in the letter that I would come up for parole again in 8 months.

Although I had suspected that the odds were not with me and I was prepared for a unfavorable decision, it was still disappointing to me. The sergeant had been in touch with Captain Gus. So, the sergeant knew about the decision and tried to console me as we had coffee together.

Stump and I were commiserating together. Stump was still being rejected for parole, and I knew that the board was gonna make him do all his time. I didn't feel like I was gonna let them string me along like him, but I knew that I didn't have a lot of cards to play. But I had one.

"What are you gonna do?" asked Stump as we waited for our ride back to the camp.

"I am gonna have to do something that I didn't wanna do. I have to go to the devil—the head devil," I said.

"Who is that?" Stump asked.

"Dunbar Harrison."

That night I wrote a very serious letter to Dunbar Harrison. I was not asking for his help, but I was reminding him what a corrupt legal system he presided over in Savannah. Particularly, I reminded him that after my death sentence was overturned, he summoned my father to his office to twist my father's arm. I reminded him that in this meeting, he told my father that I wouldn't have any trouble making parole because I was not a hardened criminal. I told him that I didn't make parole and it was because the crooked trial that I received caused me to get a death sentence.

I got a letter back from Dunbar Harrison who said that he didn't make any recommendations for parole for anyone unless the parole board personally requests a recommendation. Further, he told me that if I thought that there was something wrong with my trial, I should file a habeas corpus application.

I wrote Dunbar Harrison again, and the tone of my letter was much angrier. I told him that I knew that I had been railroaded and that the trial transcript never reflected what actually went on in the trial because the things that they all do to railroad someone are done under the table and not reflected in a transcript. I recounted specifically the things that were done by Kravitch and Drew to hurt me in the trial. I also recounted the lies told by the arresting officers and their refusal to release the transcript of the preliminary hearing which would have shown that the motion to suppress was a sham. Because I knew that Dunbar Harrison was a racist judge, I began to appeal to his racism. I told him that the decision to convict me was not really made by the jury and that this decision was made months before I went to trial by some corrupt lawyers and he was one of them. Then, I told him that a decision had been made that no favorable evidence would be presented in the trial for me, and this meant that they had indirectly whitewashed the dead person. The so-called choirboy was a member of a gang on the east side, and they kept this from the jury. So, they had whitewashed him. I knew Dunbar Harrison wouldn't like this contention. No racist would. I told him that I never should have gone to prison, and I was in prison because I had six lawyers, including him, against me. I told him that Drew had given a letter to my parents, stating that he was gonna get me out of prison. I told him that I didn't care who did it, but someone needed to get me out of prison. I included in my letter the letter that Drew wrote back in 1969.

When my parents learned that I had written Dunbar Harrison and some of what I told him, they were horrified. They were scared to death. My youngest sister told me that I shouldn't have sent Drew's letter to Dunbar Harrison.

During the next visit, I tried to reassure them.

"First, that letter is worthless. It is not legally binding and means nothing. As far as Dunbar Harrison is concerned, he can't really get mad. I told him the truth and he knows it. It is not sour grapes. They railroaded me. They know it, and I know it. Dunbar Harrison doesn't have anything to be mad about. I'm the one that was wronged, not him. Dunbar Harrison could write the parole board and tell them not to parole me because I insulted him or I indicated that I had not been rehabilitated. He might do it, but I don't think he will. He is an arrogant white man. I can envisage him calling Drew into his office and telling Drew that a nigger named Alexander wrote him. He will probably say to Drew that Alexander is that nigger that killed the other nigger over by St. Benedict Church. Then, they will probably chuckle over how they did me. Dunbar Harrison will ask Drew why he told that nigger's parent that he was gonna intervene with the parole board, giving Drew the letter that he had written years ago. I didn't write to Dunbar Harrison to ask him for a recommendation. I told him that I wanted out. I know that he isn't gonna do anything in the open. Sometimes, when you want something, you go to the main person and you don't go with your hat in your hands begging. I never expected Dunbar Harrison to write to the parole board on my behalf. He does his dirty work and then hides behind other people. That is how Dunbar Harrison and Aaron Kravitch were alike."

Everyone was still skeptical, and I didn't believe that I had convinced them that writing to Dunbar Harrison was the right thing to do. They thought that I had gone crazy and signed my death warrant. A lot of people talk about judges' power, which some have, but to me a judge was a crooked lawyer in a robe. And some lawyers are the lowest of the lowest. I had learned not to respect them and I had no fear of them.

I got a letter from the parole board indicating that I would be given a parole hearing, and I began to plan what I was gonna tell them. The hearing was conducted by two of the five board members. I was hoping that I didn't have Partain as one of my two.

The hearing was held in Reidsville in one of the front offices. It was Partain and McCall. McCall was asking questions first, and he was very low-keyed. But Partain was totally different and combative.

"Every time you tell what happened, you tell something different. I have three different versions from you regarding what happened," Partain said belligerently.

Partain read something that I had said in Jackson when I was being classified and what I told the parole investigator.

"Sir, I have not told different versions of what happened. When the parole investigator interviewed me, he told me that he only had a small space to put my version of the story. Also, I related essentially the same thing here in response to Mr. McCall's question that I said in Jackson back in 1969," I tried to explain.

"You seemed like a hothead to me, and I can see why you got into this trouble," Partain continued angrily.

"I'm not a hothead."

Then Partain's tone changed abruptly.

"Do you think that you can now walk away when trouble is brewing and not stay there like hotheads tend to do?" Partain asked.

I was about to respond to his criticism of me again, but a voice inside me told me to shut up. I had been watching them reading something in my file. First, McCall read and then handed the file to Partain. The voice inside me told me to shut up because they had already decided to let me go. The voice quickly repeated to me to make sure that I heard. "Shut up you fool. These white folks have already decided to parole you. Didn't you hear him ask, could you walk away?"

Partain's tone was completely different with me now, and this seemed to mean something. I knew his reputation.

I said what he wanted to hear. "Yes, sir, the next time that I am faced with some trouble, I will walk away," I said.

The hearing was then over.

As the guard was driving me back to Sylvania, he asked me how it went. I told him that I believed that I was going home.

I was painting the ceiling in the back bedroom when the sergeant came in smiling.

"Don't make any decisions after the end of this month; you have made parole," the Sergeant said as he was shaking my hand. "We're losing a good man, but I am very happy for you. I was just at the camp talking to Captain Gus when he got his copy of a letter to you from the parole board. Captain Gus told me and I asked if I could give you the news. Rudolph, I am happy to see you leaving, and I know you are gonna do well when you get out. If you want, you can call your parents now from here."

I went to a telephone and called home. Momma answered the telephone. I told Momma that I had just received word that I had made parole and would be coming home at the end of the month.

When I went back to the camp, the guard happily gave me the letter from the parole board. I began to tell everyone in the dormitory. I was so excited that I couldn't eat. I kept thinking that I was going home. When I went back to the barracks to continue painting, I kept smiling and saying that I was going home.

At the end of the workday, I told Stump as we were waiting for our ride.

Most people were happy for me, but Yammy was indignant. "I know goddamn well that I'm gonna make parole now. If they parole Rudolph, they gotta parole me," Yammy proclaimed.

I knew what Yammy was alluding to in his statement. He was alluding to me killing the choirboy and receiving the electric chair. He stabbed his girlfriend and was initially sentenced to life imprisonment. So, if I was paroled, he should be paroled too.

But Yammy and a lot of other people didn't know that I was railroaded to prison. The plan was for me to get life, or 20 years if I was lucky that day, but I got the electric chair because the jury went further than the lawyers had planned. White folks like to say in a trial that two wrongs do not make a right, but they believe that three wrongs make a right when they are fixing trials. There was a serious belief that if I had received a fair trial and a vigorous defense, I might not have been convicted. So, Yammy was wrong to compare me to him, but I wasn't gonna debate it with him. I was going home.

The following Sunday, my parents and some of my sisters came. They were all smiles as they greeted me and told me that there had not been that many smiling faces in the Alexander family in a very long time.

"Do you think that the letter you wrote had something to do with you coming home?" Momma asked.

"It didn't hurt me for sure. I really don't know, and I never will know. The parole board is not gonna tell me why I am being paroled. I do know that a judge or a prosecutor can get almost anyone out of prison with a letter to the parole board. They don't have to give the board a reason. All they have to write is that they want someone paroled, and the board is gonna act because it can blame that official if the person messes up bad. I don't know if that was done in my case, but I know that Dunbar Harrison would never write such a letter. I sensed that when I met with the parole board, and the hearing was just about over, that the decision had already been made to parole me. It is kind of strange that 8 months ago, my case was too serious for me to be paroled. How can 8 months change a case? If the case was serious 8 months ago, it is serious now. It goes back to something that I have been trying to explain to some guys, the board makes release decisions when it is politically feasible. Rehabilitation has nothing to do with it. I don't care how or why the board made its decision because I am coming home. But I will say that the people down in Savannah got away with a good one when they tried me. I am happy to be leaving, but I will never forget how I was mistreated."

On my last day at the barracks, a male dispatcher cooked me a very large steak dinner. I was quite full after I had finished. Also, Sergeant Kicklighter initiated a going-home collection for me. So, people at the barracks gave me money. I was touched by their kindness. As I left the barracks for the last time, I felt like I was walking on air.

When I got back to the camp, Captain Gus called me into the office to give me a last minute talk. He told me to be very careful whom I associate with when I go home and that a lot of guys associate with the wrong people, which leads them back to prison.

I assured him that I intended to stay out and would make good decisions. But mostly I listened to him.

As I was going back inside the dormitory, I knew that I wouldn't be back. I didn't have to worry about following the wrong people because I'm not a follower. Individually, I wasn't gonna rob anyone, burglarize anyone's home, or rape anyone. Any potential trouble in the free world for me would come about because I refused to allow myself to be wronged by predators. I would try to walk away from trouble, just as I told Partain.

This was my last night in prison and I couldn't sleep. I was trying to force myself to go to sleep because it would bring the morning faster. I woke up early and began to walk around. I was handed my suit, and I put it on after taking a shower. I shook everyone's hands as they came to wish me luck before going out to work. At about 8 o'clock, my daddy was there for me. I was let out of the dormitory and given a check for 25 dollars. I was going home.

Chapter 24

Daddy and I talked a lot on the way to Savannah. Pausing for a moment, he indicated how happy he was that I had gotten out. He discussed some changes in Savannah, and some of the people we knew that were looking forward to seeing me. I asked about the job situation in Savannah, knowing that a recession had occurred and that many people were out of work.

"It is kind of bad. I'm working steady, but a lot of people have been laid off, including your brother," Daddy said.

"A few months back, I was given a paper by the parole people and told to take it to Union Camp to have someone sign it. The paper said that Union Camp would consider you for a job. The supervisor at Union Camp didn't wanna sign it, but he did," Daddy stated.

"That is one of the dilemmas of being in prison and trying to make parole. At one time, the parole board said that in order to make parole, a prisoner had to have a job waiting for him. But how can someone get a job while he is in prison? Speaking of Union Camp, I heard that they do not hire anyone with a prison record. I will go out there and fill out an application anyway."

Before long, we were in Savannah. Momma was sitting in a chair, and I went over to her and hugged her.

I didn't wanna sit down, feeling that I needed to be on my feet. I went to the kitchen and got a glass of water.

Momma got up and fixed breakfast for Daddy and me. While we were sitting at the table, Daddy took out his wallet and handed me 50 dollars.

"I have a little money, Daddy."

"That's okay, but here is a little more."

"I don't need anything right now."

"Go ahead and take it, Junior," Momma pleaded.

I took the 50 dollars, but I didn't want it. I felt that I had taken enough from them, but they were looking at me as if they had not given me enough. So, I knew I had to take it.

They told me that my sister Cora Lee was working in Claxton, trying to make some money to return to Armstrong State College. Forced to find work outside Savannah, she was working at a chicken factory in Claxton and was staying with my aunt. Every Friday, she returned to Savannah and then left on Sunday.

After breakfast, I went to the telephone to call the parole department where I was supposed to report. A man who identified himself as Harry Christianson told me that I had to come to the office that morning.

Daddy took me down to the office on Waters Avenue. As we were headed south on Waters, we passed Memorial Hospital. I sensed that Daddy knew some of what I was thinking then, but he didn't say anything.

I was thinking that it was significant that we came this way. When Daddy rushed me to Memorial Hospital in January 1967, I cried when the doctor said that he had to operate on me and the nurse began taking my clothes off. Daddy was standing over me, trying to console me and reassuring me that he was not gonna leave me. But probably unknown to Daddy was that my last trip to Memorial Hospital in August 1967 was the most significant because I said to myself that this was my last trip to the hospital, and this became the catalyst for everything that followed.

When we reached the parole office, we, after a short wait, were ushered into Harry Christianson's office. He was a young looking white guy, and he quickly indicated who was in authority.

"I'm the one who is gonna send you back to prison if you mess up," he said looking at me sternly the way that white people do when they are in their intimidating posture. "I'm going over these rules, one by one, to make sure that you understand and then you have to sign this sheet, indicating that you were clearly told the rules."

He began to read the rules to me, telling me that I couldn't possess any weapons, leave the city without permission, or get married without permission. He was putting particular emphasis on some points.

"You can't stay with anyone besides your mother. On 31st Street is where you need to lay your head every night. For awhile, until I tell you differently, you can't be out at night. You can go out looking for a job from 8:00 in the morning to 5:00 in the afternoon. At 5:00, you need to be at home. I don't mean *start* home by 5:00, but *be* home before 5:00. If you are in one part of town and it is gonna take you an hour to get home, you need to leave at about 3:30. I don't wanna find you hanging down on Broughton Street on one of the street corners. I will be coming by your house to make sure you are at home when you are supposed to be there, and I will be coming by at least once a week and perhaps more. On Saturdays and Sundays, you have to be in the house. Do you have any questions?"

I only had one question for him, but I thought he misunderstood the question and thought I was being sarcastic.

"Yeah, when can I apply to get off parole?"

"You are on parole for the rest of your life. When you are paroled from a life sentence, you are on parole for life. The parole board can discharge you from parole after 3 years, but that is not a guarantee. You're on parole for life."

When we left the parole office, Daddy was visibly upset about what he had heard. He didn't say anything to me in the car, but knowing Daddy, I knew that he was upset. I was little upset myself. Although I was not complaining too much to myself, I knew that I had, in some respects, more freedom in Sylvania.

When we got back to the house, I began looking at the newspaper in the employment section. Also, there was a person at the employment agency that worked primarily with former prisoners, and I decided to see him the next day.

Later that afternoon, people started dropping by the house, having been told that I would be home that day. Percy and Francine dropped by and gave me some money.

Georgetta Baker called me later that day. Georgetta and I had gone to Richard Arnold High School together, and she was really after me for a while.

Other people came by and later my brother came too. By 9:00, I had drunk so much beer during the day that I was throwing up.

The next morning, I went to the employment office, but the man told me how tight the job market was in Savannah. He told me to keep checking with him because something could turn up at any time. When I left, I began going to any place that I could think of that might be hiring.

I went to Union Camp. I had to take a simple math test, which I passed easily and the lady told me that my score was perfect. But when she saw that I had responded yes to the question that I had been convicted of a felony and particularly that it was a murder conviction, she recoiled. I knew that I would never be called for a job there although my daddy had worked for them for almost 30 years.

Later, I was advised by the parole officer not to put anything down for the question inquiring whether the applicant had been convicted of a felony. Instead, they advised parolees to leave it blank with the hope that the parolee could get one foot in the door and get an interview. At the interview, they advised the parolee to disclose that he had been convicted of a crime.

I knew one guy who had been in prison with me, and he had worked at Union Camp for a while. He told me that I should have lied on the application and responded no. I sensed that he was able to get away with this because he was not on parole when he did this. Unlike him, I have people looking over my shoulder, and my parole officer was planning to visit me at work, if and when I found a job.

During my first Saturday being free, my daddy, who generally is out in the streets drinking on weekends, decided to stay home with me. He had a big bottle of gin on the coffee table and by noon, he was drunk. When Daddy is sober, he doesn't talk very much, but when he is drinking, he is extremely vocal. He started talking about my parole officer.

"That man told you wrong. You are not supposed to be on parole for the rest of your life. You can't live like that. He lied to you," Daddy said as he began to get angry. To him, this was a continuation of people doing his boy wrong.

"You just try to go along with him, but don't worry about getting a job. He is putting all this pressure on you to get a job. Go out looking for a job to satisfy him, but don't worry about finding a job. I'm working. Every Thursday, when I get paid at Union Camp, you'll have some money. You don't never have to work a lick as long as I am alive, and when I die, you will get my insurance money from Union Camp," Daddy said. "Anytime you need money, just ask me. If you need to use the car, all you need to do is ask. My car is kind of ragged, but it will get you where you wanna go. Also, you can borrow your brother's or sister's car at any time. Anything you need, all you have to do is say something."

I had poured a drink from Daddy's bottle and mixed it with some juice. Daddy drank his liquor straight, but I couldn't drink like him or as much as he could.

Daddy changed topics and then began to talk about Aaron Kravitch.

"I should have killed that dirty son-of-a-bitch. You don't know how many people who told me that I should have blown his brains out. I trusted him and paid him everything that he asked me for. He just lied and lied, saying he was gonna do this and that for you. But he didn't do a goddamn thing. He just stole my money. He told me that no one was gonna try your case but him. In his office, he was telling me how he was gonna argue your case to the jury and how he was gonna convince them to put your feet on the ground. I saw him the day before you went to court, and he didn't tell me anything about him not being in court the next day. Then, when I spoke to him again after you went to court, he told me that he had to go out of town and that was why he wasn't in court and had to send Drew. But he didn't have to go out of town. He was down in his office. I had Mildred call his house after the trial and Kravitch's wife said he was down at his office. She even said she had spoken to him earlier that day. Then after they had done you so wrong, he asked me for more money. I should have blown his fucking brains out," Daddy said angrily. "I had some white people I know that said they wouldn't have blamed me one bit if I had splattered Kravitch's brains all over his office. They told me that they would have done it if Kravitch did them like he did me. But they had you messed up so bad. You never should have gone to prison. If the white folks wanted someone to put in the electric chair, they could have had me. They could burn me 'til all the meat fell off my bones, and then they could have burned up my bones too."

Momma interrupted.

"Stop talking like that, Alexander. Junior is out now and Aaron Kravitch is dead. Don't bring that man's name up no more in this house. Let all that mess die. Junior's home now," Momma said.

"That's wasn't right what they did, Thelma. You know it," Daddy said.

As Daddy was talking, tears were welling up in my eyes, and I wanted him to stop, but I couldn't say much.

"Junior, I don't want you fighting anybody. If a Negro says that the sky is green and the grass is blue, you agree with him. Let him be right. Don't fight nobody and don't argue with nobody. Don't even disagree with them. If you have someone trying to start something, you tell me. I'll do your fighting for you," Daddy said as he took out a pistol he had in his pocket and put it on the table. "You didn't do anything. I'm the one who should have gone to prison. I had people who had been around you tell me that you never would have done what you did without a good reason. The lady down the street told Thelma that she had seen you with those bandages over your eyes, and she didn't blame you one bit for what you did. But there were some other Negroes in this town who wanted you dead, saying you killed this church boy for no reason. These same Negroes lied on you and lied on me," Daddy said.

Daddy poured himself another drink. My brother and his wife were over at the house now; they had brought their daughter with them. Willie Rhodes also dropped by. It seemed like we were having a party. Daddy continued to be simultaneously happy and angry.

"You know they were talking about going house to house for some donations for that woman in North Carolina," Daddy said.

"What woman?" I asked.

"That woman, you know," Daddy insisted.

"He's talking about Joanne Little, the black woman who killed the white jailer for raping her. There was some talk that the NAACP was seeking donations for her legal expenses," Joanne explained.

"Yeah, that's her. I felt bad for the woman, but I told Thelma that they bet not come to my door asking for anything. I would run their asses off my porch. No one gave me anything for you. My sisters in Ohio sent me some money to pay Aaron Kravitch. These Negroes didn't do nothing but talk bad about you. They wanted you dead. I told them if they come here begging for something, I best not be here when they come," Daddy insisted.

Shifting focus a little, Daddy began talking about the legal system in Savannah.

"They never should have tried you downtown. You should have been tried out on Eisenhower as a juvenile. Out on Wilmington Island where the rich white people live, a white boy who was your age killed another boy, but he was tried in juvenile court," Daddy said. "Ask your sister Cora Lee."

I sensed that because Cora Lee was studying criminal justice, she had learned something about the juvenile justice system in Savannah and had conveyed some information to Daddy.

But I knew that the solicitor general has discretion where to try juveniles and may do it in either court. I had also learned that favorable discretion is more likely to be exercised for white juveniles than black, and one had to be white to be given a true break.

"Alexander, don't you think that you have been talking enough? Give someone else a chance to talk," Momma said.

Daddy was quiet for a while. Then, I was getting advice from everyone on changes in Savannah, the do's and don'ts.

"Montgomery Street is now called the Strip. If you are looking for someone, take a drive down Montgomery Street, and you are likely to find them," my sister Betty told me.

Willie Rhodes had some advice for me too.

"When you go out to the clubs, never leave a drink on the table to go to the bathroom and then come back and drink from that glass again. Finish your drink before you get up to leave. If you leave the drink on the table, order you another drink. Don't drink out of that same glass. Negroes will put something in your whiskey," explained Willie Rhodes.

"You will also find people down on Broughton Street. That has become a hangout for a lot of guys. One-eyed Marshall hangs out on Broughton Street. Every time I go downtown, I see him. You will see a lot of other guys you know there too. They hang around downtown and try to hit on the women who are shopping," Willie Lee said.

Willie Rhodes asked Daddy if Daddy wanted to ride with him. This was Daddy's cue to get back into the conversation. Daddy had slid off the couch and was sitting on the floor.

"No, I'm not going anywhere today. Junior can't leave. So, I am staying home. I'm not gonna leave Junior," Daddy insisted, almost crying.

Willie Rhodes then left and told me that he would see me later.

Someone asked me what my immediate plans were.

"Well, on Monday, I plan to fill out some applications and do a little shopping. Then, I plan to go out to Armstrong to get some information on the criminal justice program. I also need to see a eye doctor," I said.

"You go ahead and see that doctor. Don't worry about the money. Tell the doctor that I will pay him," Daddy said.

"I go to Dr. Dandy on Abercorn Street. He is a black ophthalmologist," my brother said.

Boot, who I used to work with at Foodtown, stopped by.

I had seen a story about Boot on a Savannah television station that was picked up in Sylvania. I was vacuuming the carpet in the lobby area and simultaneously listening to the news when I heard a report about a Thurman Roberts being shot. I immediately recognized Boot's actual name. There weren't many details. I learned from my family later that Boot was working the midnight shift and had left for work when he decided to return home. Upon returning home, he found that his wife's boyfriend was in his house. Panicking, the guy shot Boot.

Boot poured himself a drink from the table and began to talk about his now ex-wife and his being shot.

Then, they all started talking about Union Camp. Boot and my brother both were working at Union Camp until they were laid off. They began talking about who was the quickest to stand up to unfair treatment by the white supervisors at Union Camp. It was getting quite loud in the living room.

Hog Shaw came by and told me the name of a store near the mall where I could go to pick out a shirt and a pair of pants. He told me that he had already taken care of the payment, and all I had to do was pick them out.

Boot left and told me that he would see me next week. Daddy got back on the couch and began to nod off. I couldn't help studying his face. I could only speculate at the grief that he had endured during the last 7 years and 8 months. I knew that without him and others constantly coming to see and writing to me, I would have perished in the prison system.

Even more difficult for me was knowing that I was responsible for my daddy being exploited by Aaron Kravitch and then both of my parents being used by Dunbar Harrison in that phony court scenario when he asked me to take the witness stand and then called Momma and Daddy to stand by it. My daddy had very little formal education, and he was misled terribly by a lawyer that he trusted. I had thought that it would have been better if I had not allowed myself to be arrested and was killed on Jefferson Street by Bush and Nealy. My Daddy's insurance would have paid for my burial, and I thought that after a while, he would have been able to go on.

"What you think about the trouble that they have been having in Reidsville?" Momma asked.

"I think that it has become really bad," I replied.

"Well, I am so glad that you are not down there now. It seems like we are always hearing something about Reidsville," Momma said.

I knew that she was referring to the racial trouble in Reidsville. It had gone to a new level. The attack by the white prisoners on the black prisoner and the response to it on the yard sparked a continued problem in Reidsville. In one attack, the white prisoners stabbed several black prisoners while everyone was walking down the hall headed to the yard to go to work. Some of those who were stabbed died. It was an orderly, sneak attack: the black prisoners were not looking for anything.

In retaliation a few months later, the black prisoners stabbed white prisoners who had gone to the theater. When the lights went out, they started stabbing white guys.

The white guys retaliated again. Later, some black guys stabbed some whites, including guards. One guard was killed so brutally that he had to have a closed casket.

I didn't like these attacks because of the groupness of it. One or two white guys could cause other white guys to get killed and vice versa. Probably, the individual or individuals who initiated the trouble was not harmed. I know I would have been highly upset if a white prisoner stabbed me because a black prisoner I didn't know did something to the white prisoner.

The next day Daddy went out for awhile after I assured him that I was okay.

On Monday, my brother and I went downtown, talking as we rode.

"We all are glad you are finally home. You don't know that it has been hell since you were gone. We all thought at one time that Daddy was gonna lose his mind. He cried about you for years and years," my brother related.

"Daddy doesn't quite understand that I almost didn't make it back. Kravitch and Drew's main concern when I got the electric chair was protecting themselves. I just benefited from a court case from the U.S. Supreme Court in 1968. In hindsight, the Furman case in 1972 came along and saved a lot of guys. But if that 1968 case had not come along, I would have come a lot closer to being executed. Daddy doesn't understand this and he doesn't understand the pitfalls in Reidsville. In other words, I almost didn't come back," I said. "But I have learned a lot, and I know that I will never get jammed the way I was back then. I have learned a lot about the law and now understand that it is just a theory. The reality is that lawyers decide the application of the law, and some lawyers are flat-out racist and corrupt. On paper, my being out looks good for me. Someone could point out that I shot the choirboy, got the electric chair and then life imprisonment, and paroled in 7 years and 8 months. To many people, this is a good break, but I don't see it that way."

He began pointing out guys that we knew, and just as he said, Marshall was standing on one corner trying to talk to passing women. I was shopping for some clothes because I only had what I wore from prison.

As I was walking past one store, I saw someone staring at me menacingly. I immediately recognized him and looked at him like he was looking at me.

"Who is that?" my brother asked.

"That is Alvin from the east side. I don't care if he is acting mad because I am out. Fuck him. He better not say a word to me. He was the one telling Swinton not to testify in my favor. After I was attacked by the Tornado gang, Alvin was bragging about how tough these guys were and how they kicked ass. But when one of them got himself killed for attacking me, he got his mouth stuck out. If he was so concerned about the choirboy, he should have been telling him to leave that gang alone and to leave other people alone. He and people like him encourage attacks on other people for some Mickey Mouse reason and then they get upset because their friends get killed. I even had a grown man telling me in the county jail that this gang was right to attack me for messing with their women. This is just the dumb type of stuff that causes all this trouble. They should be telling people to leave other people alone, and if a real problem occurs, then talk to the other person like a human being. A lot of black people won't do this, and then they got the nerve to get upset when someone gets killed. I know what Alvin was thinking, and I know that he knows not to say anything to me now or ever. He just thinks that he is mad, but I am mad too," I said.

When I got home, Momma was talking to me and asked me if I thought that I was gonna have any trouble from people on the east side.

"No, I don't think that if I saw any of the guys that were in this gang that they would do anything. I just saw one guy downtown this morning. He gave me a nasty look, and I looked at him the same way he was looking at me. They're not gonna do anything unless my back is turned, and they have me outnumbered."

"Willie Lee used to come home and tell me that he saw different people off the east side and they always stared at him. He would say, 'Momma, I can't go anywhere without seeing those guys.' He was always coming home, saying that he saw this person or that person and how they were looking at him," Momma said.

"I'm not gonna do anything to anyone, but I am not gonna run from anyone and I am not gonna accept that I can't go on certain parts of town if I wanna go," I said.

"When your brother first moved on the east side, someone cut his tires. He told me that he thought that one of the dead boy's cousin did it because he used to see her and she didn't look to be too happy about seeing him," Momma said.

"That's stupid to blame Willie Lee for what I did. I can't tell you about all the threats that I was hearing in the county jail and the same people who were saying that they personally wanted a chance to kill me were helping to get me convicted. His cousin should have blamed whoever talked him into getting involved with that gang and whoever nominated me for their next victim to show how tough they were," I said.

I continued to fill out applications all over town. National Linen refused to take my application, saying that its laid-off employees were gonna be called first when it had any openings.

I went out to Armstrong to talk to the guy that headed the criminal justice program. My sister told me that the head of the department was Dr. Megathlin, and he was in his office when I dropped by.

"I'm thinking about applying for admission to Armstrong and I am interested in majoring in criminal justice," I said. "I have just gotten out of prison, and I wanna come here. But I am concerned whether I would be going for nothing because I hear that a felony conviction bars one from getting a state job," I said.

"Well, we have a really good program here and would love to have you. At one time, it was tough to get a job with a record, but things are changing now. If you come here and stick to the program, a job is gonna be open to you. I'll guarantee you that if you get a degree from here that you will be able to get a job. I know some people in the city, and I can help you. We had a fellow in the program who had some legal trouble in the past, but he dropped out," Dr. Megathlin said.

"You don't have to worry about me just quitting. You know I wrote to the college months ago requesting information when I was in a prison camp in Sylvania," I said.

"You know I remember someone in the registrar office giving me that letter and I have it somewhere on my desk," Dr. Megathlin said as he searched his desk, which was quite messy. But he couldn't find the letter.

Dr. Megathlin and I talked about my case.

"Do you think that you will have any problems with the guys you had conflicts with before?" Dr. Megathlin asked.

"No."

I believed that he had asked me this question because there was a big case in Savannah involving the Brown and Washington brothers. Although it was a long time ago, I knew the Brown brothers and my sister knew one of the Washington brothers. One of the Browns was accused of killing one of the Washington brother and was acquitted. The other Washington brother spotted the Brown who was acquitted washing a car and walked up to him and killed him. I guess that Dr. Megathlin had this case on his mind, but I really wasn't expecting any trouble although Red Roberts had indirectly threatened me.

I then told him that I had heard good things about the program from my sister.

"Who is your sister?"

"Cora Alexander."

"Cora Alexander is your sister? Cora is a very good student. I had her in one of my classes," Dr. Megathlin said excitely.

I told Dr. Megathlin that I had some things to do before I could enroll in the Fall and that I needed to see an ophthalmologist about my eyes. He encouraged me to get my eyesight straightened out and then to fill out an application for admissions. I went over to the registrar's office and took some admission forms with me.

As I was headed home, my first impression of Dr. Megathlin was very positive, and I felt that my decision to come was the right decision. I had a choice between Armstrong, the so-called white school, and Savannah State, the predominantly black college. Both had criminal justice programs, but I felt that Armstrong was right for me. Savannah State was always in the news negatively, and right or wrong, I needed any edge that I could acquire. I believed that Armstrong was the tougher school and I needed that edge. Socially, Savannah State would have been better, but I wasn't going to school for a social life. Also, I knew that a reference from a white professor carried more weight than a reference from a black professor when a white person is gonna be making key decision regarding me.

Knowing that I needed to have my transcript sent to Armstrong, I stopped by Richard Arnold High School. After I told the secretary that I graduated in 1967, she began to tell me about some of the teachers who were still at the school that I would know.

"Mr. Newman is still teaching here. You ought to go by and say hello," the secretary urged.

But I didn't wanna talk to him. I wasn't angry with him or anything like that. I just didn't wanna talk about what happened after I graduated in 1967.

When I got home I made an appointment to see Dr. Dandy. When I went to his office, I was very impressed with his assistants. They were really good-looking. I filled out the new patient forms and indicated that I had had an injury to my left eye in 1967 and who my doctor was. When I got in his examination room, I told him that I had money for the examination but not for glasses at this time.

"Why didn't you follow up with your doctor in 1967?" Dr. Dandy inquired.

"I went to prison and just got out. I was seeing the doctor when I was arrested. Later, I had my eyes examined at a prison in Jackson but the doctor told me that he couldn't prescribe what I needed to see better," I said.

Dr. Dandy began to look at my left eye and the bright light caused my eyes to started watering badly.

"That was a nasty cut," Dr. Dandy said as he peered at my eye. "How old were you then?"

"Seventeen."

"The doctor that did your operation really did a good job. It was difficult surgery taking a cataract off a young person back then."

After Dr. Dandy completed his examination, he told me what I needed to see better.

"You need a contact lens on your left eye, but you can't wear a contact lens on your right eye because of its shape. So, you need to wear glasses too."

"I'm looking for a job, but I don't have one yet. I live with my parents, and my father, who works at Union Camp, can pay you a little every week," I said.

"That's okay, you can pay whatever you can on a weekly basis."

"Thank you."

"It is gonna take a few days to order your contact lens and the glasses. We will call you when they are in," Dr. Dandy stated.

One afternoon after pounding the pavement most of the day for a job, I decided to go the library on Bull Street near 37th. Before leaving, I told Momma that I was going to the library and would be back when supper was about ready. It was a little after 4:00, and I had planned to be back by 5 P.M..

I went into the room where magazines and newspapers were kept. I sat down in a chair and began to read the Atlanta newspaper. After I had read for about 15 minutes, I noticed that someone had sat down in the chair next to me, but I didn't look up. After about 30 seconds, the person touched my arm. I looked up and it was my parole officer. He then asked me to come outside because he wanted to talk to me.

"You are not supposed to be here. You are supposed to be looking for a job or at home," Harry Christianson said.

"Well, I didn't think that the library was off limits."

"You need to be out looking for work or at home unless I okay something more. If you wanted to come to the library, you should have asked me first."

"I'm sorry. I didn't think that I was breaking any rules," I said.

"OK, you are expected to be only three places—looking for a job, home, or the library. When I dropped by your house and your mother said that you were at the library, I was skeptical. You are the first parolee that I have had to be in the library reading. Most of them are hanging out on some corner. You can go back in the library," Harry Christianson said.

I went back into the library and finishing reading the newspaper. Then I went home.

"Your parole officer came by, and I told him that you were at the library. He looked at me like he didn't believe me," Momma said.

"I saw him, and he told me that I should have not gone there without asking him first," I said.

"I'm so glad you were there," Momma said.

"That could have developed into a real problem if I was on the way home when he was on the way to the library. If he didn't find me there, he would have said that I was never there," I said. "I am happy to be home, but these people are a pain."

Chapter 25

I got a telephone call one Sunday from a cousin named Roger.

"I heard, Junior, that you are looking for a job," Roger said.

"Yeah, I'm looking."

"Well, I work at Home Furnishing just around the corner from you, and we need a truck driver. Can you drive a stick shift?" Roger asked.

"Yeah, I can drive a stick," I answered.

"Okay, I will pick you up at 8:00 in the morning," Roger said.

Roger was our cousin on my daddy's side, and periodically Daddy would go over to Roger's house to drink.

Apparently, Daddy had dropped over there and told them that I was looking for a job. However, I only intended to work until September because signs were that I was gonna be admitted to Armstrong. My plan was to go to school full-time for a year, including the summer, and then work the rest of the way. This job at Home Furnishing was a good start for me because I needed some things.

Roger came by the next morning and picked me up. He told me that we would be unloading furniture when it was delivered to the store, moving furniture from the back to the showroom, and making deliveries. Zeke, another employee, couldn't drive a stick. So, I would be doing the driving.

The first day, we unloaded and stacked furniture that had been delivered to the store. At noon, I walked home for lunch and returned after an hour. We did some more work in the warehouse, looking out the side door to Anderson Street from time to time to watch women walking down the street. This was a relatively easy job.

On Friday, we had a couple of deliveries. One was on the east side, and one out in Liberty City. In making the Eastside delivery, I had to drive down East Broad Street. I was looking towards my left for the store. As I approached Oglethorpe, I knew that I had passed it and St. Benedict Church. However, I probably wouldn't have recognized them because I had not been in that area until the time of the shooting and I really had not studied the area.

We delivered a refrigerator to a home in Liberty City, and the name on the delivery slip triggered my memory. I had read while I was in prison that Earl Charles had been convicted of murder and given the electric chair in Savannah, despite solid evidence that he was working in Florida during the crime. I knew that an all-white jury had a difficult time acquitting a black man in a murder case involving a white man. Uncustomarily, after the verdict, chaos developed in the courtroom, and extra deputies had to be called.

After returning to the store at noon, Roger handed me my first pay envelope. The money was timely because my glasses and contact lens were in, and I was happy that I could pay for these myself.

I really had a difficult time putting the lens in and taking it out. The lady at Dr. Dandy's told me that I couldn't leave the office until I did it at least once by myself. After fumbling around for 15 or 20 minutes, I was able to put it in and take it out. After the experience, I decided to get me a beer for later.

I went to Minit Market on Montgomery Street to buy some beer. I couldn't help observing the differences in this store from years before. In the past, no security guards were necessary. Now, it had three armed guards to prevent robberies. One armed guard stands by the cash register. Another one stands on the right, near one of the aisles. Then, the third, armed with a shotgun, watches the cash register, too, from the rear behind a counter.

I doubted that this store would be involved in a robbery, given all that firepower. Still, I was careful not to leave my fingerprints on the counter or the door. I didn't lean on the counter and I used my palm or the side of my hand to push open doors. I had decided that whenever I go into a package shop or store, that I would try not to leave my fingerprints in the business. In case the establishment was robbed, I didn't want any detectives coming to my house. I also felt that if a package shop was robbed and my prints were found on the door that the detectives and prosecutors in this town would say that the prints were found on the cash register or behind the counter.

I had the same ideas about cars. Sometimes, when I walked by an expensive car, I was careful not to touch it, fearing that someone could be found dead in the car. I really believed that the people here in this town would lie in court and say my print was found inside the car. At one time, I thought that I was being paranoid, but I thought that a little paranoia is preventative.

I had received notice that I had been admitted to Armstrong State College for the fall quarter of 1975. In anticipation of the typing that I needed to do in college, I went to Sears and put a typewriter on layaway, although I couldn't type. With my next paycheck, I picked up the typewriter and began to practice. One weekend my sister-in-law saw me typing and told me that I was doing it wrong.

"Junior, you need to hold your fingers on the home row keys," Joanne said as she stood over me and positioned my fingers on the middle keys.

"I thought you just hold your fingers up like this so you can see all the keys," I said.

"No, the way you're doing it is wrong," Joanne explained.

I had been practicing and had been able to pick up a little speed. So, I could type a couple of sentences fairly well.

One afternoon at work, as we were standing outside the side door, a car came by with a very attractive young woman in it. She, repeatedly turning her head to look at me and turning back to see the traffic, shouted my name.

"Damn, that was a good-looking woman calling you, Rudolph," Zeke said. "Is that one of your girlfriends?"

"I wished that I knew who she was. I didn't recognize her," I said.

The next day about the same time, the same lady came down the street. This time she pulled over to the side, and I approached her car. As I approached it, I still didn't recognize her.

"How are you doing, Rudolph? I'm Eugenia, Ronald Daughtery's sister."

"I'm sorry, I didn't recognize you yesterday. How are you doing?" I asked.

"I'm fine. I am married and have a child," Eugenia said. "How long have you been out?"

"A few weeks," I said. "How is your brother doing?"

"He's fine. Look, I need to go, but I did wanna stop for a few minutes. Take care of yourself. I will tell my brother that I saw you," Eugenia said.

"You take care too and tell your brother hello."

I had been seeing various people since I had been out. Some of the people looked the same, and some looked completely different from the last time that I had seen them.

One of the most striking changes that I had noticed in some people is how badly some looked. Some were on drugs and looked quite emaciated. Some looked just plain hard; their eyes were darkened around the edges and the whites of their eyes were not white but dirty yellow. Some individuals really looked bad and looked half-dead.

One day as I was returning from the library with some books that I had checked out, I saw a guy that I had been in Sylvania with who looked badly.

"Hey man, I didn't know you were out," he said. "What do you have for the head?"

I knew he was asking me if I had any drugs, but I couldn't help him.

"The only thing that I have for the head is these books," I proclaimed.

"No, I mean drugs."

"Sorry, but I don't mess with drugs," I said.

"Ok, I'm going on down the street."

My parole restrictions were finally lightened up some. I could go out more and on the weekends. I had been going around the city, just to see how Savannah had changed or not changed.

Daddy wanted my brother Willie Lee to go places with me. My brother bought a .38 pistol. Unlike Daddy, however, my brother had a permit to carry a gun. From time to time, Daddy, when he was drinking, would ask me how I was doing and I would tell him okay. He told me that he had told my brother to accompany me when I go out and to shoot anyone that tried to hurt me. Daddy proclaimed that I had gone through hell and needed to have an opportunity to live my life. But I told my brother to ignore what Daddy had been telling him and assured him that I would be okay. I told my brother that I might call him to come and get me if I was too drunk to get home, but so far, I knew what my limit was and was able to get home before I was too drunk.

One Saturday night after I had left the movies downtown, I rode around some of the squares near downtown and down on Bay Street before going home.

The next time I was on West Broad Street to buy some clothes, I saw Lorenzo Stevens, whom I had not seen since we went to Jackson together. He didn't look too good either. His eyes were yellow.

"I saw you last Saturday night downtown. You were cruising for some women," Lorenzo charged.

"I was just riding around, enjoying my freedom and looking at the city."

"Bullshit, you were out looking for pussy. I know a pussy cruise when I see it. Enjoying the city, my ass," Lorenzo scoffed.

"Well, I guess you know," I said as I walked to the car with my packages.

Through my job, I was meeting a few women, but I wasn't taking them seriously. Most of them were looking for a man to pay their bills or buy them some appliances. I didn't have anything for them. I needed all my money for myself and didn't have any to give away.

I saw one woman walking down Anderson Street, and Roger told me not to say anything to her.

"She got a guy, and he is spending a lot of money on her. If she looks at another dude, he will beat her ass and might wanna beat you too," Roger explained.

Although I was a teenager when I left Savannah and my conception of dating girls was simple, I was not prepared for the dynamics involving men and women now. Many women's primary interest was on how much money you were gonna give them and how many of their bills you were willing to pay. I felt that this was dangerous for some women because some of the guys perceived these arrangements as owning women. They controlled who the women saw and spoke to and may not let them go if the woman wanted to end the relationship.

Around the corner from me, I met a rather attractive woman who was in her early twenties. She was living with a guy in his sixties who was paying all her bills and giving her money. However, she didn't like him that much and tried to quit him. The man told her that if she ever tried to leave that he would kill her. She tried to leave, and he shot her in the face, the bullet exiting near her jaw. She and I went to a motel, and she was trying to persuade me to be patient while she delicately extracted herself from this older guy. But I didn't see her anymore after that one night together. I wasn't interested in being shot for some silly shit like that, and I wasn't gonna be paying her bills.

One day, a young guy came to the furniture store and told the manager that he was not gonna make any more payments on the furniture he had purchased and wanted the store to come to his house and pick it all up.

So, instead of delivering furniture, we were picking up furniture that day. When we got to the house with the list of items to pick up, I could see that we were gonna take almost everything. I could also see why this guy had come to the store to ask that the furniture be picked up. He and the woman he was staying with were breaking up.

"Take it all. I bought it on my credit, and this bitch hasn't paid a goddamn cent on this furniture," said the guy angrily.

Within a short period, we had everything loaded up on the truck and the small house was completely empty.

"Now, let's see what you are gonna do now, bitch," the guy stated.

The woman mumbled something to the guy, and he quickly jumped up in her face.

"Bitch, you want me to raise hell?" he shouted just inches from her face.

I was hoping that she didn't repeat what she had said because I didn't wanna see him hit her. She was a frail young woman and she had three small children standing around her in this now empty house. After standing menacingly near her, the guy left the woman and the children in the empty house. I felt sorry for her.

We returned all the furniture to the store and began to clean it up for resale.

A few days before school started, I quit my job at the furniture store.

Unofficially, my sister advised me and told me many things about the school and the criminal justice program. She informed me that Armstrong had an honor code, and professors would often give examinations and then leave the classroom. She told me that it was a violation of the honor code to know that someone has cheated and not report it. She said that when she is taking a test, she keeps her eyes on her paper and does not wanna know what others are doing. She advised me to do the same.

Officially, Dr. Megathlin became my advisor. Consulting with him, I decided that I wanted to take typing first. So, I registered for Beginning Typing, American Government, and Introduction to Criminal Justice.

I really enjoyed my American Government class, which was being taught by an Asian professor. On the first day, I had a difficult time understanding him, but by the second class, I understood him very well. The professor of this class had a practice of announcing all students who made an A on the exam. For each exam, he would recognize me and a few others before the class and then recognize me for making the highest score.

I did well in his class because for the past 8 years, I had watched the evening news on a regular basis and had read the newspaper for a long time. Thus, when he discussed the executive branch and Congress, I knew what he was talking about. Also, when he discussed the judiciary, I already knew the structure of the federal courts, having pursued habeas corpus relief in state and federal courts personally.

In the other classes, I made a B in Introduction to Criminal Justice and a B in Typing. I had the speed and the accuracy to get an A in typing, but during one typing examination, my book fell from the stand. It was slowly slipping, but I couldn't stop to steady it and was hoping that I could finish the exam before it fell. When it fell to the floor, I had to stop typing. The teacher saw that it had fallen and told me that she was sorry. However, I didn't ask for any second chances or special favors.

After my first quarter, my GPA was 3.4. Feeling confident, I asked Dr. Megathlin about me taking an overload. I had to take a noncredit remedial English class, having failed an admission test before enrollment. However, I thought that I should have passed it and gone right into beginning English. Additionally, I was taking Psychology, Sociology, and Algebra.

The school was giving the English examination again, and I decided to retake it as I was taking the remedial class. This time I passed. So, I requested at midterm to get out of the remedial class, and the teacher told me okay because I didn't need to be in a remedial class. She told me that my essays were way above average for the class, and I only needed to work on my verb tenses as I had a tendency to use the wrong verbs.

At the end of the quarter, I had a C in Psychology, a B in Sociology, and an A in Algebra. My Algebra instructor spoke with me at the end of the quarter about changing my major. She told me that I had potential to be a good mathematician. However, I told her that I had already decided upon a major.

During the spring quarter, I had my most challenging and interesting quarter. I had enrolled in Art, but I was completely lost. The professor would lecture on a piece of art and talk about the depth and recession, and I didn't know what the hell he was talking about. I stared at the painting, twisting and turning my head to see what the professor was seeing. I had only taken this course as an elective and didn't need it. So, I dropped it.

The other class, a history class taught by Dr. Duncan, was to have a lasting impression upon me. When I told my sister that I had enrolled in Dr. Duncan's class, she told me that I had made a serious mistake.

"Students have been complaining about him for years. Some say that he is a racist, and he is extremely hard," my sister Cora advised.

"I signed up for his class because it was a convenient time for me. My goal is to take as many classes as I can, and I am not that concerned about a professor's toughness or grades. I wanna do well, but my plan is to get as many credits as I can as fast as I can."

"Okay, you'll see. Don't say that I didn't warn you," my sister Cora stated.

"My name is Dr. Duncan. Besides teaching students, my goal is to get rid of students who don't wanna be here. Education is for the serious. If you are not serious, you shouldn't be here, and some of you are not serious. We've have students who are only at this college because their parents want them to be here, but the students don't wanna be here. Also, we have students here because the government pays their way. I intend to get rid of you students who don't wanna be here. As far as my grading, I do not have a grading system. You get what I give you regardless of what your test scores might say. I know an A student from a B student from a C student from a D student from an

F student. My examinations are short answer, explanation, and true/false. With respect to the true/false, don't guess on a question if you don't really, really know it. If you don't know it, leave it alone because I take off one correct answer for every wrong answer. So, if there are twenty True/False questions and you get ten right and ten wrong, you get zero points. I do this because a monkey can take a true/false examination and get half of them right. Also, you are going to have a map test, in which you have to bring crayons to color your map like kindergarten students. Also, you have to write two papers. On Thursday, we're gonna have our first examination, and it will cover the first nine pages of the book. Now, you may leave," Dr. Duncan announced.

So, on the first week of class, we were having an examination. More than half the class failed, including me. When Dr. Duncan returned the exam papers the next week, he crumpled up some students' exams, told the class that the individual had 32 or 28, and threw the exam to the student. Because I was in the front, he handed my paper to me. One of the black female students angrily told him that she didn't give her permission to announce her score, but he ignored her. When he had returned all the exams, he stated that this would drive out some students and now he was about to get rid of some others.

"In 1619, a Dutch man-of-war ship brought 20 niggers to America, not blacks but niggers. If you need help spelling it, it is N-I-G-G-E-R-S, niggers," Dr. Duncan said.

"What year was that?" I asked.

"1619," he responded.

Dr. Duncan also stated that the first white child born in America was Virginia White Dare and for us to put this very historical event in our notes because it would definitely be on the exam.

I looked around the class briefly, and the black female student was looking very intensely at Dr. Duncan. Her eyes had narrowed so much that only the slits of her eyes were showing. If looks could kill, Dr. Duncan would be dead. He saw her looking at him, but he just smiled. I knew that he had her.

Whenever a student dropped his class, he would announce it happily at the beginning of class.

Then, Dr. Duncan went after other students. He made disparaging comments about the Irish, Italians, and Jews. One day he was talking about the "Honkies" and how they leave the city to buy overpriced, rinky-dink houses in the suburbs. A white student asked in a soft Southern drawl where did he lived. He stated that he lived in downtown Savannah and told the class that all the great minds have come out of the ghettos of the world and nothing has come from the suburbs. Another white student, inquiring about the Honkie statement, asked what was he.

"Whatever, I am. I'm not one of you," Dr. Duncan said.

At midterm, I had an F, but I decided not to drop his class. In fact, in a perverse manner, I was enjoying it. I didn't consider myself a humorous person, but he did make me laugh sometimes with his comments. I thought he was a white, overweight Richard Pryor. Although he initially used the word,

Niggers, and targeted black students first, I didn't think he was racist. He definitely tried to shock students, and even admitted that he had to do it after students had come from the "hot house," his term for high school.

By midterm almost half of the class had dropped. Only the serious students were left. So, he stopped with some of his antics. He was now referring to black people as blacks.

"You know, I went to New York recently. While some people wanted to see the United Nations Building and the Empire State Building, I wanted to see Harlem. I had goose bumps walking down 125th Street in Harlem with all those black people. It was like walking down West Broad Street here in Savannah on a Saturday night," Dr. Duncan reported.

He was lecturing about slavery this day and had digressed, but he returned to the topic.

"There were some slaves who were allowed to return to Africa. You know, when they got back to Africa, they acted just like the white man," he stated.

I thought that this was similar to what the Muslims had said—that black people, once they've been around the devil, frequently act like him. I found myself frequently comparing his version of history to the Muslim's version of history.

"Another thing about black people. They are so docile when it comes to white people. They get in front of the white man and start Uncle Tomming."

Then, he stood in front of the class and started scratching his head and shuffling his feet. He looked at me and asked me is this the way we Uncle Tom. I laughed and told him that he was doing it okay.

I buckled down even more in Dr. Duncan's class and really began to get deep inside my textbook. My grades came up and at the end of the quarter, I had a C in his class. He really liked the papers that I wrote. I was so proud of this C and felt that it was a much higher grade than the A's that I had received. I also felt that I had learned a lot and knew that I had what it would take to finish.

I was always studying, at home and at school. Sometimes on the weekend, I would go to Forsythe Park to study, the same park that I was supposed to have been spotted running from the east side. As I was walking towards a bench, I heard someone shout my name. Looking in the direction where I heard my name, I saw two people from a distance walking towards me, but they were too far for me to determine who they were. I stopped and waited. As the two people came closer, I recognized Iceman, who was dressed in a pimp-like hat with a Superfly-type coat and who was carrying a greasy grocery bag, and a woman, who was dressed in cheap, bright-green pants, a yellow blouse, and cheap shoes sprinkled with shining pieces.

"I knew that was you. I couldn't see your face from way over there, but I recognized your walk. No one else in the world walks like you do. I want you to meet my woman, Minnie," Iceman said as he was pointing towards the woman. "How long have you been out?"

"Nice to meet you," I said looking towards Minnie. "I've been out about a year. What're you doing in Savannah?"

"Well, me and my woman Minnie just getting off the road. We were up north and we passing through Savannah on the way back to Brunswick," Iceman said, rubbing his face with one hand as I remembered he did on detail in Reidsville while talking about slick things.

Then, Iceman reached into the greasy bag and pulled out two stale-looking pieces of bread with some bologna between it.

"Hey man, how about let me hold a few dollars? We're trying to get back to Brunswick," Iceman asked.

"I'm sorry, Ice, but I don't have any money. I'm not working. If I had anything, you could get it," I stated.

We chatted a little more and he asked about Giles. Then, he and Minnie walked towards Whitaker Street. It looked as if they were heading south and headed in the direction of Highway 17, which would take them to Brunswick.

I thought that when a person returned from being on the road, he should have a pocket full of money and riding. I wondered what type of filmflam games he and Minnie were playing on the road. Whatever games they were playing, these games didn't work very well, and they needed some new ones. They were walking back to Brunswick, hungry, and eating bologna sandwiches out of a greasy bag. I knew if Iceman got busted and returned to Reidsville, he would be bragging on a detail how slick he was on the road, how much money he made playing various con games, and what type of car he was in when he rode through Savannah on the way back to Brunswick.

At school, I studied a lot in the cafeteria between classes. In the cafeteria, most of the black students had a section that they occupied and no whites sat there. Because they were much younger than me and because I saw school as a job, I sat by myself and studied with a cup of coffee on the table. A black female student began to come to my table and introduced herself as Debra Samuels. Every time she would see me, she would come over.

Debra told me that she was impressed with my seriousness and liked my maturity and wanted me to call her. At first, I was a little resistant, but I relented and called her a few times. We went out a few times and would walk around campus sometimes. One day while I was at Debra's house, Debra told me something that shocked me.

"You know, Rudolph. I just learned who you really are. I didn't make the connection until I recently learned that you are Cora Alexander's brother. The person you killed was my first cousin. In fact, here is his picture on this coffee table. His mother is my aunt, and she and my father are brother and sister. But I am not mad with you. I'm in love with you. When I met you, I didn't know who you were. I thought that you were good looking, mature, and serious. I had grown to like you a lot, and what happened years ago can't change how I feel about you now," Debra related.

After getting over my initial shock, I knew that I had to terminate this relationship.

"I think that you and I shouldn't see each other any more because some of your relatives might not see things the way you do. It is gonna cause hard feelings between you and your aunt and perhaps your father. It could cause a problem if I ran into your aunt at your house. I am not gonna apologize to her because I feel that I was the one treated wrongly. Your cousin initiated that conflict and his friends in that gang kept it going. Your relatives might still be mad, but I am mad too. This could lead to a problem. For this reason, we shouldn't be seeing each other anymore," I said.

Debra started crying and telling me that we could still see each other, but I persisted and told her no. I didn't wanna deal with what could happen.

During the summer quarter, I decided to take another overload by taking 15 hours at Armstrong and one at Savannah State College. My parole officer commented that I had an ambitious schedule by leaving Armstrong during the day, going to Savannah State, and then returning to Armstrong for an evening class. But my goal was to take as many classes as possible because I intended to switch to taking evening classes and working during the day. It was a sacrifice now because I didn't have much money but I believed that it would pay off in the end.

At Savannah State, I was taking a Philosophy class, which students at the college told me was taught by a very difficult professor. Although Savannah State was predominantly black, some of the professors there were white, and this philosophy class was being taught by a white professor named Dr. Smith. At the end of the quarter, Dr. Smith stated that four students had an opportunity to get an A in his class, and this was the most students with an A average that he has ever had going into the final examination. I was one of the four and received an A after the final examination.

During the time I was in summer school, there was a scandal involving the police department, and several police officers were fired from the force. Ordinarily, I wouldn't have been too concerned except that one of the officers fired was Bush, the same son of a bitch who lied at my trial. He was fired for taking gifts from some gambling figures. Bush lied on black defendants for the white prosecutors. Now, when Bush was caught with his hand in the cookie jar, he couldn't call in those favors to save his job.

I was not having much of a social life, but I had somewhat planned it that way. I had another one of my black female classmates flirting with me. I thought that she was a little too young for me. In a conversation about relationships, she told me that she wouldn't go with a guy and make love to him unless the guy was buying her clothes and giving her money. When I told her that I wouldn't buy her a handkerchief, she stopped talking to me.

Her girlfriend Sharon was not as bold, and I liked her quiet style. Interestingly, she was the granddaughter of Officer Nealy, the officer who arrested me. I told her that I knew her grandfather, but I didn't tell her how I knew him.

At the end of the summer quarter, I began looking for a job. I went to some businesses that reported that they help college students, but I was not hired. I began pounding the pavements again, looking for any daytime job.

After a while, my parents were getting concerned about me. One day, Daddy asked me to ride off with him, and we went to Percy's house. While there, they started talking about going home and decided to go the next weekend. I was gonna do the driving. We would leave early Saturday morning and come back Sunday night.

I called my parole officer to tell him that I was going to my daddy's hometown and would be back Sunday night. I learned that I had a new parole officer. He told me to let him know when I was back in town.

We left Savannah about 4:00 in the morning and headed to Crawfordville, Georgia. When we got there, we dropped Percy and Willie at their sister's, and Daddy and I went into town for breakfast. Long ago, when Daddy's brother was living, we would arrive in time for breakfast. After he died and Aunt Emma moved away, Daddy would eat breakfast at a truck stop, but this time, we decided to eat in downtown Crawfordville at a restaurant.

"Excuse me, are you a member?" asked a white waitress.

"No," I said slowly, looking at Daddy.

"This is a private restaurant, and you have to be a member to eat here," said the waitress.

"Okay, but could I use your restroom?" I asked.

"You have to be member," the waitress declared.

Daddy and I left the restaurant laughing.

"Damn, you have to be a member to use the bathroom," Daddy said as we laugh.

"Well, this is your hometown, not mine," I joked.

"Yeah, but I thought that things would have changed by now," Daddy said.

"It had changed, Daddy. In the past, it was NO NIGGERS ALLOWED and this was clearly communicated. Now, you can eat there but you have to be a member. What they won't say is that only whites can be members. That's change."

We went to the truck stop and the waitress took our orders.

Daddy still had a cousin near Crawfordville called Dorsha, and we went to her house. When we got there, she had visitors from Cleveland. I had heard Daddy talk about these people for years, and I was finally able to meet them. He called me into the room and introduced me to Boy Red, Putt, and Chicken—all from Cleveland. Afterwards, I went back into another room, I began to nod off because I was sleepy. I could hear one of Daddy's cousins asking Daddy if I were the one that was in "trouble." Daddy said yes and stated that I was his heartstring.

When we got back to Savannah, I called my parole officer to inform him that I was back. He told me that he didn't mean for me to call him at home, and I could have called him at the office the next day. I apologized and hung up. I thought that when he said to call him when I got back, he meant exactly what he had said. Better safe than sorry, I thought.

Chapter 26

One morning as I was looking through the want ads, I saw a very brief advertisement for a truck driver. When I called, I was told to apply at Gonchar Produce Company at the State Farmer's Market on Highway 80.

I went that day and filled out an application. It was a small produce company, and the warehouse smelled awful. There were numerous cats in the warehouse, and the place reeked of cat shit. I was relieved somewhat that there was no question on the application asking about any felony convictions, but I knew that my completed application looked suspicious. It showed that I had worked for three months in 1975 at Home Furnishing, and the previous employment was in 1967.

"How come you stop working in 1967?" asked Gonchar.

"I was in prison," I responded.

"For what?"

"Homicide."

I had decided not to use the term murder for a couple of reasons. Foremost, I never accepted the idea that I was proven guilty of murder in a fair trial. Secondarily, I thought that homicide was a more euphemistic term than murder. Homicide doesn't necessarily connotate guilt, but murder does. Also, a homicide may be justified under the circumstances but not murder.

"Well, they didn't keep you very long," Gonchar stated.

"You got Lamy down as a reference, I know a Lamy. Is he in his sixties?"

"No, I believe that this Lamy is in his late twenties or early thirties. Maybe you know his father," I said.

"Well, we pay minimum wage here. We open at 6A.M. and we worked until 5P.M.. But I generally let the drivers go about 1P.M. or a little later. We also work on Saturdays for a half of a day," he explained.

"I can get here at 6A.M. every morning, and I don't mind working on Saturday either," I said eagerly.

"Well, I am still taking applications, and I will hold yours."

As I was leaving, I thought that this job would be ideal for me. The pay wasn't good, but evening classes at Armstrong begin at 6P.M., and I could work full-time and get to class in time. But I didn't think that this guy was gonna call me first. I decided to call my parole officer and ask him to call Gonchar for me since Gonchar may know his father. Lamy called Gonchar and recommended me for the job. After a week, when I didn't hear anything, I started looking again. I saw something in the newspaper and was headed out of the door to apply for it when the telephone rang. It was Gonchar wanting to know if I could start work the next day at 6A.M.. I told him yes.

The next morning I was at the Farmer's Market a few minutes before 6A.M.. A few minutes later, Gonchar drove up, opened the door, and disarmed the burglar alarm system. He handed me a time card, told me to punch in my card in the clock just outside the door, and handed me the withholding forms to fill out.

I quickly learned that Gonchar had serious problems with his drivers. Although they were supposed to be at work at 6A.M., they came in at different times. Fields, who lived down the street from the Farmer's Market, came to work at about 8A.M.. Spike came in at about 9:30A.M. or 10A.M. and the other driver named Earnest, who drank a lot, came in at about 10:30A.M.. Gonchar had a problem keeping drivers because the pay was low, and he didn't have to pay overtime because of the smallness of the business. I also heard that Gonchar was planning on getting rid of the drivers as soon as he could find some others to replace them.

During the first day, I was helping to load the three trucks that Gonchar operated and put up lettuce and tomatoes that Gonchar had ordered. I would also go into a freezer in the back where Gonchar kept meat and get items that he was gonna send out. Gonchar also had a trailer backed up to the ramp where he kept meat in too.

Gonchar was asking me about various businesses around town and if I knew where they were. When I told him no, he was angry, saying that I didn't know where anything was; therefore, he couldn't let me deliver. So, I worked around the warehouse mostly.

Two of the drivers, Fields and Spike, were robbing Gonchar blind. They justified their stealing by saying that they were making things right since Gonchar was not paying much.

"Why do you park your car way over there? Why don't you park by the trailer, and he could load up your car," Fields commented.

"You're not putting anything in my car," I said. "What you and Spike do is your business. I'm not gonna tell, and I am not gonna help you or be a lookout."

"What are you, some type of good nigger? I heard that you were in the joint. You should be down with us," Fields charged.

"I learned a long time ago from studying other guys not to do anything with anyone. If I were to steal, I wouldn't do it with you or Spike because I know that Negroes like you will roll over on people," I said. "Further, it is just not worth it to me to have someone coming to arrest me for stealing hamburgers or a box of bananas. If someone comes for me, it has to be for something far more serious than small-time thievery, and when that happens, I am not likely to go. So you and Spike do whatever. But don't involve me in any way."

The next morning, Spike and Fields stole some steaks out of the freezers. They took about ten boxes and threw them over the wall in the back. Then, they went around the back of the warehouse and threw them over a fence. When they left that morning to make deliveries, they went behind the Farmer's Market first and picked up the steaks.

Gonchar knew that he was losing merchandise and took inventory once a month. He tried to watch the drivers, but he couldn't do it. There was no one there but his assistant Jack, who was primarily in charge of selling meat and didn't care about thievery. Jack said that Gonchar promised him a portion of the profits, but won't let him see the books. So, Jack was not interested in helping Gonchar and would go outside and badmouth Gonchar to the drivers. Gonchar's wife, Rosalee, came to the business at about 10:30 or 11 A.M..

Gonchar sent me into the freezer to bring out three boxes of steaks. I knew the steaks were gone, but I went in looking for them anyway.

"There are no steaks in the freezer," I said.

"Yeah there are. You just overlooked them," Gonchar said.

I went back in to carry out the charade of looking again for the steaks.

"I've looked but there are none in there," I insisted.

Gonchar took out his inventory book and told me that he was supposed to have twelve boxes in the back. He got up and went with me into the freezer, but he couldn't find them either.

"I'll be goddamned. They're gone," Gonchar said.

He went back in the office and told Rosalee and Jack. Gonchar sensed what had happened and tried to trick Spike and Fields. The first person to return from making deliveries was Fields, and Gonchar gave him the key to the freezer and told him to go get three boxes of steak. Fields, acting cool, took the key and went to the freezer. Gonchar was watching Fields' reaction, but Fields sensed what Gonchar was doing. After a few minutes, Fields came back and told Gonchar that he was out of steak and needed to reorder some. When Spike came back, Gonchar repeated his test, and Spike was cool too.

The next day, Gonchar told me to go with Earnest to learn the route and where businesses were located. It was a fun day. We made a delivery at St. Benedictine School, and the cook gave us a large glass of beer from the Fathers' keg. This was the first time that I had learned that Catholic priests drink. We also went to the Landings, a country club for rich white folks. The cook there gave us some food that he was preparing.

Gonchar later announced, much to my dislike, that he was only gonna have one person going into the meat freezer and that was gonna be me. He also moved the freezer key to his desk, and I had to get it from his desk and put it back. I didn't like it so much because that freezer was cold, and I had to keep wiping my glasses when I came out. Spike and Fields were not pleased that they couldn't go into the freezer anymore and blamed me. I knew that they were talking about me, but I didn't care.

Gonchar, feeling a little desperate with his drivers, rehired Willie Mims, whom he had fired in the past for stealing two chickens out of a box. Willie Mims, as Gonchar related to me, made a delivery to a business, and the cook called to complain that the chickens were short. Initially, Gonchar thought that the chickens were shorted at Fries Chicken, where Gonchar had purchased the box. Willie Mims overheard Gonchar talking to a Fries salesperson and panicked. After work, Willie Mims went to a woman's house where he had dropped the two chickens, retrieved them, and then took them to the business that was supposed to have them. Willie Mims was almost retarded. So, he thought that he was doing a wise thing. When the cook told Gonchar what Willie had done, Gonchar fired Willie. Now, Gonchar had hired him back, sensing that at least Willie Mims would come to work on time and everyday, although he had to be watched.

School had started back, and I was taking only night classes. I was getting off at work at about 2P.M. or 3P.M.. As soon as I returned home, I would take a bath and head to Armstrong. I would use the time before class to do some additional studying. I was also studying early in the morning. Sometimes, I would get to the Farmer's Market at about 5A.M. and drink a cup of coffee in Kesseler Restaurant, which was located inside the market. I felt that I could absorb material best early in the morning.

One of my classes was juvenile delinquency, and a requirement of the course was to work as a volunteer probation officer. The class was being taught by a federal probation officer. Because I sensed that my status as a parolee might have some bearing on whether I should participate in this volunteer program, I confided to the instructor about my background and status. When the representative from the juvenile court came, he told me that Judge Dickey probably wouldn't want me to participate because the judge had some strong views about offenders. I thought that I would be given an alternative assignment, but Dr. Megathlin intervened, and I was allowed to participate in the volunteer program.

I was assigned a young man who lived four blocks from me that had broken into a barber shop. In fact, he broke into the shop where I got my hair cut. I began checking up on the young man and began to take him places with me. We went bowling once, and I also took him on campus. I was supposed to be committed to the program for 10 weeks, and thus, I had to take an incomplete in the course. The director of the program, after the 10 weeks, told me that I was doing a good job with this young man and asked me to continue. So, I continued working with the young guy though it was no longer a course requirement.

All the classes that I was taking now were criminal justice classes. I enjoyed these more and was making very good grades. Many of the students in the classes were police officers and they expressed, as expected, some very conservative views about what was wrong with the criminal justice system.

Dr. Megathlin and I were discussing this one day. We agreed that law enforcement people tend to say very punitive statements in class and in the public, but some of them ironically will help prisoners who work around police barracks. We both agreed that it is easy to sometimes dislike and condemn people that one doesn't know. But once someone is around some prisoners, they see them a little differently and sometimes think that these prisoners are somehow different from other prisoners.

Gonchar finally sent me out alone to make deliveries, making sure that I knew where every stop was. One delivery was to be at the county jail. Gonchar remarked that he never had to tell any of his past or present drivers where the jail was, and they all knew. The drivers might not know where some businesses were, but everyone knows where the jail is.

I acknowledged to myself that this was indeed true. Black people knew where the jail and the emergency room were. I thought that it would be wonderful to live in a city where I didn't know where these two places were.

I was feeling good as the fall quarter ended, until I saw in the papers that Lionel Drew was chosen to be the next judge of Recorder's Court, which conducted preliminary hearings. A crook with a robe, I thought to myself. I bristled every time I saw Drew's name in a case. In one case, the newspaper stated that Drew was quoted as saying that should a lawyer on trial for killing his wife be found guilty that the state would be asking for the death penalty. However, the lawyer was acquitted. I thought that Drew should have had the death penalty asked for him. I believed that it was a mistake to make him a judge.

A few days after this announcement in the newspaper, I saw Drew downtown walking back to the courthouse. I was making deliveries and had parked the truck on a side street. Just as I was looking at my clipboard, I happened to see Drew strolling towards the courthouse. I couldn't help remembering all the dirty, nasty things he said to me and what he did to me.

I also saw James Head, who was also now a judge. I was making a delivery at a country club when he and I passed. I was surprised that he spoke to me although he didn't know me. I never saw him back in 1968 and had only spoken to his associate, Mr. Boney.

At work, things had changed considerably. Gonchar had stomach problems, and he was getting sicker. Sometimes, after the trucks were loaded and had left, he would go to his car and lay down. One morning, as he was bent over, he told me that he needed my help. He asked me to finish loading the trucks and told me that he was counting on me.

By that time, I had become the only person that he knew wouldn't steal from him. His wife told me that Gonchar was not gonna admit it to me, but he had just starting making money since I arrived. She said that Gonchar knew he was losing merchandise but was just trying to keep it to a minimum. Thus, the business was not making much of a profit. Rosalee told me that they were making money now that I was the only person going in the freezer.

Later that day Gonchar went into the hospital. The next morning, Rosalee came at 6A.M. and told me that she wanted me to stay at the business with her and help her run it. She gave me keys to the front door and the burglar alarm and told me that I could leave to go to school whenever I wanted to leave. Thus, Rosalee and I would load the trucks and then I would sit in the office with her. She would send out for lunch for both of us, and she also gave me permission to go into the money bag in the morning to buy coffee and biscuits for everyone. The first day, I told her how much money I got out of the pouch, but she told me that I didn't have to tell her. She would just readjust it.

The other drivers were even more jealous of me now and were angry. One day Rosalee decided that she had enough of Fields. She told him that she didn't need him anymore and he was fired. Earnest, who was out on a drunk, missed work for 3 days. When he came in at about 10:30 the morning afterward, he was speculating how many hours he had in and would have by payday. However, Rosalee stated that she was gonna give hours to the people who were coming to work on time and every day. So, as soon as the trucks were loaded, Rosalee told Earnest that he could clock out about an hour-and-a-half for that day. The next day, Earnest was working down the ramp at another produce company.

Sidney Brown came back as a driver. I had heard about him and had read about him in the newspapers. Sidney shot and killed his wife. His daughter, Linda, was a student at Armstrong, and I had seen her around campus. When Sidney went to trial, Linda was a witness for the state and the jury convicted Sidney of manslaughter and gave him 9 years. Sidney's attorney filed an appeal, and now Sidney was out on appeal bond. The first day at work, Sidney had an announcement to make.

"Any motherfucker snitches on me, that will be the last snitching he'll do," Sidney announced angrily.

I sensed that he was talking to me, and I also sensed that he had been talking to Spike. Because I knew that I had not snitched on anyone, I didn't say anything to Sidney. He didn't scare me with his announcement, but I didn't think that I needed to defend myself.

Later, we started talking, and I took the opportunity to talk about Fields and Spike after Sidney brought up Spike's name. I simply repeated what I had initially said to Fields, expecting Sidney to understand that whatever he did at Gonchar that he was not to involve me. After Sidney learned that I went to Armstrong with his oldest daughter and we knew some of the same guys in prison, we began to talk more and got to be a lot friendlier. In fact, we started hanging out together a little on Saturday after work.

I really felt sorry for Sidney. He was drinking a lot, but unlike Earnest, he would be at work at 6A.M. every day. I suspected that he was drinking so much to deal with the guilt of killing his wife. One Saturday after work, I went over to Sidney's father's house. As I walked onto the porch, I could see Sidney inside the house sitting at the top of the stairs crying. Another one of his daughters was leaning over to him and talking softly to him about killing her mother. She told him that she hated what he had done, but she still loved him. All Sidney could do was cry. When he saw me, he acquired the energy to get up and leave with me. In my car, he told me that he couldn't say anything and had to sit there as he wiped his eyes. He said that he was happy that I had driven up. I told him that he needed another drink, and we headed to the package shop.

Sidney also knew that he was responsible for one of his boys having a psychiatric break down. The strain of his mother dying was too much and this triggered the breakdown. All of Sidney's children were staying with his father. So, every time Sidney went over to his father's house, he saw his son, who didn't speak and had a blank stare on his face. So, Sidney was drinking everyday. I suspected that either alcohol was gonna kill him or someone on the street.

Sidney had a very quick temper, and though he was in his early forties, he had no hesitation about fighting. One day, Willie Mims told Sidney to go to hell. Sidney attacked Willie in the warehouse, biting him in the face, and hitting him with his fists. I had to break it up and tried to tell Sidney to let that kind of stuff go.

"I can't do that. No one is gonna talk to me that way," Sidney insisted.

"You and I both know that Willie Mims is retarded and he is harmless. Willie Mims just talks a lot. Ignore him," I suggested.

"No, I can't allow that," Sidney repeated.

"That is one of the differences between you and me. I don't care if someone tells me to go to hell. I am only concerned when blood is drawn or about to be drawn. I don't like seeing my own blood. Words from someone like Willie Mims, I can ignore. On the other hand, you feel that saying 'go to hell' is enough to fight someone, which could lead you to serious trouble," I stated.

I had another view of things in this area, which is when people have wronged me, I want them to be upset with me later because that means that I did something about it and just didn't lie down and take it. I want them to curse me every time they bring up my name and say that they wished that they had killed me. The angrier they are, the more it means that I didn't roll over like a licked dog. But I decided not to tell Sidney this part.

As much as I tried to give Sidney another way of viewing and responding to people, he wouldn't accept what I was saying. He insisted that the line in the sand should be where he had drawn it. Sidney was just that way.

One morning he stated that he had rode the bus, and some teenage boys were in the back of the bus raising hell. The bus driver, whom Sidney was talking to, was afraid to say anything to the boys. But Sidney wasn't. He went to the back and told the boys to sit their behinds down and behave themselves. The boys sat down. Sidney stated that if the boys had talked back to him, he would have kicked their asses. I knew that he meant it.

One day, when I went to over to Sidney's father's house, he and I walked up to a pool hall and beer joint on the corner of Gwinett and Waters Avenue. I was just gonna have a beer and didn't plan to play pool because I couldn't play well. I was watching Sidney around the pool table with other guys, and

I knew that one day he was gonna get killed or he would kill someone. His presented demeanor was that he was the 800-pound gorilla, and all it took was another gorilla for something to develop.

Sidney confided something to me one day when I was standing in front of his father's house, and I told him not to ever repeat it to anyone again.

"Years ago, I stabbed a guy in the stomach and he died. The person who saw me do it just died, so there are no living witnesses. Therefore, I can talk about it now," Sidney announced.

"No, don't discuss it and don't ever repeat what you just told me. You don't know that only one person saw you. It could be that someone else saw you that you didn't see. You don't know who is watching us now. It doesn't look like anyone is around, but someone could be peeping out the window or from under a house. Another thing, there is no statute of limitation on a homicide. You can always be tried for murder regardless of how many years ago that it happened. Your admitting to a killing might be all that is needed to put you in the penitentiary. I have heard a lot of guys in prison talk about the law, and a lot of times, they were dead wrong. One guy said that no murder charge can be brought if there is no body and a dumb guard told him that was true. But it was wrong, and you are wrong to think that you can't be tried. Trust me Sidney, don't repeat what you just said," I insisted.

"Okay, I know you are studying law and criminal justice. So, I won't repeat it. Thanks for telling me," Sidney stated.

He did switch the subject and started talking about his daughter Linda and her running for Miss BAM at Armstrong.

I had heard about Miss BAM and knew that it was a position that some black females were running for and was connected to a black organization on campus. But I had no interests in student activities. I was just there for a degree.

According to Sidney, Linda told him that she lost Miss BAM because her competitor had a bigger behind.

"She told me: Daddy, you know black men like women with big behinds and the person who won had a big behind," Sidney said, laughing.

"That sounds like sour grapes to those who are not at Armstrong. But let me tell you that there might be some truth to it. I am not that interested in student activities, but I can see. The young lady who won, indeed, has a big behind. If I had voted, I would have voted for the other person too. Her behind looks like she got basketballs in her jeans. She is also a cheerleader for the basketball team. I was at the game one night when the team was losing, but some of us were satisfied seeing her with that little skirt on. I saw her at a social function once and I believed she was with her boyfriend. One guy looked at me and I looked at him. You know how when you see a real fox and with a guy, and you're looking at the guy trying to figure out how he got so lucky. So, don't dismiss what Linda said because she might have been right. That girl's behind belongs in the Hall of Fame," I said.

One day at work Sidney asked my advice on another issue.

"I've been thinking about withdrawing my appeal and serving my time. One guy asked me why I let the 9 years hang over my head, and if he were me that he would go do the time and get it over," Sidney stated. "What do you think?"

"I don't know who you have been talking to, Sidney, but whoever it is, stop. You don't wanna go anywhere and get anything over with. Let that 9 years hang over your head until the cows come home. Live the best you can, until it is time for you go. Anyway, you probably won't go to prison. If the white folks really wanted you in prison, you would be in prison. There are guys in prison for killing their wives or girlfriends, and they wanna get out badly. I left a guy in prison named Yammy who had life for killing his girlfriend. He was angry when I made parole. That's how badly he wanted to get out and there are others. Yet, you are thinking about going in. Also, if you withdraw your appeal, you will hurt other black defendants. In a future case involving a black defendant in which the outcome can go either way, a white judge would say that black men don't wanna be free, thinking about you. So, in a borderline case, this person will go to prison. As I said, I don't think you will have to do the 9 years, especially if you don't get into anything. That's why I tell you to ignore some stuff, like that scrape you got into with Willie Mims. If they wanted you in prison, you would be in prison now. Just be thankful you are out," I said.

I wasn't sure that Sidney really wanted to do the time as much as he wanted to get away from his children. They were killing him with love and he had to regularly look at his son who had had the psychiatric breakdown. I felt that I might have been a little selfish in that I didn't want him to withdraw his appeal because of my feelings about the legal system in Savannah. I knew that a negative aspect of Sidney being out was that it might influence some other guys to kill their wives or girlfriends, thinking that they could get the type of deal Sidney got. But I also knew that Sidney was not really getting away with anything and that he was being punished more by being free, and sending him to prison would be less punishment. But I thought that I would advise him like a lawyer who was a hundred percent concerned with his client and not concerned with societal implications. I concluded that I told him right, and I believed that he was listening.

One day when I was in the Piggy Wiggly Supermarket on the east side, someone behind the food area called my name.

"Hello, Rudolph," said Sylvia.

"Hi, Sylvia," I said as I immediately recognized her.

"How long have you been home?" she asked.

"A little over a year," I said.

Sylvia and I talked awhile, reminiscing about when I first went to her house and had to leave at 9P.M. when the coo-coo bird came out of the clock. I also reminded her that I had to put my shirttail in before I could come in her house. She told me that she got married, had two daughters, and now was divorced. Before I left, she gave me her telephone number and urged me to call her. I called her and began going to her house.

She had a pregnant white girl living with her that was named Joy and who used to dance at one of the clubs downtown. Sylvia also had a black homosexual friend who would come over to her apartment and talk about his relationship with a high school teacher. Sylvia had some other friends over who smoked marijuana with her. I told her that I didn't smoke it, but I would drink a beer if she had one in her refrigerator. They were passing around the joint, and I passed it to the next person without smoking it. Some of Sylvia's friends got up and left, swearing to Sylvia that I had to be an undercover police officer. As they were leaving, they told me that the names that they had told me in the introductions were not really their names. I laughed at them and their implying that a black man who didn't smoke marijuana had to be an undercover police.

I didn't mind too much Sylvia smoking marijuana because it increased her libido, although she didn't need an increase. She told me that she liked sex and liked the way the penis felt. I thought that she was my type of woman. You never had to beg her and there was no "I don't feel like it tonight." Sometimes, when I rolled off, she would roll over on me to maintain our connection. Sex with her was good, and it was even better when she was high on marijuana. Although sex was good, I never really spent the night with her. I would always get up and go home. Sometimes, I would leave at 3 or 4 in the morning. Then, I would go home and get ready to go to work. Part of the reason I didn't stay was that I was still on parole, and the other reason was that Sylvia was talking about us moving in together. I liked her, but I didn't wanna marry her or move in with her.

My parole regulations were becoming more liberal. I didn't have to report every month and could send in a written report every month and then go in to see my parole officer every 3 months. I had also learned that I might be able to get off parole after 2 years. I was planning to graduate in June 1977 with my A.S. degree in criminal justice, and I was gonna ask that I be released from parole for exemplary behavior.

I was taking penology during the winter quarter and part of the requirements for the course was a class trip to Reidsville. I debated whether I should go, considering that I might be recognized by some of the prisoners. But I decided to go. I also thought that the young guy that I was working with might benefit from going too. So, I contacted the director of the volunteer program at the juvenile court, and he, after consulting with the judge, okayed me taking him.

On the visit, the girls in the class were not allowed inside the prison and received a very limited tour. The males were escorted through the L Building and the M Building. When we passed through the L Building, I looked into the cellblock in which I was a prisoner from 1969 to 1971. The inside still looked the same. We were taken to the back where we passed both the buildings where I had worked—the tag plant and the MDTA training. As we were walking, one guy who was in L2 with me recognized me and asked was I out now. I told him yes. He asked me for my watch, but I told him no.

The group was taken back near the front and we got on the elevator to go the fifth floor, where the electric chair was. The guard began to explain the procedures involved in an execution. Considerable emotions erupted in me, but no one knew. The guard showed the steps involved in the "last mile" which really was about 15 yards. I was careful not to touch the big, wooden white chair and stood back a little and allowed my classmates to huddle around it. The guard explained the purpose of the wedge that was in the back of the chair. He stated that it was designed to hold the prisoner tight in the chair as he struggled and keep the prisoner from rocking too much as the current went through him. I could visualize myself struggling and the wedge dropping further and further down the back of the chair and holding me tighter and tighter. The guard stated that after the execution, the prisoner was put on a table that was in the room and stated that the wooden block he held in his hand had held many prisoners' heads. I could also visualize me stretched out on the table too with my head being held by the wooden block. Much to my disappointment, my juvenile friend sat in the chair. I don't believe in bad luck so much, but he never should have sat in that chair. On the way back to Savannah, I told him that he shouldn't have sat in that chair because a lot of black men had died in it. Although I was feeling many emotions, I was not sorry that I went.

At the end of the winter quarter, my sister and I both made the Dean's List, and all students who did were published in the Savannah newspaper. I could have made the Dean's List in the fall quarter too, but I had to take the incomplete in juvenile delinquent course. My employer saw it and a lady that momma worked for saw it, too. Momma was really proud that two of her children were on the Dean's List at Armstrong State College and this white lady told Momma that her daughter had to drop out because she couldn't pass the courses. I had a natural high that lasted a long, long time.

Chapter 27

One night I was returning from the theater and was traveling down Abercorn Street. I saw a car in the median waiting to turn on Abercorn Street. Just as I was about to pass this car waiting to pull into the traffic, the waiting car pulled out and hit my driver's side door. I pulled over and the car pulled behind me. The driver was a white teenager who stated that he wanted to call his father. I went to a telephone and called the police. When the officer arrived, he cited the teenager. We were scheduled to go to court in a few days.

I dreaded going to court, however.

"You shouldn't be concerned since the guy hit your car and there is no way that you are gonna be found responsible for the accident," said my brother.

"That's not what concerns me. It's Lionel Drew. I don't wanna see Drew and don't wanna appear before him," I said.

I really had to prepare myself to go to court for this accident. I didn't wanna tell this man anything, knowing what I know about him.

When the day came for me to go to court, I arrived before court started but wouldn't go in. Instead, I stood just outside the door. I decided that I was not gonna stand up for Drew when he strolled into the courtroom and didn't wanna be the only person in the courtroom who refused to stand for the judge. Other people were going in the courtroom and sitting down. When the door was opened again, I could see that Drew had come into the courtroom, and everyone was sitting down. At this moment, I walked in and sat down.

I was staring at him and remembering my very first conversation with him and what he said to me. I also remembered what he said to me on the morning of the trial when I was in the sheriff's office and the purpose of his verbal attack. Before I could relive anymore, the case against the teenager was called, and I was called as a witness to stand before Drew.

I was not too attentive to the court proceedings. I was looking at Drew, and for a few moments, we had eye contact. I was sure that he didn't remember my face, but I could sense that he sensed that this black man standing before him was not in awe of him and was not a fan of his. My heart was pounding so hard that my chest started hurting, causing me to have difficulty breathing. I wanted to reach up to him and snatch his ass off the bench. He did not deserve to be deciding anything for anyone. I knew how they throw cases and helped fix trials.

I was asked what happened and I told how my car was hit. As I was testifying, I was thinking about Drew and him telling me at one time that he didn't give a goddamn. In a matter of a few minutes, the case was over, but I didn't remember what was said. We were ushered out of the side door, and then I recalled hearing that the teenager's father saying that the case was dismissed because it was a civil matter.

I was so immersed in my feelings about Drew that I had not remembered that this was the same court in which I had my preliminary hearing, and my being bound over to superior court in 1967 was my last appearance in this court.

I met with the insurance adjustor, and he indicated that he was gonna recommend to the insurance carrier that the boy's family pay for my damages. In a few weeks, I received a check to cover the damages to the driver's side of my door.

Sylvia had been complaining that I was not spending much time with her, and she was beginning to get on my nerves.

"Are you coming over tonight?" Sylvia asked.

"I can't. I have a test coming up, and I need to study," I explained.

"You know, I don't see you very much," Sylvia whined.

"I would like to see you more but it is tough. I'm working about 50 hours a week at Gonchar, 6 days a week, and I am going to school at night. Besides just going to class, I need to read and keep up. Those professors at Armstrong kick ass and take names. I have to study," I said.

"But I wanna see you. Why don't you bring your book here and you can study here. That way I could look at you," Sylvia said.

"Okay."

I took my book and went over to Sylvia's house. I suspected that she really wanted to have sex, and this was why she wanted me to come over. When I got there with my book, she allowed me to study for about 15 minutes, and then she came over and sat on my lap. Within a few minutes, we headed to her bedroom.

The next day at work, Sidney and I were discussing women. At some point, but I wasn't sure when, Sidney remarried after killing his wife. However, he may have just moved in with a woman that had a baby from him. In addition, he was chasing women too. Almost every morning, he talked about some pussy that he had gotten the previous night. He seemed as if he was afraid that his appeal was gonna be turned down, so he was gonna get as much pussy as he could.

"My woman Georgia called me and told me that she had given a dude some pussy who had been begging her for it, but he didn't do anything with it. 'Sidney,' she said, 'he didn't do nothing but play with my pussy. I still wanna fuck. Sidney, come on over and fuck me.' So, I went over there," Sidney said.

"That is the black man's burden," I said.

"You know what that bitch told me she did. She tried to get the guy fired by calling his job and telling the guy's boss some shit about some stuff the guy was supposed to have stolen," Sidney said, laughing. "She tickles me when we get in bed. She'll grab my dick and say 'Sidney, I gonna kill this motherfucker.' She acts like it some kind of snake."

"That woman is dangerous. You better leave her alone. You're getting older and you're drinking a lot. One day, your dick is not gonna get hard, and she is gonna kill you over there. I'll be reading about you in the newspaper and the title of the story would read that, 'Man killed after his dick wouldn't get hard.' The lawyer would probably plead her not guilty due to temporary insanity," I said.

Then, I began to talk about Sylvia.

"Man, Sylvia is getting on my nerves, and I am thinking about dropping her," I said.

"You're gonna quit that little sugar?" Sidney said in amazement.

"I might have to. She is pressuring me and wants me to quit school although she hasn't come right out and said it. She wants to go out more, but she really wants me to move in with her. It's tough to work here, go to school, and run women. If I had to give up one thing, I would give up Sylvia. Although this job doesn't pay much, I need it. I also need school now. Sex with Sylvia is extremely good. At one time, I thought that being in bed with Sylvia was like being in paradise. Then, I made the Dean's List and that was better than sex. Making the Dean's List felt better and it lasted much longer. It's kind of funny, a few years ago, it looked like I might never see another pussy, and now I'm turning it down. Now, I wanna pass on it sometimes and read," I said.

"Man, you've been in those books too long. Nothing is better than pussy. But if school is better than pussy, I wouldn't want it. I'd rather be a dumb motherfucker," Sidney proclaimed.

I finally quit Sylvia. She had been getting weirder and weirder. Her roommate told me once that Sylvia reads my horoscope every day to try to figure me out. One night, I was over at her place and we were in bed together. Sylvia had been drinking in addition to smoking pot. So, she was high. I decided to leave and got up and began dressing.

"Where are you going?" She slurred.

"Home."

"No, you're not," she said angrily.

"Watch me."

I had my pants and shoes on and was putting on my shirt as I was walking out of Sylvia's bedroom. Sylvia, still naked, followed me. Pushing past me, she stood in front of the door.

"Please move out of the way. I'm going home," I said.

"You're not going no goddamn place," Sylvia screamed.

As I tried to reach around her to unlock the door, she pushed me backward. "I told you that you're not going no goddamn place."

"Move out of the way, Sylvia," I insisted.

"You're not going," Sylvia repeated as she continued to push me back.

I didn't wanna hit her, but I was getting close. Sylvia had discussed her marriage with her ex-husband Slim, and she told me that she and Slim would get into knock-down, drag-out fights. Sylvia said that sometimes she would kick Slim's ass, and she could be just as tough as a man. I had never hit Sylvia, and I sensed that she felt that I wouldn't.

I had managed to unlock the door. Grabbing Sylvia by the shoulders, I was able to push her from the door and walk out quickly. Sylvia didn't wanna come outside naked. So, she accepted that I was gone and slammed her door.

As I was walking to my car, I decided that I wouldn't be back and would call her the next day to tell her that it was over.

I liked some things about Sylvia, but she had a substantial amount of flaws. Although initially I liked the mood that marijuana tended to put her in, I was not comfortable with her and her friends' drug use around me. On one side, she was very amorous, but tonight, I knew that I had seen the other side. This other side canceled out the first. Then, she finally admitted that she wanted me to quit school so that I could spend more time with her. For these reasons, I felt that it was right to quit her. Smiling, I remembered what Partain told me when I was up for parole—walk away when trouble is brewing. But sometimes, it is not easy to walk away.

There had been major changes in the structure of the parole system. The parole officers were employed by the Board of Rehabilitation and Corrections; however, advocates of the parole board believed that parole officers should be responsible to parole officials. So, the legislature made a change in state policy. The parole officers became probation officers attached to the county, and the parole board hired new people to supervise its parolees.

My new parole officer was Garnell Pace, a former classmate of my brother. At Beach High, I was in class with Garnell's sister, Gloria. So, Garnell and I hit it off right away. I related to him that the previous administration had promised to support my termination of parole when I had completed 2 years in 1977. Also, I told him that I was scheduled to graduate in June with a A.S. degree in criminal justice, and I wanted to end parole supervision, hoping that it would help me find a job. However, this idea was nixed by Garnell's supervisor, and Garnell was quite disappointed that I was not given support in terminating parole supervision. I thanked Garnell for his support and acknowledged to him that he had done the best that he could.

During the spring quarter, my last before graduation in June, I had to take 15 hours. I knew that I was in for a full load of work. In one sense, I was looking forward to it, but I was not too thrilled by one class. This class was in the judicial process. I felt that I would do well in the class, but I was not thrilled by it being taught by an assistant prosecutor from the Chatham County Solicitor General office. The instructor's name Joseph Newman, who had not been in the office when I went to trial. I sensed that this instructor was gonna give the class a lot of bullshit. But I was quite wrong.

On the first day of class, Newman stated that he was happy to be teaching the class and looking forward to it. He stated that after he was approached by Dr. Megathlin about teaching the class, he went to Solicitor Ryan to seek guidance on what he could really say in the class. Newman asked if he could tell the class how the system actually worked in Savannah, and Ryan had given his okay to say how the system really operated. However, Newman stated that there was one restriction, which was that he couldn't be too specific about some things and had to talk in general.

In most classrooms, instructors try to be specific, but in this class it was gonna be reversed. I understood.

I understood that he had to give himself some wiggle room so that he could deny some things if they were repeated outside of class. I liked Newman's class and I liked Newman personally although he was a prosecutor. I had no problem with anyone in law enforcement as long as the individual was doing his job. Police officers are supposed to arrest, and prosecutors are supposed to prosecute. That's their job. A defense attorney has a job to do too, but as I knew, some of them do not always do their jobs. My problem was when these people don't do their jobs and instead do other people's jobs.

Newman seemed to be a fair-minded person. He mentioned his previous private practice in a small Georgia town and how one of clients was unfairly treated because the judge in one town was a private attorney in another town and had opposed Newman in a case. Newman stated that he was sure that the judge mistreated his client to get back at him.

Newman also discussed Chatham county. He stated that the prosecutor's office operated much better now because Dunbar Harrison was no longer around to intimidate the prosecutor's office. Newman stressed that a superior court judge was one of the most powerful political figures in Chatham County.

Newman said more about Dunbar Harrison after a story appeared in the *Savannah Evening Press* about a case that Dunbar Harrison, who was retired but available to do work in other counties, was being challenged from serving as a presiding judge in a small town. The story, entitled "Expert to Interpret Harrison's Testimony," stated that "Harrison said he was a member of two all-white clubs, and he objects to school integration. He also said he wouldn't entertain a black at his home."

Newman said that he couldn't have commented before on Dunbar Harrison's racial views, but since Dunbar was now on record, he could discuss more specifically Dunbar in class now. Newman said that everyone around the courthouse was aware of how Dunbar Harrison felt about black people, and he was shocked to hear the virulence of many of Dunbar Harrison's comments about black people, not just black defendants but all black people.

I later acquired the transcript of what Dunbar Harrison had said to cause the defense attorney to want to have Dunbar's testimony interpreted by a psychiatrist. There was nothing in the *Savannah Morning News,* and only a little in the *Savannah Evening Press*. But I knew that there were a lot more details that the Savannah papers wouldn't publish.

The case was a capital case and Dunbar was being considered as a trial judge. The defense had done its work and knew the real Dunbar Harrison, pulling the sheet off him.

At this hearing, Dunbar Harrison stated that he would never address any black person as Mister. He had a history of telling lawyers in the courtroom not to call a black person Mister or Missus. When invited and encouraged to call the defendant Mr. Henry Willis, Dunbar refused to do it. Dunbar was asked about his black maid and he said that he wouldn't allow her to sit at the same table with him in his home and drink a cup of coffee with him. He said, however, that when the maid died, he took his children to her funeral because his children loved her. Dunbar testified that he would never vote to allow any black person to become a member of the two all-white clubs that he was a member. Discussing the school system, Dunbar stated that he was opposed to school integration because black people don't want to be educated. He said black children walk the streets when they should be in school and thus, school integration didn't do anything but mess up the Savannah schools. Dunbar invited anyone to come to Savannah and see black children walking the street during school hours. When asked about how his testimony looked to black people in the courtroom audience, Dunbar stated that he didn't care what no black person thought.

Dunbar Harrison was further asked about a specific case in which he was reported to be sending signals, through a court deputy, instructing the prosecutor which jurors to select. When the prosecutor allowed one black juror to be selected, Dunbar told the prosecutor, "I worked hard to see that this young nigger who committed this terrible crime didn't have any niggers on his jury, and you let one get on the jury. If you lose this case, I don't want you back in this courtroom." Dunbar stated that he wouldn't talk that way to a prosecutor, but he didn't see anything wrong with a deputy signaling the prosecutor because defense attorneys have help in selecting jurors.

After reading this in the transcript, I felt that there was a strong possibility that this was my case that was being alluded to in this challenge to Dunbar Harrison. My jury had one black juror, and I couldn't remember any other major criminal case that had one black juror. All the major cases in the past in Chatham County were decided by all white juries. If this was my case, it now made more sense to me.

The stories in the newspaper and what Newman said caused me to recall that sham when I was sentenced to life imprisonment and Dunbar Harrison called me up to the witness stand, and then my parents. He was pretending to be sympathetic, caring, and fair. Dunbar hated all Black people with a passion, and this courtroom theatric in 1969 was just to fix the transcript and get a favorable story involving him in the newspaper. I also remembered what Drew had said about Dunbar Harrison at Norris Hodges' habeas corpus hearing. Then, Drew was explaining why he left Norris in the courtroom while the prosecutor was giving the closing summation. He explained that the prosecutor would never say anything improper, and if the prosecutor did, Dunbar Harrison wouldn't let the prosecutor get away with it. This was totally bullshit. Dunbar Harrison didn't give a damn about Norris Hodges and would do anything to help or protect a black defendant. They all lie and protect each other.

I knew that Dunbar Harrison hated that this defense attorney had pulled the sheet off his Ku Klux Klan ass.

I had been talking to Dr. Megathlin about my future and I told him that I felt that my best chance at being successful was to leave Savannah. Dr. Megathlin disagreed and felt that I could succeed in Savannah, and it might not be as difficult because he and other professors at school could speak up for me. I respected Dr. Megathlin, but I knew that I had to leave Savannah to be successful.

I felt that if I stayed in Savannah, eventually I would perish. All I ever wanted from anyone was to be treated fairly and like a human being, and I would certainly reciprocate.

Besides talking about Dunbar Harrison, Newman also discussed in general terms a defense attorney whom he had opposed several times. Newman stated that he felt sorry for defendants who had this attorney because this attorney didn't know anything. As an example, he stated that this attorney was trying to plead a young boy guilty to selling drugs to an uncover agent on Rivers Street. However, it was not really a drug sale. The agent, to ingratiate himself with certain people on the street, gave the boy some money, and the boy, gratified by the specious friendship, gave the officer some drugs. Although money and drugs were exchanged fairly close together, it was not money for drugs. But the defense attorney didn't know the law.

Newman said that they refused the guilty plea just before trial, and the prosecutor table became the defense for this boy. After some careful balancing, they were able to get the judge to dismiss the case while pretending that they were prosecuting.

I believe that this would be the type of lawyer that would be appointed to a capital case and then everyone, from the prosecutor's office, the attorney general's office, and the Georgia Supreme Court would say what a highly skilled and competent lawyer this was.

Newman also explained the theory of what is supposed to happen in court. He stated that the defense attorney is supposed to challenge him, and out of this conflict, the right thing is supposed to be done. The right thing may be an acquittal or a guilty verdict. But Newman stated that this is not always the case, and some cases are decided long before they come to trial. He also stated that when potential jurors are questioned on voir dire, some of them would be electrocuted if they were hooked up to lie detectors. He stated that it was easy to get a conviction in some cases when the prosecutor has twelve good 'ole boys on a jury. According to Newman, there are always racial and social undercurrents operating in a criminal case, but he can never publicly acknowledge that this is the case.

Newman stated that not all cases are supposed to result in a conviction, and some cases shouldn't even be prosecuted. However, for various reasons, the case is prosecuted. He stated that he went to Ryan to tell Ryan that he didn't want to prosecute a particular case, but Ryan overruled him and ordered him to proceed. From what I had gleaned, in one case a boy had been discovered performing oral sex on a willing girl, and the girl's mother was pushing prosecution. The boy was charged with some type of perversion but was acquitted at trial.

Newman stated that some defense attorneys are very accommodating to the prosecution and received their rewards on down the line. I immediately knew what he was referring to by this statement. If the prosecution has an important case and wants a conviction, the defense attorney would permit, for example, police officers to testify falsely without challenging them. In return, in a lesser case that is not highly publicized, the defense attorney can call in chips for helping the prosecution. This translated into money, I knew, for the defense attorney.

I was making the highest score in the class. So, Newman was talking to me some, and I would talk to him before class.

"Is it true as I have read that the current pay of judges keep good lawyers from wanting to be judges?" I asked.

"No, that is not true. What you read is just a line to get the county to pay more. Good people will take judgeships at the amount that is being paid. Some lawyers are going to always want more, and some will leave the bench to make more money, in say, private practice," Newman said.

I was speaking to him out of class just outside the class building when he told me something else. Newman volunteered some information about a recent killing that was in the newspaper. A clerk in a liquor store downtown was found dead on the floor. There appeared to be no witnesses, but a subsequent story appeared in the newspaper stating that a certain person was a prime suspect. Newman revealed that this person's fingerprints were found in the store, which was not in the newspaper but was why he was named as a suspect.

I didn't say anything, but I knew that my paranoia had been justified. If one has a criminal record, it is not good to leave prints in a liquor store or a convenient store because these establishments are frequently robbed. An important issue is where the prints are found but they can always say that the print was on or behind the counter or on the cash register, whether it was or wasn't.

I was relating to Sidney some of what Newman had been saying in class. Particularly, Newman discussed all the letters the prosecutor office gets from inmates wanting to swap information about drug dealers in Savannah in exchange for some type of deal. I told Sidney that the people in the jail wanting to make these kinds of deals are the same people who are talking the loudest about snitching and what needs to be done to a snitch.

There were a couple of cases that reinforced my beliefs about the dual nature of the justice system in Savannah. One involved a doctor who killed a man who was involved with the doctor's wife. The story the doctor told was that the man requested to speak to him in the park late at night. The doctor looked for a security guard to accompany him but couldn't find one. He then decided to take a pistol to the meeting and subsequently shot the man numerous times in the head. The doctor was allowed to plead guilty, was placed on probation, required to pay the funeral expenses, and required to establish a trust fund for the children of the victim. With a black person or someone from the lower class, this would have been called premeditated murder.

In addition, in the list of court activities, I saw a name that I had recognized from several years ago. This individual, the son of wealthy people, attempted to rob a guy collecting money for Savannah State College and subsequently killed the guy by dragging him under the car. Although Georgia law says that the killing of a person in the commission of a robbery is murder and murder is punishable only by death or life imprisonment, this individual was found guilty of manslaughter and given a few years. Now, I saw his name in the newspaper for selling drugs, and he was put on probation.

Reading these stories really irked me because individuals are always insinuating how black defendants get all these breaks in the legal system. Furman contended that the killing was an accident, but he received the electric chair. Stump was convicted of selling drugs and couldn't make parole. Despite the con game that white people like to run, no ordinary black person receives a break from the legal system; to really receive a break, one has to be white.

While I knew it already, Newman's assertion that there are always racial and social undercurrents operating in a case certainly rang true.

Graduation was approaching. The school had begun to give all graduating criminal justice majors an exit exam to establish norms for graduation and to assure that graduates knew what they were supposed to have learned. I had to take the examination that students who were graduating with bachelor degrees were taking. Although I had not taken many of the courses that bachelor degree candidates had taken, I made the highest score of all students that year and the previous year. Dr. Megathlin kidded with me about it and told me that I had messed up their norm.

Both my sister and I were graduating—she with a bachelor's degree in criminal justice and me with an associate degree. My parents attended the ceremony and were quite proud of both of us. It really was an exciting evening as we took pictures in our caps and gowns with our parents.

Almost immediately, my sister found a job. She had applied for a job as a correctional officer at the South Carolina Department of Corrections at the beginning of the week and that same week the department called to offer her a job. I was looking too and applying, but I was not having any luck. Through Dr. Megathlin, I had an interview at a juvenile detention center in Dekalb County Georgia. The director knew of my background and told me that I could relax. The questions he posed to me were quite tough, and he told me that if he hired me, he would be forced to tell other employees about me. The director wanted to know how I would handle it. As best I could, I told him that I hope people would judge me by what I am now and not what happened back in 1967, 10 years ago. The director told me that he was gonna make a decision in a week and told me that if he didn't call in a week, then I would know that I was not hired. When the week was up, he had not called, and I was extremely disheartened. My sister was leaving Savannah, but I was staying.

That Saturday, I stopped at the package shop and bought something to drink. As soon as I got home, I started drinking. I took a bath and headed over to Sidney's house to pick him up. Lately, I had been doing the driving when Sidney and I were together. It was because I had learned that Sidney kept a shotgun in the trunk of his car. With his temper, I didn't wanna be with him if someone told him to go to hell. I had bought a 1976 Grand Prix, and I told Sidney that we could pick up women easier in my car than his. But the real reason was that he had a weapon in his car, and I didn't.

By about 10:00p.m. I was as drunk as I had ever been. Sidney and I were in a night club, and as I was returning from the bathroom, I felt a strange sensation slowly going from my head and down my body. I knew then that I was very drunk and couldn't drive. I stumbled back to the table where Sidney was.

"Sidney, I'm fucked up and can't drive. Call my brother for me. I'll think of his number in a minute," I said slurring my words.

"I knew you were fucked up. I've seen you get high when you're drinking, but I never seen you drink this much," Sidney said.

"Call my brother, he'll come and get me."

"Man, you don't need to call your brother and get him worried. I'm with you. Tonight, I'm your brother and I'll take care of you. No one is gonna fuck with you as long as I'm here," Sidney promised. "Give me your car keys."

I fumbled in my pocket and gave Sidney my car keys. I laid my head on the table, and Sidney, grabbing me by the arm, told me that we were leaving. I kept telling Sidney to call my brother and was trying to tell him my brother's telephone number. Sidney kept telling me that he was my brother. When we got outside, he put me in the passenger side and began to drive. The cool night air felt good on my face, but I didn't know where I was. In a few minutes, we were at Sidney's house. Sidney pulled me up the stairs, telling his wife that I was with him and I was drunk. He told her to get some blankets for the couch for me. Just as he said that, I threw up in the living room, and Sidney asked his wife to bring a towel. I tried to apologize, but Sidney told me to get on the couch. Within a few minutes I was out. The last thing I heard was Sidney laughing at me.

The next morning, I apologized to Sidney and his wife and told them that I had exceeded my limit. With a throbbing headache, I drove home and got in my bed to sleep some more.

Chapter 28

Daddy finally retired from Union Camp after working there more than 30 years.

After he retired, he didn't know what to do with himself. In the past, he would only drink on the weekends. Now, he was drinking during the week.

He joined a social club of other retired black men and would go there to play checkers. They had a competition one day and Daddy brought home the trophy for being the best checker player.

While Daddy was involved with the social club, he came across former Officer Nealy, who had retired. Having never forgotten that Officers Bush and Nealy lied at my trial, Daddy confronted Nealy about how they altered their testimony at my trial. It wasn't a loud confrontation, but Daddy wanted him to know it was wrong what they did.

Daddy never cared much for black police officers because they tend to do more than their jobs at times. Years ago, my youngest brother announced that he might be a police officer when he grew up, but my Daddy told him that a black police officer was the sorriest person there is.

Daddy didn't have a problem with black officers doing their jobs, but some of them hurt other black people unjustifiably to curry favor with whites. This is what Daddy always criticized.

One day as I was making deliveries at a drug store that operated a sandwich shop near the courthouse, I saw Joseph Newman. I stopped with my handcart to talk with him. After leaving, I could sense that he appreciated my working and having a job.

In class, Newman had expressed puzzlement about why some guys rob the mom-and-pop stores and take the chances that they take. He said if they were gonna take chances, at least they should be going for the big money. Newman stated that a recently conducted survey revealed that the average robbery in Chatham County netted the robber 22 dollars.

I wanted to explain partly why I thought some guys targeted mom-and-pop stores to rob, but I didn't wanna speak up in class. Mostly, I listened and did the work. I didn't engage in the class debates about criminal justice issues.

But I believed that poor people do not have the conception of money that white people have. To a poor person, 50 or 100 dollars is a lot of money, whereas to a middle class or upper class person that amount is peanuts. White people steal millions, and black people steal peanuts.

In a lot of the classes, many of the police officer students had very strong views about what is wrong with the criminal justice system. They criticize offenders as not wanting to work and that these offenders prefer to rob and steal. Then, they would point the finger at the prosecutor's office for not being tough enough.

In one meeting in the community that was alluded to in class by a police student, Newman stated that he didn't make enough money to take the abuse that was leveled at him during this meeting.

During the fall of 1977, I called Dr. Megathlin to discuss my coming back into the criminal justice program to get my B.S. degree. He told me that it was a good idea and that the B.S. degree would make me a stronger applicant. So, I told him that I would be back, beginning the winter quarter of 1978.

Dr. Megathlin told me about some law enforcement assistance funds that I would have available to me to help pay for tuition. He didn't seem too concerned that I had not found a job and believed that something would come up later. Specifically, he told me that he had done favors for several people and that he was gonna call in one of those favors for me. Although I believed him and knew that he had a very good relationship with many individuals in Savannah, I decided that I would do some looking myself, and I would be looking out of state.

In my last quarter at Armstrong during the spring of 1977 just before I graduated, one of my professors related in class that a graduating student had complained that she couldn't find a job. Requested to list the places that she had looked, the student mentioned two or three agencies in Savannah. The professor said that students need to be aggressive and look for jobs in other states too. As an aid, he mentioned that Sam Houston State University, where he had graduated from, published a list of jobs in corrections and law enforcement from all over the country and that students looking for jobs should consult it.

I began to look at it too and read about an advertisement for a job that I thought fit my qualifications and interests. It was a job in Houston as a parole aide working with offenders. I sent a resume and a cover letter, detailing my education and prison background, but I never received an acknowledgement or a rejection letter. I continued to look at this publication, which the library received, every month when it came out.

I had been keeping in touch with my sister Cora in Columbia. She had heard from the Federal Bureau of Prisons and was being offered a job at a federal prison in Butner, North Carolina. So, she decided to quit her job at the South Carolina Department of Corrections and relocate to North Carolina.

When January 1978 rolled around, I decided to take a full load of classes in addition to still doing my job at Gonchar Produce. I wanted to finish as fast as I could.

Gonchar had returned to work after his surgery and recuperation at home. Rosalee told me that not only did they not start making money until my arrival, but she believed that the business would have gone under when Gonchar got really sick if I had not been there.

Then, she related what happened a few years back when Gonchar was sick during another time. She stated that a friend of hers was helping her, but they lost a tremendous amount of money. All of it was due to theft.

Because of how Rosalee felt about me, she treated me much more differently than Sidney or Willie Mims. Gonchar, upon his return, put a stop to me going in the money bag in the mornings to buy breakfast for everyone. Also, he told Rosalee to stop giving me money for lunch. However, Rosalee would come out on the ramp with money crumpled in her hand and slide it into my hand.

Sidney saw her doing it once and smiled. Later that morning, Sidney said that he had been curious for a long time why Rosalee was so nice to me and wondered whether we had something else going on. Sidney said that he asked his wife if it was possible for a woman to be that nice to a man and not be fucking him. Based on what Sidney told her, she opined that there was something else going on between Rosalee and me. Despite my denials, Sidney continued to believe that when Gonchar got sick and was hospitalized I was going over to Gonchar's house and was screwing his wife.

I tried to explain something to Sidney about trust and the reciprocal nature of it. I told him that it meant a lot to me that this woman treated me as a human being and showed me that she had a tremendous amount of faith in me. Although I never told her anything about anybody, she was appreciative of my work, dependability, and honesty. Sidney didn't grasp what I had said and insisted that I had to be fucking Rosalee.

On some days, I was working a little later than usual and was scrambling to get home, bathe, and go to school. Also, when I had to work late, this cut into my study time. As a result, my first quarter back was not spectacular, but I did okay. I received two B's and a C.

In one of my classes, a history professor approached me after class one day and asked if I was related to Cora Alexander. I told him yes and that she was my sister. He told me that my sister was a very "sharp gal" and it was a pleasure to have had her in his class. He asked me what she was doing and I told him that she was working in North Carolina.

During the next quarter, another person asked me if I was related to Cora Alexander. This was a student in my Group Processes class.

"Are you Cora Alexander's brother?"

"Yes, I am."

"Are you the one that was in trouble several years ago?"

"Yeah, that was me."

"You may not remember me but I used to come by your house to see your sister. She and I were really good friends. At that time my hair was really short and you may not remember me anyway because I was about 10 or 11 then."

I pondered, but not seriously, whether the next time someone asked me if I was related to Cora that I should admit it.

There were several stories in the newspaper involving people that I knew. I read that Rudolph Heard was found dead in his cell at Reidsville. The authorities believed that it was a suicide, but someone I was discussing it with speculated that he might have been killed. Regardless of whether it was suicide or not, I was not sorry to read that he was dead. At one time, I had decided that if I had to kill him that I was gonna kill him myself, and I knew that this would have been the end of me.

Honey was in the newspaper after killing a guy following a gambling game. Apparently, Honey and the guy got into a fight earlier in the morning while gambling and Honey broke the guy's leg. Then, later that day, the guy returned to the gambling house with a gun, but Honey, also armed, was a little quicker. I didn't expect Honey to be convicted in this case.

Earlier, I had read another story involving Honey in a nightclub near Bay Street. In that situation, a guy supposedly was bending over and was putting his ass in Honey's face. When Honey said something to him, the guy gave Honey a smart remark. So, Honey left the club, went to his car to get his gun, and came back in the club, and shot the guy in the ass.

A few months back, I had read about Willie Robinson. Willie Robinson had walked away from Chatham prison camp. A few months later, he shot a guy six times. However, the guy didn't die. I thought that this incident would send Willie Robinson back to Reidsville and may cause him to spend the rest of his life in prison. But he would be content there. Prison was all he knew. After being sent there so young, he got indoctrinated into the prison culture and values. He couldn't replace it with anything else. His entire mentality was based on prison values.

Many guys I knew in prison I didn't see that much on the street. If I did see some of them, I would speak to them and chat with them a little. But I didn't socialize with them because we had different goals.

One day, a cousin of mine, who was on the police force, came by my house and was asking questions about Glenn Jenkins. He wanted to know if I had seen Glenn around. I told him no and that I had not seen Glenn since we were in Wayne Correctional Institution.

"Why are you looking for Glenn?" I asked.

"He raped a woman on the east side who went to school with you all. He broke into her house and told her that he should kill her because she knew him. When she was interviewed, she pulled out her Richard Arnold yearbook to show us Glenn's picture, and I saw your picture in the yearbook too. We know Glenn likes to play basketball, and we are watching the parks. But I wondered if you had seen him," he asked.

"No, as I said, I have not seen Glenn. I am sorry what happened to the woman. I remember her. I find it strange that Glenn is out raping women. In prison, he was prostituting himself and was considered to be a woman himself. I'm really sorry that he is doing that."

I always had somewhat mixed emotions about some of the guys who were going back to prison. Some of the guys, like Willie Robinson, I felt should be in prison. But some guys I wanted to stay out of prison because I felt that they were too strong to be wasting away in the white man's penitentiary. If these guys had a break here and there, they could have been doing some fantastic things in the community and could have been making major contributions.

Some of the guys were doing well. I see Willie Joe Newton a lot at the library. He had become a Muslim and really looked good. His skin and eyes looked good and you could tell that he was into clean living. He told me that he had quit drinking and had gotten married. I really felt good talking to him and comparing him to how he used to be.

In a similar manner, I had come across Wyman Gordon. In jail, he called himself the Cincinnati Kid because he was good at cards. He told me that he had stopped doing a lot of things and was now living for the Lord. Around his neck was a cross, and he touched it as he talked about being a Christian now. I was happy for both Wyman and Willie Joe.

Finally, I was able to get off parole after being on it for 3 years. The only known incident that I had had was initially going to the library without permission.

Technically, I broke one regulation by going to bars. But I was very careful which bars I went to. I would avoid any bar in which the crowds tended to get rowdy. I just went to bars in which I could have a quiet beer without anyone bothering me or wanting to fight because I accidentally bumped into him. For this reason, I started going into a few bars on River Street near the waterfront. There were mostly white people on River Street, but they never bothered me and I didn't do anything to them. A friend of mine warned me that I might be attacked by some whites and thrown into the Savannah River. Although I knew that this was a possibility, I also knew that if I went into ten black bars and ten white bars that my chances of being hurt were greater in the black bars.

A few weeks after my parole had ended, I received an order from the parole board that restored all my civil and political rights. So, now I could vote and run for political office.

When Carter was running for president in 1976, I wanted to vote in that election, but I was told by my parole officer that I couldn't vote. I guessed that my vote would taint the political process.

During the summer, I decided to take my internship. Among my three choices was the Chatham County Juvenile Detention Center. I chose it because I knew that I could fit this in my work schedule and do my internship from 3P.M. to 11P.M..

Although I was told that I had done a good job as a volunteer probation officer, the judge of the juvenile court didn't want me in the facility. The volunteer coordinator, the director, and the judge met for about two-and-one-half hours to discuss whether I could do my internship at the detention center. I patiently waited as they discussed it. When they had finished and I was called into the office, the judge left before I arrived. The volunteer coordinator and the director told me that I could do my placement there provided I could get letters of reference from my professors at Armstrong and I not disclose any information to the staff about my background. The director stated that they needed the letters of reference just in case the newspaper learned about me. When I told the director that one of their staff members knew me and that we had gone to school together, he was called into the office and told not to talk about me with other staff.

The internship went okay except the judge never spoke to me. Occasionally, the judge would come into the detention facility, but he wouldn't speak to me although he spoke to the other staff members. Although I had no reason to dislike this juvenile court judge like I disliked Dunbar Harrison, I didn't care if the judge never spoke to me.

Sometimes, I would sit in the courtroom and observe cases being tried in the afternoons. In one case, an 11-year-old boy had an adjudicatory hearing for hitting his female teacher and knocking her glasses off. The boy, crying steadily, testified that the teacher was squeezing his arm, and he hit her because she was hurting him. The teacher, a young black female, testified that she was escorting the boy by the arm and was not squeezing it. I felt the teacher was lying and that she had indeed hurt this boy. Also, I took a telephone call the previous night in detention from a child who was trying to tell me about an incident in class in which the teacher was lying. I was sure that this child was a witness to the case that I was sitting in on.

It was an interesting hearing, and I was shocked by the aggressiveness of the prosecuting attorney when cross-examining the boy. This prosecutor really went after this boy, calling him a stubborn bully. He was more aggressive with this boy than Barker had been with me when I was tried. Then, the judge got into the act. The judge stated that he knew that more went on in the classroom than what the teacher testified to, but there was no justification for hitting the teacher. So, the judge leaned over the bench and sternly lectured the boy before placing him on probation. The judge had put on a good show.

Later, one of the black female probation officer was talking to me in her office about the juvenile court system in Chatham County. She stated that the judge was nothing but a politician who would do anything to further his career.

She told me that she was assigned a case involving a white boy from a well-to-do family and had left the file on her desk at the end of the day. The next day, the file was missing. When she inquired about it, she was told that it had been "administratively handled." She said that this was the code word that the judge had given this case special attention, and as a result, the file was gonna be destroyed. She said the judge was always doing things like this for juveniles who came from wealthy families.

She said that when she first came to work there that she was enthusiastic about helping juveniles, but now she didn't care anymore because of the unfairness of how some cases were handled.

I told her I didn't mind too much that white juveniles receive preferential treatment and I expect white people to help their own more than others, but I hated it when officials insinuated that black youths were getting all kinds of breaks from the legal system. Whatever breaks that are available to mete out, the lion's share goes to white people. Little goes to black individuals although white people are constantly trying to convince black people that they have been given all kind of breaks.

I know that it takes resources to get breaks for the legal system—political resources, social resources, and financial resources. White people have those and black people do not.

Another black employee, fed up with the racial handling of cases, told me that a white teenager came to the detention with a shotgun to force the release of another white youth. However, this incident was never published in the newspapers. The black employee said that if this was a black teenager who had done this, the story would have been put on the front page and the teenager would have been thrown in the system to rot. However, unlike the female probation officer, this employee was not demoralized and understood the practices as just white folks being white folks.

One night I took a very interesting call in the control room. It was Solicitor General Ryan, the same prosecutor who gave the closing argument in my case, held his hands to the ceiling, and told the jury this was when I shot the choirboy. He was very dramatic when he said it. Ryan wanted to know would I do him a favor and I said, of course, I would. He told me that a police officer was on the way to the detention center with a boy and to have the officer call him at home. He then gave me his home number. About that time, I buzzed in a man who told me that his son had been arrested and was on the way there. He asked to use the telephone. I let him and was listening to him while pretending that I was doing something else. I didn't know who he called, but he began the conversation by saying, "Guess what, they arrested my boy, my boy," the man said in astonishing tone while emphasizing the words "my boy."

I was certain he was implying that it was okay to arrest the juvenile delinquents but not "his boy."

The officer arrived with the boy and I gave him the message. He was not saying much, but, "huh" and "okay" as he spoke to Ryan. Of course, this boy wouldn't be in detention very long.

Near the end of my internship, the situation became a little more interesting when a job opened in detention. The director of detention, a black woman, told me that she liked my maturity and skills and encouraged me to apply for the opening. In my presence, she told the director of the court what a wonderful job I was doing and had mentioned to her that I should be hired for the job.

After talking with Dr. Megathlin, I applied for the job. I wanted the job because I felt that I could finish school while working and that this would be a good first job for me. But I told Dr. Megathlin that I suspected that Judge Dickey wouldn't approve me working there because he wouldn't even speak to me when he would come in the detention center. Dr. Megathlin acknowledged that it was a sticky political situation, but he, citing my good work as a volunteer and my internship, believed that he could persuade the judge to give me the job.

At the same time, I was still looking at the National Employment Listing Service and read about one job in Texas that I thought I was qualified to do that served emotionally disturbed and delinquent boys. It was a live-in counselor job in a wilderness program in east Texas with a main office in Houston. The application that I received from the agency in Houston didn't ask about felony convictions, but I disclosed it anyway in a lengthy cover letter.

The fall quarter had started and I enrolled in Business Law, Criminal Law, and Civilization. The Criminal Law class was being taught by Joseph Newman. Unlike the earlier class that he taught, I didn't find this class to be illuminating. Much of that was me because my mind was on getting away from Savannah.

Early in the quarter, Newman announced that he was requiring us to write a paper and that he was gonna assign us a case to research and write about. As he was calling each student's name and telling each student which case was assigned, I slowly began to recognize the names. All the assigned cases were capital cases in Georgia, and I had read about them at one time or another.

Ordinarily, I wouldn't have minded writing the paper, but I suspected that Newman had a political motive in assigning capital cases.

A few weeks ago, Earl Charles was released from the county jail after being in jail several years under a death sentence. I suspected that the prosecutor's office was concerned that potential jurors in future cases might be hesitant to bring back death sentences, remembering that Earl Charles was given a death sentence and later determined to be innocent.

Also, Newman had discussed in class a case that resulted in a disappointing verdict for the prosecution. After the case was over, Newman said that one juror told the prosecutors that one particular juror stated that he didn't believe police officers always told the truth in court and believed that they had planted evidence against the defendant. This juror's name was given to the prosecutors by the snitching juror and Newman said that this juror, who had qualms about the truthfulness of police officers and believed that police officers were capable of planting evidence, would never serve on another criminal case.

As I expected, the judge, despite Dr. Megathlin's strong advocacy, refused to authorize hiring me. The detention center hired someone else instead.

But I got a response from the agency in Texas and flew out there for a job interview. I had been saving money—money that I called my freedom and relocation fund. So, the $142 that it cost to fly to Houston and back was not too much for me. The personnel director had made a mistake in scheduling my interview because I had to stay at the wilderness program for a day to see if I liked it and to see if the director thought that I would work out. She was an extremely attractive black woman with long hair and a split skirt that showed some of her thighs. She was apologetic for the scheduling problem, but I wasn't angry about it. She said that she was going to see if the director would hire me without a visit. She called the camp and asked for the director. After she had spoken a few minutes, she seemed to be less anxious about the scheduling problem. She told me that the director of the camping program was on the way to Houston and she would ask him to interview me here in Houston.

When the director arrived, the circumstances were explained to him and we met in the personnel director's office. He introduced himself as Lyndy Langford. As he was looking at my application and accompanying cover letter, he asked me what happened that led me to going to prison. I told him what happened.

After we talked about young people, their problems, and how to help them, Lyndy told me that he liked what I said.

"I have a good feeling about you. But the 2-day visit to the camp is essential. Could you stay until the camp reopens on Tuesday and stay until Thursday?" Lyndy asked.

"No, I can't stay. I had only made plans to stay until Sunday. I have a job in Savannah and I am still in school," I said.

Thinking quickly, I told Lyndy that I would return next Friday, and he promised to let me know whether I was hired or not on the day that I left, which would be Sunday.

The following week, I was back in Houston and stayed for the weekend at the camp in east Texas. The program was unusual in that it was not like anything that I had read about in my juvenile delinquency class. However, I knew about reality therapy, which was the counseling approach used with the boys.

There were ten boys in a group, and they had five groups spread out in the woods. I was escorted to the Rangers' campsite and introduced to the boys and the counselor, Loy. In the campsite, there were three tents for the boys, and one for the counselors. The tents were essentially four shaven pine trees covered with a canvass, and each tent for the boys had three or four beds in it on a wooden floor. There was a cook tent that I understood the boys did their own cooking 2 days a week, a small tool shed, and a latrine. In the middle of the campsite were some logs that were placed in a rectangle with an opening for the group to walk inside. Problems were discussed inside the logs in campsite and the logs were used to settle a group down and organize them for leaving the campsite.

The first problem that occurred happened when the group was asked to line up to go up front to play football before supper. Some of the boys were pushing and shoving to get in front. Loy called a "huddle-up" and this was a call for everyone to go the logs to sit and talk about the problem. I had been told to jump into any discussion because I was a counselor too. Loy began by reminding the group that this issue of shoving and pushing to be first had been previously discussed, and everyone decided that being first in line was unimportant. I stated that everyone is going to get to wherever they're going about the same time and pushing is unnecessary. I also stated that it could cause a fight. The boys who were pushing agreed that it was unimportant who was first in line, and we lined up. We played football behind a building that everyone called the "chuckwagon." After the game, we washed up for supper and sat on some logs waiting for someone to call us in to eat. When the tables had been set, we were called in to eat. I got a chance to see the other four groups and saw that one group was older and the others were younger. The youngest group of boys looked to be about 10 years old and the oldest group about 16 or 17 years old.

When we finished the meal and had cleared the table, one of the counselors got up to ask each group what they did that day. One of the guys in the group mentioned that I was visiting and discussed the football game. We headed back to the campsite and it was quite dark then. Lanterns were lit when we got back in camp, and within a short time, someone said it was time for "pow wow." Everyone went to another set of logs and lit a small pile of wood. Then, each person evaluated his day and how he was gonna do better the next day. Then, they went to bed. Loy told me that this was the most important time of the day, and so I followed him as he went into each tent to congratulate the boys and to shake their hands. I did the same. Then, Loy took his guitar from the tent, sat on the logs, and began to sing.

The next morning, the boys were different. They were argumentative and becoming agitated. I noticed it and asked Loy why. He told me that he was leaving at 12 noon to go on time-off and the boys knew it. Thus, they were feeling insecure. At noon, Zak came into the group and some of the guys went up to him to hug him. When Loy left, the group disintegrated. It became chaotic, and I could see that Loy could control the group much better than Zak. Zak had to run behind some of the guys and had to restrain one of the boys.

On Sunday morning, Zak told me that I could share a house with him and some others if I were hired. He told me that he lived in Nacogdoches, which was about 50 miles from the camp. I told him that I would keep it in mind.

In talking with one of the camp supervisors during an exit interview, he told me that the resume and letter that I had written, and specifically my letter, was one of the most impressive presentations that he had ever read. He said that everyone was impressed with my letter.

Among the things that I discussed was my philosophy about the helping process. In addition, I asserted that I had never used any unprescribed drugs, not even marijuana, and I had been around people who did. Further, I told them that although I had been in prison for almost 8 years that I have never had homosexual contact with another male in any form during my stay in prison, and they could be assured that I would be safe to have around their clients. I told them further that I would be willing to take a polygraph examination in Houston on the drug or homosexual question if they wanted me to take it.

At the end of the visit, I was told that I had the job. I was ecstatic on the plane ride back to Savannah and enjoyed sipping a screwdriver and reflecting on my life. On Monday, I told Gonchar that this would be my last day working for him. Because he knew that I was planning to leave Savannah, I didn't think that he was being put in a bind.

The next day I was on campus at Armstrong State College getting forms to drop all my classes. When I told Mr. Newman that I was dropping his class, he was curious where and whom had hired me. He offered to write a letter of reference for me, but I told him that I had sufficient references.

As I was looking for the professor of my civilization class to get his signature, I happened to look out a window facing Abercorn Street. On the sidewalk talking were Dr. Megathlin and Judge Dickey.

I could imagine what they were talking about. Dr. Megathlin had strongly recommended me for the job at Chatham County Juvenile Court, and Judge Dickey was explaining to him, I thought, why he couldn't hire me. I stood at the window and watched them talking. After a few minutes, they shook hands and Judge Dickey got into his car. Dr. Megathlin was walking back to his office.

Even if I had been offered the job at the juvenile court, I would have turned it down if I had simultaneously received the job in Texas. I needed to get away from Savannah.

I decided to leave on Wednesday, having mapped out my trip to Houston.

The night before I left, I visited my sister-in-law in the hospital because she had just given birth to her second daughter. I didn't like going in hospitals, but seeing my new niece was rewarding. She was just as cute as could be.

On the morning that I was packing, my parents were in my room. Both of them were sitting side by side on my bed, staring at me as I packed. I had never seen them like this before, and I was a little surprised that Momma was not helping me pack. When my sister Cora moved to Columbia, South Carolina, Momma helped my sister to pack. But she was not helping me.

My sister called, having been told that I was leaving Savannah that morning.

"Hello, brother, I just wanted to say that I am happy for you and wanted to wish you well out in Texas," my sister Cora said.

"Thanks. You ought to be here to see Momma and Daddy. They are just sitting on the bed like they are in a trance. I thought that Momma might help me pack, but she isn't," I said.

"Their baby is leaving. That's why they are acting this way," my sister reported.

"I had applied for a job at the juvenile detention center, but they wouldn't hire me," I said.

"That's their loss," she said. "Well, I need to go. I just wanted to say good luck and have a safe drive to Texas."

"Thanks and I will drive safely.

When I returned, my parents were still sitting on the bed. After I had packed, I began loading my things in the back seat. Daddy did help me bring my clothes and stereo out. I hugged Momma and shook Daddy's hand.

Momma and Daddy were acting as if they would never see me again. I had been telling Daddy for a long time that I had planned to leave Savannah. I told him that when I left, I would always come back to see him and Momma, but I would never return to live in Savannah. I had also decided that when I died, I didn't wanna be brought back to Savannah to be buried. But I didn't tell him this part.

I got into the car and headed to Ogeechee Road where I was gonna take Highway 17 South. I passed the building where Bon Air Restaurant used to be and where I had worked in the mid 1960s. It was fitting that I would come this way. I turned on Highway 84 and headed for Ludowici where I had worked on a prison gang bumping curbs in town and cutting grass along the highway. I went through Jesup, where we would silently crave, from the back of the prison truck, women walking down the streets. I continued on Highway 84 through Waycross and then to Valdosta Georgia and then to Thomasville. There, I got on Highway 319 and headed toward Tallahassee, Florida. There, I gassed up and got on Interstate 10 and headed west to Houston, Texas. With the Funkadelics playing "One Nation Under a Groove" on my eight-track, I headed towards Houston. I felt the same euphoric way that I did when I was leaving prison.

Chapter 29

In Pensacola, Florida, I checked into a motel for the night and continued to Houston the following morning. I arrived in Houston at about 2 P.M., and called Daddy from a pay phone to tell him that I had arrived.

"I didn't know that I would get here about this time. I thought that it would take longer," I said.

"Well, I'm just glad that you got there okay. I want you to know that if you need anything, just call me. Also, if things don't work out for you out there, you can always come back home," Daddy announced.

"Thanks, but I know things are gonna work out for me here. I'll keep in touch. Also, tell Momma that I am okay," I said.

I know Daddy was a little worried. But I didn't have any intentions of returning to Georgia, except for a short visit. I had a foot in the door and intended to make the most of it.

I really didn't need to stop in Houston because I was gonna be staying in Nacogdoches, Texas, but I wanted to stop there to personally thank the personnel director. Also, I wanted to see her again because she was so beautiful. Too bad she was already married.

Then, I headed north on Highway 59 to Nacogdoches. It was night when I got there. I found my way to the house where I was gonna be staying with some of the other counselors, but no one was home. I understood that there were about five people staying there. I left to get something to eat and returned later. But no one was there. I waited in the car until about 10 o'clock and then left to find a motel.

The next day I drove around Nacogdoches to check it out. A sign indicated that the population was about 30,000 and there was a college there too, Stephen F. Austin University. I filed that away in my mind just in case I had an opportunity to return to school later to complete my bachelor's degree.

Just before I left Savannah, Dr. Megathlin told me that it might be possible for me to take classes in Texas, transfer the credits to Armstrong, and get my degree from Armstrong. I only had about a year worth of work left to do to get my bachelor's degree. I was gonna keep it in mind for later, but because the counselor job that I had taken was a live-in position, my schedule wouldn't allow it.

Someone was at the house and introduced himself as Mike. He had worked at the camp, but had recently quit. I learned that a number of personnel at the camp were upset and planning to leave. But I also learned that in the past, people had quit and then come back 4 or 5 months later.

I was initially assigned to the group that I had visited, being warned that the group was gonna be a problem for a while. The group had gone through a lot of counselors, and there was a considerable amount of insecurity in it. I was told that they would raise hell for a while, but they would settle down later.

The boys did exactly that. They raised hell incessantly for a week. Fearing that I might quit, the supervisory staff took me out of the group and put me in another group, a younger, stable group. The group that I was leaving was upset when they were told that I was being moved. One boy called Chico said that I was a good counselor because I wouldn't get mad at their testing.

So, I got a reputation for being laid-back. My new group had a female counselor and an established counselor named Joe. They began to teach me how to manage the group and the camp policies. Joe told me not to feel badly about the group that I left because they had been unstable for a long time, and it was gonna take awhile to get them to function as a cohesive group again. Joe told me that he had similar problems with our current group, and it took awhile for the group to test him and then settle down. I thought it was very similar to a substitute teacher taking a class and students taking advantage of the teacher's inexperience.

The group had planned a week-long van and camping trip to San Antonio and Austin. This was gonna be the first time that I had slept in an outdoor, cloth tent. It wasn't too bad except one morning after getting up near San Antonio it was quite cold.

In Austin, we had an opportunity to visit the University of Texas and tour the campus. I was curious about the tower where Charles Whitman had shot all those people in the 1960s. We were told that we couldn't go up to the tower, but it wasn't because of the shootings. Someone told us that suicidal students were going up there and jumping off. So, the tower became off limits, and no one was allowed up there anymore.

After we returned to the camp, we only had a few more days to work before taking the Thanksgiving holidays. Because the camp didn't take holidays during the year, all holidays were taken during Thanksgivings and Christmas.

Although there were three other black counselors working at the camp, I seldom had an opportunity to talk to them and so I didn't know them very well. I believed that all of them lived in Houston.

One Friday, I decided to go to Houston although I didn't know anyone well enough to go their house. I decided to ride around town a little, staying close to Highway 59 to keep from getting lost. I didn't know where I was, but I stopped into a bar. It was a black bar and the music was good. I started drinking screwdrivers. I left after drinking two and decided to drive around some more. I stopped at another bar and had a few more drinks. By then, I was feeling high and decided to return the 140 or so miles back to Nacogdoches. After I had driven about 50 miles, I decided to pull over and sleep a little. So, I locked the car and slept for about an hour-and-a-half on the side of the highway. Then, I felt okay enough to finish the drive, but I was already having a severe hangover. I decided that in the future, I would do all my drinking in Nacogdoches where I didn't have far to go to get back home.

I began to explore Nacogdoches more during the Christmas holidays. I went to the campus of Stephen F. Austin and looked around. I visited the library and was impressed with its size. I also attended a basketball game on campus and recalled that the basketball team in the past had been nationally ranked.

One day when I was shopping downtown I walked into a clothing store and a black female clerk was helping me. I decided to talk to her a little, and she gave me her name and telephone number. Her name was Joy, and she told me that she was from Center, Texas, but she lived in an efficiency apartment in town. I visited her in her apartment and learned what an efficiency apartment was. It was quite small, but certainly large enough for one person. The sofa doubled as a bed. To get ready for bed, you just took the sofa pillows off and pulled the bed from the wall shelf. I understood that most of the people living there were college students. After I visited her a few times, it was obvious that we had no chemistry. I later learned that she was in love with a married guy, and he was coming over there and sleeping with her. I decided to continue talking to her, however, because I might get lucky when she got mad with him.

I found a couple of clubs to go to that was out in the country. I heard someone mention one and asked where it was. It was about 30 miles from Nacogdoches, and it was far back in the woods. It was a real country juke-joint. It had a juke box and benches against the wall for people to sit. The place only sold beer. After a few beers, I introduced myself to three women and told them that I was a stranger to Texas. I felt that this would be a good ice breaker, and it was. Before long, they were telling me how friendly black Texans were. They looked as if they were all over forty, and two were extremely fat. They wanted me to take them to another beer joint, and I said okay. The two fat women got in the back and were complaining about how there wasn't much room in the back. Later that night, I took all of them home. I was glad that the fat women asked me to take them home first. The one that was left in the car began to flirt. So, the next day, I went back to her house and picked her up. We went to a Holiday Inn. While we were there, she began to tell me about her love life.

"You know, every man that I had has done me wrong," she said.

I thought that I would do a little counseling.

"I know that was disappointing to you," I said sympathetically.

"Yeah, but the next man to do me wrong, I intend to do some time for him," she said angrily.

When I took her home, I told her that I would see her next week. But I didn't have any intention of seeing her again. She wasn't gonna do any time because of me.

The other club that I found was closer to Nacogdoches and was just out of the city limits. From the outside, it looked like a warehouse and was made of sheet metal. In the inside, it had regular tables and chairs, a dance floor, and a disc jockey playing music. It didn't have heating, except for a couple of wooden stoves in which someone put wood in, from time to time. If it wasn't so cold, it would have been okay. When I ordered a beer, the waitress brought me a quart bottle and a plastic cup.

On other occasions, I began to look around the town more, riding town the streets or sauntering down the sidewalks of the reputed oldest town in Texas. I wondered where the sweet women were that were easy to get along with. Good women, I knew, were hard to find. I did meet a woman at the library, but she and I didn't hit it off.

As in Savannah, I would go the public library on my time-off and read back issues of the Dallas and Houston newspapers. One of the women who worked in the library was black, and it seemed that she was always putting newspapers out when I was in the reading section of the library. She later admitted that she would wait until I came in before putting them out. But she didn't have to admit it, I knew when a woman wanted to engage in a conversation while pretending that she was just doing her job.

So, I began to talk to her and invited her to a movie. We went to the movie, and frankly, I enjoyed the movie more than her company. The movie was called "Magic" and it was about a man who allowed his ventriloquist dummy to control him. When he used the dummy to beat another man to death and the dummy was complaining about having a headache, I laughed so hard that I almost slid out of the chair. I laughed even more when the guy bandaged the dummy's head. I was enjoying the movie more than her.

But the real problem with the librarian was that she thought that I should be running behind her and showering her with gifts. But she didn't know that she had the wrong black man. She must have thought that I fell off a watermelon truck on the way to Houston. Besides, she didn't look that good anyway. So, I started going to the library at Stephen F. Austin University and reading its newspapers.

I began to do a little research on future jobs because I had only given a year commitment as a wilderness counselor. I learned that some job applications indicated that an applicant could omit admission of a felony conviction if the offense occurred when the person was a juvenile or the person was given a complete pardon. I had learned in Georgia that it restored a convicted felon's civil rights with an order of restoration and a first offender pardon. I knew that the pardon didn't erase the conviction, but I knew that other people wouldn't necessarily know it. All they would wanna know is whether I had a full pardon, if the conviction issue came up.

So, I applied for a first offender pardon from the Georgia Board of Pardon and Paroles, citing my education and current achievements. Within a few weeks, I received the first offender pardon. In examining it, I noted that it had virtually the same language as the restoration order that I received when my parole was terminated. But now I could, on some applications, omit answering that I had been convicted if the application stated that the offense had occurred when the person was a juvenile or the applicant was given a full pardon. I also knew that I was legally a juvenile when I was arrested and could have been tried in juvenile court, but this would be a little more difficult to handle on an application and later explained.

The weather was getting a little colder, but it was not unbearable to be living outdoors. I never would have thought that I could live outdoors. While wooden heaters were available, Joe told me that it was best not to have them because you would sweat when the tent was warm and then as the fire died down you would get cold. So, we didn't have a heater in the counselor's tent, but it wasn't bad because I had a lot of covers on my bed. When I was leaving for my time-off and headed back to Nacogdoches, the trees on both sides of the highway were covered with icicles. I was looking forward to a hot bath. But there was no hot water in the house when I got there because the bills had not been paid. Feeling unclean and desperate, I felt that I had to wash. So, I went to Joy's job and asked her if I could use her shower. I wasn't sure what she would say, but I wasn't afraid to ask her. All she could say was no, but she didn't. She handed me the keys to her apartment, and I told her that I would bring them back in about 45 minutes. The shower was invigorating, and I decided then that I would get my own place. I returned Joy's keys and thanked her.

I later asked the manager about a vacancy, and she told me that there was one on the third floor. So, I filled out an application and was quickly approved. Within a few weeks, I moved into my efficiency apartment, a floor above Joy.

I had to buy a few things and went to Kmart. When I was there, I bought a small trash receptacle and a few utensils. The clerk was a black woman, who looked to be in her thirties. She had to get my check approved. While we were waiting on the check approval, I decided to flirt with her a little. After I got home, I realized that I needed some more items. So, I went back to Kmart. While we were waiting on my check approval again, I asked her for her phone number. She gave it to me and told me that she lived in Lufkin and had five daughters. Within a couple of weeks, she was coming over to my apartment after work. We would have sex, and then she would go home. I went to her house once in Lufkin and met her daughters. She told me that she didn't wanna have sex at her place because she needed to set an example for her daughters, and I told her that I respected her position. So, we would only have sex at my place. Before long, she decided that I wasn't a good prospect given my work schedule.

One day when I went over to see Joy, she excused herself, quickly going out of the door. A few seconds later, Joy had a woman with her that she introduced as Ira. I immediately sensed that she was trying to set me up, and I chatted with Ira a little. Ira told me that she was a school teacher and taught in an elementary school in a small town north of Nacogdoches. She also stated that she lived a few doors down from Joy.

After Ira had left, I decided to return to my apartment. Within a few minutes, I thought that I heard a very faint knock on the door, but I wasn't sure if it was a knock. I went to the door, intending to confirm whether someone had knocked. When I opened the door, it was Ira.

"I decided to drop by and talk some more," Ira said as she slowly strolled into my apartment with her hands behind her back and sat down.

I began to study her more. She wasn't that good-looking, but she wasn't bad-looking either. She was in between. She had a denim dress with straps over both shoulders. I sat down on the couch next to her and immediately concluded that she was looking for a boyfriend. Because I wasn't seeing anyone, it might as well be me. I began to make a move on her, letting her know that I was available too.

"Do you have a boyfriend?" I asked.

"No, I'm not seeing anyone," Ira responded.

"Neither am I. So, you and I have a lot in common. I know Joy, but she is the only person that I really have met in Texas. If I had not gone in the clothing store, I never would have met Joy. It is hard to meet people in this town," I said.

Ira was staring at me, and I could sense that she would have sex with me if I asked. I had read something that women know within 5 minutes whether they would sleep with a guy. So, I asked her.

"Let's make love."

"We just met less than an hour ago," Ira said, astonished.

"So what does it matter when we met? I don't believe in the line that 'we need to get to know each other first.' You are not seeing anyone, and I am not seeing anyone. More importantly, I can sense now that you and I have some chemistry. But if you feel differently, then you are certainly free to leave. I'm not gonna force you to do anything you don't wanna do," I explained.

"You're right," Ira said as she began pulling the straps of her dress over her shoulders. We began to kiss passionately, and in a few minutes, we were having some serious sex.

I would get in Nacogdoches at about 2P.M., and Ira would get home about 4:30P.M.. After a few minutes of small talk consisting of her students and my boys at the camp, we would turn the sofa into a bed. It was good being with her, but I began to get a little worried.

Ira began telling me that she loved me, and she would tell me this when we were not having sex. I told her that I really, really liked her, but this was the best that I could say at the moment. I began to get concerned because I knew that she was from the country, and many country women believed in roots. I didn't believe in roots, but I know that people who do, do strange things, such as putting junk in your food or liquor. But as of yet, I had not eaten or drank anything that Ira gave me.

Ira, as expected, talked about Joy's love life. She told me that Joy had gotten pregnant from this married guy and had an abortion. She said also that Joy had been complaining because every time the guy came over that he would begin taking the sofa pillows and cover off the sofa and making the bed as soon as he arrived. There was little talking, hand-holding, or foreplay. I told Ira that a married guy can't stay too long and has to hit and run back home. Joy should know that.

One day I was at Ira's apartment when Joy came in. Joy was visibly upset and asked to use Ira's telephone. She called her brother in Center and asked him to bring his gun to her. Sensing that Joy wanted to ventilate to Ira, I left. After an hour, Ira came up to my apartment and told me that Joy really broke down and cried furiously after I left. According to Ira, Joy and the boyfriend's wife got into a fight. Joy was beating the wife when the boyfriend held Joy while the wife beat up on Joy. Joy felt betrayed because she realized that the guy cared more about his wife than her.

It was now well into 1979. I had been keeping in touch with my family in Savannah and my sister. She was now back in South Carolina. Initially, when she left Savannah after graduation, she obtained a job with the South Carolina Department of Corrections as a correctional officer, and she was living in Columbia, South Carolina. After working at a South Carolina prison for 6 months, she took a job as a federal correctional officer in Butner, North Carolina. She worked there for a year and then quit to return to Columbia as a bank teller. She also had enrolled in the University of South Carolina to work towards a master's degree in criminal justice. After a quarter or two, she had quit school and was just working in the bank. I was a little worried about her.

At work, I was getting better with the group. I had gotten considerably better after Joe and Annette left the group, and I attended counselors' training at the girls' camp and a canoe training trip for counselors.

The canoe training trip consisted of counselors from the girls and boys' programs. The purpose of the trip was teach counselors how to handle a group on the river, but it was also to instill confidence in the counselors.

One of the counselors on the trip was a black counselor named Les and he and I got to be better friends. He was from Houston and had started work about the same time that I did. He also was having a hard time with his group initially, but had gotten stronger too.

After our canoe trip was over, we stopped in Austin to celebrate with pizza. I didn't take any money with me, thinking that there would be no place to spend it. At the pizza shop, Les paid for my pizza and told me not to worry about paying him back for it. I knew then that he was okay.

I learned that my sister was planning to visit Savannah in April, and I decided to go too. I negotiated my time-off for April so that I could take a week off.

I had decided to return to Georgia a different way than from when I first drove to Texas because I was in Northeast Texas and a different route would be shorter. I intended to leave for Georgia as soon as I got home and took a bath. I decided to stay in Jackson, Mississippi for the night and continue on to Georgia the next day. As night fell and I was beginning to get tired, I stopped in Jackson. However, the motels near Interstate 20 were full, and I didn't wanna drive too far from the Interstate. So, I continue to drive. It was the same story in Meridan, Mississippi.

Before long, I was in Alabama and had gotten on Highway 80 as I had planned to do. As I approached a bridge, I stopped my car and pulled over to the side of the road. It was very dark but I could see that the bridge was only big enough for one car. There were lights going on and off near the bridge, but I wasn't sure what they meant for me to do. So, I studied the bridge and waited. A car came up behind me and then waited at the bridge. It waited until a truck had come from the opposite direction and the lights had changed and then the car went across. Feeling more confident, I pulled up to the bridge and drove across.

In Selma, Alabama, I found a Holiday Inn that had vacancies. I was glad because I was so tired that I was numb. It was close to midnight, and I had driven about 11 hours. The room was extremely clean, replete with furniture, and a king size bed. Crawling into the huge bed, I fell asleep quickly. The next morning, I took a shower and went down for breakfast. In looking around the restaurant, I realized that I was the only black person in the restaurant eating. Although I knew the historical significance of Selma when I approached it, it really hit me more as I was eating breakfast, and some white people in the restaurant were looking at me but weren't really staring. Just as I was leaving the city, I went across the bridge that was made famous by the attack on the civil rights demonstrators in the 1960s, which I had seen numerous times. In other parts of Alabama, I could see fields on either side of the highway engrossing small shacks. In some fields, I saw black women and men with their backs bent over and their sacks dragging the ground.

The next town that I passed through that triggered memories was Tuskegee, Alabama. I knew that there was a black college there, but I also recalled that it, or a nearby town, had a black mayor who married a white woman, and this story had been big news at one time. I also knew that the "Commodores" and Lionel Ritchie had their roots there. Riding through this town made me think about Sylvia because she used to play a lot of their music.

In Macon, Georgia, I got on the portion of Interstate 16 that led to Savannah, feeling that I was getting closer to home and picking up my speed. The excitement in me began to grow because I was eager to see my parents and my brothers and sisters. When I was a few miles from Savannah, I knew that I was on a very familiar road as I exited on 37th Street. Although I had seen this street many, many times, it now looked small. When I turned on Jefferson Street, it, too, looked small, as well as 31st Street. I had been gone 6 months, and all the streets seemed narrower and the houses seemed closer together.

When I walked into the house, I hugged Momma and told her how glad I was to see her. Daddy was at a social club that he had joined since his retirement. Before long, he was at home and I shook his hand. He was grinning, and as he was, his cheekbones became prominent as I had seen numerous times and had seen a few times in his brother, who had died a few years earlier.

I told him about my trip, including the Alabama bridge and staying in Selma. I asked about everyone and how they were doing. I also discussed my job and how it was going. Before long, my brother Willie was over at the house, and he caught me up on what had been going on in Savannah.

The next day, I went over to Sidney Brown father's house looking for Sidney. As I drove up, I could see Sidney and some other people sitting on the porch. I parked the car and went up to the porch.

"As soon as I saw that Grand Prix with Texas tags, I knew that was you," Sidney said as he extended his hand to me. "How you doing out in Texas?"

"I'm doing okay," I said. "The longer I stay away from Savannah, the better things are for me."

I spoke to the people that were on the porch with Sidney and we made some small talk. They had a bottle on the porch, and Sidney got a glass to pour me a drink. They invited me to eat dinner with them, and I said okay and then followed them into the house. I asked Sidney's mother not to give me very much, knowing that Momma was cooking all my special foods. After everyone had been served, Sidney was asked to say the grace, and he did so effortlessly.

As I bowed my head in respect to their family tradition, I wondered how religious Sidney was. He and I had talked a lot, but he never suggested that he was religious. The closest he came to discussing anything spiritual was when he told me that after he killed his wife, she came to him one night and choked him. He told me that this was the only time that she had bothered him.

Sidney finished the grace, and we began to eat.

"Oh yeah, I wanna tell you while you are here that you were right about me not having to go back to prison. I don't have that over my head anymore. My lawyer called me one day and told me that the case was over and I wouldn't have to go to prison. You told me not to withdraw my appeal and go to prison to get it over with, and you were right," Sidney stated excitedly.

"Well, I know white folks. When white folks really want you in prison, you go to prison, and they do not let you out on appeal bond. Some cases get special handling and some cases don't. But I just knew that no black man should volunteer to go to prison. That is absurd and ridiculous," I explained.

Sidney asked me if I wanted to join him and a few women at a club on Waters Avenue later that night. I said okay and later returned. We had a few drinks at the club and just laughed and talked.

My sister from South Carolina had arrived, and we got caught up on everything. I was interested in what she was doing in South Carolina.

I had only planned to be in Savannah for a week, and it went very quickly. It seemed that I had just gotten to Savannah and now it was time to return to Texas. As I was leaving, I was not unhappy to be returning to Texas. I told them that I would be back at Christmas.

My job in Texas was getting considerably easier. I had become the senior counselor in the group, which meant that the group felt more secure with me and wouldn't act up. The junior counselor in the group was a guy named Fletcher, who was quite good but who was very stressed about the turmoil in the group whenever I left. The boys in the group knew when my time-off was scheduled. So, at about 11A.M., the boys started getting agitated, and Fletcher would have a really pitiful look on his face. One time, he jokingly begged me not to go. I told him that the boys would stop soon, and this was an experience that all new counselors had to go through. As I left the campsite at noon with my bags, I could hear the boys screaming and Fletcher trying to get them to the logs. Three days later when I returned, I could hear the turmoil in the campsite as I entered. As soon as the boys saw me, they would come up to me, hug me, and begin telling me how badly Fletcher ran the group in my absence. Fletcher had a very haggard look on his face and told me that the boys raised hell for the last 3 days. I told him that he had done a good job, but a few days later, he quit.

Fletcher's quitting reminded me how high the turnover was with counselors. Although the camp asked for a year commitment, most counselors didn't stay a year. Also, a few had to be fired because they got too rough with the boys.

One day, a supervisor came to me and told me that they wanted to move me to the oldest group, which consisted of 15- and 16-year-old boys. I was told that there was some concern about how the counselor in the group was performing and the staff felt that the group could benefit from my laid-back style. The staff wanted me to run the group according to the philosophy of the camp, and the staff didn't believe that the current counselor was following policy. Also, this group was planning a major canoe trip, which was to last for 4 weeks, and the staff wanted someone else in the group. I also was told that this was a move up for me and would put me in line to be promoted. I really didn't wanna go because I had a good group, but I said okay.

When I got into the oldest group, I readily saw that there was a problem. The senior counselor in the group name was Terry, and he had some unorthodox ways of handling the group. Slowly, I began to do things a little differently and some of the boys complained that I had brought unnecessary rules from my old group.

The group was planning two canoe trips. One was for 1 week and the other was for 4 weeks. The week trip was over very quickly and there was little problems although I had gotten sick. The other trip was down the Sabine River. We were taking 2 weeks of food and had scheduled to have the last 2 weeks of food brought to us. On the day we put in the river, it was raining and it rained for the next 3 days. Thus, everyone's tent, sleeping bag, and clothes were wet. We felt like real outdoor-men when we had to build a fire to cook our food when everything was wet. If we had not done it, I wouldn't have believed that a fire could be started in that type of weather.

After the sun came out, the trip became really exciting. We were being given catfish by some fisherman that we had met on the river. But it was a little scary when we saw an alligator in the water, and I told the boy who was in the canoe with me that he better not tip over the canoe. We reached the end of the river where it emptied into the Gulf of Mexico and the boys were really excited by our accomplishment. I was excited too. We found a telephone and called the camp. When we were told that we would be picked up a day early, the group was ecstatic and some boys were dancing in the road.

But the last night was awful. The mosquitoes were numerous and a small, smoking fire wouldn't run them away. I had never seen mosquitoes like that and shining a flashlight revealed how numerous they were. They were in the tent and their buzzing was too much for me to go to sleep. The boys couldn't sleep and many of them were walking around, fanning their heads. No one slept well that night. I couldn't sleep because of the mosquitoes.

When I saw Ira, she was about as happy to see me as I was to see her. She thought that she was in love with me and told me how badly she had missed me during the last 4 weeks. She really began telling me how much she loved me and began hinting about us possibly getting married.

One day, she told me that she was gonna cook me a special dinner. I feared that she was not gonna wait for me to propose to her and she intended to propose to me. I wondered if this was leap year and had to think whether it was or not. She told me that she would call me when everything was ready.

When she called and I went down to her apartment, it was pitch dark except for a candle in the middle of the table. It was so dark that I could not see well what she was serving. As we began to eat, I tasted sugar in the string beans.

"These string beans have sugar in them," I said in amazement.

"I know. I like to put sugar in my vegetables," Ira responded.

Fearing that she had put something in the string beans and was trying to cover it up with sugar, I turned on the light and blew out the candle.

"It's too dark in here," I said.

She looked hurt. But I wanted to see what I was eating. All this talk about marriage and her being from the country made me suspect that she had put something in the food. I wasn't gonna eat any more of her vegetables. I picked at the other foods, but I knew I was not gonna clean my plate.

A black woman who believes in roots and who wants to get married will put something in the food. Even if she hadn't, blowing out the candle and turning on the light dampened her marriage ideas, if these were in her mind to discuss.

Later, I related the incident to Les about Ira's dinner and what I did and why. He laughed in that deep belly laugh that was characteristic of him. When he returned from his next time-off, he told me that he had told his girl-friend, and she told him that if he did anything like that she would kill him.

Chapter 30

The new year, 1980, had just begun, and I had feelings that this year, and thus the beginning of a new decade, was gonna be extremely good for me. To some extent, I felt like I did when I was about to go into the beginning of 1967, the last leg of my senior year in high school. But unlike what happened in all of 1967, I knew 1980 was gonna be different. But I had a jolt that made me think differently for a while.

The Texas Department of Human Resources regulated treatment programs in Texas and there was some concern about treatment employees who had lied about their backgrounds and had later been determined to have been abusive with children. So, there was some attention being given to personnel records. Lyndy, who had hired me, told me that the Department of Human Resources was looking at personnel records. I told him that I had been given a pardon by the Georgia Board of Pardon and Paroles. Lyndy asked me for a copy of it just in case questions arose about me. I gave it to him, and he, after making a copy, put it in my personnel file and returned the original.

I had been given an indication why I was hired. I was told that they had hired some people with legal problems in their background, though not as serious as me. Mostly, the issue was drugs. All the people did an outstanding job for them and there were no problems. Lyndy, who was from Oklahoma, claimed to be part Indian. He told me that his Indian blood was conveying a favorable impression of me and he knew that I would be good. When he said something similar about a guy he hired who had no criminal background and had to fire, I tried to console him by telling that his Indian blood was right at least one time.

I was given a promotion. I became noticed primarily because I could write. I had always been told that my counselor evaluations were the best written of all the counselors. Later, there was an incident involving one of the boys, and I had to write a detailed report. I welcomed the opportunity, and one of new administrative staff members told me that he didn't know that I could write so well. So, my writing, combined with my dependability, made some people think that I would be a good choice whenever a promotional opportunity arose.

I was promoted to roving counselor. In this position, I was now not assigned to a particular group and floated from group to group in a supervisory capacity. I now slept in a small bedroom in the main building and supervised the counselors when the other staff members left at 5 P.M.. Also, I had supervisory responsibilities on weekends.

This promotion was quickly followed by another promotion to group work supervisor. In this position, I was entitled to weekends off and basically could leave in the evenings provided everything was running smoothly.

I immediately realized that this was my opportunity to return to school. Stephen F. Austin had a criminal justice program, but I was leaning towards Sam Houston State University in Huntsville because it had a national reputation.

However, I was faced with a dilemma. If I chose Stephen F. Austin, I should remain living in Nacogdoches or Lufkin. But if I chose to go to Sam Houston State, I should live, perhaps, in Groveton where a co-worker named Mike had invited me to share a two-bedroom apartment with him. Groveton was a very small town, with a population of about 2,000. It had about fifteen or twenty units of one and two bedroom apartments.

The camp was the center of my life and I basically decided that I needed to live between school and work. So, this meant either Lufkin or Groveton. But when word got around that I might move to Groveton, one of the white camp teachers begged me not to move there.

"I heard that you are thinking about moving in with Mike in Groveton, Rudy. Please don't move there. You're too nice a person to deal with what you will have to deal with there," she said as she held my hand.

"I really appreciate your concern, but I will be okay if I move there," I said reassuringly.

"But you don't know those people in Groveton. They are some very prejudiced people there and they give black people a very hard time there. I have heard about some of the mean things that some of them have done, and I don't wanna see it happen to you. Please! Please! Please! Don't move there. Stay in Lufkin or somewhere else," she begged.

"I really appreciate your concern, and I consider your warning to be an indication of friendship. But trust me when I say that I will be okay," I said.

I told Mike that I would move in with him and share the expenses.

Other people around the camp were teasing me and telling me that the real reason that I wanted to move to Groveton was to be near Fay's, a prostitution establishment on Highway 287, which was about a mile from Groveton.

"Rudy wants to be near that pussy. I bet you will be down at Fay's every night," someone joked.

I just laughed along with them, but I, as a matter of principle, had no intention of going to Fay's. I didn't discuss it with anyone, but I could never go there.

The main problem for me with Fay's was that it had only black prostitutes and local law enforcement had told the owner that she could stay open as long as she didn't have any white prostitutes there. While I didn't have any desire for a white woman, I couldn't go somewhere where only black women could work and any low-life white man could go. I had passed by Fay's and had seen unwashed, dirty white truckers stopping there. Any white man could go. That place had unpleasant racial overtones for me. It reminded me of how I felt when I was reading *The Godfather,* and one of the Dons said that he tried to keep drugs in the dark people's neighborhood. Fay couldn't give me any of her girls for free.

When I told Ira that I was returning to school and moving to Groveton, Texas, which meant that our relationship was over, she cried angrily. She called me all kinds of names. But I never promised her anything. She knew that one day I would leave.

I had been in contact with the criminology program at Sam Houston State and had had my transcript from Armstrong sent there to learn what courses it would accept as transfer credits. I was unsure how the courses would fit because Armstrong was on a quarter hour system and Sam Houston was semester. But when I met with the chair of the criminology and corrections program, I was very satisfied how my courses transferred. In fact, I was given more credit than I had earned. I could be finished in a year and had planned to begin in January 1981. My goal was to be finished by the end of December, which meant that I had to take full loads and attend during the summer. But I knew that I could do it.

I was entitled to weekends off, but I negotiated with Lyndy taking my two days off on Tuesdays and Thursdays, which coincided with classes at Sam Houston State.

In September, shortly after I moved in with Mike, he decided to get married and move out. It was one of those quickie relationships. He met someone, and a few weeks later they were married. So, I had a two bedroom apartment to myself.

About a week later, I just happened to look out my bedroom window where my car was parked. It didn't look right. One side was low. When I went out to investigate, I saw that one tire was going flat and the hubcap was gone. Examining the tire closer, I could hear air coming out and could see that it had been cut. I immediately knew that a white person had done it, and this was what I had been warned about.

But I knew that I was not gonna move. I had not done anything to anyone and only moved into this small town to facilitate my returning to school. I was not about to move or change my college plans from Sam Houston State to Stephen F. Austin.

I thought that whoever cut my tire was less than a man anyway and not someone that I should run from. If he had any guts, he would have come up to my face and told me that he hated niggers and wanted me gone. I didn't think that I was so tough and bad, but I stopped believing long ago that I should run from anyone.

There was no mail delivery in this small town, and mail had to be picked up at the post office. So, I had been seen a few times in town, and I suspected that whoever cut my tire was someone who was on the main street a lot. So, I went to the small hardware store and asked to buy a box of hollow-point .38 bullets. I knew the store didn't sell them, and I had no weapon to put them in. When the clerk told me that he didn't sell bullets, I knew that word would quickly get around town that I was looking for bullets and I wasn't planning on leaving.

I was asked to change my two bedroom apartment for a one bedroom apartment across the courtyard. There was a family consisting of a white man, his son, and his daughter living in a one bedroom apartment. The daughter was about 12, but she was precociously developed. Management had some concern about this girl not having a bedroom for herself. So, I agreed to change apartments. They helped me moved and were very polite. The boy was about 17 or 18, and he called me Mr. Rudy. It made me feel old.

All the units had thin walls and less than sturdy doors. That night I heard the white couple upstairs arguing, but it was mostly the man. He was asking where she had been and was calling her a tramp. I could hear it well and then the arguing seemed to be headed toward the front door. I peered out of my window and saw the guy roughly pushing the woman towards the stairs, calling her a tramp and slut. The woman started down the stairs as the man slammed his front door. Perhaps thinking that he would call her back or trying to figure out where to go, the woman sat at the bottom of the stairs for about 10 minutes. Then, she began walking across the courtyard.

The next night, I saw the guy escorting a different woman inside his apartment. A few minutes later, I could hear his bed bumping loudly above my bedroom ceiling. After about 10 minutes, the bed was still.

An elderly white man in his sixties became friendly with me and invited me to his place for a drink. Unafraid and sensing that he was being sociable, I went over to his unit, and we shared a bottle together. While I was there, he showed me a nine-shot 22 pistol that he owned.

As I was returning to my unit, I thought how many white people are painted with the same brush. Undoubtedly, there were some racists in this small town, and many white people will lie, cheat, steal, flimflam, and betray a black person. But there were also a few white people that were decent people. While I don't expect all white people to be friendly, my only expectation was that they either leave me alone or treat me like a human being when I was forced to deal with them. Even if they were not friendly, that was okay with me. White people could pass me and not speak to me. As long as they were not doing anything to hurt me, I had no problem with them. Just being white was not enough for me to hate or dislike a white person.

One day at work, a black caseworker named Marsha from the Department of Human Resources in Conroe, Texas escorted a boy to the camp for a visit. As I was talking to her, the conversation turned social. She told me that she had just been divorced, and she gave me her telephone number.

I called her and she invited me to attend a football game at the Astrodome involving Texas Southern and Grambling. Then, she told me that I could spend the night with her after the game.

Naturally, I said okay to her invitation. She had a 12-year-old son who was looking at me very suspiciously. I could sense that he didn't like me and didn't want someone fooling around with his mother.

The only unpleasantness about the evening was that I didn't like the smell in her hair. She had some type of grease in it that smelled awful. It was hard to make love to her because of how her hair was in my face and nostrils. Also, her moaning and exhortations while we were making love seemed insincere. "Oh Rudy, Rudy, this is so, so good" she repeated over and over. I felt that she was trying to make me think that it was better than it was. It was okay but it was nothing to write home about. In the morning, she got out of bed early and went into the living room. Later, she came back and told me that she had to lie to her son. After she told him that I was sleeping in her bed, he asked her where she slept. She told him that she slept on the sofa. Although he was not awake when we came in, he knew that his mother had lied. I realized that guys that age don't want their moms doing it with strange men.

I called her a few more times, but the relationship didn't develop. She lived about 70 miles from me, and I wasn't gonna be driving to see her on a regular basis. It was a friendly realization on both our parts.

When 1981 came, I was very excited. During my first quarter at Sam Houston State, I enrolled in five courses—American Government, English, Probation and Parole, Human Behavior, and Legal Aspect of Corrections. My classes started early in the morning and were back-to-back. I had to schedule them one after another because I was gonna be able to take classes only on Tuesdays and Thursdays.

On the morning of examinations I was really tense because I was afraid that my car might not start and I was 40 miles from school and had no one to catch a ride with. I had joined AAA, just in case I had morning car trouble. Despite my anxieties, my car always started. At the end of the semester, I had two A's, 2 B's, and one C.

Of my first courses, I really enjoyed the English class because I had always liked reading short stories and analyzing them. For this English class, as well as at Armstrong, I was struck by stories in which a character faced a forked road and was forever changed by taking one road instead of another. But the most intriguing story that we analyzed was Dante's *Inferno*.

Although I was not religious, I enjoyed reading about Dante's journey into, and emergence from, hell. According to the professor, sinners were placed in hell according to the degree of seriousness of the sin. The most egregious sinners were placed closest to the devil. I agreed that treacherous individuals, especially those in positions of trust who combined their treachery with greed, belong closest to the devil and were more despicable than individuals who had shed blood. I agreed with the devil's treatment of Judas,

Brutus, and Cassius. As Dante passed them, his guide pointed to some stairs as the way to rise above such evil and to ascend into the shining world again.

My situation was akin to Dante's journey. He went to hell and so did I. I wondered if we went to hell, who would be closest to the devil, Drew, me, Kravitch, Dunbar Harrison, or members of the Tornadoes? We did some other stories, but I liked *Inferno* the best. It made me think.

I had heard a rumor that I was gonna be asked to transfer to Houston as a caseworker. As a caseworker, I would interview boys and parents for the wilderness camp and write intake studies. Also, I would function as a liaison between parents and the camping program and would conduct monthly parent meetings in Houston. I wanted it, but I had just started Sam Houston State University. When I was told that I would be given some flexibility so that I could finish the program at Sam Houston State, I quickly said yes to leaving the camp and relocating to Houston, Texas.

I looked through a Houston newspaper for advertisements about apartments, and one advertisement caught my eye because it said $100 will be taken off the first month's rent. When I looked at the apartment complex in Southwest Houston, I found it acceptable and signed a lease. It looked okay, had swimming pools, and a security gate.

After signing the lease, I found out why it had offered $100 dollars off the first month's rent. There had been two really brutal murders that were still unsolved. In both cases, the women who were killed had been decapitated.

But these unsolved cases didn't cause me to change my mind and move out. I did notice that the people, especially the women, who still lived in the complex exuded fear. I had not seen anything like it since I was in prison. Some prisoners I had served time with had fear written all over them. Some of my new neighbors had the same type of fear. One time, I watched two sisters who lived across from me get out of their car, their heels clicking rapidly as they made a dash to get behind the locked door of their apartment. I spoke to them once, but they ignored me, their clicking heels intensifying.

Soon after I moved to Houston, I was trying to get in touch with Les. Les had quit the agency and the word out on him now was that he was pimping. One afternoon, he dropped by my apartment with a guy and a woman scantly dressed in a micro-mini skirt. I sensed that the story about him pimping was true. After a few minutes, they left. As the woman was going out the door, Les put his hand in her behind and goosed her. In his deep belly laugh, he stated that he liked doing that because she didn't like it. The guy with Les never said a word as he followed them out.

A few weeks later, a co-worker told me that Les had been killed the previous night. Subsequent reports were that a friend had killed him, and I suspected that the friend was the same person that he had brought to my apartment. Although I wasn't there, I suspected that they may have had a dispute about money. Regardless, I attended Les's funeral, and this was the first funeral that I had ever attended.

One night my brother called me to give me some news from Savannah.

"I'm not gonna talk long. I just wanted to let you know that your friend Sidney Brown was killed a few days ago, and I thought you wanted to know," my brother Willie said.

"I'm not really surprised and I kind of expected it. What happened?" I asked.

"It happened near 37th Street and Jefferson. Sidney was with some sisters who were looking for a third sister who had not been seen in a couple of days. They suspected that she was over at her boyfriend's place and was in trouble. The boyfriend lived on 37th Street and Jefferson. The woman was there and had a broken leg after getting beat up by the boyfriend. Also, the newspaper said that Sidney used to go with the woman with the broken leg. Well, the two sisters went into the apartment, which was upstairs, and Sidney stayed in the car. The sisters learned that their other sister was indeed there and they started arguing with the boyfriend. After awhile, Sidney went inside the apartment with a .38 pistol, but the guy had a shotgun. He shot Sidney in the chest and Sidney died on the way to the hospital. I went over to Sidney's father house to take the family some sodas and told him that I was your brother. Sidney's father was torn up by how Sidney died and said that it could have been avoided."

"Well, like I said, I'm not surprised. I'm sorry to hear that he's dead," I said.

On another occasion, my brother called me with news of another killing. This time it was George Wilson.

"Two police officers went to George's house to arrest him, but, according to the newspaper, George pulled a gun. One of the police officers, in trying to shoot George, shot the other officer. George died a couple of days after being in the hospital. The police officer who was killed was Detective J.J. Brown. Did you know him?" my brother asked.

"Yeah, I knew Detective Brown."

"I wanted to ask you something. When George was in the hospital, the chief of police stated that if George lived, George was gonna be charged with murder. Can they do that since George didn't kill the detective?"

"In some states, yes. But I am not sure if Georgia has that type of law. I remembered reading that a guy in the northeast got into a shootout with the police, and one police officer accidentally shot another officer. When the shootout was over, the guy involved was charged with murder and they later executed him. The law in that state was that if someone creates or causes a situation that leads to death, then that person is responsible for that death although he may not have actually killed anyone. So, if Georgia had a similar law, George could have been tried for causing Detective Brown's death. It's a good thing that George died. I would rather see him die that way than to see him die in the electric chair. Years ago, when we were both at Wayne Correctional Institution, he told me that he wasn't gonna do any more time. Apparently, he meant it."

Mike, who I was supposed to move in with in Groveton, was living in Houston and working as an adoption worker. Mike came by my apartment and told me that his wife didn't want him to come because of the unsolved murders at the complex. He told me about a good-looking woman who worked at his agency and invited me to drop by his job one day. I did, but she was not there that day. Mike stated that there was another single woman there, but she too was gone that day.

Mike later called me and told me about a jazz concert in a club on Scott Street near the University of Houston. I had a bottle of Seagram Seven and had been drinking it when I fell asleep on the couch. When I awoke, it was almost time for the concert. I quickly showered and left.

When I got there, the place was full, and it was dark. I began to walk around, looking for Mike. He was not hard to find, being a white guy in mostly a black crowd. I went over to his table where three other couples were sitting. Mike introduced me to everyone, but there was only one person that stood out, Mike's co-worker.

However, she was not single that evening because she was hanging on to a guy's arm. When Mike introduced me to her, my eyes zeroed in on her sparkling eyes. She had been drinking and it had changed her eyes. But there was something else about her that appealed to me. I had not been too impressed with the women that I had dated, but this lady impressed me and I thought that I was looking almost at my match.

Although she had a date, I knew that he was not her match. He had an alligator on his shirt pocket. No true black man dresses socially with foxes and alligators on their shirt pockets. I knew that he had gotten it from Sears or JCPenney. She probably was out with him because she didn't have anyone else to ask her out for this event.

I was still worried about my sister because she didn't seem to be doing too well. She was complained about her job in South Carolina as a teller. So, I thought that she might like to come to Texas.

"Sis, why don't you come here? There are a lot of opportunities out here. You can live with me, if you don't mind sleeping on the couch. You don't have to pay me anything and you can stay until you get on your feet," I proposed.

It didn't take her long to say yes. She got my youngest brother Sylvester to drive with her and had made plans to pay his airfare back to Georgia. I gave them directions and they came straight to my place. I didn't have to go get them because they were lost.

I warned my sister about the two decapitations in the complex and told her to be careful in any place that she went. There was a lot of crime in Houston. People were always getting killed, robbed, and raped.

After a few weeks, my sister found a job as a security officer for Joske Department store. She asked me if she could continue living with me to save some money. I told her that she was free to stay as long as she needed.

In the meantime, I had taken a summer class at Houston Community College and attended a summer workshop for credit at Sam Houston State. The most exciting and entertaining feature of the workshop was an evening with G. Gordon Liddy. I started not to go because he had worked in the Nixon

Administration. But to my surprise, he made the best presentation of all the presenters.

When the summer was over, I needed 18 hours or six classes to finish by the end of the fall quarter. My sister was concerned that I was doing too much, driving the 70 miles to Huntsville and working at my caseworker job. But I felt that I could do it. I contracted to take one independent study and agreed to do a specific number of book reports for a C. I took Criminal Law, Organized Crime, Research, Interviewing, and Human Sexuality. At the end of the fall semester, I had 2 A's and 3 B's. More importantly, I had a bachelor's degree in Criminology and Corrections from Sam Houston State.

When I graduated from Armstrong, I went to the graduation ceremony, and it felt fabulous marching across the auditorium stage. But this time, I decided not to attend the graduation ceremony at Sam Houston State. I had the school mail my degree, and I picked it up at the post office.

Just before leaving Sam Houston State, I spoke with my advisor about a graduate degree, and she, having a doctoral degree in social work, advised me not to get a master's degree in the same field that I was getting from Sam Houston. Although the courses were graduate level, they were the same as many of the courses that I took as an undergraduate. She advised me to get a master's in social work and stated that it would do more for me. Taking her advice, I applied to the Graduate School of Social Work at the University of Houston.

My sister finally moved out and got a place on the other side of town.

I decided to move too. I wanted to move a little closer to the University of Houston. So, I moved to Broadway Square apartments near Hobby Airport. It was really huge, consisting of over 5,000 units and taking up several streets. I really liked it because it had security systems in their apartment and the grounds were kept neatly trimmed and were clean. Later, my sister moved to Broadway Square and was in the next block from me.

I was invited to a black political luncheon one Saturday and told my sister about it. So, we went together. As soon as we were seated and I looked around, I spotted someone that I recognized.

"I know that lady sitting over there," I said.

"Know who?" my sister asked.

"There is a lady sitting over there that I met 7 months ago at a jazz concert. She had a guy with an animal on his shirt pocket with her then, but it looks like she is alone now," I said. "I was high then and the club was dark, but I remember her."

"You recognized someone from 7 months ago?" my sister asked.

"Yeah and I am going over there in a few minutes to reintroduce myself," I stated.

"Well, you go ahead, brother. I wanted to take some of these mints home," my sister said as she started putting what she thought were mints in her purse.

"Those are not mints. They are pats of butter. Don't embarrass me. I see that I have to call Daddy and tell him on you," I joked.

I got up and went to the table of the lady that probably wouldn't remember me.

"You may not remember me, but you and I met at the Jazz-on-the-Cob last summer. You were sitting with Mike Mink, and he introduced us," I said. "Maybe we should reintroduced ourselves. My name is Rudolph."

"My name is Arlinda Turner. It is good to meet you again. I remember the concert, and I remember meeting some people."

We talked about the speech that we had heard, and I later went back to my table. I made sure that she knew that I was with my sister in case she looked over at my table.

"Well, we reintroduced ourselves. I intend to call her Monday or Tuesday and invite her to lunch." I did call and she said yes to lunch on Thursday. It was the beginning of the deepest and most serious relationship that I have ever had with a woman.

I was accepted at the University of Houston and started during the summer of 1982. Roy, whom I worked with at the wilderness camp, was a beginning student too. Roy also lived at Broadway Square. We also met another black student from Philadelphia named Nate.

As I have always done, I took as many classes as I could. Although I was taking classes, I was still doing my job. I was able to take classes during the week and work in the office doing my paperwork on weekends. So, on many Saturdays and Sundays, I would be in the office by myself.

I gave the parents my home number and would call them at home on the weekend. Some parents were really impressed, telling me that I worked every day and they didn't know anyone that worked on weekends like me.

So, I had a few parents with whom I had very good relationships. One of the closest relationships was with a white parent. One woman co-worker, after observing us talking, told me one day that this parent liked me. This co-worker was convinced that this parent had a crush on me. While I denied it, I suspected that she did, but I didn't do anything unethical. All I did was talk to her.

As I received reports from camp or was up at camp, I would call some parents and tell them how their sons were doing. I would also make contact with parents to learn if their sons had written letters home, which we encouraged, or had said something in a letter that was a concern.

Some parents would talk to me about personal problems. One parent was thinking about divorcing her husband, which I thought was a mistake. On occasion, she called me to tell me about her nonexistent marital problems and I listened.

She was complaining that her husband lies on the couch on the weekends and does nothing. He would take her out if she asked him and was not jealous of her going out with her girlfriends. He just didn't volunteer to take her out on Saturdays and this was bothering her.

Although counselors are not supposed to give advice, I decided to do it anyway, given that she and I had a friendly relationship. First, I told her to list his strengths and weaknesses. She said that he didn't chase other women, he didn't drink, he paid the bills, and he was good in bed.

I added that he didn't hit her.

What about his weaknesses? I asked.

All she could bring up was this couch thing.

"You don't have a problem, and it is all because you have been reading those women magazines and listening to those women complain on those talk shows about the couch potatoes. Tell me, would you be happier with a man that likes to take you to the bars, but he chases other women, does drugs, and hits you?"

"No."

"No individual is perfect, and we all have some flaws. Some women complain about not having a good man, and these same women wouldn't know a good man if they had one. I would be very disappointed with you if you divorced this guy for the reasons that you told me. If you said that you didn't love him anymore, that would be better, but not what you told me. I got a black neighbor who divorced her husband because he played basketball in the evenings after work. She said that she had a problem with a grown man playing basketball. I asked her should he have been playing tennis, golf, or something else to exercise? The guy was working and her primary problem with him was that he played basketball. Now, she is complaining that she doesn't have anyone and can't meet anybody. There are some guys out there with problems, but some women are gonna create something to complain about. There is nothing wrong that I can see. He works hard doing physical work and he wants to relax on weekends. But he still will take you out and do things with you, but you just have to ask him. Big deal. Ask him. That's just part of your role in the marriage. Just like his role may be to go outside when you hear a noise late at night outside the trailer. I am willing to bet that he will never complain and will never say 'why you don't volunteer sometimes to check the noises?' And 'why do I always have to be the only one going outside?' Some people assume or take certain roles. It doesn't have to be fifty-fifty on every single issue," I said. "If he was mistreating you or the children, that would be a different story. But he is not. Throw those magazines away and stop watching those shows. That is your problem."

There was a long silence on the telephone, and I knew that I had convinced her that these thoughts were foolish.

Chapter 31

Arlinda and I were going out on a regular basis, but our relationship didn't blossom into a serious relationship at first. After several dates, I told her that I really enjoyed her company and enjoyed being with her. I also told her that I liked her very much. This was a mistake.

She seemed to withdraw at that point, accusing me of pressuring her into a relationship but evincing confidence that she had the upper hand. I had read a theory about power in a relationship that stated that the person who most wants the relationship possesses the least amount of power. This person continually accommodates and yields to the other person to further and maintain the relationship. Hence, the other person possesses the power and controls the relationship.

However, with me there was a limit. While I could tell a woman that I liked her a lot, it didn't mean that I would be willing to do anything and everything to win that person. At one point, Arlinda told me that I didn't know how to court a woman and suggested that my behavior toward her was not indicative of someone who liked her. I tried to explain it to her, but she didn't understand what I was saying.

Exacerbating the situation, I related to her that a married friend told me that he asked his wife out for 6 months before she agreed to go out with him. I told her that I wouldn't repeatedly ask a woman to go out with me when she has told me no initially. Arlinda said that I had the wrong idea about women and didn't understand them and what a man's role was. Thus, Arlinda and I didn't grow closer together, and we were confined to occasional dates that were nonromantic and friendly.

We grew further apart when my family came up from Georgia and I invited Arlinda to a barbecue at my place to meet my brothers and my daddy. Arlinda didn't come and didn't call. I was extremely hurt, and she apologized profusely, saying that she simply forgot. I knew that she woudn't promise to come and deliberately stay away. I believed that she forgot because she was busy doing a lot of things. I knew that she showed houses for a real estate company and was very involved with Amway. Unlike some women who wanted the good life, Arlinda was trying to get it and she was ethical about it. But my brothers and my daddy were very important to me, and Arlinda forgetting them was too much for me to brush off. At that point, I distanced myself further from her and stopped calling her.

While my social relationship was not going well, I was finding considerable success at the University of Houston. I was doing well in my classes, but I was feeling tired. After having some political trouble with my research project, I was tired of school. A couple of people mentioned that I should pursue a doctoral degree, but I said hell no. I was tired of school, but I kept plugging ahead. In 1984, I graduated with my class, but I chose not to march. I had the school mail my degree to me.

I was meeting other women, but none excited me. They were all lacking in something. They were not Arlinda. I had never kissed or slept with Arlinda. We never got to that point, but I felt good just being with her and being with her was more stimulating than some of the women who spent the night at my apartment.

My friend Marsha from Conroe called me, informing me that she had been dispatched to Galveston to help deal with the aftermath of a hurricane that had recently been in this area.

"My co-worker and I felt like going out and socializing, but we didn't wanna spend our prime-time with white folks," Marsha said. "Would you like to meet us up at Cody's during happy hour?"

"Yeah, I'll meet you up there," I said.

Cody's was a jazz club that was quite popular. Arlinda and I would go there often.

"My co-worker is also meeting a guy up here. She is not married, but she is living with another guy," Marsha said.

Marsha's friend was in the restroom and joined us at the table. Then, they started talking about men and relationships.

"When I go home today, I have to undress in front of the guy I'm living with because he would be suspicious if I immediately went into the shower after getting home. So, I have to undress in his presence so he could see that I have all my underclothes and there aren't any unusual stains on them," Marsha's friend said.

I started laughing and both of them looked incredulously at me.

"What are you laughing about? That's all part of being married. Where have you been?" Marsha asked.

"I've been here. But, if I were married, I woudn't be checking my wife's underwear. You two probably get into that underwear checking too. I bet that you two, instead of looking for lipstick on the collar, are looking for stains on your guys' shorts," I said laughingly. "Now, I understand why some couples fight all the time."

They stared at me as if I were from Mars.

Then, Marsha said something that made me angry.

"You're paying for my drink," she said matter of factly.

"Wait a minute. If you want me to buy you a drink, ask me. But don't tell me I have to buy you a drink," I said.

"I don't need to ask. A man is supposed to buy a woman's drink. My aunt told me to never pay for a drink when a man is at the table," Marsha said confidently.

"You and your aunt have been fooling with the wrong black men. Given your attitude, I have no intention of buying you a drink, and I won't pay for it," I stated quite seriously. "I wish that I met your aunt. I would have straightened her out."

"Yeah, you will pay," she responded.

When the waitress came to the table with the drinks, she told me what the total was.

"Lady, I only ordered one drink and that's all I intend to pay for," I said to the waitress.

Marsha looked at me in amazement. She thought that I was not serious, but now she knew that I was dead serious. She stared at me and then reached for her purse to pay for her drink.

Later, Marsha called me to process the evening.

"I thought about what happened at Cody's, and now I realize that you are not like most black men. Other black men make things tough for you, I bet. Many black men will just cave-in when women are stern with them, but not you. I didn't know you were like that," Marsha said.

"Well, now you know. Anytime a woman, or a man, tells me that I better do this or that or else, I say bring on the else."

I was still doing my parental counseling. A Hispanic woman had her son in our program and she lived with her boyfriend for 6 months. The boyfriend, whom I met at the intake interview, would lock her in the house. He would put a padlock outside the door as if it was a chastity belt. The house had burglary bars and if there had been a fire, there was no way for her to get out. She told me that he carried a pistol with him all the time. He decided to sever the relationship with him and let her leave. The issue was that she felt entitled to some of his furniture and appliances for staying with him for 6 months. I told her no and her mother got on the telephone to help convince me that her daughter deserved something for her ordeal.

I told the boy's grandmother that what she was advising her daughter to do would get her killed. I told the grandmother that if someone took some of this guy's furniture, that someone would get killed. Either he would kill someone or they would have to kill him and that it was not worth it for a portable television and a coffee table. I told her to be happy that her daughter was out of this relationship. But the grandmother insisted that her daughter had a right to some things for living with him for a few months. I was hoping that they would heed my advice. I had seen this dude and I knew he was a serious guy.

Periodically, I would call Arlinda and we would catch up on what each of us had been doing. Occasionally, we would go out, but I was mostly dating other women that I met. She called me one day at work and asked if we could have lunch together. When I met her at the restaurant, she began filling me in on what she had been doing.

"I met a guy recently and he seemed to be interested in me. But I found out later that he was married, and he, in effect, was looking at me as his mistress or something. I quickly terminated that situation," Arlinda said. "What about you? Are you seeing anyone?"

"Well, I haven't been seeing any married women, but I have been talking to a divorcee who is a juvenile probation officer," I said. "She is nice and attractive, but we haven't committed to anything permanent or serious. We are still out on the fringe."

Then, she dropped a bomb on me.

"I was wondering if it is too late for us and if it would be possible for us to have a relationship now," Arlinda asked. "This is why I asked you to lunch."

I had to collect my thoughts quickly.

"Frankly, I wasn't expecting this when you called," I said, still trying to organize my words. "I told you several times that there is a lot about you that I liked. Presently, I'm not seeing anyone on a regular basis. So, it might be possible to have a relationship."

Before the lunch was over, we decided that we were gonna embark on a different relationship from which we had had. In the parking lot, we lightly and quickly kissed on the lips. This was the first time that we had kissed, 3 years after we first met.

Arlinda and I started spending more time together. She had always been involved in Amway, thinking that it was gonna lead to riches and the good life. She asked me about going to a meeting and I went. However, I couldn't get into the enthusiasm that they exhibited in this meeting. Arlinda was jumping up and down. It was almost like a church revival. She also wanted me to go to church with her and I went there too.

For Christmas, I gave Arlinda a nice watch. I couldn't remember the last time that I had given a gift to a woman. With Arlinda, I didn't mind giving it. She was very excited, as she was putting it on and came over to kiss me.

"I know if I don't act right that you are gonna ask me for this watch back," Arlinda said.

"No, I won't. First, when I give it to you, I lose rights to it legally. It becomes yours. Second, I'm bigger than that. If you and I stopped seeing each other next week, I will not ask you for the watch back. That's childish. The watch is yours," I reassured her.

Arlinda later asked me if I wanted to go with her to New Orleans. She told me that she had placed a child in New Orleans, and she needed to make a home visit. We would leave on Friday and return on Sunday. I told her that it would be fun.

But we had one problem area to straighten out. After Arlinda and I started seeing each other seriously, she told me that she was not ready to have sex. I said okay, but I would ask, from time to time, to see if she was ready. I was sure that she wasn't a virgin, but I suspected that she didn't wanna appear to be too easy.

"Regarding our sleeping arrangement when we go to New Orleans, we can sleep in the same room, but we have to have double beds," Arlinda said.

"That sounds awkward to me," I said.

"No, it is not awkward. I just don't think we should sleep in the same bed," Arlinda said.

"Okay, if you say so. But I don't feel comfortable with sleeping in a room with someone that I am going with and we have separate beds. It seems odd to me," I said.

Although Arlinda was making an issue of the beds, I had no doubt that she was planning to make love in New Orleans. I was so confident that I was planning on packing some rubbers in my bags.

We stopped in Baton Rouge and Arlinda showed me around Southern University where she attended as an undergraduate student. We finally got to New Orleans and checked into the motel. The beds were separated by a lamp stand. When we got ready for bed, Arlinda said that we could hold hands between the beds. I told her that this was comical and so she said that I could move the lamp stand and push my bed next to hers. I did while thinking that we could have had one bed instead of this charade that she wanted to go through. After a few kisses, we were making love. The next day she told me that she was on the pill, and I didn't know that she would make love. I told her that I knew she would and showed her the rubbers that I had in my bags. She then playfully hit me on the arm.

After Arlinda visited the family of the child she placed, we went to the French Quarters. We stopped into a restaurant and Arlinda ordered a Long Island iced tea. After drinking two, her eyes began to sparkle. They looked just like they did when I first saw her. We went back to the motel and she wanted to make love again. Later, we went back to the French Quarters to see it at night, and it was so enjoyable. I really enjoyed it, and it was made more special because I was with Arlinda.

After we returned to Houston, I began wondering about the future and whether Arlinda and I had a future. As much as I wanted it, I knew that the odds were against us. We still had some major differences. I was feeling subtle and not so subtle pressure from Arlinda that I should be altering my life so that I, or rather we, would have considerable financial wealth. She had this idea of being rich when I met her and she still had it.

One night I was talking to my friend Roy and he told me that he wished that he could return to school and get his doctoral degree. He stated that he couldn't because he and his wife were expecting twins, but if he could go back to school, he would.

After talking with Roy, I thought here was a man who wanted to return to school but had family obligations and here was me. I was single and I had saved some money. There was nothing standing in the way. That night, I decided that I was returning to school and planning on getting a doctoral degree in social work. I was so excited by my decision that I couldn't sleep.

While I had made this decision, I decided not to tell Arlinda initially about it. After thinking about possible schools, I decided that the University of Minnesota was best for me because I had read good things about the state of Minnesota, and I wanted to study in a place that I thought the state officials were pursuing progressive social policy. I knew a little about some of their criminal and juvenile justice policy. I also knew a little about their drug policy. So, I intended to move to Minnesota to go to school.

Deep down, I didn't think that Arlinda would go although I wanted to be with her. One night, Arlinda was at my place and saw some material that I had on my love seat about the University of Minnesota.

"What is this?" she asked.

"This is some materials on the doctoral program at the University of Minnesota. I am thinking about going," I announced.

"You can't make any money with that degree," she said. "How can you make these kinds of decisions without discussing them with me?"

"Well, I haven't applied and I have not been accepted. So, at this point, I haven't made any firm decisions," I said. "Of course, I was gonna tell you, but I was waiting on the right moment."

A few weeks later after returning from a date, Arlinda told me that we didn't have a future and told me that we shouldn't continue seeing each other. She told me that I seem stagnated, and she needed someone who was going places and trying to better himself financially. The next day, she called me to tell me that she was upset and didn't know if she had made the right decision. She wanted to talk some more. I knew that this was an attempt to put more pressure on me and to change my direction. We did talk but it was no use. She was a wonderful person, but we had different goals in life. I respected her goals and hoped that she respected mine. Sometimes, this happens.

After taking a few days to get over my hurt, I began making serious plans to leave Texas. While I had some money saved, I decided that I needed to pay off my car loan. About a year-and-a-half before, I bought a new Toyota Supra and had taken out a 4-year loan.

I called my daddy and told him that I was leaving Houston and planning on going to Minnesota to go to school. He didn't say anything, but I knew by his silence that he didn't understand. Later, when I spoke with my brother, he told me that Daddy told him that he thought that I was making a big mistake and that I didn't know that the weather was rough in Minnesota. Willie Lee said that he told Daddy that this wasn't a snap decision on my part and that I knew what I was doing.

I began looking for a weekend job to earn more money to pay off my car loan. In November 1985, I found a weekend job as a mental health worker in a hospital. When I got off the telephone confirming that I was being hired, I called Delta and made reservations to go to Savannah that afternoon, knowing that I wouldn't be able to go for Christmas.

When I began working at the hospital, I was now working 7 days a week. I was working at the hospital from 7A.M. to midnight Saturday and Sunday and I was always tired. Everything that I was earning on my second job was going on my car loan. I also had a small loan that I took out to buy a computer and printer. When I left Houston, I wanted to be completely debt-free. So, I didn't have any problems with my schedule. I was doing it for me.

I had my application material in early and learned that the department of social work at the University of Minnesota only takes about 9 students a year. I was confident that I would get in. My grades were good, I had research experiences, I had paid work experiences, and I could write. I was so confident that I didn't apply to any other school. In February, I was notified that I was accepted for the fall quarter of 1986.

In July, I went shopping at a mall. As I was in the mall, I saw a black nurse named Claudia who worked at the hospital occasionally. She thought that this was an omen. So, we went out one Friday night, and she spent the night at my apartment. She told me that she was so sorry that we hadn't met earlier and she knew that I had a lot of money because I was single and working two jobs.

In August, I quit my job at the hospital and then flew to Minnesota to look for a place to stay. I decided to rent a place in Crystal, Minnesota, which was about 10 miles from the campus.

As I was about to return to Houston, I was sitting at a bar at the airport in Minneapolis, confident that I had made the right decision. As I was sipping on my screwdriver, I happened to look around and saw people looking at me. I was the only black person in the bar and I then noticed that there were not many black people walking down the aisle toward the luggage area. As I realized that people were watching me, I wondered if they thought that I was a pimp who was here recruiting white girls. I recalled that there was a movie about the "Minnesota Strip" and teenagers going to New York as prostitutes.

Arlinda called me to wish me well and asked if I could meet her at Cody's later for a farewell drink. On the day she wanted to go, I couldn't go. However, if I was free to go, I would have gone. I wasn't upset with her.

I had asked my brother Willie to come to Houston and help me move. I knew that he had never been on a plane before, so I paid for his plane ticket to Houston and paid for his flight from Minneapolis back to Savannah. I was gonna rent a truck and pulled my car behind it on a dolly.

On my last day at work, my colleagues at the youth agency took me out for a farewell dinner. I was really touched by it. I had worked at this agency for 8 years, and I was a little saddened to be leaving. It had made a major change in my life, more than a lot of people knew.

My brother flew in that Friday night, and I decided to take him out. But really it was mostly for me. I wanted to see Houston at night one more time. We went to a few places and ended up at a nightclub that I had started going to. On a few occasions, a friend and I had met some of the nurses at this club. We were dancing to Peter Gabriel's "Sledgehammer," and it was a fun night.

The next day, we loaded all my furniture on the truck, and I drove my car on the dolly. I was so concerned about my computer that I had it up front between the driver and passenger seats. We had to stop at a nearby service station to have a mechanic disconnect the drive shaft of my car. When this was done, I got on Interstate 45 and headed north. I told my brother that we were gonna drive nonstop. While I didn't plan it, we had time to talk about a lot of things, my going to prison and the effects it had upon him, his troubles with Daddy years ago, and his children.

When we got to Iowa, the weather got noticeably colder. We had to turn on the heater and stop to get a blanket from the back of the truck. As we entered Minnesota, I told my brother that I knew a guy from Albert Lea, Minnesota, who had worked at the camp and quit after discovering that he had cancer. We stopped in Albert Lea for gas at about 7 in the morning, but I decided that I would come back later to see him. At about 11A.M. we pulled up at the apartment where I was gonna be staying. We were told that we could back up the truck to the balcony, and as a result, moving in was easy because we slid all but one piece over the balcony.

Afterward, we went out to eat and I drove him into Minneapolis to see the University of Minnesota, as well the dome stadium, which we passed first. When he left the next day, I began making preparation for school. I had a fellowship for the first year and decided that I was gonna load up on my courses the first year.

After I got my telephone connected, I called the former co-worker at the camp who lived in Albert Lea, Minnesota, and who was being treated for cancer. Then, I called my parents to give them my new telephone number. During my conversation, I mentioned to Momma about my former co-worker who lived in southern Minnesota and how sad it was to watch the way his brother acted when he came to Texas to see him. I told Momma that I promised Tom that I would come see him as soon as I was settled. Momma stressed that if I promised to go see him to keep my word, and I assured her that I would.

When I was settled, I called Tom and got directions to his house. Leaving early Sunday morning, I drove the 90 miles to Albert Lea. As I saw him, I hugged him, telling him how glad I was to see him. Tom introduced me to his parents, who seemed very friendly. I stayed for 5 or 6 hours and had dinner with them. Tom told me that he might move to Minneapolis, and I told him if he did to let me know where he was staying.

The first year was busy but I was making steady progress. I liked that the school was on a quarter-hour system, but I always had the feeling after the first week that I was behind. I had problems in one class, but the others went very well. I decided to go during the summer of 1987, and by the end of it, I had completed most of my course work.

At the end of the summer, I decided to work and found a job at a halfway house for mentally ill adults as a mental health worker. I worked in the evenings and continued to take classes in the mornings.

During the Christmas holidays of 1987, I went home. I decided to go out with my brother and he took me to a bar where we found Honey. He looked the same, except older, and he bought us some drinks. I started asking him about some of the guys that we both knew from prison. He told me that Chick was dead. I felt sick when he told me that Chick was killed on the east side about 2 years ago. He said that he tried to talk to Chick about something Chick was doing, but Chick wouldn't listen. His refusal to listen and his insistence upon dealing with the wrong person cost him his life.

Honey also said that he had been arrested for another killing. I knew that he had shot and killed someone following a gambling game, but I had expected him to get out of it because the other person came at him armed. In this other case, he stated that he got into a fight with a guy on the waterfront, and the guy went into the river. His lawyer was successful in arguing that it was accidental, and he was able to walk away from it. However, he mentioned that he was leery of the family of the guy, hinting that someone had threatened him. Also, he told me that he was still gambling and had made over $100,000 the previous year playing cards.

Unlike most of the guys that I had met in prison, Honey was one of the smartest, and this may be why he has survived as long as he has.

But my thoughts were on Chick. I felt the same way about Chick dying as I did when Larry Shanks was killed in Reidsville. Shanks died because he was a decent guy but strong and couldn't be pushed around. Unlike Shanks, Chick was a little mixed up in his approach. But he had the status of a god in Reidsville, and when he was out of the yard, he acted the part. Guys had genuine fear in their voice when they talked about Chick from Savannah. I felt badly about hearing that he was dead because he was a strong black man, and if he had been steered in a positive direction, there would have been nothing that he couldn't do. He had the type of mental toughness that if he wanted to do something, he would do it. What a waste.

In 1989, I started looking for a job. Initially, I thought that I might find a job in an agency and perhaps teach part-time at a local college. But after teaching a class in social welfare, I decided that teaching was fun. So, I started looking for a full-time teaching job. I had decided that I wouldn't return to the South and was looking for a job on the West Coast, some place other than Los Angeles. I thought that Oregon or Washington would be a pleasant place to live. However, I learned that Ohio State had several openings and I applied. Fortunately, I had published two articles in academic journals, and this persuaded the search committee to invite me for an interview. At the end of the interview, I informed the dean about my background. I told him that the primary reason that I was telling him was that I intended to write about it one day and it was not going to make some people happy. He thanked me for being open and honest. About a month after the interview, I was offered a position as an assistant professor beginning in the fall quarter.

However, I was not finished with school and was in the midst of completing my dissertation. But I was confident that I could be finished by the time that I left Minnesota at the end of August. So, I began making preparations to leave Minnesota.

I had decided that I wanted to buy a place in Ohio instead of renting, but I was short on money for a down payment, so, I called Daddy.

Daddy's health had been declining for the past few years. He developed glaucoma but didn't seek treatment until it was too late. Because his eyesight was poor, he stopped going to the social club and was spending more and more time in the bed. He was always getting sick, but I still could count on him.

"I wanna buy a condominium before I move to Ohio, but I am short of money," I said.

"How much do you need?" he asked. "You can always have whatever I have. I will give you the last nickel that I have. How much do you need?"

"About 1,400 dollars," I said.

"When your brother gets off from work, I'll have him go to the bank and withdraw it. I'll have it wired to you this afternoon. If you need more, tell me. I have some money."

"No, that's enough."

"I can't tell you how proud I am of you. Someone was talking about you with me recently and said that you were so unusual. He said that it was remarkable that after they mistreated you so badly here, that you went off and did all that time, and then got out of prison and made something of yourself," Daddy said.

"The success that I am having now, I owe a lot of that to you, Momma, and the rest of the family. You wouldn't give up on me. I wouldn't be in the position that I am in now without you," I said sincerely.

"I'm also glad that you found a job in Ohio. When you get there, go see my sisters every chance you get," Daddy said.

"I will."

Daddy mentioned that his sisters in Ohio were planning a family reunion in Cleveland in July. So I decided to go. I had never seen many of the relatives on my daddy's side, and I wanted to see them. My sister was flying in from Houston and we managed to make the same connecting flight in Chicago to Cleveland. Additionally, my brothers and sisters were coming from Savannah in a van that they had rented. After learning that I was coming, my first cousin who lived in Cincinnati and whose mother was in the courtroom when I was sentenced to life imprisonment, decided she wanted to see me. We all had a good time, and I got a chance to see people that I had not seen before.

I left Minnesota at the end of August, but I was not finished with my dissertation. Really, I was finished, but the committee had not given me its final endorsement that my dissertation was ready to defend. My deadline with Ohio State for finishing was the end of September, and after some discussions with the chair of the committee, my defense was scheduled for the last week in September. I returned and the committee quickly passed my dissertation, deliberating less than 5 minutes. Now, I was officially Dr. Rudolph Alexander, Jr.

I began to get more into my classes. Unexpectedly, I was nervous my first quarter and made some mistakes. Gradually, I began to get better.

After being in Ohio for a year, I received a call that I didn't want. I was down in the basement using my computer when my telephone rang upstairs in my living room. I decided to keep working because I had my answering machine on and I could hear the person talking. It was my sister in Houston, and she told me that I needed to call Savannah right away. Walking slowly up the stairs and fearing the news from Savannah, I called home and stood in the middle of the floor as the telephone rang. My sister-in-law answered the telephone and gave it to my Momma. Momma had trouble talking.

"Your, your . . . your daddy died at 1:30 this afternoon," Momma said and then started crying.

I could hear Willie Lee in the background.

"Let me talk to Willie Lee," I said calmly.

When he got on the phone, I asked about funeral arrangements. Then, it hit me that Daddy was dead. I began to shake, my legs felt weak, and I dropped to one knee, crying.

My brother told me that he would call me back in a little bit. I continued to cry and after composing myself, I called him back to tell him when I would be in Savannah.

I flew to Savannah on Saturday, and my youngest brother was driving from Atlanta. Momma told us that Daddy didn't have a good suit to wear, and when Sylvester came in from Atlanta, she wanted us to go buy him a suit. I didn't wanna cry in front of Momma. So, I got up and went in the hall. Tears were rolling down my cheek.

When my brother Sylvester got in, we went to National Tailor to buy Daddy a suit for his burial. I wasn't much help because I continued to cry. All I could say was okay to the suit that my brothers picked out. We bought him a suit, white shirt, tie, and a belt. It didn't dawn on us that a belt was unnecessary until the undertaker gave the belt back to us. We didn't want his pants to fall down.

We had relatives from Atlanta, Cincinnati, and Cleveland come. We were all in the bedroom talking, and I suddenly realized that the funeral was in about an hour. I didn't want my daddy to go. I got up and went in the hall to cry, knowing that the time of the funeral was getting closer and closer. When the funeral cars came for us, I wasn't sure that I was gonna be able to get through it. Internally, I was saying no, over and over again. After a nurse came over near me and starting fanning me, I was able to compose myself to get through the funeral.

Later that night I heard that one of my nieces had taken pictures of Daddy in his casket, and I was asked if I wanted a copy. I was angry that she had done this. I didn't want a picture of my daddy dead.

When I returned to Ohio, I continued to think of Daddy. One day in Mc-Donalds, I started thinking about him. Without realizing it, I was crying and I got up and returned home. Ten months after Daddy's funeral, we had another reunion, but this was one was in Atlanta. I felt Daddy's spirit during this reunion and was on the verge of crying, but I held it in. I rode with my brother and his children to a shopping mall. As we were leaving the parking lot, I broke down and sobbed loudly. My brother didn't say anything and my brother's children didn't know why I was crying like that. Later, when they asked him, he told them that their uncle was crying about Granddaddy.

Two years after Daddy died, I still was crying occasionally, and I thought that I might need some professional help. I made sure that I was composed around Ohio State, but I was not okay at home sometimes.

I suspected that I was having a hard time with Daddy being gone because I remembered when he stood by me when I was about to be operated on at Memorial Hospital in 1967. I also remembered he and momma standing with me at my preliminary hearing, I remember he and momma standing by me at Dunbar Harrison's charade. I wasn't ready for him to go.

Finally, I began to feel that my severe grieving had ended, and I began to feel stronger. As I was walking to my mailbox one day and looking up at the beautiful sky, I realized that I had ascended the stairs and taken the correct route. Everything would be all right from here on.